BORN TO RULE

Born to Rule

The Making and Remaking
of the British Elite

AARON REEVES &

SAM FRIEDMAN

THE BELKNAP PRESS OF
HARVARD UNIVERSITY PRESS

Cambridge, Massachusetts
London, England
2024

Library of Congress Cataloging-in-Publication Data

Names: Reeves, Aaron S., author. | Friedman, Sam, 1984– author.

Title: Born to rule : the making and remaking of the British elite / Aaron Reeves and Sam Friedman.

Description: Cambridge, Massachusetts : The Belknap Press of Harvard University Press, 2024. | Includes bibliographical references and index.

Identifiers: LCCN 2024001882 (print) | LCCN 2024001883 (ebook) | ISBN 9780674257719 (hardcover) | ISBN 9780674297708 (pdf) | ISBN 9780674297715 (epub)

Subjects: LCSH: Elite (Social sciences)—Great Britain. | Educational sociology—Great Britain. | Educational equalization—Great Britain.

Classification: LCC HN400.E4 R448 2024 (print) | LCC HN400.E4 (ebook) | DDC 305.5/20941—dc23/eng/20240319

LC record available at https://lccn.loc.gov/2024001882

LC ebook record available at https://lccn.loc.gov/2024001883

For our partners, Beth and Louise,
and our parents,
Sarah and Richard, and Pat and Andy

Contents

Introduction   *1*

PART ONE   *Aristocratic to Ordinary*   *19*

1   Who Are the British Elite?   *21*

2   A Life Less Ordinary   *39*

3   Cultural Chameleons   *64*

PART TWO   *How to Make an Elite*   *93*

4   Silver Spoons   *95*

5   Old Boys   *115*

6   Bright Young Things   *135*

PART THREE   *Why Elite Reproduction Matters*   *155*

7   How Elites Think   *157*

8   Radical Women   *179*

9   Centring Race and Empire   *200*

Conclusion: Who Rules Britain?   *221*

Methodological Appendix   *241*

Notes   *263*

Acknowledgments   *307*

Index   *309*

BORN TO RULE

Introduction

"Complete rubbish." Henry, a recently retired corporate lawyer, is visibly offended.[1] For nearly two hours, he has spoken amiably and animatedly about a long and highly successful career (he was once described as a "Giant of the City" by a national newspaper).[2] But suddenly the atmosphere has changed. We have just asked him a question we put to nearly 150 highly successful people we interviewed for this book: "Do you consider yourself a member of the British elite?" His irritation is palpable:

> I've never considered myself to be one of the elite. I consider myself, justifiably or not, to have been a successful professional. I don't consider that elite . . . This belief that there is an elite that can dominate society, I have considerable doubts about that. If you are a successful lawyer, a successful banker or whatever you are within your profession, yes you have a fair amount of push, but do you have a general influence? No, none at all . . .

There is something a little incongruous about Henry's outrage. Maybe it is that we are sitting in the "drawing room" of his seven-bedroom townhouse in Bloomsbury. Maybe it's the huge self-portrait that hangs opposite us as we talk, or the fact that we know that his wealth extends beyond £10 million. Or maybe it's something about his background and life trajectory. His father held a senior post in the civil service (as did his grandfather). He went to one of Britain's most prestigious elite boarding schools (where his father was also a pupil). He attended Oxford. And for more than thirty years he was a senior partner at a Magic Circle law firm, before more recently taking on a range of non-executive board roles.[3]

Or maybe it is just that as we speak, despite his protestations to the contrary, it quickly becomes abundantly clear Henry is hugely influential. His personal networks include senior figures at the Bank of England, a former Chancellor of the Exchequer, and several members of the royal family. And he talks of "several mobilisations" where he was "able to lever principally my position I think, and to a degree my reputation" to bring about change in his industry and beyond. One example, he recalls, was in the early 2000s, when he was part of a group who organised a series of meetings with senior ministers to "rant" about amendments to a new Act of Parliament which he felt would "harm my clients." The result, he explained, was that the government agreed to "take the teeth out" of the legislation.

Henry appears, to us at least, to be the embodiment of the British elite, both in origin and destination. But, like the vast majority of people we spoke with for this book, this is not how he sees himself. Certainly, he acknowledges, he is from a "classic upper middle-class" background. But he is keen to stress that this was not always the case in his family. In fact, he spends several minutes telling us how his great grandfather rose from humble beginnings in rural Scotland to eventually become the president of one of the Royal Colleges for medical professionals in the United Kingdom. "So my direct family has been astonishingly successful," he concludes. "But," he adds with emphasis, "mostly through their *own ability*." Henry also rejects the notion that privilege has played any significant role in his own success:

> I don't think economic resources did much because, you know, I was not penniless, but I wasn't, I never inherited much money. When my father died I got a little bit of money, enough to put a deposit on a ruin. So, I did have some money but not by any standards significant . . . and I had no connections in the City, so it wasn't as though I had any, you know . . . I didn't know anybody.

The story Henry tells of his career is notably meritocratic. This is not to say he doesn't touch on other factors, such as the role of luck ("I had a few breaks") and education ("oh yes, makes a big difference"). And it isn't that he is somehow arrogant or pompous. On the contrary, he is positively charming and thoughtful throughout our interview. But there is a clear narrative to his story, a sense of almost romantic struggle against the odds. "I had to build my career from scratch," he notes. "By about '87 I had a number of clients, all of which I brought in; I wasn't given a single one; I wasn't given a single thing."

Key to his success, by his estimation, was a unique set of skills and character traits that set him apart. He was "ruthless" and forged a reputation for "aggressive" client advocacy. He was "innovative" and "unorthodox" in managing a range of takeovers. And he "worked astonishingly hard year after year." Henry sees himself as an exemplar of a more meritocratic era in Britain, particularly in the corporate centre of the City of London. As he explains:

> The City has changed enormously . . . Undoubtedly, if you go back a generation before mine, there were a number of people who became partners who would never have, but they had been to . . . they had connections and everything else. Now they wouldn't, by about the middle '90s they never had a hope. Meritocracy had come in. Properly.

The narrative Henry offers of life at the top is striking. While the British elite may be skewered as a closed establishment, an old-boy, snobbish, out-of-touch chumocracy, for those like Henry such tropes are hopelessly outdated. This couldn't be further from the dynamic, meritocratic, highly professional picture that he and others paint of contemporary Britain.

But are these perspectives really accurate? Our aim in writing this book is to hold such progressive narratives to account. Drawing on a unique analysis of how Britain has made its elites over the last 125 years, we show that there is a troubling disconnect between how elites see themselves and seek to present themselves in public, and what we find when we carefully analyse patterns of elite recruitment among the 125,000 people who have shaped Britain since the turn of the twentieth century. Certainly, Britain's upper echelons are no longer as closed as they once were. Since the end of the nineteenth century, the elite has become meaningfully more open when it comes to elite schooling, and significantly more diverse in terms of gender and (to a lesser extent) ethnicity. But the main takeaway from our analysis is the persistence of elite reproduction—the propensity for elites to be recruited from very privileged backgrounds—particularly in recent decades, where progress on opening up has clearly stalled. We show that white men from elite backgrounds who have all too often attended a tiny group of private schools and highly selective universities remain profoundly over-represented in the contemporary British elite.

This matters because it has important implications for the type of elites we get, and for how they think and behave. Our analysis clearly shows that elites from privileged backgrounds tend to tilt to the right politically and culturally, and that these leanings are accentuated if the individual, like Henry, combines positional power with extreme wealth.

So why are elites like Henry so keen to convince us that they are ordi-nary?[4] One answer we suggest, building on the work of others, is that re-cent rises in economic inequality and the pulling away of those at the very top have made people like Henry insecure about their legitimacy and sensi-tive to public concern that they are elitist and motivated only by economic self-interest.[5] In this context, public expressions of ordinariness—in the way you tell your back story, express your cultural tastes, or articulate your meri-tocratic legitimacy—could be seen as a logical strategy of impression man-agement.[6] Showing that you are just like everyone else forges cultural con-nections across class and dissolves very real economic divisions between your experience and that of most other people.[7] Now, of course, public expressions of ordinariness can sometimes backfire. We saw this at play recently when Rishi Sunak—the son of a doctor and educated at the elite Winchester College—tried to hark back to his immigrant grandmother to ground himself in a rags-to-riches story during the 2022 Conservative Party leadership campaign. Such claims do not always land with the public. But the fact that elites across various social domains feel obliged to *try* to appear ordinary is itself a manifestation of a strong symbolic market for ordinari-ness.[8] And beyond this, when this performance of ordinariness works, the implications can be powerful. As we will show, elites who successfully con-vince people that they have risen from humble origins or have mainstream cultural tastes are more likely to be viewed sympathetically—as more relat-able, intelligent, hard-working, and even to some extent competent.

A Project That Nearly Never Was

It is not lost on us that there is a certain irony to two white male profes-sors from Oxford and the London School of Economics (LSE) writing a critical book about the British elite. Yet as sociologists who have spent most of our careers studying the ways inequality shapes Britain, this felt like a logical (and pressing!) extension of our previous work. For the last fifteen years, Sam's research has explored the long shadow that social class casts over people's lives, both in who gets on but also more widely in terms of people's identities and lifestyles. In 2019 he brought these interests together in *The Class Ceiling* (co-authored with Daniel Laurison), which showed that even when those from working-class backgrounds make it into high-status occupations like law and finance, they face a powerful class pay gap. Like Sam, Aaron also works on social class but with a focus on how policy decisions affect those living in poverty. Often this has meant uncovering how the classed assumptions built into policy design fail to take into account the experiences of working-class communities or those living on low incomes.

One theme that connects our work, we realised when we began working together at LSE in 2016, is an interest in how patterns of inequality are connected to the decisions, ideologies, and behaviour of those who wield power and influence. But who precisely are those people, we asked ourselves, and how do we go about studying them? The go-to source in Britain, we quickly discovered, is *Who's Who*—the leading biographical dictionary of "noteworthy and influential" people which has been published every year since 1897.[9] The information in *Who's Who* had formed the backbone of several small-scale studies of British elites, but these had all involved researchers trawling the pages by-hand to conduct small-scale projects. What if we could get access to the whole database, Aaron asked? We created a script which could scrape all available data from the *Who's Who* website, which we duly attempted in late September 2016.[10] At first, everything seemed to be fine. We had intentionally set the script to run slowly so that we would not overwhelm the servers, and we had made it clear to the webmaster that we were researchers. But several days later, things were not fine. Far from it. Not only had the offices of *Who's Who* blocked our scraping operation, but their parent company, the publishing giant Oxford University Press (OUP), had temporarily shut down the entire LSE subscription to OUP books and journals. The *Who's Who* team called us in for a meeting. They were angry, we presumed. And this was surely the end of the project. We were wrong. Yes, *Who's Who* didn't want us to scrape their data. But at the same time, they were intrigued by the project and wanted to support us. In late 2016, after extensive discussions, we successfully brokered access to data on everyone who has ever been in *Who's Who,* some 125,000 people.

Who Counts as Elite?

But why *Who's Who*? One of the perennial problems in writing about elites is figuring out who exactly you're talking about.[11] "The elite" are frequently invoked but rarely properly defined. In many ways this is understandable. After all, there will always be some contestation about where power and influence lie in any given society. But if we are going to make bold statements about the elite, we need to be clear who we mean.

Who's Who provides a good measure of the British elite, we outline in Chapter 1, for three key reasons. First, it preserves an appropriate order of magnitude, consistently representing only about 0.05 percent of the UK population. Second, it is theoretically coherent in selecting members based on widely recognised positions of national influence. In this way, around 50 percent of entrants are included automatically: Members of Parliament, peers, senior judges, ambassadors, FTSE 100 CEOs, poet laureates, fellows of the British Academy, and many others are included by virtue of their office. The other 50 percent are positional elites selected based on reputation by a board of long-standing advisors.[12] Finally, inclusion in *Who's Who* acts as a marker of consecration in its own right, both reflecting and actively constructing a widely recognised public-facing elite.[13]

We are aware that, for many, *Who's Who* may still feel too big to really represent a national elite. The latest edition includes some 33,000 people. Our analysis therefore goes one step further to identify those within *Who's Who* who hold exceptional wealth. Here we draw on the theories of Karl Marx, Gaetano Mosca, and C. Wright Mills to define a *wealth elite* who are both positionally elite in the sense that they are included in *Who's Who* and economically elite in the sense that they occupy the top 1 percent of the national wealth distribution.[14] As we explain in Chapter 1, we estimate that this wealth elite is made up of approximately 6,000 individuals, or 0.01 percent of the UK population.

So, these are the two groups we are working with—a positional elite made up of 33,000 people and a smaller wealth elite of around 6,000 people, combining both positional and economic power. Our aim was to examine these groups both quantitatively and qualitatively, and to see how they may (or may not) have changed over time. For those interested, we explain this complex research design and the range of analytical techniques employed during our seven-year study in detail in the Methodological Appendix.

On the quantitative side, the bedrock of our project was the analysis of the biographical profiles of all 125,000 entrants in *Who's Who* since 1897.

We looked at things like gender, location, family background, schooling, university, stated recreational pastimes, and occupation. *Who's Who* is significant not just for its extraordinary temporal scope but also because it contains information that is not generally available elsewhere. For example, it often provides the name of the school each person attended, unlike survey data which only examines school type. This allows us, as you will see in Chapter 5, to look at the propulsive power of specific schools, particularly Britain's nine most elite schools—Charterhouse, Eton, Harrow, Merchant Taylors', St Paul's, Rugby, Shrewsbury, Westminster, and Winchester, collectively known as the Clarendon Schools.[15] *Who's Who* is also the only data source we know of that systematically collects data on the "recreations" or cultural tastes of elites, allowing us, in Chapter 3, to provide a unique window into changes in elite culture in Britain.

We decided to supplement *Who's Who* using several other sources. First, with the help of Naomi Muggleton and a small army of research assistants, we examined probate records, allowing us to see not only the wealth of *Who's Who* entrants but also the wealth of many of their parents. This critical information allowed us, in Chapter 4, to look at the changing impact over time of being born into a wealthy family. Because *Who's Who* does not collect data on ethnicity, we also employed an algorithm, Onomap, that estimates the correlation between names and self-identified ethnicity in census data and allows you to predict ethnicity when you only have someone's name. There are a number of limitations with using this approach, which we outline in detail in Chapter 9, but it is important to state up front that we only use this algorithm to estimate the proportion of people from different ethnic groups over time and not to assign ethnicity to individuals.

Another key source of information was a survey we sent to current entrants of *Who's Who* between February and June of 2022. The survey was completed by 3,160 people, a response rate of approximately 13 percent. This sample was not a perfect mirror of everyone in *Who's Who,* but as we show in the Methodological Appendix (see Table A.1), the people who responded were demographically quite similar to those who did not.

The survey allowed us to glean important pieces of demographic data not present in *Who's Who* profiles, most notably self-identified ethnicity. We also asked a range of questions about policy preferences and "culture war" issues that are central to several discussions in our book, notably the political ideology of elites in Chapter 7, gender and sexism in Chapter 8, and racism and empire in Chapter 9. Finally, the survey allowed us to conduct a series of experiments, testing, for example, whether people would change their description of their cultural tastes when we increased the salience of income inequality.

Finally, we combed through a number of other data sources that illuminate specific aspects of Britain's elite, like the music tracks chosen by the 1,200 people in *Who's Who* who have appeared on the long-running BBC radio programme *Desert Island Discs,* or the 467 judgments made by the UK Supreme Court since it was established in 2009 and their possible connection to the class backgrounds of its judges. And we traced the descendants of a small number of elite families to see how many extended family members also ended up in the British elite.

Armed with this information, we then conducted 214 in-depth interviews. Our aim was again to understand changes over time, so interviews were organised into four birth cohorts: 1900–1920, 1921–1940, 1941–1960, and those born after 1960. It is worth saying that only a handful of our interviewees were born after 1980. This is because people tend to reach elite positions when they are older (the average age of new entrants to *Who's Who* is 52). This makes sense. Reaching the types of positions we are studying in this book takes time and experience.

Interview data was collected in two ways. To capture the narratives of those born in the early part of the twentieth century, most of whom have died, we read through seventy interviews carried out with individuals included in *Who's Who* that can be found in the British Library's *National Life Stories* archive. Because these interviews are publicly available, we do not anonymise these individuals. We supplemented this with a further 144 semi-structured interviews with people currently in *Who's Who* who expressed interest in being interviewed after completing our survey. The people we spoke to operated in a range of sectors, and included government ministers, permanent secretaries, university chancellors, senior judges, FTSE 100 CEOs, newspaper editors, and television presenters. These interviews, which are anonymised, were conducted either by ourselves or by post-doctoral researchers Eve Worth, Katie Higgins, and Vladimir Bortun.

Change and Continuity: The Case of the British Elite

This book sets out to tackle a big question: How has Britain's elite changed over the last 125 years? And more specifically, how has it changed demographically? Is it still dominated by wealthy public school boys? Is it still marked by the same culture? Does Britain's elite think and behave in a particular way—is it ideologically coherent? Before we attempt to answer these questions, it is important to understand what we know already. Certainly, we are not the first to ask these questions. In fact, an array of fine thinkers have tackled them over the years. Their contributions are rich and varied, but reading across them, one key point of divergence pertains to the basic question of how much the British elite has changed over time.

On one side are those who stress continuity.[16] These commentators tend to point to two critical facts that have maintained the status quo. First, the British elite has never been subject to a significant rupture that has stripped the power of the ancien régime and replaced it with a new one.[17] As a number of historians have noted, elites in Britain did not face the kind of violent revolutions or wholesale expropriation of elite institutions that so profoundly altered the lives of their contemporaries in countries like France and Germany.[18] This absence of rupture, many argue, has furnished powerful families in Britain with an unusual capacity to reproduce themselves over time, even as the society around them has undergone profound change. There has also been a remarkable persistence in the key institutions that have produced elites in Britain—exclusive boarding schools like Eton, Harrow, and Winchester and prestigious universities like Oxford and Cambridge.[19] The durability of these institutions has been key to the maintenance of a distinct ruling class or power elite.

A key figure on this side of the debate is Ralph Miliband—the LSE academic and father of Ed and David Miliband, who both competed to be leader of the Labour Party in 2010. Writing in 1969, Ralph Miliband argued that the rise of the democratic state in Britain may have given the appearance of genuine change, but this merely masked the perpetuation of a "ruling class" drawn predominantly from privileged backgrounds that had "a markedly disproportionate share of personal wealth" and sought to ensure the state acted in its interest.[20]

In the early 1990s, following a decade of Thatcher-led Conservative governments, sociologist John Scott returned to Miliband's thesis and argued that Britain continues to be "ruled by a capitalist class whose economic dominance is sustained by the operations of the state."[21] The shared social backgrounds of this ruling class—the "relatively uniform pattern of socialisation" they received, first within elite families and then at boarding schools— "establish a bedrock of meanings which become the basis of a legitimating framework of ideas" concerning the maintenance of the status quo.[22] These common channels of elite recruitment, Scott argued, provide the settings for "ideas to congeal into the internal cement, the consensus that binds [the ruling class] together."[23] To be clear, it wasn't that authors like Miliband and Scott saw no changes in the British elite, more that they viewed such changes as a cover for a far more fundamental stability in who rules Britain.[24]

Against this view are a set of more change-focussed commentators who concede that elites in Britain emerged less bruised than other European elites by the reforms, economic shocks, and social upheavals of the last two centuries, but argue that this does not mean that they traversed these crises unscathed.[25] These writers hold that Britain's elites today may bear some superficial resemblance to those of the past, but in many important respects they are decidedly different.

Anthony Sampson is probably the most popular exponent of this view.[26] The various editions of his classic book *Anatomy of Britain* offer a fascinating picture of elites in flux. Sampson's initial portrait of the early 1960s describes a group of fragmented gentleman amateurs, ill-suited to the problems of the day, who are gradually replaced by a less privileged and more merito-cratic elite throughout the 1970s and 1980s. Fast forward to the final edition of his book, however, released in 2004, and we find him lamenting the arrival of a new elite, one that reversed the trends of the first half of the twentieth century and now looked "much more unified" and far more closed.[27] As Sampson re-examined the British elite at the dawn of the new millennium he was surprised to discover that "a small number of familiar names keep reappearing" and the key people seemed to be quite easily found "at a few clubs, dinner-parties, or gatherings" all within a few "postal dis-tricts in London."[28] In many ways, Sampson prefigures an observation more trenchantly expressed in Matthew Goodwin's recent book *Values, Voice and Virtue*.[29] Since the 1970s, Goodwin argues, we have witnessed the rise of a "new elite" who are "utterly different" from "the old elite."[30] Hereditary titles have been replaced by university degrees. Small-*c* conservatism has been replaced by "liberal cosmopolitan if not radically progressive cultural values."[31]

There is much to glean from these insightful accounts. But they also suffer from a number of common weaknesses. The most important is simply empirical scope. Many are purely theoretical, while others rely on data that are often ad hoc.[32] This is understandable. Elites are notoriously hard to study in a systematic way and are too small to show up in the kind of large-scale survey data we tend to use in much social scientific research, pushing researchers to rely on other source materials.[33] Often, this has led to small-scale studies that only give a snapshot of the British elite or, when change over time is addressed, accounts that are confined to a single elite profession.[34]

The problem with these more targeted studies is that they fail to give us a sense of the elite *as a whole.* This means that when people in Britain ask— as they frequently do—"Has our elite changed over time?," the only answer we can give is rather uncertain. It is this uncertainty that we want to address in this book. We want to provide a more systematic and overarching account of the British elite: who they are, how they have changed, and why this matters.

The Shifting Sands of Elite Distinction

Sociologists may define elites in particular ways, but that doesn't mean the people they write about see themselves in the same way. It is on this question that Part One of this book begins. Elite distinction, what the French sociologist Jean-Pascal Daloz calls "the necessity for dominant social groups to display cultural signs of superiority to signal their upper social position," has long been a foundational concern in social science.[35] Certainly, scholars have long argued that distinct lifestyles, identities, norms, and codes have been key to marking out the dominant classes, what the feminist historian Leonore Davidoff called "status theatre."[36] Such work has tended to look at elite distinction from two directions: first via the broad lens of elite identities, examining how a privileged group understands its dominant social position, draws symbolic boundaries with other groups, articulates its deservingness, or sets itself apart via particular embodied and racialised ways of being, such as accent, inflection, gesture, posture, styles of dress, etiquette, and manners.[37]

By contrast, others have focused more squarely on the question of elite culture and how taste and lifestyle act as a vehicle through which elites signal their superior social position.[38] Here many recent studies have emphasised that today's upper middle class actually tends to have an omnivorous cultural palette, grazing on both highbrow and popular forms.[39] Yet the significance of this omnivorousness is strongly contested, as sociologist Jennifer Lena chronicles in her forensic study of twentieth-century shifts in the art field.[40] For some, this is evidence that those in privileged social positions no longer operate as highbrow snobs, while for others it is simply evidence of the evolution of elite distinction.[41]

In Part One we tackle the question of elite distinction from both these directions. In Chapter 2, we look at how the British elite *sees itself* and how explicit notions of eliteness have waxed and waned in its members' identities. The contemporary elite, we show, strongly (and often angrily) push back on the idea that they are elite.[42] Many are instead keen to present themselves as ordinary, meritocratic, and upwardly mobile. Most articulate this claim in one of two distinct ways: through elaborate origin stories that downplay their privileged upbringings and seek to forge affinities with more humble extended family histories, or by positioning themselves as the beneficiaries of a more open Britain, the kind of people who would never have succeeded among the stuffy aristocratic elites of the nineteenth century.

Is this posture of ordinariness really any different from the past? Beneath the veneer of British modesty, our data suggest a very clear shift in self-presentation.[43] Elites born at the beginning of the twentieth century are much more comfortable talking about their class privilege, are often unapologetic about being the beneficiaries of nepotism, and at times seem to positively revel in expressing a highbrow cultural identity.

We take up the issue of elite taste in more detail in Chapter 3. Here people's stated hobbies and pastimes reveal three historical phases of elite culture: first, a mode of aristocratic practice forged around the leisure possibilities afforded by landed estates, which waned significantly in the late nineteenth century; second, a highbrow mode dominated by the fine arts, which increased sharply in the early twentieth century before gently receding in the most recent birth cohorts; and, third, a contemporary mode characterised by the blending of highbrow pursuits with everyday pastimes, such as spending time with family, friends, and pets.

Yet this rise in cultural omnivorousness does not necessarily indicate the end of elite distinction. Indeed, we found that today's elite may simply be a new, stealthier kind of snob. This is partly reflected in the careful selection of *popular* culture. The music tracks played on *Desert Island Discs* show that although elite tastes have shifted away from classical music and opera, the popular artists and tracks selected on the programme still tilt notably towards the critically acclaimed. Another issue here is the gap between the private lives of elites and what they choose to disclose in public. We show, for example, the disconnect between the unashamedly highbrow persona many elites project in our anonymised interviews and the ordinary cultural pursuits they chose to write about in their public *Who's Who* profiles.

Members of the British elite now signal their status in fundamentally different ways. While earlier elites were largely unapologetic about their status, and actively deployed culture to signal their distinction, today's elites strive to distance themselves from this traditional image. They work hard, in various ways and with uneven success, to present themselves as ordinary. But why? Well, ordinariness we argue performs an important signalling function for elites in settings in which they interact with a wider public. Drawing on a range of experiments, we show that elites who successfully convince people that they have risen from humble origins or have mainstream cultural tastes are more likely to be viewed favourably by their colleagues, peers, and constituents. Ordinariness, in other words, represents a rich form of cultural currency.

The Resurgence of Elite Recruitment

Today's elite *may see* itself as more ordinary and meritocratic, but do their claims of progressive social change stand up? The second part of this book tackles this question head-on. We assemble a range of innovative quantitative data sources to look at how the power of three key channels of elite reproduction—wealthy family backgrounds, elite private schooling, and Oxbridge attendance—have changed over time.

For much of the twentieth century this type of research—known as the sociology of elite recruitment—was one of the discipline's signature areas of enquiry.[44] From the 1980s onwards, though, this tradition was eclipsed by new approaches to social stratification—particularly in the United Kingdom. Sociologist John Goldthorpe and his colleagues argued forcefully that by focusing solely on the social composition of "who gets ahead," earlier approaches failed to place patterns of elite recruitment within the context of broader patterns of social mobility. Goldthorpe's approach, which has since become dominant, instead emphasised the importance of analysing national mobility rates using representative survey data.[45] Elites, too small to show up on such surveys, largely "slipped from view."[46]

Rising inequality during the latter part of the twentieth century and early years of the twenty-first century—particularly at the very top—has prompted a strong renewal of interest in economic elites across the social sciences.[47] Yet, analysis of the social composition of those at the very top has largely been absent from this new research agenda, particularly in Britain. Some policymakers even believe we have an unhealthy interest in "the top" in Britain. The chair of the UK Social Mobility Commission, for example, has argued that this should be replaced by a broader focus on "short-range" upward mobility and "levelling up" regionally.[48]

We would not dispute that social mobility is a much wider topic than elite recruitment and that a focus on access and progression in other areas of the labour market is crucial. However, we believe that turning the analytical lens away from elites is a dangerous step. It leaves those with the most power and influence unscrutinised and unaccountable.

In this book we aim to revive interest in who gets to the very top and to refine the way the topic is studied in three important ways. First, previous work has tended to provide only a snapshot of elite recruitment, whereas our analysis looks at trends across 125 years.[49] Second, we capture for the first time the propulsive power of specific backgrounds (rather than broad measures of parental occupation) by examining how the chances of reaching the elite vary if you were born into the top 1 percent of the wealth distribution. Finally, we look at the relationship between key channels of elite formation. While previous work examines the association between *one* type of institution and elite recruitment, our approach in Chapters 4, 5, and 6 allows us to understand the way elite origins, schools, and universities often work in concert to propel elite trajectories.[50]

Chapter 4 begins with some fairly extraordinary results: despite the dramatic equalization of wealth over the course of the twentieth century (largely through the expansion of home ownership), the relationship between wealth origin and membership in the elite has declined, at most, only modestly. If you hail from the top 1 percent of the wealth distribution, you have consistently been about twenty times more likely to reach the British elite than others in the UK population born at a similar time.

These findings are particularly significant when they are put into conversation with those in Chapter 5, which examines the propulsive power of Britain's most elite schools—the nine most famous, historically male-only Clarendon Schools, the twelve most prestigious girls schools, and a further group of 200 elite schools that make up what—until recently—was called the Headmasters' and Headmistresses' Conference (HMC).[51] At one level our analysis stresses that the Clarendon Schools remain tremendously powerful channels of elite formation, and remain more propulsive than the most elite girls schools (even though students at these schools tend to perform just as well academically). Yet we also show that the power of the Clarendon Schools has declined significantly over time.

How, then, do we make sense of these somewhat diverging trends? Our tentative suggestion is that they illustrate the shapeshifting capacities of wealth. As we explain in Chapter 5, while educational reform and democratising cultural change over the course of the twentieth century may have dented the ability of schools like Eton and Harrow to effortlessly propel their old boys—particularly the less academic ones—into elite positions, this hasn't really weakened the ability of wealthy families to convert their wealth into advantages for their children via other means. The rise of super-state schools in expensive postcodes in London provides a clear indicator of this trend.[52]

Finally, in Chapter 6, we examine Britain's other main channel of elite recruitment, Oxbridge, as Oxford and Cambridge are colloquially known. In some ways, this again reveals a similar picture: Oxbridge graduates re-main profoundly over-represented in the British elite. Yet this chapter reveals two other storylines. First, it shows that the propulsive power of Oxbridge relative to those who didn't go to university has actually fluctu-ated a lot over the last 125 years, starting from a very high base, declining significantly among those born in the 1930s and 1940s, and then becoming increasingly pivotal to elite reproduction again among those born from the 1950s onwards. Next, we show the *cumulative* power of Britain's channels of elite recruitment, where the sum is more than its parts. In particular we look at whether the advantage of attending one of these universities is the same for everyone or whether distinct advantages flow from following the pathway from schools like Eton, Harrow, or Winchester, or being born into wealth. We also consider whether women or people of colour who attended Oxbridge have the same chances of reaching the elite as men or white people. There are, we conclude, arguably two Oxbridges: one for a closely networked group of (largely white) old boys, and one for everyone else.[53]

Why Elite Reproduction Matters

Where you start in life continues to play a fundamental role in who gets to the top in Britain. Despite the profound changes that have taken place in society over the last 125 years, the main channels of elite recruitment—with the exception of a few schools—remain almost as effective today as they were more than a century ago. But why, we ask in the last part of this book, does that matter?

We care, of course, about equality of opportunity and the fair allocation of rewards. But reducing the importance of elites to a narrow focus on social mobility misses something fundamental. Elites are not just significant because they enjoy more wealth and status than the rest of us; they matter because they wield power and influence over our lives in ways large and small. Who they *are* therefore matters because it has an important bearing on *how they think, what they do,* and, by extension, the lives that all of us are able to live. Social scientists have long hypothesised that where elites are drawn from narrow social backgrounds, they are more likely to develop "a unity and cohesion of consciousness and action," which may have profound implications for the exercise of power.[54] These issues continue to animate public debate in Britain. Owen Jones's revival of the idea of the "establishment," for example, was particularly influential because of its assertion that this group is bound together "by common economic interests and a shared set of mentalities" oriented around "protecting the concentration of wealth in very few hands."[55] Similarly, the impact of Matthew Goodwin's notion of a "new elite" seemed to rest in large part on his assertion that this group work together in a coherent, almost conspiratorial, fashion.[56]

The empirical basis for such claims is not as strong as we might think.[57] In Chapter 7 we therefore draw on our bespoke survey data to address these questions directly. Our analysis reveals that, in many areas, the British elite are fairly aligned with the UK population. They are, for example, equally concerned about inequality and more in favour of extra public sector spending—although, tellingly, they think tax rises should fall on everyone, while the public think the rich should shoulder the burden.

But there are key political divisions *within* the British elite, and it is here that we see the importance of identifying our wealthy faction within the British elite because it helps us uncover traces of what the US philosopher Olúfẹ́mi O. Táíwò has called *elite capture,* "when the advantaged few steer resources and institutions that could serve the many toward their own narrower interests and aims."[58] We show that the wealth elite skew significantly to the right compared to the rest of the British elite. This is important, we argue, because these individuals have a greater ability to further their political agenda. Not only are they more politically active, but their wealth gives them a unique platform to exert power and influence.[59]

Political orientations also map directly onto the question of elite reproduction. We find that elites from privileged backgrounds tilt to the economic right and tend to be more culturally conservative, whereas those from working-class backgrounds mostly orient the other way (although this is modulated by whether they are themselves in the wealth elite). In Chapters 8 and 9 we turn our attention towards women and people of colour in the British elite to explore their distinct political identities. Our data shows that women are notably more progressive than their male counterparts, which may become increasingly important in shaping the character of the British elite as they become more prominent within its ranks. And in Chapter 9 we argue that the rising number of elites of Black and Asian heritage may have important political implications going forward as they tend to be more radical in foregrounding issues of racial inequality and decolonial thought, and have often used their platform to push for change in these areas.[60] And yet, as the sociologist Nirmal Puwar has argued, there are reasons to be cautious about presuming that "women" and "ethnic minorities" are homogenous groups that can generate "a mimetic politics from their shared experiences."[61]

The British Elite as a Lens

This is a book about the British elite, but it can also help us think about elites in a broader international context. After all, Britain's colonial past, as Pere Ayling and Aline Courtois have shown for Nigeria and Ireland, to take just two examples, means it has played an outsized role in the development of elites in many other parts of the English-speaking world, particularly the Commonwealth but also the United States.[62] Indeed, during much of the imperial period we cover in this book, the British elite *was* the elite in many colonial contexts—or at least dominated positions of power and influence. British elites have thus been critical to the spread of certain types of state institutions (for example, the Arts Council model in Australia, New Zealand, and Singapore), the proliferation of now-global sports (such as cricket, tennis, and rugby), and the dissemination of particular models of education, notably exclusive, fee-paying schools.[63] In this way, understanding shifts in the British elite may offer important insights into how and why elites have changed elsewhere.

In fact, the story we tell in this book is not entirely disconnected from what has happened in other parts of the world. Britain is one of many

countries that witnessed a dramatic decline in wealth inequality throughout
the first half of the twentieth century, only to see the rich once again recap-
ture a larger share of national income since the 1980s.[64] In many countries
this initial decline was driven, as in the United Kingdom, by the rise of the
property-owning middle class.[65] The fact that such a dramatic equalization
of wealth did not fundamentally alter elite reproduction in the United
Kingdom suggests that such changes may have been insufficient to increase
elite openness elsewhere. Similarly, there are very few countries which have
not seen dramatic increases in access to education over the last 200 years,
and we would be surprised if this had not similarly dented the link between
elite schools and elite destinations. The United States is particularly relevant here, with prestigious boarding schools like St Paul's, Groton, and Phil-
lips Exeter modelled in many ways on Britain's Clarendon Schools.[66] And,
finally, Britain is also one of many countries where the entrenched nature
of elites is cited as a key driver of recent populist political revolts. Here, as
Cas Mudde has argued, the ideological root of populism is the belief that
society is split into two groups: "the pure people" and "the corrupt elite."[67]
Whether elites today are actually more corrupt than in the past is hard to
document, but there is certainly a perception in a large number of countries
that elites are out of touch and excessively self-interested.

So, yes, this is centrally a book about the British elite. But we also aim
to shed light on the contemporary character of elites in general, and on how
certain institutions—families, schools, universities—actually make elites
and, pivotally, how they might be remade so the elites we get are the ones
we need.

PART ONE

Aristocratic to Ordinary

1

Who Are the British Elite?

In 2003, the sociologist John Scott suggested that *elite* is "one of the most misused words in the sociological lexicon."[1] Fast-forward twenty years and Scott's damning indictment feels more relevant than ever. Popular interest in elites has never been higher.[2] Yet flanking this is a maddening conceptual fuzziness. We hear constantly about the dysfunctions of the "woke metropolitan elite," "the establishment," or the "super-rich" but are rarely told where these formations actually start and finish.[3]

The most frequently cited definition comes from the American sociologist Shamus Khan who describes elites as those with "disproportionate access to, and control over, a range of economic, social, cultural, and political resources."[4] This definition is both entirely reasonable and unhelpfully broad. Certainly, it has led to elites being imagined in widely varying ways— from individuals in high-status occupations, to those with advanced levels of education, to people with superior stocks of "capital."[5] Such groups are not only conceptually disparate but are often far too large to meaningfully represent an elite.

A recent high-profile example of this comes from the political scientist and popular commentator Matthew Goodwin. Goodwin argues that Britain is in the grip of a "political revolution," with influence increasingly wielded by a "new elite" who have "risen to positions of immense economic, political and cultural power."[6] This new elite, according to Goodwin, makes up as much as 25 percent of the population. Yet there is an obvious contradiction here. How can 25 percent of the UK population—some seventeen million people—occupy "positions of immense economic, political and cultural power"?[7] The numbers just don't add up.

There will always be challenges in identifying where the boundary should be drawn between elites and non-elites.[8] And there will never be one uncontested and all-encompassing definition. Indeed, attempting one would miss something crucial about the nature of power and the way it manifests along any of the dimensions Khan alludes to. This is because the varying *degrees* of power and different *types* or *bases* of power change over time.[9] Britain, for example, used to be an agrarian economy with power rooted in land ownership, but it transitioned to an industrial and then to a knowledge economy, and in the process the bases of power were fundamentally altered.[10] The malleability of these two dimensions also means that drawing hard boundaries will always miss some people who have "access to" or "control over" some resource at any given moment in time.

Yet we would maintain that the term *elite* can play an important role in how we think about how societies operate. But to do so its meaning must be clear and coherent, and an appropriate order of magnitude preserved.[11] After all, trying to pinpoint what we mean by *elite* is not just a dry academic exercise. It helps us delineate precisely who (both individually or as a group) exercises a disproportionate degree of control over the societies in which we live, and enables us to figure out what is at stake in allowing them to continue to do so.[12] In other words, identifying the elite is an essential task if we want to understand the inequalities that shape our societies. Are the elites we have the ones we want? And if not, can we do anything about it?

Our primary conception of the British elite in this book comes from *Who's Who,* the leading biographical dictionary of "noteworthy and influential" people, which has been published in its current form every year since 1897. *Who's Who* was created as an explicit rejection of similar volumes that defined the British elite as only the aristocracy. Instead, it aimed to document those who achieved positions of influence in British society, rather than just those who happened to be born to barons or earls.[13] And it has maintained this basic orientation ever since. The book has consistently represented approximately 0.05 percent of the UK population (or 1 in every 2,000 people). Our analysis includes all 125,000 entrants from the past 125 years.

Who's Who's decision to choose its members primarily based on their positions of influence is quite similar to how some academics define elites.[14] This idea is associated with the Italian scholar Gaetano Mosca, who famously argued that elites are best understood as "ruling minorities," empowered by their ability to exercise authority over others and who usually occupied top positions in organizational hierarchies.[15] In this way, around 50 percent of the entrants in *Who's Who* are automatically included based on their jobs or positions. These include members of Parliament, members of the House of Lords, King's Counsels (senior trial lawyers), ambassadors, national newspaper editors, university chancellors, FTSE100 CEOs, poet laureates, heads of public bodies, dames and knights, members of the aristocracy, and fellows of the British Academy, among many others.[16] While these positional elites are diverse in their fields of influence, they are individuals whose actions can be said to hold a certain significance beyond their specialised areas (as might be the case for certain top athletes and celebrities).[17] In other words, we study positional elites who have *national influence;* which is to say that their actions are at least somewhat significant to the character and development of the nation.

The other 50 percent of entrants are positional elites chosen on the basis of their reputation. Here, a board of long-standing advisors makes a reputational assessment of an individual's professional impact on British society. This reflects the idea, popular among many scholars, that elites are more usefully identified as people *thought to be* powerful by those "in the know" or as individuals occupying some form of centrality in high-status networks.[18] Many of the people we interviewed underlined the fact that reputation is central to how perceptions of eliteness circulate in Britain. As Douglas, a Black British broadcaster born in the early 1950s, explained:

> I think the way the British elite defines itself and closes itself off—it asks itself, who's good? And I think the decision-makers . . . we don't just make decisions in abstract and purely on the merits. We also make decisions with a test of how, in our subconscious minds, how will my peers take this decision? And therefore who our peers are really matters. And the test for who our peers are is, "oh such-and-such, he's really rather good isn't he?" Now I think Germans and Americans don't quite have that, but we do. And we have this sort of sense of what's good and meritorious is . . . well . . . we end up worrying about the reaction of a very limited group of people . . . and that's a very peculiarly British thing.

Reputation is important, as Douglas takes care to explain, because assessments of "merit" in elite gatekeeping decisions often have this social dimension. Like members of a jury endlessly gauging the response of their fellow panelists, elites are often more preoccupied with how their peers might assess a prospective candidate than they are with their own assessment of that person's merits.

The reputational part of the *Who's Who* selection process is shrouded in mystery and has been the subject of much media speculation.[19] In an effort to gain a more transparent understanding of the process, we spoke, in May 2017 and again in November of 2019, with the coordinator of the selection process. She clarified that inclusion is not influenced by politicking and entries cannot be purchased: "It's our job to reflect society, not to try and shape it," she explained.[20] She underscored that advisors make decisions at annual board meetings where they are provided with short biographies of a long list of potential entrants (compiled by *Who's Who* editorial staff) who have recently achieved a noteworthy professional appointment or who enjoy sustained prestige, influence, or fame.[21] Each potential entrant is discussed in turn by the board and inclusion is based on a majority vote. Individual board members have the power to veto any single decision if they wish. While the coordinator declined to provide detailed information about the board, such as their demographic makeup or average tenure, she did tell us that the gender composition has been stable over the past fifty years. This cautiousness about the board was, she argued, because "the continued integrity of the publication depends on the total anonymity of the advisory board."

Focusing on people who have had "sustained influence" or who occupy pivotal positions means that the people admitted to *Who's Who* are older than the population on average. Around 25 percent of new entrants are under 46, 50 percent are between 46 and 58, and the remaining 25 percent are over 58. People are included in the book until they die, at which point they move into another volume called *Who Was Who,* which, for the purposes of our analyses, we treat as basically one dataset. One consequence of this process is that *Who's Who* contains some people who are above what we typically think of as retirement age. Yet one thing that was striking in our interviews was that the people we spoke to who were in their seventies (and even some in their early eighties) had remained both active and influential in their fields.

Who's Who may choose its entrants based on a mix of positional and reputational considerations, but all those so chosen are then united by inclusion itself, which acts as a marker of consecration in its own right. *Who's*

Who doesn't just catalog individuals who have reached particularly prominent positions, it publicly anoints them. So we would dispute *Who's Who's* claim that they don't shape notions of eliteness. The book has played a unique role in actively constructing a widely recognised national elite for at least a century.

This has been demonstrated in various ways over the years. Most importantly, *Who's Who* has among elite scholars long been considered the most valid catalog of the British elite.[22] But the book has also maintained a wider signalling power. A conversation with Ashura, a Black British academic (born 1960–1965), illustrated this clearly:

> *Ashura:* I think [*Who's Who*] is the quintessential marker of elite status . . . it's the British establishment, isn't it? That is what *Who's Who* really is; I remember being on committees in Oxford colleges, committees to elect heads of college. And the instructions to potential heads of college were always "send us your CV," or, if applicable, direct us to your entry in *Who's Who.*
>
> *Interviewer:* It had real currency?
>
> *Ashura:* Oh, yeah, absolutely. There was always a copy of *Who's Who* in the senior common room of every Oxford college. And the implicit question that British people always ask is, a certain type of British person, is he a good chap? I mean, that's the fundamental question. And one piece of evidence of whether you were a good chap was what your *Who's Who* entry said about you.

In this way, new entrants continue to be the subject of widespread national media attention and *Who's Who,* as a phrase, has even passed into everyday parlance as a casual byword for social prominence.[23] During the Second World War, Winston Churchill personally intervened to ensure its publication would not be affected by the paper shortage, arguing its circulation was a matter of "national importance."[24] And its signalling power has occasionally had quite tangible effects, as the feminist intellectual Germaine Greer found in the 1970s:

> Once when I was in Khartoum, I was grabbed by the presidential guard outside President Nimeiri's palace. I protested that I had an

appointment with someone in the government and was only trying to find him. They took me to an office where I was left waiting to be chucked out. *Who's Who* was on the official's desk. I asked him to look me up, hoping against hope I was in it. He smiled in disbelief but I insisted that he look up the name in my passport, and there I was! Suddenly there was a reception committee, red carpet, drinks, the lot! *Who's Who* has its uses.[25]

So, Who Are the British Elite?

What does the contemporary British elite, as identified by *Who's Who,* actually look like? Examining this group in detail, and chronicling how it has changed over time, is of course one of the central aims of this book. But for now, to set the scene for the analysis that follows, we outline the demographic coordinates of the current entrants of *Who's Who,* based on their biographies and answers to the survey we sent out to them in 2022. The first thing to say is that, unsurprisingly, this is a very small and select group. There were about 33,000 people in the latest edition.

A few further observations can be made from the snapshot in Figure 1.1. No one would be surprised to discover that the British elite is predominantly made up of men. Although the proportion of women has increased significantly over the past century, a phenomenon we will return to in detail in Chapter 8, men still make up more than 80 percent of current members of *Who's Who.*

Its membership is also overwhelmingly white. While 90.3 percent of those over 50 in Britain are white, the figure among the contemporary British elite is 96.8 percent. This has been changing slowly over the past few decades, as Figure 1.2 shows, but the change has been much faster for white women than it has been for people of colour and women of colour in particular. For instance, white women made up more than 25 percent of new entrants to *Who's Who* over the past few years, whereas only 3 percent are men of colour and around 1 percent are women of colour.

Figure 1.3 also illustrates that the elite overwhelmingly live in a small number of places. London is over-represented with around 35.9 percent of the elite living in the capital (compared to just 13.1 percent of the population), although they are predominantly located in neighbourhoods in the north and the west of the city. Oxford and Cambridge have high concentrations too, as does Edinburgh—and Manchester to a lesser extent.[26]

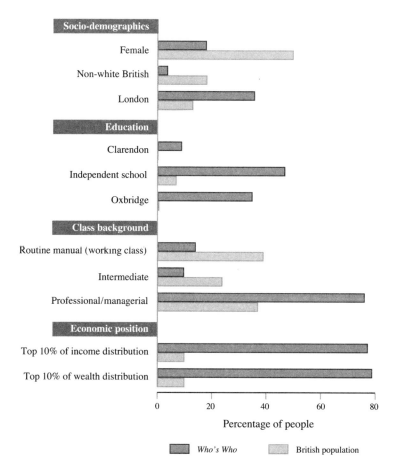

1.1 The people in *Who's Who* are not like the rest of the population.
Note: "Intermediate" is the term used by the British government in their official statistics on social class and describes occupations such as secretary, clerical worker, or small business owner.

The elite is also privileged when it comes to socio-economic origins and destinations. Seventy-six percent are from professional or managerial backgrounds, in terms of what their parents did for a living (compared to approximately 37 percent in the UK population), and 47 percent were educated at private schools (compared to 10 percent in the UK population).[27] Nearly 9 percent attended one of the nine elite Clarendon schools and around 35 percent attended either Oxford or Cambridge, compared to less than 1 percent of the British population. They are also affluent. Over

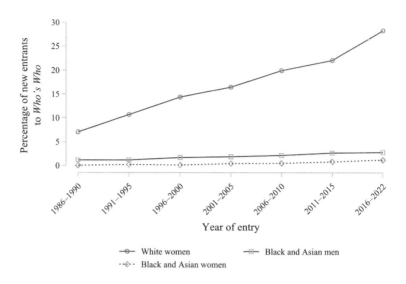

1.2 The percentage of women in the elite has grown, but there have only been modest improvements for people of colour.

75 percent, according to our survey data, have income and wealth that would put them in the top 10 percent of these respective distributions, and 16 percent earn more than £175,000 per year (putting them in the top 1 percent a few years ago). Over 12 percent have more than £4 million in household assets (again putting a couple in the top 1 percent).[28]

Are the elite drawn more from certain sectors of British society? Figure 1.4 shows that, in fact, the current British elite—as compiled by *Who's Who*—are drawn broadly from the fields of business, politics, and law, as well as to a lesser extent education, creative industries, the military, and religion.[29]

This occupational composition has changed in important ways over time. The power of the clergy (down from over 15 percent) and the military (down from over 20 percent) has waned in particular since the end of nineteenth century, as shown in Figure 1.5. Other occupations have expanded. Law and government have together increased to around 25 percent over the past 125 years, while people in the media have increased too.

It bears mentioning that *Who's Who* is not a definitive measure of the British elite. Its focus on occupational achievement and influence is only one way of looking at eliteness, and like any data source, it has its limitations. Some have argued, for example, that it tends to under-represent elites in newer professions or sectors of the economy, such as technology or IT,

1.3 Elites live in central London, Oxford, and Cambridge.

Note: Each hexagon is a constituency, a geographical region which corresponds to an electoral unit. Constituencies do not all have the same population, but they are designed to be of similar sizes. Hexagons with a thick black outline are inside London. Darker colours correspond to more elites living in that area.

or those who wield significant influence but don't have (or want) a public profile, such as certain lobbyists, consultants, or philanthropists.[30]

It is also true that the reputational criteria used to select *Who's Who* entrants are somewhat ambiguous. This opacity helps maintain the editorial independence of the publication, but it also limits our ability to scrutinise the validity of the selection criteria.[31] The demographic composition of the

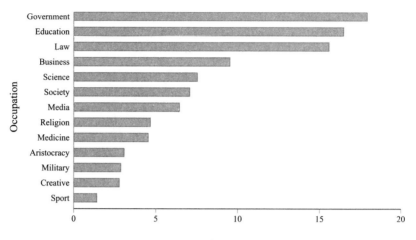

Percentage of people in *Who's Who*

1.4 The elite is drawn from a broad range of occupational fields.

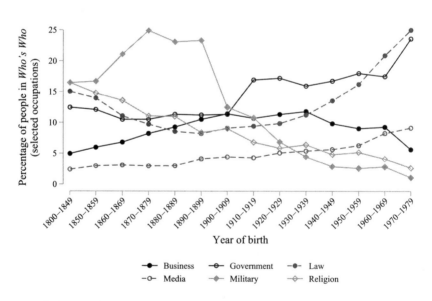

1.5 The legal, political, and media elite have grown significantly over time.

Note: Occupation fields are defined according to the categories in *Who's Who* and are based on the occupation which led to their inclusion.

board of advisors, and how this has changed over time, may also affect who is included. To partly address these uncertainties, we selected a sample of entrants who were automatically included based on occupational position and compared these to all others in *Who's Who.* Reassuringly, results across a range of questions we addressed in this book are similar for both groups.

One final limitation of *Who's Who* is that it fails to capture the economic dimension of elites. The recent revival of elite studies—much of it inspired by the work of such economists as Anthony Atkinson, Thomas Piketty, and Emmanuel Saez—is dominated by economic definitions of elites.[32] This work tends to focus exclusively on economic thresholds, such as the 1 percent, the super-rich, high-net-worth individuals, or members of various Rich Lists.[33] Such conceptualisations have the virtue of being precise, but at the same time they ignore the importance of positional or reputational elites operating in fields such as politics, culture, media, and academia, where power does not always correlate with wealth. Having said this, we recognise that economic capital is also a key dimension of both eliteness and the exercise of power. To account for this, we sought to bring together economic and positional definitions to identify a distinctive British *wealth elite.*

A Brief Detour into Elite Theory

Who's Who represents a miniscule proportion of the British population. Yet at 33,000 members, it may still feel too large to be described as a national elite. Surely, the *real* elite—those who hold real power—are a much smaller group? In part, this intuition is sound. As Khan writes, elites are those with "disproportionate access to, and control over, *a range of . . . resources.*" And while many of the people in *Who's Who* are very influential in *one* domain of British life, they may not have disproportionate control over resources in *multiple* domains.[34]

This is important because different forms of power often interact with one another. Consider Baron Michael Ashcroft. Ashcroft is tremendously wealthy, having amassed a huge fortune (valued in 2023 at £1.3bn, making him Britain's 133rd richest person) through various business acquisitions. Yet his success in the corporate world has also enabled him to leverage economic power into political influence. He is a major Conservative Party donor and was made a baron (making him a life member of the House of Lords) in 1999.[35] And when Prime Minister David Cameron snubbed him for a senior position in 2010, Ashcroft paid a journalist £500,000 to write what the *Guardian* branded a "Jacobean revenge biography" aimed at Cameron.[36] What Ashcroft's example makes clear is that different forms of power often reinforce each other. His wealth accentuates his political influence, and his political influence accentuates the power of his wealth. In this sense, power frequently has a kind of multiplicative relationship. Increasing power on one dimension can increase it in others.[37]

If we accept that there is some interaction between different forms of power, then it becomes critical that our analysis goes further than simply identifying those in the highest-level positions. We need to identify individuals who wield the most power or hold a ruling position *within* the elite. We are not the first to seek to do this—many scholars have tackled this idea of the elite-within-the-elite. Here there are broadly three schools of thought, all of which inform the approach we take in this book.

The first is typified by Karl Marx's conception of the "ruling class."[38] This view is characterised by a capitalist class (the owners and controllers of capital) that is able to exert disproportionate influence over the state, either directly, by occupying positions of power within the state, or indirectly, through the state's subservience to the will of this class. Indeed, Marx and Engels's *Communist Manifesto* asserts that "the modern state is but a committee for managing the common affairs of the whole bourgeoisie," by which is meant the capitalist class.[39] Notably, Marx was strongly critical of Palmerston's UK cabinet in the 1850s, which famously contained "ten lords and four baronets," precisely because it was constituted of the kind of ruling class he railed against.[40] Whether the state is entirely subservient to capital has been debated a great deal among those working from the "ruling-class" perspective, such as John Scott and Ralph Miliband, but the core assumption remains that a capitalist class exists whose members, in Miliband's words, "participate in the exercise of political power" and whose "operations are sustained by the operations of the state."[41]

In response to this idea of a "ruling class," the Italian social scientist Vilfredo Pareto and his student Gaetano Mosca developed an alternative view which sought to ground eliteness not in economic power but in the idea of excellence in some dimension of social life.[42] Here, elites are afforded status via their exceptional ability. This does not mean that all elites are important at a societal level: You may be exceptionally good at completing a Rubik's Cube, but this doesn't make you part of what Pareto and Mosca called the "governing elite."[43] With this distinction, they tried to identify those who by virtue of their excellence (and their capacity to organise themselves as a group) were able to become the rulers of a given society by occupying positions of power and influence.[44]

One crucial difference between Marx's ruling class and Pareto and Mosca's governing elite is its degree of fluidity. The "ruling class" is certainly not entirely static—after all, such a group came into existence and would eventually disappear, according to Marx—but it is durable.[45] This group is largely successful at reproducing itself and maintaining its power over time. Pareto and Mosca, by contrast, had a more dynamic conception of elites. They were keenly interested in what they called the "circulation" of elites—that is, the ability of new generations of elites to replace older generations and take control of the means of power.[46] For them, elite circulation was far more rapid than it was for Marx, in part because the economic bases of power had changed and in part because the cultural norms of old elites had become out-of-sync with this new economy. It was stories of this kind that, in many ways, underpinned the flurry of studies of elites in the 1950s and 1960s.[47] These narratives described Britain's post-war decline as rooted in the failure of the old elite to adapt to the new world and to resist pressure from new elites.[48]

The third school of thought, in some respects a combination of these two perspectives, is most closely associated with the work of the American sociologist C. Wright Mills, who famously introduced the term "power elite" to describe the set of actors who occupied "the strategic command posts" of US society.[49] Mills defined the power elite as those who held "pivotal positions" in government, business, and the military.[50] This emphasis on "pivotal positions" resonates with Pareto and Mosca's "governing elite" but, like Marx, Mills was attuned to the salience of economic interests. He recognised that the heads of major corporations exerted huge influence over the interests and orientations of this power elite, and that, as documented by his compatriot and fellow sociologist Michael Useem, there was an "inner circle" of interconnected and politically active corporate directors and business owners who work together to promote a favorable political environment.[51] More than this, Mills argued that the very rich were able to deploy the "institutional powers of wealth," allowing "economic power . . . to be translated directly into political party causes."[52]

One important theme across all three perspectives is an emphasis on the centrality of both positional power *and* economic power—that is, of identifying those who have disproportionate control over both these kinds of resources. Marx's ruling class is made up of capitalists (the very rich) who are able to exert influence over people in positions of power (either directly or indirectly); Pareto's governing elite are those whose exceptional abilities enable them to occupy positions of power and to be economically rewarded for these attributes; and Mills's power elite are those occupying pivotal positions but who also possess high levels of wealth and prestige.

Flowing from this, we have identified a group in this book which we have called the *wealth elite*. We define this group as people who are both positional elites in the sense that they are included in *Who's Who* and economic elites in the sense that they also occupy the top 1 percent of the national wealth distribution. The wealth elite, in other words, sit at the top of both positional and economic hierarchies.

We have identified the wealth elite using two different sources. To identify this group historically, we analyze the entire corpus of probate records in the United Kingdom, covering some eighteen million records from 1855 to 1995. A probate record reveals whether a person left a financial estate when they died, and if so what its value was. We used the value of these probate records to produce a probate wealth distribution and placed individuals within it.[53] Finally, we matched the probate records with people in *Who's Who* to identify those who were also in the top 1 percent of the probates recorded in the year of their death.

To identify today's wealth elite, we of course cannot rely upon probate records. Instead, we turn to the bespoke survey that we circulated to *Who's Who* entrants in 2022. Here, among other questions, we asked respondents about their total household wealth and then cross-referenced this with a recent analysis of wealth in Britain using the Wealth and Assets Survey to identify a group of *Who's Who* entrants who also occupy the top 1 percent of the wealth distribution (that is, those with over £2 million in total household assets or £4 million in joint assets).[54]

Who Are the British Wealth Elite?

Now that we have established what exactly we mean by the British wealth elite, it is time to interrogate this very select group. Who really rules Britain today? Unsurprisingly, the answer is a very small number—about 6,000 individuals (18 percent of the people in *Who's Who*) or 0.01 percent of the UK population.

Again, demographically, this is a highly skewed group. As Figure 1.6 indicates, aside from their slightly more prestigious educational trajectories, their much higher likelihood of living in London, and their higher incomes, the wealth elite are not all that distinct demographically from the rest of the elite.

The wealth elite are, however, somewhat different occupationally. Figure 1.7 shows that business leaders are most likely to combine positional

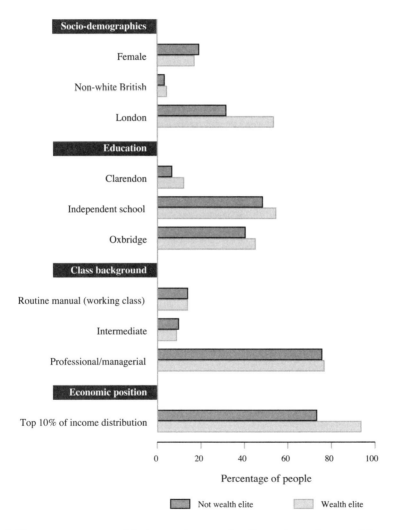

1.6 The contemporary wealth elite are demographically similar to the rest of the elite.

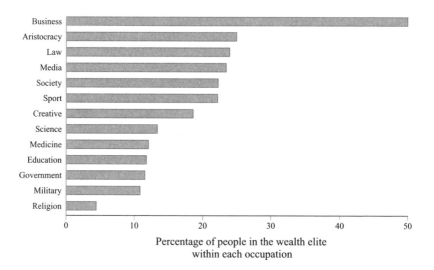

1.7 Business, the aristocracy, and law are over-represented among the wealth elite. *Note:* Eighteen percent of the people in *Who's Who* are in the wealth elite.

and economic power—making up 24 percent of the wealth elite. More intriguing is the presence of those in law, who are also significantly over-represented. Conversely, those in education (mainly academics) and civil servants are under-represented.

Notably, the occupational composition of the wealth elite has changed significantly over time. In Figure 1.8, we combine members of the wealth elite into three fractions: economic occupations (business leaders, finance, and so on), cultural occupations (artists, those who work in the media, educational professionals, scientists, and sports stars), and everyone else (including lawyers, politicians, and military). We then track the size of these groups in the wealth elite over time.

Figure 1.8 shows that during the first decade of *Who's Who*'s existence there was very little difference in the occupational composition of the wealth elite and the rest of the elite. This started to change, however, with the rise of the industrialist class in the United Kingdom during the middle of the twentieth century and then diverged sharply after the Thatcher era—with the business fraction of the wealth elite becoming more and more dominant over time.[55]

Again, this conception of Britain's wealth elite is not without its limitations. Our reliance on *Who's Who* may mean we are missing some wealthy positional elites in new fields like tech or less visible sectors of the economy,

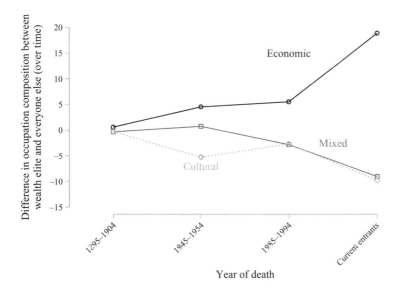

1.8 Business elites have become increasingly dominant within the wealth elite.

Note: Economic occupations (business leaders, finance, and so on), cultural occupations (these include artists, those who work in the media, and educational professionals, as well as scientists and sports stars), and mixed (including lawyers, politicians, and military).

such as lobbying, that may contain individuals in the top 1 percent of the wealth distribution. And there are of course important gradations of power within our wealth elite which we do not discern here. We also do not attend to those in the top 1 percent of the wealth distribution who, for whatever reason, are not in *Who's Who.* These are likely quite different from the rich who are—they may be wealthy because they own properties in expensive parts of the country or work in high-salary fields (such as finance), but they do not necessarily have the most powerful or influential jobs in those fields. Money, of course, provides some dimension of power in itself, but simply owning an expensive house was not considered sufficient for inclusion in the positional elite we study here.

Despite these caveats, we think that pinpointing a wealth elite sheds important new light on Britain's power structure, allowing us to identify the demographic characteristics of those who have both positional and economic power. For one thing, it clearly shows how the business community has come to dominate this group over time. It also allows us to address a foundational issue in elite studies—whether this wealth elite can be considered an ideologically coherent group who seek to exercise power in a unified way. Specifically, how does this wealth elite think? Are they worried about inequality? Do they want higher taxes? Are they in favour of trans rights? After all, the existence of an ideologically coherent wealth elite may be particularly concerning if it is actively using its power to further a distinct policy agenda that diverges from other groups in the population. This is what we consider in Chapters 7 through 9. And, as we will show, there are ample reasons for concern.

We have made the case for defining the British elite in two ways, and in this book we work with both definitions. Yet while we, as sociologists, may think about elites in these ways, this does not necessarily align with how elites see themselves. Do Britain's most powerful people see themselves as elite? What versions of themselves do they tend to project in public? And how have their identities changed over time? In the following chapter we seek answers to these questions, finding that today's elites, unlike those of the past, are extremely anxious about being perceived as elitist. Indeed, many of them labour fairly elaborately to present themselves as regular, ordinary, and meritocratic.

2

A Life Less Ordinary

In March 2022 we began reaching out to members of the British elite. Around 1,500 of the people included in the latest edition of *Who's Who* had indicated on the survey we'd sent the previous month that they would be happy to be interviewed, so now we were following up. Our ask was simple—we were interested, we wrote, in "exploring the experiences, attitudes, and beliefs of influential individuals in multiple fields." The vast majority wrote back quickly and enthusiastically. Yet there was also a curious tenor to some responses. People were happy to be interviewed, but before proceeding many were eager to make one thing very clear—actually, they were not very influential at all. Many were keen to explain this is in some detail:

From: [Recipient]
Date: Thursday, 31 March 2022 at 13:46
To: [Research Team]
Subject: Interview
Dear Professor Friedman,
I found your initial questionnaire fascinating. However, I do have serious reservations. Most importantly, I do not consider myself in any way whatsoever to be either "a key decision maker" or "in a position of influence in British society." I have simply made a small contribution to my own, somewhat narrow, field. I think that it would be a pity if you wasted one of these on somebody who has no illusions of authority.
With kind regards,
[Recipient]

From: [Recipient]
Date: Thursday, 31 March 2022 at 16:15
To: [Research Team]
Subject: Questionnaire
Dear Professor Friedman,
The thought of my being an influential individual would be for both my family and my closest friends the best laugh of the week. But if it's useful for you to have backed one horse that fell or refused at one of the early fences . . .
Yours sincerely,
[Recipient]

Was this just a very British mode of humble-brag? Perhaps. But these responses mimicked a wider theme we were seeing across both our own and others' research, reflecting a contemporary elite keen to position itself as regular, ordinary, and meritocratic, and often doing so by positioning itself against a caricatured image of an older and more traditional aristocratic elite.[1] In this chapter, we explore this projection of ordinariness. We look at how it manifests itself in the way people distance themselves from notions of eliteness, how they tell elaborate origin stories that act to deflect from inherited privilege, and how they construct their meritocratic legitimacy by setting themselves against the stuffier elites of Britain's past. We also show that this quest for ordinariness has not been a perennial preoccupation of elites. Delving into accounts from the early twentieth century, we find a much more unabashed upper-class identity. These earlier elites were comfortable with their privilege, proud of their highbrow cultural palette, and appear largely unashamed of the nepotistic processes that often flanked their recruitment to elite careers.

Elite Ambivalence

One theme that unites the contemporary British elite is a deep discomfort with the term *elite*. Nearly all of the people we interviewed pushed back strongly when we asked if they consider themselves "a member of the British elite":

> I don't see myself as elite . . . I'm not elite, not at all. (Samira, education, born 1965–1970)

I'm just a chap sitting in a little house in a suburb whose life is, as you've discovered, normal . . . quite ordinary. (Raymond, finance, wealth elite, 1935–1940)

I'm very cleared eyed about this, I'm not part of the elite at all. I have very limited influence and almost no power. (Anthony, business, wealth elite, 1955–1960)

As you can see here, even those in the wealth elite—the 0.01 percent who fall both in *Who's Who* and the top 1 percent of the wealth distribution—reject the label elite. Many seemed offended, maybe even a little angry, at the suggestion. Such responses are perhaps understandable. After all, "elite" is almost always a pejorative term in public life today. It is a formulation that, as Owen Jones has noted, often simply signals "those with power who I personally don't agree with."[2] On the right, for example, we hear constantly about the dysfunctions of a new, radical woke elite, while the left decries "the ruling elite," or its corollary "the establishment." It is no great surprise, then, that people resist the imposition of this somewhat toxic identity.

It is also not particularly unexpected considering what we know from the sociology of elites.[3] Sociologists have long shown that people tend to locate their social position by comparing themselves to those in their immediate social vicinity. This leads them to see themselves as "normal" or "average" regardless of their objective status or privilege.[4] American sociologist Rachel Sherman has noted that elite disidentification can also be part of a strategy to claim moral worthiness.[5] In the quest to see themselves, and be seen by others, as a good person, the very wealthy often try to obscure their economic advantage.

Yet the expressions of ordinariness we were seeing went beyond simply disavowing snobbery and elitism. They were wide-ranging and intertwined with how people articulated their meritocratic legitimacy. This played out in two ways. First, via the expression of upwardly mobile origin stories which downplayed interviewees' own (often elite) upbringings in favour of more middle- or working-class extended family histories. And second, by counterposing one's own elite trajectory with a caricatured vision of the early twentieth–century British elite.

Deflecting Privilege

The British have always had a rather complicated relationship to class identities. In many parts of the world, people tend to identify upward, reporting that they feel middle class even when this contradicts their more disadvantaged socio-economic position.[6] People in the United Kingdom, by contrast, are more likely to identify downward.[7] For example, nearly half of British people employed in solidly middle-class professional and managerial jobs see themselves as working class. And more strikingly, 24 percent of those in these middle-class jobs who also come from middle-class backgrounds *still* identify as working class.[8]

This trend is also evident among the British elite, particularly those from elite origins. Our survey shows that only 3 percent of those in *Who's Who* see themselves as coming from an upper-class background, although we know from our analysis of historical probate data that nearly seven times that number—approximately 20 percent—hail from families within the top 1 percent of the wealth distribution.[9] Even more significantly, 34 percent of those from middle-class backgrounds report their class origin as less advantaged than the standard way they would be classified based on their parents' occupations (that is, they describe their background as "working class" when their parents had professional or managerial jobs like teachers or engineers, or as "lower middle class" when their parents did higher professional or managerial jobs such as doctors or lawyers). Or to look at it another way, 43 percent of elites who say they are from working-class backgrounds actually come from professional, middle-class families. Notably, this is equally the case for men and women, and among elites of colour.

We can also see this inclination in other ways too. In one of our survey questions, we asked respondents to imagine that a close friend of theirs had recently been appointed as the CEO of a FTSE 250 company. The friend, we said, is looking for some advice concerning an online profile that she has been asked to write that will be shared with all of the company's employees. We then gave them a few facts about this fictitious friend and asked them to pick which ones they would advise her to mention. Three concerned slightly conflicting dimensions of her family background; a) that she grew up in a mining village where her grandfather had worked in the pits, b) that her father was a headteacher, and c) that she received a partial scholarship to a private school. Tellingly, over 86 percent of our respondents thought that she should mention her grandfather, while 63 percent thought she should mention her father. And only 38 percent thought she should mention her private schooling. Even in this stylised setting, then, elites would, whatever their motivations, advise their colleague to tell a story about their life that has the consequence of deflecting privilege.

Why do so many members of the British elite identify (or misidentify) downward in this way? Some clues emerged in interviews when we asked people to discuss their backgrounds. Specifically, we began interviews with two simple questions: "What did your parents do for a living?" and "Do you think of yourself as coming from a particular social class?" Many answers to these questions were direct and to the point, describing their parents' occupations (and any relevant changes during their childhood) and then identifying a class background that closely matched their "objective" social class origin.[10] Among those from distinctly elite families—who had either gone to a top private school or whose families were in the top 1 percent of the wealth distribution—this often meant an explicit acknowledgment of privilege:

We were very well-off. (Stephen, business, wealth elite, 1950–1955)

I was a very fortunate child, raised in a privileged background. (Atonye, religion, 1955–1959)

My parents were very wealthy. (Sharon, business, wealth elite, 1960–1965)

Yet for a significant minority, including many from elite origins, these questions were uncomfortable.[11] Answers were stilted rather than direct, elaborate but vague. Some began with awkward qualifications such as "This is going to sound really bad" (Michael, politician, wealth elite, 1940–1945) while others, like Kevin, a business executive (1955–1960), acknowledged: "Class things, they just make me feel innately uncomfortable." Barbara, a celebrated professor from an aristocratic background (1945–1950), was particularly thrown when asked to describe her class background:

Barbara: I mean I don't know . . . I'm certainly not, I mean upper middle, I don't know what you call it. I mean [my father] probably thought himself as upper class but communist. You know I don't particularly . . . I don't think of myself as a class, but I'm clearly not working class or lower class. And I, you know, I don't particularly want to think about class, but I must have come from a privileged background . . . I mean do you think I've got a slightly . . . I mean I'm sometimes slightly shocked when I hear a recording of my voice that it sounds a bit upper . . .

Interviewer: It's got a middle-class sound, but it doesn't sound super posh to me.

Barbara: Well, good, well I don't want it to.

What is striking here is not only the palpable awkwardness but also Barbara's desire to not appear "posh." Like Barbara, many we spoke to attempted to deflect from, or downplay, aspects of their upbringing that might signal privilege. This deflection tended to take place in two ways.

For those educated at elite private schools, discussions of background were often discussed relationally, with one's privilege muted by comparison with more conspicuously advantaged classmates.[12] By any standard measure, the vast majority of these people were from highly advantaged backgrounds. Yet within an institutional environment characterised by extraordinary wealth and privilege they often recounted visceral memories of feeling culturally and socio-economically "other." Peter (academic, 1945–1950), for example, recalled being mocked at Eton because his family didn't own a car, while Terence (CEO, 1950–1955) recalls the embarrassment of feeling like his father—a successful small-businessman—"was the poorest parent" at St Paul's. For others, such comparisons were less concrete and rooted in a more abstract sense of feeling like they were outside an inner circle, either at school, university, or in the workplace, often imagined in somewhat fuzzy and caricatured terms as an "establishment," "old boys club," or "upper class." As Michael explained:

[my background] felt very normal and ordinary. Because my father was a judge . . . I never thought of myself as coming from a sort of upper-class background . . . none of my friends at Rugby were sort of hunting, shooting, fishing types, they were mainly London professionals. So I think I very much thought I came from—not a working-class background—but I absolutely didn't want to come from, sort of, *that* background.

Such distancing allowed interviewees like Michael to describe themselves as coming from "normal" or "ordinary" backgrounds—despite hailing from the top 1 percent of the wealth distribution. Brian (scientist, 1945–1950), whose father was a surgeon and who had been educated at Harrow, made a similar claim:

I thoroughly dislike [class] terms, but they do mean something . . . I would call myself middle class. Because I am neither lower-class nor upper-class. So, slap bang in the middle.

The second way our participants deflected their privilege was by placing their upbringing within the context of a much longer family history, incorporating grandparents and sometimes even great-grandparents. These interviewees typically sidestepped, or only briefly addressed, questions about parental occupation. Instead, they located themselves within extended family stories of working-class struggle and upward mobility. Helen (academic, 1960–1965), for example, whose parents were both teachers and who had been privately educated, described her background as "working-class," but did so by focusing on her parent's upbringings. Many of the people we spoke to constructed such elaborate origin stories, and foregrounded their parents' backgrounds as the primary source of their class identity rather than their own.

This tendency was perhaps best exemplified by our discussion with Cerys (1965–1970), an Indian British barrister. Cerys's father was a successful doctor who had initially trained as a surgeon before later running and owning a large GP practice; her mother was a nurse but also the manager of the practice. Yet Cerys characterised her background as "lower middle-class," foregrounding her mother's extended family, particularly her grandmother, who had worked as cleaner. This was key to her sense of being upwardly socially mobile:

Interviewer: Do you think you've experienced social mobility in your lifetime?

Cerys: I think the spread is more between the generation which is the level of my children compared with my mum and her family, so my grandparents in Wales, we demonstrate a nearly vertical trajectory . . .

my mum of course left school at 14, so that was the first change, and then my grandparents in Wales would have left school before senior school, so it's definitely pinned to education, as far as I can see. I mean we've not made money any other way than education, going into professions, working hard, you know.

We should be cautious in what we draw from this. Such subjective understandings of class origin are not necessarily "incorrect" or cynically strategic.[13] They clearly reflect "real" lived experiences of multigenerational upward mobility and "real" relational inequalities with colleagues or classmates from more elite origins. As the American social psychologist Robyn Fivush notes, our sense of identity is not only shaped by our own autobiographical memory but also by the stories we hear during childhood about the lives and characters in our extended family. These elements scaffold what she calls our "intergenerational self."

This intergenerational self was particularly complex for people with a migration story in their extended family.[14] The upward story most of these people articulated was rooted in the downward mobility their parents or grandparents had experienced when migrating to the United Kingdom. These relatives may have been relatively advantaged in their origin country, but upon migrating had been forced to take lower-paid or lower-status work, which had left an important mark on their identities. Samira, an educational leader, explained that her parents and grandparents had been "extremely wealthy" before migrating from India. "I suppose, according to the British way, we'd have been upper class," she explained. After the family migrated to the United Kingdom, her father got a job as a civil engineer. Yet Samira described her upbringing in the United Kingdom as "lower-middle class" and the downward mobility she associated with migration seemed to strongly inform this sense of self. As she put it, "We had to start from scratch."

Deflections of privilege, then, are not necessarily calculated or even straightforwardly intentional. They clearly reflect authentic feelings and experiences. Yet we would maintain that these kinds of origin stories nonetheless have tangible effects when they are expressed in everyday life. Whether intentional or not, they act to downplay one's class privilege in the eyes of others, especially in the face of questions that, if answered directly, would reveal such advantaged origins in fairly unambiguous terms. Transposing a question about one's own upbringing into a narrative about one's grandparents, then, allows interviewees like Helen and Cerys to construct an origin story of romantic upward progression.[15]

The Meritocratic Legitimacy of an Upward Story

Claiming multigenerational upward mobility not only functions as a means of telling a humble "origin story." This intergenerational self was also present in interviewees' accounts of their subsequent life course, and particularly how they made sense of their career. These individuals often presented themselves as classed outsiders who had overcome significant barriers at work. To return to Cerys, she characterised her career at the bar as beset with economic barriers rooted in the fact that she came "from a background with no base in economic security." This sense of struggle seemed to morph into an awareness that her career trajectory should be read as unquestioningly meritocratic. As she summed up: "I think it is a meritocratic elite that I am in, I worked for my position, I wasn't born into it."

This link between deflecting privilege and the claim of meritocratic legitimacy also came through clearly in our survey data. Those who identified subjectively as being less privileged than their parental occupation would suggest were more likely (by 5 percentage points) to tell us that merit had been "very important to their success." Ian, a banker (1965–1970) who reported his ethnicity as "white other," offers a telling illustration of this kind of sentiment. He answered questions about his background by focusing on his father, who "was born into relative poverty and lived a life of deprivation," although later in the interview he acknowledged that his father had gone on to be a successful business owner. Yet the idea that his own subsequent success had involved "escaping" from the "confines" of his background was central to his sense of self:

Ian: But you wouldn't consider me to be the British elite would you?

Interviewer: Well this is what I wanted to ask you how you, how does that word land with you?

Ian: No I find it—I find it utterly jarring and almost like offensive. What's it got to do with me? I don't regard myself as that . . . This is not a question of modesty, immodesty. I regard myself as kind of like you know yet another middle-class, well-educated boy who managed to escape the clutches of the confines of their background, the restrictions of their background and do something a little bit more interesting. So I don't regard myself as elite. I'm not that at all. I regard myself as a thoroughly middle-class guy who you know has found where the escape hatch is and has tried my very best to make something interesting of a life that could otherwise perhaps not have been that interesting . . . I don't think of myself as different, I just think of myself as kind of solidly in the middle class of people who are striving to do something useful with their lives.

What is striking about this conversation with Ian is not only his disbelief at the suggestion of being labelled elite but also how this is bound up with a particular upwardly mobile self-understanding.

Notably, these kinds of narratives strongly echoed feelings of dislocation and imposter syndrome expressed by interviewees who had risen to high-ranking positions from more unambiguously working-class or disadvantaged backgrounds. Yet there were subtle differences in narrations of imposter syndrome among interviewees from different class backgrounds. For those from disadvantaged backgrounds, imposter syndrome was described as a more chronic condition. These individuals reported fairly enduring, often paralyzing, feelings of insecurity and inferiority during their careers. Consider Paul, a senior civil servant (1955–1960), who grew up in a very poor, single-parent household:

I always felt an outsider, even when I was being written up as the next permanent secretary and I can vividly remember virtually every time I walked along Downing Street, a thought popped into my head which was, what the fuck am I doing here? And that never leaves you, and the truth is it eats at you in a negative way . . . because you're never quite at home, never quite settled.

In contrast there was a strong theme of resistance among interviewees from more privileged backgrounds. To return to Ian, he explained that he had refused to be made to feel like an outsider and had strived to keep pushing forward in his career:

Look, I don't have the right name, I don't have a title, I don't have form, I don't have old boys networks, I don't come from Eton, I didn't go to Oxbridge. What do I have going for me? I work like a dog, okay. I know a lot of people do but I really work hard.

In these accounts, we see how narrations of upward mobility allow interviewees like Ian to position themselves as uniquely meritocratically legitimate. In order to "escape the clutches" of his background, Ian asserts that he has had to "work harder," "work longer," "be better," and therefore, by implication, is *more* deserving of his success.

We are not passing judgment on people like Ian. After all, why should we expect people to understand their class privilege in the first place? And more specifically why would we assume people see themselves in the same terms as sociologists? These are important questions. Yet the point we would return to is that, generally, discussions of privileged backgrounds in interviews, and particularly elite origins, felt uncomfortable, awkward even—particularly when such privilege was objectively fairly extreme. There was a sense that the elites we spoke to instinctively moved to cast their origin story in a more humble light. This was often subtle, mentioning some aspects of their upbringing and not others or downplaying aspects of their upbringing that might signal privilege; the inexpensive nature of their private schooling, the periods of economic uncertainty their family had faced, or the working-class struggles of their ancestors. They wanted, it seemed to us, to tell an upward story, or at least a less seamless account, to claim a particular meritocratic legitimacy for their success.

One unusually frank conversation with Mary, a CEO (1945–1950), illustrated this sentiment. Mary had been educated at an elite boarding school but explained that throughout her career she had hidden her education from colleagues, even going so far as to omit her schooling from her *Who's Who* profile:

Interviewer: Why did you not put it in your Who's Who entry?

Mary: Because I didn't want to draw attention to the fact I'd been to private school.

Interviewer: Why is that, do you think?

Mary: I can't remember for sure. There probably was an element of not wanting to draw attention to it . . . I think I'm more comfortable about it now than I was. But yes, there probably is an element of not wanting people to make assumptions about my background, based on the school I went to.

We would argue that these accounts of concealing, disavowing, and downplaying elite backgrounds are significant because, whatever their purpose, they still deflect attention away from the inherited privilege these individuals enjoy, both in their own eyes and among their colleagues. At the same time, one consequence of framing their lives as an upward struggle "against the odds" is that their subsequent life outcomes may appear more worthy, more deserving, and more meritorious. Whether this is intentional or not is of course hard to adjudicate, and we must be careful not to smuggle analysis behind the backs of our respondents. But whether this is a matter of how people make sense of their origins *or* how they choose to tell their story in public, either way it tells us something significant about the quest for meritocratic legitimacy among the contemporary British elite.[16]

Narratives of Opening Up

Ordinariness, as a claim to legitimate fortune, was not only articulated via origin stories. It was also forged by positioning one's own life experience against a distinct imagined vision of elites from Britain's past. Here the prevailing narrative was that the elite institutions one had experienced—be they elite schools, universities, or employers—had once been closed and socially exclusive, but that things had changed, and become more markedly meritocratic. Such comparative narratives were not necessarily about the recent past—most did not think Britain had become more open in the last twenty or so years. Instead, most made comparisons with Britain in the 1970s, 1980s, or even earlier.

Thomas, for example, a senior civil servant (1940–1945), explained that when he joined the service in the 1970s the institution functioned similarly to the way it was caricatured in the BBC TV comedy *Yes Minister*—with a "band" of posh "Sir Humphreys" dictating who progresses.[17] Yet during his career this changed dramatically, and the fact that he had been to an elite public school (Winchester College) had "not been relevant at all." Similarly, William, a newspaper editor (1950–1955), counterposed his own experience of the British media to the portrait painted by Anthony

Sampson in *Anatomy of Britain*. There was a fundamental "mismatch," he noted, between the "stuffy establishment ruling Britain" portrayed by Sampson and his own experience of a media elite that "was already quite porous, and becoming more porous all the time." Michael, an influential policy advisor to several governments, observed a similar trend in politics and academia:

> The truth is there's been masses of [social mobility] . . . so when I was young the number of top jobs were very limited. Nowadays there are so many top jobs there are plenty of ways in which you can move up. I mean if I was thinking about a certain elite from the 30s, 40s, 50s, 60s, then a really large number of people would've got there through a boarding school. And that would be a way you would identify people . . . now you wouldn't dream, I mean I can't imagine asking what school someone went to.

These narratives of opening up are significant for several reasons. First, they show how contemporary elites perceive Britain to be a country that has experienced significant progressive change over time. This allows them to see those at "the top" of contemporary British society as qualitatively different to the elites of the past. They are less "stuffy," less "posh," less dominated "by what school you went to"—in other words, more meritocratic.[18]

A second, related reason is that such comparative accounts have a subtext which acts to frame their *own* trajectories in a more meritocratic light. Echoing the findings of elite scholars such as Elisabeth Schimpfössl in Russia, Lauren Rivera in the United States, and Katharina Hecht in the United Kingdom, a notable feature of the career narratives we heard was that they were meritocratically achieved.[19] This is not to say that accounts did not touch on other factors, but we were struck by most interviewees' insistence that, ultimately, the decisive factor in understanding their own personal achievements was merit. This was echoed in our survey data, where merit emerged—as Figure 2.1 shows—as by far the most important factor in elites' understanding of their own success. This is consistent even among elites added to *Who's Who* in the last few years.

Again, what was interesting was that when elites spoke about their own accomplishments, their reflections were often flanked by references

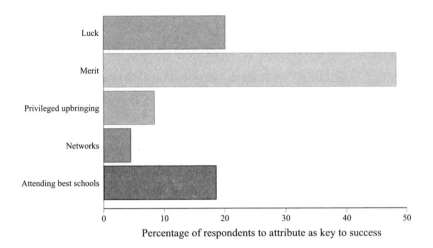

2.1 The elite see merit as the main driver of their success.

to the past. Mark, for example, an influential political advisor (1965–1970), explained that central to his success had been his abilities as an original and creative thinker, someone who had acted as a disruptive ideational entrepreneur:

> I think in policy terms I probably would be seen towards the entre-preneurial end of the spectrum . . . the way I was probably able to differentiate myself a bit was when things went bad and we had crises which I have always welcomed because that's when the window of op-portunity opens up to reconfigure things . . .

Yet for Mark, these ideational talents had only been recognised by his colleagues because he was part of a new and different generation in British politics:

> It's a different network, it's not the old boys network, it's not the social circle network. There's more of a market for ideas now, and even political people are less ideological than they were, they just want stuff that's going to work basically and that's quite lucky for someone like me, basically, who essentially is apolitical but has had thoughts about one or two things. So I think those barriers are fewer than they have been.

Highbrow and Entitled: Early-Twentieth-Century Accounts of Elite Identity

Those in positions of power may strive to present themselves as emblems of upward mobility and progressive change. But hasn't this always been the case? Haven't the positional elite always been keen to deflect attention from their privilege? Our interviews with those born in the first few decades of the twentieth century, most sourced from the British Library and therefore not anonymised, provide unique insight into these questions.

Reading across these interviews, rhetorical claims to ordinariness are certainly evident in some accounts. A discussion with the celebrated architect Denys Lasdun, born in 1914 to a very wealthy family and educated at Rugby, reveals a familiar deflection of class privilege:

Interviewer: Do you think the war had a democratising effect on you? Because up to the war you had had a rather upper-middle-class background.

Lasdun: Not upper middle, I would say just middle. Well, whatever, you can say what you like. But yes, I'm sure mucking around in the war with your fellow men and the great bond that you had because you were fighting . . . it was a good salutary way of meeting all kinds of people, and I don't have any middle class feelings at all about people, I mean, it doesn't enter my value systems, we are just people . . . Rugby would be responsible for not feeling elitist in any way because Rugby didn't have an elitist ethos, it had Midlanders, all kinds of people you know, a real mixture.

By and large, though, these interviews paint a very different picture of elite identity. Most interviewees talked openly (and often proudly) about the influence and successes of their parents and wider families. Jeremy Morse, a banker and later university chancellor born in 1928, offers a notable example. Not only did he agree to be interviewed in his home, an imposing townhouse in Kensington (in Central London), he talked happily about the inherited wealth that had shaped his life:

And we bought this house in Drayton Gardens, and we still live in it . . . we both had capital, I mean, I had quite a lot of capital, both from my father and my mother's side, and my wife has inherited, from her grandfather, one of the farms in Gloucestershire, and also had some other capital. So we have never been short of money. And my father was always very insistent on that, he said, "If you have some capital, it gives you some freedom, you're not at the beck and call . . . ," and I note that the tax system in this country has been extremely light on capital. So, anyway, I've never been other than comfortably off, and I've never felt I have to, you know, take every penny from my work, etc., etc. And that's just a bit of luck.

The breeziness with which Morse discusses his and his wife's inherited wealth here, and their ability to live off capital income, sits in stark contrast to the uncomfortable discussions shared earlier in this chapter. It is also clear from the accounts of Morse and others that these earlier cohorts embraced a more self-consciously upper-class identity. This is difficult to illustrate directly as the British Library interviewers did not ask explicitly about class. Yet the moment one starts reading these transcripts (or listening to the audio) it becomes abundantly clear—linguistically in the distinct speech, diction, and turn of phrase, and more generally through the particular manner in which these people describe their lives.

Two areas are worth highlighting. First, we were struck by the way these interviewees described their lifestyle and tastes. Most were unashamedly highbrow and happily paraded their knowledge of, and interest in, opera, theatre, ballet, classical music, and visual art, and occasionally more aristocratic pursuits like shooting, polo, and horse-riding. For many, like Alan Carr (born 1936), a senior partner at the law firm Simmons & Simmons, these tastes and pursuits were rooted in a particular upbringing:

Carr: I was reasonably literate certainly at a very early age.

Interviewer: And you mentioned theatre and opera as being an enthusiasm of your parents. Did they pass that on?

Carr: Yes they did, very much so . . . I can remember my first 'Tosca' at the Ostend Casino, remember going to 'La Traviata," it was probably the first thing I remember vividly at home, because I could read the programme, I must have been about 11 or 12. My father had by this time got a car, a very nice car, and I remember a very beautiful Armstrong Siddeley with wonderful curving wings, and he driving us on one of our holidays down to Saint Jean de Luz and into Spain . . . And we went to France quite a lot, but quite remoter parts of France, Annecy we drove to one year. And, the south of France, Côte d'Azur, Provence. I went to Paris quite a lot, my father knew Paris very well . . . We also went, I'm talking early Fifties '52, '53, just before I went up to Cambridge, I went with my parents to Italy, and we went several times to Venice; we went to Florence and Rome, the usual major cities.

What is notable here, especially in comparison with our contemporary interviews, is not just how rarefied the cultural palette of people like Alan Carr is—his confident reference to high-art touchpoints, but also the mon-eyed nature of the recreations he describes. He fondly remembers elabo-rate holidays in Paris, Provence, and the Côte d'Azur, regular participation at cultural and sporting venues, and expensive restaurants. Indeed, these often act as key contexts for formational life experiences. Anthony Mal-linson (law, 1923) describes how he met his wife after eyeing her throughout the cricket season at Lords, while John Maxwell Kennedy (law, 1934) de-scribes how sharing a love of opera with key colleagues was central to his promotion to partner. And what is perhaps most salient, when compared to more contemporary accounts, is the unapologetic manner in which this highbrow orientation is expressed. There is no concern about the exclusivity or snobbishness that these kinds of pursuits might signal. Being "cultured" is proudly paraded as a badge of honour.

The second way we detected more self-conscious upper-class identities in these earlier interviews was via a distinct sense of entitlement. Family legacy played an important role in shaping the expectations people had re-garding their future careers. Frank (a pseudonym because he was one of our interviewees) was born in the early 1930s and recalls distinctly how, at the age of 8, he decided to become a politician. He remembers asking about a photograph on the wall of the family home of a statue of a man. Frank was told that this man was his great-great grandfather and that the statue recognised his twenty years of service as an MP. "Well," Frank responded, "I shall become one of those."

Unlike the quest for meritocratic legitimacy expressed in later accounts, these individuals also happily recounted how their careers were advantaged by nepotism and favouritism. This was particularly key in transitions between university and entry into professional firms:

> Well, my father having been in the City and my grandfather having been in the City, I suppose there was always an expectation that I might have an opportunity to get a job in the City. And a half-brother of my mother's was a director of a small insurance broking company, and he asked me if I would like to go and start with them, which I duly did. (David Scholey, banking, 1935)

> I was up at Cambridge, and I began to think then, what I am I going to do? And I got a very clear message from my uncle, he said, "I can introduce you to George Dennehy, who with Gordon Simmons is one of the two senior partners at Simmons & Simmons. I think you would be a very good solicitor, and I think he will take you and will be very glad that he has taken you. You'll have status, you'll have a good income, you'll have a great deal of scope for your talents," and that is what happened. He introduced me to George Dennehy. And I did go there. (Alan Carr, law, 1936)

What is striking in both of these accounts is how comfortable these interviewees are in describing how they benefited from egregiously nepotistic recruitment processes. It tells you something about a particular upper-class culture that existed at the time, where giving one's friend's children a leg up was normalised as simply "the way things are done."

It is of course hard to fully convey the intricate texture of this kind of elite identity. Perhaps the best way to illustrate this is via an extended example. Consider John Henderson, chair of the investment management company, the Henderson Group, born in 1920. Educated at Eton and Cambridge, he first had a successful career in the army, rising to become aide-de-camp to Field Marshal Bernard Law Montgomery (Monty) in World War II. Central to this military success, and particularly his relationship with Montgomery, he explained, was a sense of shared upper-class culture:

> *Henderson:* And so Monty said, "Well, what do you want to do [after the war]?" And I said, "Well, I thought I might go in the City." And he said, "Well, that won't do you any good. All they do is think of making money. All they want to do, on the 1st of January, is put in

their diary when grouse shooting begins, and the dates of Ascot and Wimbledon." And I said, "Well, that sounds rather good to me!"

Interviewer: Did that irritate him?

Henderson: Oh Lord, no! Good Heavens, no!

Interviewer: So do you think that social background was important in enabling [you] to converse, be relaxed, with someone like Monty? I mean, was it useful to have been to Eton?

Henderson: Well, oh, yes, yes. I mean, you either do or don't, don't you. I mean, I don't think it's anything you can change your attitude of, to life. I mean, either you are fairly free and easy about things, or you're not.

What is telling here is how Henderson understands the notion of shared upper-class culture. Rather than any concrete social or cultural touchpoints, it is a more diffuse "attitude to life," a "free and easy" experience of the world. Henderson went on have a successful career in the City, where he evidently felt very much at home:

Interviewer: What about your, your school day chums from, from Eton, were they visible in the City?

Henderson: Yes, oh yes. Oh yes . . . , I mean, a lot of them are all there.

Interviewer: Is that a convenient thing for you, though, just to have all those friends dotted around in useful . . .

Henderson: Well, of course it helps, mmmm.

Interviewer: Do you think that the City is rather a cosy sort of place?

Henderson: Would I say it was a cosy sort of place? Mmmm. If you want it to be cosy, it can be cosy, but if you don't, it's not. No, it's not cosy to everyone. I mean, today, it's much more competitive and, I mean, it hasn't got the charm that it had.

Interview: What would you describe as charm?

Henderson: Well, charm, you had the enjoyment of a deal with friends, and . . . today, I mean, everything has to go up on the screen straightaway.

The suggestion of a shared class culture is again not explicit here—it is referenced opaquely, via terms such as "cosy" and "charm"—but neither is it obscured or deflected. Henderson is quite candid about the commercial utility of being surrounded by fellow old Etonians, and the pressures and inconvenience of contemporary market transparency (where "everything has to go up on the screen straightaway"). Such accounts are reminiscent of the wealthy US women in Susan Ostrander's classic *Women of the Upper Class,* one of the only other qualitative studies of elites born in the first few decades of the twentieth century. Not only were these women largely comfortable with their eliteness but this also translated into a more general sense of "being better than other people"—"a moral, as well as social, superiority."[20]

The Symbolic Market for Ordinariness

Our analysis so far suggests a notable change over time in the expression of ordinariness. But a key question remains. Why does the contemporary British elite strive to present itself in this way? One potential explanation is that there is a strong symbolic market for ordinariness in everyday life. Specifically, ordinariness may perform an important signalling function for elites, especially in settings where they interact with the general public or those they lead in organisations.[21] A number of sociologists, including Shamus Khan, Rachel Sherman, and Oliver Hahl and his colleagues in the United States, Anu Kantola and Hanna Kuusela in Finland, and Magne Flemmen and Vegard Jarness in Norway, have made this case in recent years.[22] One takeaway from this work, we would argue, is that as contemporary elites have pulled away economically, and as more attention has been focused on the lives and opportunities of the 1 percent, many have begun to suffer from an insecurity about their moral legitimacy in the eyes of wider publics. To offset the new narrative that elites are principally motivated by status, money, or power, they seek to present themselves as ordinary and authentic.

They do this, Flemmen and Jarness claim, because non-elites and working-class groups in particular, often distinguish between elites whom they see as decent, open, and accommodating towards others and those whom they see as snobbish and who look down on others, with the former clearly valued over the latter.[23] It is thus not so much that elites are viewed with suspicion because they are elite; rather, it is their perceived smugness or elitism that rouses negative reactions. In this way, it is possible to see efforts to present oneself as ordinary as effective because it acts to dissolve (at least temporarily) the actual cultural and economic boundaries between elites and others. This is what Pierre Bourdieu called "strategies of condescension": in downplaying difference, elites can "derive profit from the objective relations of power" in the very act of obfuscating the relation.[24]

But is there really a symbolic market for ordinariness? The theoretical logic may be compelling but the evidence base is fairly weak. To get at this question, we conducted a series of experiments in January 2023 with a nationally representative sample of 500 people from the British population. The experiments were simple. We presented people with short descriptions (vignettes) of imaginary elites and then asked them to rate these people on a number of different dimensions.

The first experiment aimed to identify whether ordinary people are more sympathetic and admiring of elites if they think they have been upwardly socially mobile. More specifically, people were assigned one of these two vignettes about a fictitious academic:

Imagine you see an academic on TV who is talking about their research. In the TV show, they talk a little bit about how this academic developed their research interests. You find out that her father worked as a maintenance assistant and it was his experiences that informed her research. She has been working at the University of Manchester for five years now and she did her PhD in Sheffield, the university where her father worked in maintenance.

Imagine you see an academic on TV who is talking about their research. In the TV show, the academic explains how they developed their research interests. You find out that her father was an academic and it was his experiences that informed her research. She has been working at the University of Manchester for five years now and she did her PhD in Sheffield, the university where her father was a professor.

We then asked people to rate (on a scale of 100) whether they thought the notional academic was "very intelligent," "hard working," "would listen carefully to someone like me," and does "research that is useful to everyone in society." How respondents reacted to these two hypothetical people was surprisingly different (see Figure 2.2). People were significantly less sympathetic to the academic born into privilege. They not only saw her as less meritorious in terms of intelligence and hard work, but they were also less sympathetic to her research, believing it was less likely to be beneficial to society as a whole. Tellingly they were also much less likely to believe that this academic would listen to someone like them.

This suggests that there is indeed a strong symbolic market for deflecting privilege. It is a strategy that may actually work. Those elites who successfully convince ordinary people that they come from more humble backgrounds (even if this is not actually the case), are likely to be viewed as more

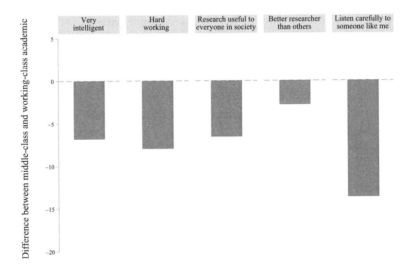

2.2 The British public sees an academic from a privileged class background as less intelligent and hard-working than a "working-class" academic. Negative scores imply middle-class person scored lower.

Note: The *p*-value for these contrasts was less than 0.001 except on the question asking whether this researcher was better than other researchers, which was great than 0.05. We explain what *p*-values mean in the Methodological Appendix but most researchers would treat *p*-values less than 0.05 as evidence that the difference we are observing between two groups is unlikely to explained by random chance (or more concretely, the idiosyncrasies of the particular people we surveyed in this experiment).

meritorious and as doing more meaningful work. Downplaying privilege, then, is not just about a very British discomfort around discussions of class and privilege. It also represents an effective strategy of impression management. Mary, who we met earlier in the chapter, may have been absolutely right to assume that people would make negative assumptions about her if she had acknowledged she had been to private school.

We also asked people to evaluate another vignette. This one was not explicitly concerned with class but instead focused on two CEOs with different cultural profiles:

Imagine you are working in a large company. You do not know much about the CEO but you have heard that he is a family man. He loves spending time with his partner and his kids, having a drink at the pub, and walking the dog. He has been in charge of the firm for five years now and was at one point a middle manager in the same firm.

Imagine you are working in a large company. You do not know much about the CEO but you have heard that he is someone who loves high culture. He regularly visits the opera with his wife, enjoys classical music with his friends, and plays musical instruments with his kids. He has been in charge of the firm for five years now and was at one point a middle manager in the same firm.

Again, there were clear differences in how people assessed these two CEOs. In fact, in this example (Figure 2.3), the differences were even more stark. People were much less likely to think that the highbrow CEO would "look out for people like me" and that he was "down-to-earth." They were also less likely to believe that he knew what it was like to "struggle to make ends meet" and were more likely to believe he was motivated by money. The currency of ordinariness, this shows, is not just channelled via humble beginnings but also via culture—through your taste and lifestyle.

Wanna Live Like Common People

In 1995 British Britpop band Pulp released their iconic hit "Common People."[25] The song satirised the elite longing to be ordinary, describing an art-school love affair between Pulp frontman Jarvis Cocker and a Greek sculpture student from an elite background. "You wanna live like common

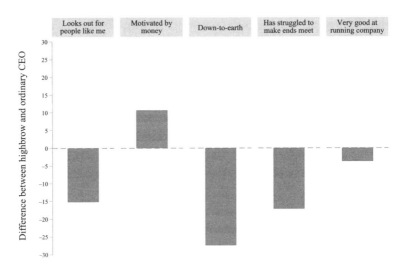

2.3 A CEO with highbrow tastes is viewed less favourably than a CEO with ordinary tastes. Negative scores imply highbrow CEO scored lower.
Note: The *p*-value for these contrasts was less than or equal to 0.01. We explain what *p*-values mean in the Methodological Appendix.

people," sang Cocker. "You wanna see whatever common people see, Wanna sleep with common people, You wanna sleep with common people . . . Like me."

In this chapter we have illustrated that this cosplay of ordinariness extends far beyond the aesthetic affectations of art school students. It is central to understanding contemporary elite identities, scaffolding how they tell their backstories, how they make sense of their success, and how they distinguish themselves from those who held similar positions in the past.

This is not necessarily an intentional strategy. But whether it is conscious or not, the fact is that elites are right to be anxious about how they come across. Our two experiments reveal that appearing privileged or elitist does alter how the general public perceives you, whether they think you're relatable or likely to care about them, perhaps even whether you are competent or not. Nowadays, revelling in nepotism or casually dropping high cultural references, as elites in the past were more likely to do, can have serious negative consequences.

Yet one of the perils of performing ordinariness is that the public do not necessarily buy it. As Cocker sings: "Rent a flat above a shop, Cut your hair and get a job, Smoke some fags and play some pool, Pretend you never went to school, But still you'll never get it right." Pulling off this posture of ordinariness, as this illustrates, is often a question of culture; a matter of taste, recreations, and lifestyle. In Chapter 3 we will take up this question of elite culture in more depth, analysing the evolving ways in which Britain's elites have used culture to distinguish themselves from others.

3

Cultural Chameleons

The Bank of England's Court of Directors is one of the most hallowed sanctums of the British elite. From the founding of the bank in 1694 to the present day, the court has met every few weeks to discuss the administration, strategy, policy, and operation of the United Kingdom's central bank. Its handful of members have long provided a window into the shifting character of the corporate inner circle. Consider, for example, three bankers who have served on the court over the last 125 years.

Henry Grenfell, governor from 1881, was an exemplar of the blue-blooded era of the City—when banking was, as Walter Bagehot famously observed, "an inheritance."[1] Grenfell's father had been a member of the bank's court and his son Edward went on to join the court between 1905 and 1940. Grenfell's cultural life was also distinctive. He lived in a large country house near Henley and his favourite pastimes, according to his *Who's Who* profile, were simply "hunting and shooting."

Fast forward 100 years to 1981, and in some ways not a lot had changed. David Scholey, who joined the Court of Directors that year, had also made his way to this position via a top public school and Christ Church College, Oxford. He also shared Grenfell's love of hunting. But Scholey, our 1992 interview reveals (he is still alive), was also quite a different banker. He was self-consciously "cultured"; he lived in Central London and had active interests in classics, literature, opera, golf, and tennis. These highbrow interests even impacted his City trajectory. In perhaps the key moment of his career, he explains, he was introduced to a City legend, the CEO of investment bank S. G. Warburg and Co., Siegmund Warburg, over "a cup of tea" in 1963. The pair talked for several hours, "ranging over history and literature." Only days later did Scholey learn that this had been a successful interview for a job at Warburg, where he went on to become chief executive.

Then there is Ian, one of our anonymised interviewees, who sat on the court in the early 2010s and 2020s. Not only are Ian's credentials distinct—he was neither educated privately nor was he a student at Oxbridge—but his cultural profile is notably different. The first recreation listed in his *Who's Who* profile, for example, is "family." It is not necessarily that Ian completely eschews traditional legitimate culture—he also mentions a taste for "visual arts"—but it is more that the cultural self he projects is often in direct opposition to the aristocratic and highbrow orientations presented by Grenfell and Scholey. He stresses, for instance, his ordinariness and inclusivity ("I don't think of myself as different . . . there's nobody I would treat differently, you know, from an ice cream vendor to a prince") and sees himself as an exemplar of a changed City—one that is less snobby, and more meritocratic:

> I don't give a damn about "recreations." Genuinely don't give a damn, the City has moved on and that suits me fine. If it were about clubs, codes, recreations or fitting in I would have got nothing.

We highlight these three bankers because their stories provide a neat illustration of wider changes that have taken place in elite culture, and elite (cultural) self-presentation, over the last 125 years. In this chapter, we document these changes via a range of unique data sources. We start, as we have done before, by using data from *Who's Who,* which not only contains biographical data on its entrants but also, crucially, asks them to comment on their "recreations," providing us with insights into the cultural lives of the 70,000 entrants who answered this question. We have supplemented this information with more fine-grained data on elite musical tastes drawn from the archive of *Desert Island Discs*—a radio show broadcast on the BBC since 1942, as well as attitudinal and experimental data from our own survey and in-depth discussions about culture with our 214 interviewees.[2]

Understanding Elite Distinction

Before we plunge into the cultural lives of elites in Britain, it is worth pausing to consider why we should be interested in the tastes and lifestyle of these people in the first place. How does this relate to the wider questions of who reaches the elite and how they get there? The answer is that culture has traditionally been a key vehicle through which elites signal their superior social position.[3] Yet debates have long raged about how this process of elite distinction actually works. Three accounts dominate the conversation.

The first theory, most often associated with the economist Thorstein Veblen, centres on social emulation. This is the simple idea that people tend to imitate others they see as socially superior to themselves by adopting their recreational pastimes. In response, elites engage in a process of what Veblen called "invidious distinction," differentiating themselves by continually developing ever-more expensive and elaborate tastes.[4] *Scarcity* is key to this process, with elite recreations traditionally carrying strong economic barriers to entry. But there are also cultural barriers. Attempts to mimic elites, for example, are often considered crude.[5] Take the often-cited example of the nouveau riche. Although these upwardly mobile individuals may have the economic capital to adopt elite culture, they are still mocked or excluded by incumbent elites because of the "mistakes" they supposedly make in their execution of taste, the excess of their efforts, or the insecurity of their conduct.[6]

The second model counters that the key process in elite distinction is not cultural emulation but misrecognition.[7] Here, socially subordinate groups do not so much imitate elites' culture as accept their tastes and lifestyles as superior. It is not that elites themselves are considered inherent cultural paragons, then, as in the emulation model; rather, they have the ability to generate widespread belief in the intrinsic value of their own tastes and recreations. This is achieved, according to key proponent Pierre Bourdieu, by elites occupying precisely the positions in society that allow them to establish this legitimacy.[8] For Bourdieu two "agents of legitimation" are particularly important: 1) the state, which plays a central role in consecrating culture via funding and subsidy but also actively canonizes certain cultural items in educational curricula via subjects like literature, music, and art, and 2) cultural intermediaries, that is, taste-making critics, journalists, publishers, scouts, agents, marketers, and so on, whose job it is to generate belief in the value and prestige of certain cultural goods.[9] In this misrecognition model, therefore, elites have the resources at their disposal to imbue their own cultural preferences with widespread legitimacy that can then be used by themselves, and dominant social classes more generally, to demarcate themselves from other groups. Elite tastes, in other words, become what sociologists Michelle Lamont and Annette Lareau call "widely-held high-status cultural signals" that operate as a socially valuable form of cultural capital.[10]

Finally, a more recent model takes a different tack. Its advocates argue that elite distinction may be disappearing in the contemporary era. They point to several empirical studies showing that today's elite are generally cultural omnivores—grazing happily on both highbrow and popular forms of culture.[11] This is evidence, these scholars argue, that elites are no longer highbrow snobs and have ceased to use culture to pursue distinction from lower-class groups.[12]

Yet, the significance of cultural omnivorousness is strongly contested.[13] Some argue that it simply represents an evolution in elite distinction, and point to the fact that omnivorous elites tend to opt disproportionately for *critically acclaimed* popular culture or tend to employ a distinctly highbrow style of appreciation even when consuming popular culture.[14]

This is a very lively area of debate, but we actually know very little about the specific tastes of elites, how these may have changed over time, and the implications of potential shifts for processes of elite distinction. Our aim was to address these questions.

Keeping Up Appearances, 1890–1920

Our analysis begins at the end of the nineteenth century, when elite culture had a distinctly aristocratic character. As Figure 3.1 shows, elites in this period—and especially those in the wealth elite—had a particular taste for hunting, shooting, fishing, sailing, yachting, rowing, horse-related activities (for example, horse riding, horse racing, polo, dressage, or eventing), and golf. Note that we organise this data by the decades in which people turned 20, as this is widely considered by scholars as the age by which our tastes stabilise.[15]

These trends reflect the fact that throughout the nineteenth century dominant social groups would congregate at the manicured estates of the landowning aristocracy and take part in activities like hunting, shooting, and fishing.[16] Consider, for example, these recreational profiles from the period (we use real names because these are listed publicly on the *Who's Who* website).

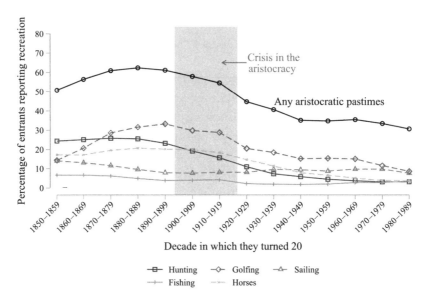

3.1 The ascendancy and decline of aristocratic culture.

Note: The top line is the summation of all the activities reported in the figure and other less common but still aristocratic activities, such as "motoring."

Hunting, shooting, polo, fencing, boxing, lawn tennis, golf, fishing. (John Crawfurd, civil service, born 1834)

Cricket, field sports, hunting, shooting; bred most of the horses in his stables, both carriage horses and hunters. (John Digby, politics, born 1859)

Many of these activities were also institutionalised through the "Season," a set of regularized events that dominated the leisure time of the aristocracy and the landed gentry.[17] This began in May with the Royal Military Tournament (shooting) and continued with the Epsom Derby (horse racing), Ascot (horse racing), and the Fourth of June events at Eton (cricket). In July, there would be polo at Hurlingham and the Henley Regatta. From August onwards, events would move towards the country, with hunting the focus until the Oxford-Cambridge boat race in March. Participating in the Season required considerable economic resources, and therefore throughout most of the nineteenth century, these economic barriers ensured that aristocratic practices remained the preserve of the traditional landowning elite, albeit with some marginalised participation by members of the gentry and the middle classes.[18]

Elite cultural distinction in this first period rested on the principle of *scarcity*, which endowed activities like hunting or polo with a sense of rarity that set elites apart. At the same time, notions of ascribed class position prevailed in Britain, with the aristocratic elite enjoying a widespread, although not complete, deference in the eyes of other social groups.[19] Entry to elite circles in this period, then, largely rested on what Veblen called "pecuniary emulation," that is, one's financial capacity to take part in, and ape, the cultural practices of existing elites.[20]

Yet this model of elite distinction, premised on exclusivity and deference, was threatened at the turn of the century. Threats came in the form of American (and to a lesser extent British) industrialists, who had amassed fortunes often surpassing even the wealthiest landowners, and gradually began to buy their way into high society—purchasing country estates and marrying the children of the landed gentry.[21] Many traditional landowners resented these parvenus, but there was no formal way to exclude them. Economic capital was the only real barrier to entry, but the British aristocracy was in the midst of profound economic decline. The cost of labour, combined with falling agricultural prices, left many of the great estates bankrupt, forcing aristocratic families to sell off large sections of their land.[22]

With this context as a backdrop, the dominance of aristocratic culture began to wane in the early years of the twentieth century—as illustrated in Figure 3.1. A reconfiguration of elite social and cultural life began to take place, with the social and cultural centres of Britain moving from the countryside to the cities, and London in particular.

The Rise of Highbrow Culture, 1920–1950

At the turn of the twentieth century, at the same time the hold of aristocratic culture began to loosen, we see in our data an increasing importance of "highbrow" cultural activities. As Figure 3.2 illustrates, starting around 1920, before slowing down after 1950, we see a marked increase in preferences for theatre, classical music, literature, opera, and the arts, although this rise was delayed among the wealth elite.

Particularly influential in understanding this shift was a generation born between 1900 and 1929, heavily influenced by the Bloomsbury Group, an intellectual collective that came to define a new mode of elite culture.[23]

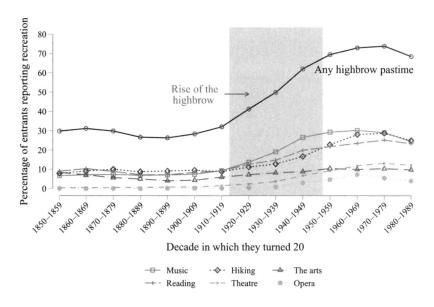

3.2 The rise of highbrow culture.

Note: The top line is the summation of all the activities reported in the figure and all other highbrow words listed, such as jazz.

Many of this new elite cohort were educated at the same institutions as earlier generations, going to Eton and Winchester, Oxford and Cambridge, but they were strongly critical of the "philistinism" of leisured aristocratic culture.[24] Instead, they embraced a set of emerging cultural forms—abstract art, theatre, and ballet—promulgated by, among others, prominent Bloomsberries such as Virginia Woolf, D. H. Lawrence, and Roger Fry. As poet Ezra Pound proudly proclaimed in 1918: "the old aristocracies of blood and business are about to be supplanted by the aristocracy of the arts."[25] The recreational profiles of many born in the first decades of the twentieth century provide a useful window into this emerging highbrow orientation:

> Writing (several plays, stories; criticism, etc.; translations), music, art (pen paintings called shapes), theatre, opera, reading, chess, lecturing, conversation; travelling, promoting good causes, fond of good food and wine. (John Calder, business, born 1927)

> Classical music, opera, theatre, cinema, photography. (Naim Atallah, business, born 1931)

Travel to archaeological sites and art centres, classical music, food and wine. (Alexander MacWilliam, religion, born 1923)

These highbrow recreations not only represented a new mode of elite culture but also a new mode of elite distinction—premised on misrecognition. What united these new cultural practices was a particular modernist aesthetic premised on a "disinterested" privileging of artistic form over emotional function.[26] The Bloomsberries and other tastemakers were strongly convinced of the intrinsic value of this modernist aesthetic and believed it should play a "civilizing" role in society. They believed art had the ability to change the human character, but to do so, to bring about human flourishing, people needed to adopt the "right" kind of stance. This orientation was bound up with a wider shift towards meritocracy. Enjoying highbrow culture was a mark of merit. The capacity to engage with art at this level was, for some, evidence that you possessed some kind of generalised intelligence and refinement.[27]

Crucially, this cultural avant-garde began to institutionalise this vision and had an enormous influence on the ethos of a number of emerging cultural institutions. One of the most prominent members of the Bloomsbury Group, economist John Maynard Keynes, was the first head of what is now known as the Arts Council, the main public body responsible for administering state funding to the arts. In this role, Keynes reduced support for local cultural activities and argued stridently that "it was standards that mattered."[28]

The influence of the Bloomsbury Group can also be seen in the early ethos of the BBC, and particularly its first director, John Reith. Reith explicitly rejected the lowbrow populism of American broadcasting. Instead, like Keynes, he turned his focus to "standards." He aired classical music, theatre, poetry, and elite sports, while shunning football, and argued that the BBC's core mission should be to share "all that is best in every department of human knowledge, endeavour and achievement."[29]

This belief in the civilizing force of high culture also informed efforts to standardise educational curricula. By 1950, for example, students were required to pass a humanities exam to receive their School Certificate (the first generalised, pre-university qualification). The humanities had long been valued in elite schools and had been central to the curricula at both Oxford and Cambridge. Although the centrality of the humanities within Oxbridge had started to wane by the middle of the twentieth century, as the hard sciences (and to some extent the social sciences) became more important, the standardization of the educational curriculum was both an attempt to formalise and expand the importance of certain subjects, such as English literature and art history, and to broaden the number of students encountering these subjects during a period of expansion in secondary schools.[30] One consequence of this standardisation was that it explicitly connected knowledge of high culture to educational attainment.[31]

To understand the strong rise in preferences for high culture in the early twentieth century, it is thus imperative to consider the processes of legitimation and institutionalization that flanked the adoption of this highbrow mode. This is not to say there was not some misrecognition of aristocratic culture, or that highbrow culture did not feature at all in the lifestyles of earlier elites. But what is distinct about this period was the concerted efforts of a particular set of elites, operating in the fields of politics, education, and the cultural industries, who not only acted as early adopters and first movers in relation to this new highbrow culture, but were also central in institutionalizing its value and producing a widespread belief in its intrinsic superiority.[32]

A somewhat snobbish belief in the value of one's own highbrow palette is also possible to discern in the profiles of some of those who made their careers in this period:

Chinese ceramics, music, poetry, art, wine, the championing of unjustly neglected writers. (David Solomon, senior partner, law, born 1930)

Visiting second-hand furniture and bookshops, collecting modern pictures and Chinese porcelain, music. (Clare Hollingworth, journalism, born 1911)

Reading, theatre, opera, films, concerts and art galleries, swimming, watching the best of television—and sometimes, for clinical reasons, the worst. (Roy Shaw, creative, born 1918)

What is notable here is the manner in which these entrants chose to describe their recreations. Whether it is adding detail to showcase the depth of one's cultural knowledge ("modern pictures and Chinese porcelain") or asserting the value of one's own judgment ("the championing of unjustly neglected writers," "watching the best of television"), all confidently parade their highbrow taste.

One further striking thing emerges from this highbrow period. Among *Who's Who* entrants who turned 20 between 1900 and 1950, the propensity to report one's recreations increased dramatically, from around 40 percent to about 80 percent of entrants. Clearly, as the institutionalization of highbrow culture gathered pace, so too did the propensity of elites to take a certain pride in expressing their tastes in public.

The Decline of Deference, 1950 Onwards

Although highbrow tastes and recreations appear to dominate elite culture in the early to middle part of the twentieth century, there is an intriguing break in the 1950s and 1960s. Figure 3.3 shows that the proportion of the British elite who expressed *only* highbrow recreations began to fall in the mid- to late 1950s.

Many have written about this period, and their accounts emphasise several factors that help us understand this decline. These include aesthetic

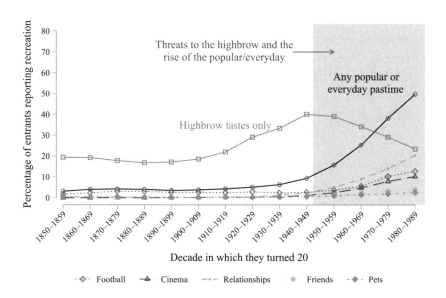

3.3 The rise of popular and everyday recreations.
Note: The highest line at the end of the period is the summation of all the non-highbrow activities reported in the figure and all other popular/ordinary words, such as listening to the radio.

shifts within the cultural and creative industries where many artists and tastemakers (from the Beatles to Richard Hamilton and Andy Warhol) challenged the supremacy of highbrow culture and began to aestheticize popular cultural forms.[33] There were also huge generational changes in norms that precipitated a decline in deference to elites.[34] Finally, this decline coincided with important shifts within many of the institutions that had previously been so instrumental in generating belief in the value of highbrow culture. The BBC, for example, and to a lesser extent the Arts Council, began to change aesthetic course, increasingly promoting, programming, and funding more popular cultural content.[35]

Yet, Figure 3.3 not only details a move away from the dominance of highbrow culture. It also shows, from the mid-1950s onwards, a rise in preference for more "popular" cultural forms, such as football and cinema, and everyday cultural practices, such as spending time with family, friends, and pets. These ordinary recreations may not have been superseding more conventional elite pursuits, but their significance to our analysis is rooted more in their *integration* with traditionally dominant modes of elite culture.

In Figure 3.4 we employ a form of semi-automated computational text analysis that allows us to look at the way elites combine particular types of recreations.[36] This shows that emerging modes of elite culture increasingly involved retaining a penchant for more traditional forms of elite culture and, at the same time, combining these with more popular and ordinary forms. Consider these examples:

Family, theatre, opera, walking, skiing, sailing, four grandchildren—two boys and two girls. (Lynda Addison, business, born 1945)

Theatre, cinema, playing tennis, supporting Tottenham Hotspur. (Anthony Giddens, sociology, born 1938)

Art, television, books, dogs, family. (Monisha Shah, media, born 1969)

What is striking in these profiles is the distinctive juxtaposition of the highbrow and the ordinary. These contemporary elites happily place a love for art alongside a love for pets, and keenly signal their authenticity via a commitment to specific football teams and caring for family.

The British elite, then, appears to have become increasingly omnivorous in its cultural tastes over the past fifty years.[37] The question, of course, is

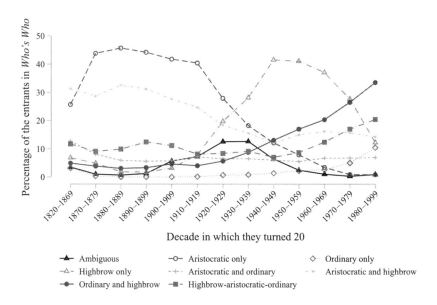

3.4 The rise of the elite omnivore.

Note: These estimates were calculated using ReadMe after both authors hand-coded 600 responses. The solid black line with solid triangles at the bottom of the graph is the proportion of people who reported participating in ambiguous activities, such as gardening. The dashed grey line with hollow diamonds measures the combination of the aristocratic and the ordinary, but this never really reaches above 10 percent of responses.

what does this omnivorousness mean for debates about elite distinction? Although this is difficult to answer definitively, our data provides some useful clues.

De Gustibus Non Est Disputandum

Recall that, for some, the rise of the omnivore is evidence that elites no longer use culture to pursue distinction from lower social class groups. Yet when we turn to survey questions posed to contemporary elites, we see the distinct lingering of snobbery. Specifically, we asked respondents whether they believed "one person's taste is as good as the next" and whether the "old snobbery around culture in Britain has been eradicated." We then compared their responses to a nationally representative sample of British people who answered the same questions.

As Figure 3.5 shows, contemporary elites and particularly those in the wealth elite are significantly snobbier than the average British person, in

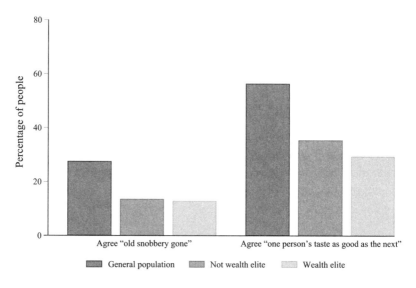

3.5 The elite (and wealth elite) are snobbier than the UK population.

terms of both their sense that all taste should be valued equally and on whether Britain has eradicated its snobbery. This is partly about age. Older elites on average are slightly more snobbish. But it is worth noting that even younger elites are far more snobbish than the general population. We also explored these questions in interviews. Most were very careful to refrain from making explicit claims about the superiority of their own taste or lifestyle. Yet at the same time, most struggled to fully accept the idea that "one person's taste is as good as the next." A conversation with Michael (politics, born 1935–1940) was illustrative:

Interviewer: Is it possible to distinguish good and bad taste?

Michael: De gustibus non est disputandum [translation: there is no accounting for taste] . . . I mean, of course I do not use the word good or bad taste [laughs] . . . But do I think people can have good or bad . . . ? It is very interesting. There's a very famous German historian called Cocker, have you heard of Cocker? No, don't worry I'm not going to mark you down [laughs] . . . And he says the fascinating thing is that some people have been brought up to go into a room and see that there's a beautiful carpet there and roughly date it and things like that. And I can do that. Because that was how I was brought up, so the answer is yes in that relative sense. I mean there are tastes and judgements but there are also facts . . . a business of taste in relation to antiques or how a room is arranged.

What is striking here is the apparent contradiction between Michael's initial statement that he "of course" would not "use the word good taste" and then the discussion that follows, where he demonstrates that he *does* believe it is possible to discern a certain intrinsic value in greater cultural fluency. Not only does his overall manner here signal a certain cultural distinction (for example, the use of Latin, name-dropping German historians, checking if the interviewer shares his cultural knowledge) but he argues that, in some cases at least, good taste is simply a "fact." These subtle and carefully veiled judgments were evident throughout interviews, albeit often flanked paradoxically by an explicit rejection of cultural snobbery.

Another, more understated, form of cultural distinction was evident from the way many expressed their recreations in *Who's Who*. Many choose to report their recreations in ways that go beyond a simple list: they actively "play with the form" of their entry, describing their interests in a knowing, humorous, or slightly ironic way. Consider these examples:

[The] usual. (Admiral Sir Edward Ashmore, military, born 1919)

Gluttony, sloth. (John Cleese, creative, born 1939)

Loud music, strong cider. (Jonathan Ashley-Smith, civil service, born 1946)

Tennis, guitar, cycling, skipping, herb-surfing, dendron-leaping, portacenare. (Richard Addis, journalism, born 1956)

Collecting money. (Benjamin Zephaniah, creative, born 1958)

Tennis, guitar, making martinis for The Wastrels. (Selvaraju Ramasamy, law, born 1970)

Watching and playing tennis, bad surfing, hiking, memorising poetry, 20-minute meals, reading. (Allegra Stratton, journalism, born 1980)

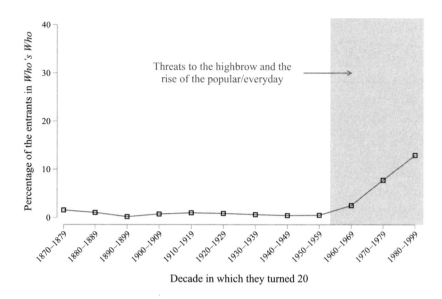

3.6 The rise of *Who's Who* entrants "playing with form" in the recreations entry. *Note:* These estimates were calculated using ReadMe after both authors hand-coded 600 responses.

While some of these entries may be technically omnivorous, they also use humour to express their cultural omnivorousness in a highly knowing way. By dramatizing their pastimes and deliberately drawing attention to the apparent incongruity between "tennis and The Wastrels" or "memorising poetry and 20-minute meals," these entrants actually flaunt their cultural capital in the very act of seemingly downplaying it.

We would argue that these entries represent subtle acts of distinction, as people demonstrate their aesthetic confidence by knowingly playing with the form. In Figure 3.6 we estimate the proportion of people in each cohort expressing their recreations in this way over time. Strikingly, this kind of playing with the form is largely nonexistent among entrants who came of age before the 1950s, and far more common in more recent cohorts.

Mining *Desert Island Discs*

When most people express their recreational tastes in *Who's Who* they do so via art forms or activities such as "theatre," "football," or, most commonly, "music." But the obvious problem with this is that most cultural forms contain many internal gradations of status based on critical acclaim or popularity. We wanted to unpack this complexity in relation to music, so we turned to another unique dataset—the archive of the iconic BBC Radio show *Desert Island Discs* (*DIDs*). The format of the show is straightforward. Each week a "castaway"—usually a noteworthy and influential person—is asked to choose eight songs or pieces of music they would take with them if they were to be stranded on a desert island. *DIDs* is therefore particularly useful because it allows us to move beyond generic preferences towards a more granular analysis of music tastes. Specifically, we merge *Who's Who* with data from *DIDs* to analyse the individual musical tracks played by 1,200 *Desert Island Discs* guests who were also in *Who's Who*.

Two findings emerge. First, we coded artists into genres and examined how the songs played on *Desert Island Discs* change over time and by birth cohort. This genre-based analysis echoed the trend towards omnivorousness shown in Figure 3.4. Specifically, the vast majority of entrants played at least one piece of highbrow classical music, but the percentage who play classical music *and* tracks from less legitimate genres, such as pop, rock, folk, electronic, world, and country, grew significantly over time. Among entrants who turned 20 between 1896 and 1939, 10 percent combined classical music with other genres. In contrast, among entrants who turned 20 after the 1960s, over 40 percent combined tracks from classical and more popular genres.

What does this movement towards musical omnivorousness look like in practice? Well, consider the musical choices of two celebrated British intellectuals—the philosopher and historian, Isaiah Berlin (1907–1995) and broadcaster and peer Joan Bakewell (1933–present):

Isaiah Berlin tracklist:
1. Modest Mussorgsky, "Clock Scene" from *Boris Godunov*
2. Giuseppe Verdi, "Ah, fors' è lui" from *La Traviata*
3. Johann Sebastian Bach, "Violin Concerto no. 2 in E major"
4. Ludwig van Beethoven, "Piano Sonata no. 32 in C minor"
5. Gioachino Rossini, "*The Italian Girl in Algiers* Overture"
6. Ludwig van Beethoven, "String Quartet no. 14 in C sharp minor"
7. Franz Schubert, "Piano Sonata no. 21 in B flat major"
8. Wolfgang Amadeus Mozart, "L'ho perduta" from *The Marriage of Figaro*

Joan Bakewell tracklist:
1. Jimi Hendrix, "Voodoo Child"
2. Thomas Tallis, "Spem In Alium"
3. Richard Strauss, "Marie Theres'! Hab' mir's gelobt"
4. Peggy Lee, "Where or When"
5. Bob Dylan, "Blowin' in the Wind"
6. Franz Schubert, "String Quintet in C major"
7. William Shakespeare, "Shall I Compare Thee to a Summers Day?"
8. Benjamin Britten, "Four Sea Interludes" from *Peter Grimes*

Berlin's tracks are exclusively classical music and opera, and unambiguously highbrow. This is matched by his words on the show. Berlin repeatedly passes judgment on the intrinsic quality of music. Thus, Bach's "Violin Concerto no. 2," we learn, "is foundational to music" while Beethoven's "String Quartet no. 14" is "one of the profoundest works of man."

Bakewell too opts for mainly classical music and opera, with a nod to Shakespeare, and there are notable similarities in the way she and Berlin talk about their choices. Like Berlin, she talks about the form and texture of the music (Chamber music is "focused," Schubert "concentrated," and Britten "lyrical") and offers confident value judgments (Peter Grimes is "probably the greatest post-war opera").

But notably Bakewell, who was born twenty-five years after Berlin, also includes two pop songs from Jimi Hendrix and Bob Dylan. Yet her choices are anything but indiscriminate. Both tracks are highly critically acclaimed; Hendrix's "Voodoo Child" is ranked 101 on the *Rolling Stone* list of "The 500 Greatest Songs of All Time," and Dylan's "Blowin' in the Wind" is included in the Grammy Hall of Fame.

This issue of popular legitimacy brings us to the second finding from our analysis of music played on *DIDs*. Specifically, we examined the critical acclaim of the musical artists played by analysing their average score on the music website *Metacritic,* which aggregates reviews of albums by professional critics. Artists played by *Who's Who* entrants consistently rate higher in their *Metacritic* score than the average musical artist. Indeed, they are consistently in the top quartile. For example, consider the tracks played by two important contemporary cultural figures— writer and actor Sharon Horgan (1970–present) and model Kate Moss (1974–present):

Sharon Horgan tracklist:
1. David Bowie, "Rock 'n' Roll Suicide"
2. The Smiths, "The Queen Is Dead"
3. Mic Christopher, "Kid's Song"
4. The Fall, "Telephone Thing"
5. The Charlatans, "The Only One I Know"
6. Metronomy, "Everything Goes My Way"
7. Arcade Fire, "The Suburbs (continued)"
8. Kate Bush, "Moments Of Pleasure"

Kate Moss tracklist:
1. Soul II Soul and Jazzie B, "Back to Life (Sunday Service Mix)"
2. King Curtis, "A Whiter Shade of Pale"
3. Neil Young, "Harvest Moon"
4. David Bowie, "Life On Mars?"
5. The Velvet Underground, "Oh! Sweet Nuthin'"
6. The Rolling Stones, "Sympathy For The Devil"
7. George Harrison, "My Sweet Lord"
8. Van Morrison, "Madame George"

What is notable here is that while both Moss and Horgan play only popular music, their choices are all critically acclaimed. Bowie's "Rock 'n' Roll Suicide" is included in *Acclaimed Music*'s list of "most celebrated songs in popular music history," the Smiths' *The Queen Is Dead* was named the Greatest Album of all Time by *NME,* the Metronomy album *The English Riviera* was nominated for the Mercury Prize, Arcade Fire's album *Suburbs* won a Grammy for Best Album, and the Fall album *Extricate* was widely lauded, including by *NME* and *Melody Maker.*

Also striking about these guests is how they speak about their music preferences. While their tracks may well be critically acclaimed, they refrain from presenting them as such, or indeed talking about the structure or form of the music. Instead, they talk exclusively about how the music is connected to key people or life events in their biography. Horgan explains that she chooses a Bowie track because it reminds her of her family ("I wanted something to connect with my parents, brothers and sisters because I love them madly"), while she chooses the Smiths "because it makes me think of my best friends at school." Moss similarly picks "Whiter Shade of Pale" because this was the song played when her parents "walked down the aisle at their wedding," while playing Soul II Soul takes her back to "when I was 14 and my best friend had an Escort Mark 1 with roll bars and speakers in the back, and we would blast it down Croydon High Street and thought we were the absolute coolest."

Spotlighting how music commingles with key relationships or life events is notable here because—whether intentional or not—it is likely to be relatable for most listeners. Unlike Berlin's discussions of form and quality, which may act as a cultural fence for many listeners, the privileging of more mundane lived experience acts as a way of erecting a bridge to the general public.[38]

Although elites today may be increasingly integrating modern popular culture into their taste repertoires, the individual artists they choose often still tilt towards the legitimate (even if they choose not to spotlight this in the way they talk). This insight is supported by a number of other contemporary studies that have looked at how class similarly maps onto more fine-grained tastes for television, comedy, and food.[39] Today's elite omnivore then may simply be a new kind of snob; a somewhat stealthy popular culture snob.

Publicly Ordinary, Privately Distinct

The data presented so far provide evidence that there may be more than meets the eye when it comes to cultural omnivorousness. When elites express omnivorous tastes, in other words, this does not mean that they have abandoned cultural distinction. Instead, what we see are various processes that sit alongside this seemingly popularizing tendency—the private harbouring of snobbish feelings, the careful selection of legitimate popular culture, and knowing ways of expressing taste that purport to distance oneself from highbrow modes of distinction-signalling but paradoxically act to showcase one's aesthetic prowess.[40]

But it is important to recall that many of the non-highbrow recreations that show up in Who's Who (see Figure 3.3) are not forms of conventional cultural consumption. Most are more everyday activities, such as spending time with family, friends, and pets, that are not normally considered in debates about cultural omnivorousness.[41] Among the most recent entrants to Who's Who, it is these everyday recreations that are rising most significantly, and much faster than any given taste for popular culture. Figure 3.7 unpacks this rise to look at the role of both cohort (a group of people all born in the same few years) and period effects (the moment in time when the data were collected).

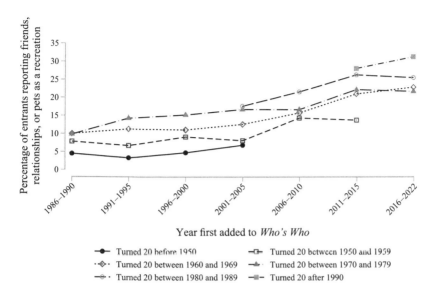

3.7 The rise of everyday recreations since 1986.

Note: The year *Who's Who* entrants were added to the volume is only available for individuals added after 1986.

Two patterns are clear here. Younger cohorts are far more likely than older cohorts to report these everyday recreations, but such reporting increases for all cohorts over time—particularly among entrants who were added to *Who's Who* after 2000. This suggests that the rising expression of these distinctly ordinary recreations is not just about the generation in which elites grew up, but also the distinct period in which they enter *Who's Who*. Some of the most recent entrants demonstrate this trend:

Family and friends, walking, spa days. (Monica Galetti, creative, added 2022)

Cookery, family, pets. (Victoria Huston, business, added 2007)

Playing and watching sport, cinema, family, friends, local community. (Sadiq Khan, politics, added 2007)

Singing, dancing, drinking beer, seeing friends and family. (Victoria Wakefield, law, added 2019)

How should we make sense of this new trend? Turning to our interview analysis suggests that this might be at least partly about when and where elites actually express their tastes in social life. We were struck in particular by the disconnect between the ways in which people described their cultural lives in an anonymised interview setting and what they chose to foreground in their public *Who's Who* profile. Many who spoke extensively and passionately about highbrow interests in their interview chose not to include any information about their recreations in their public profile. Although this discrepancy was never discussed explicitly, some, like Elizabeth, a professor (1955–1960) who chose to include nothing in her profile, seemed conscious of how others might interpret her more high-art tastes:

> My husband and I are both of us, just utterly stereotypical high culture people, you know. We love opera, we love classical music, we like high end literature, you know. Absolutely. I mean we like all sorts of down grade things that, you know, popular things as well. But we are, you know . . .

Others projected subtle but tellingly different versions of themselves. Kevin, an entrepreneur (1955–1960), lists his recreations publicly as "simply messing about on the water." Yet in his interview he talked of a "deep love for culture" and ranged widely on the subject of literature, theatre, and revue-style comedy. Similarly, Amanda (media, 1960–1965) told us in her interview that she was passionate about theatre, classical music, and opera and was unapologetic about her highbrow orientation:

> Opera, theatre, I mean they tell you something fundamental about human beings. And I think this kind of government anxiety about the canon, the sort of willingness to chop classical music, I mean it's absurd. The amount of money that goes into the Arts Council is peanuts, it's peanuts. It's three hundred and fifty million pounds a year the Arts Council gets for the great concerts of the nation. Rishi Sunak's eat out to help out was seven hundred and fifty million, what is that about? I don't want to go to my grave knowing I have had a meal out somewhere. But I want to go to my grave knowing that I have sat through the last act of the *Marriage of Figaro*.

Yet, in her public profile Roisin mentions none of these highbrow interests. Jeffrey, a CEO (1950–1955), explains that this kind of public–private disconnect is common among people he knows in *Who's Who*. "What the recreations in people's *Who's Who* profiles tell you," he summed up, "is basically what people want other people to think they do."

This might seem uncharitable, even mean. After all, we can't know for sure why these cultural profiles vary in the way they do, and it is unlikely that they all reflect deliberate attempts to conceal highbrow tastes. Certainly, elites are not entirely unique in their propensity to modulate their self-presentation in this way. The widespread phenomenon of "guilty pleasures" is a clear manifestation of this kind of cultural code-switching.[42] Nonetheless, we think these mismatches suggest that there is sometimes a gap between the private cultural lives of elites and how they choose to present themselves in public.

This theme also came through in interviews. Chris, for example, an MP (1980–1985), recounted his amusement when learning that several of his parliamentary colleagues, who he knew considered themselves "very cultured," had listed "drinking beer" in their *Who's Who* profile. This, he argued, perfectly illustrated their (ultimately unsuccessful) attempts at publicly "signalling" ordinariness:

Chris: There was a little diary piece months ago saying five or six of my colleagues had put drinking beer as an interest [in *Who's Who*] and that's just bollocks. That's not an interest, right? That's no more an interest than pizza. It's just signalling.

Interviewer: Why do you think that is?

Chris: Well, it's the number one accusation to throw at a politician, you know, you're out of touch, you don't know how the other half lives, you're all the same. So, I understand why they did it. They're constantly told they're out of touch, you've probably got private health care, you've probably got this, that and the other . . . So they say, oh, well, I'm interested in beer, just like you. But people who drink beer wouldn't call beer an interest. Where I grew up, they wouldn't say, oh yes, beer is really my interest. It just doesn't work. On the other hand, did I need to put I was a Liverpool season ticket holder in my entry?

It's the same spectrum: you think because I went to Oxford, I'm a certain kind of guy, but actually hey I'm not.

This type of signalling works both ways. While some discussed the importance of projecting ordinariness in public settings, others like Peter and Amanda stressed the continuing importance of highbrow tastes, or projecting an aura of cultural "sophistication," in elite circles:

I think again the word sophisticated comes in, not necessarily because . . . I don't think there's anybody that I encountered in the establishment that was impressed by knowledge of Renaissance painting, although I do seem to remember the *Ring* cycle, yes, having several conversations about Wagner and the *Ring* cycle [laughs]. But in general giving the impression of being a sophisticated, cultured individual—that did have an impact on my working career, particularly during Number 10 and after Number 10 . . . (Peter, policy, 1945–1950)

I go to places and I immediately feel at home because there is a sort of code, an unwritten code . . . Like if I say I have just seen *Rosencrantz and Guildenstern Are Dead,* that person, an insider, will know what I'm talking about. They will know. They will know not only that it's a modern play but who it's by and what its title refers to. And if you are not in that charmed circle, you are out because you will feel weird and you won't be able to sit down and have a cup of coffee with that person, they are talking a different language. (Amanda, media, 1960–1965)

What these accounts demonstrate is the importance of taste in shaping different kinds of social relationships. As Omar Lizardo has shown, popular culture can act as a social bridge—facilitating weak ties across a range of social backgrounds.[43] Recreations like beer-drinking may be favoured by politicians, then, because it can help them to appear down-to-earth. In contrast, highbrow tastes—like Wagner's Ring cycle or *Rosencrantz and Guildenstern Are Dead*—act more as a fence. These more legitimate tastes are more available to those who have had the kind of upbringing or education that provides the aesthetic tools to enjoy it—so they tend to strengthen ties among those operating in more exclusive settings. Knowing when and where to deploy different cultural references, in other words, can be pivotal to contemporary elites' ability to accumulate social capital.

Rising Inequality and the Expression of Highbrow Taste

One big question looms in the background here: why has it become so important for elites to know when and how to deploy different cultural tastes? Well, one of the striking patterns in our analysis so far is that the rise of ordinary elite distinction—marked by the twin pursuits of distinction *and* ordinariness—is most clear-cut from the 1990s onwards, and particularly acute among cohorts that came of age after the 1960s. At the same time, most of the people in Chapter 2 who displayed self-consciously upperclass identities were interviewed in the late 1980s and early 1990s, suggesting that the desire to downplay elite tastes has emerged since then. We have already described the profound changes to British society that occurred during this period, including the decline of deference, the rejection of ascribed privilege, and the increasing importance of working-class culture. This rise of ordinary elite distinction is operating against this backdrop but it also coincides neatly with the pulling away of the top 1 percent of the income distribution in Britain, following a more general increase in inequality through the 1980s.[44] Our tentative claim is that these patterns may be plausibly connected. Put simply, as elites have pulled away economically, they may have become more insecure about their moral legitimacy, and increasingly sensitive to public concern that they are only motivated by self-interest.[45] We have already seen that how elites present themselves can have quite significant implications for how the general public views them. We saw in Chapter 2 that a CEO with a penchant for classical music, for example, was seen as less "down-to-earth" and more "motivated by money." And it is telling that it is the wealth elite who are slightly more likely to include ordinary activities in their *Who's Who* profiles.

Now this is a big claim and one that is hard to test. To do so we again turned to a survey experiment, asking *Who's Who* entrants to imagine what they would do if they were asked to appear on *Desert Island Discs*. We invited them to list their favourite music track, explain why they chose it, and choose a book to take with them. Half of our respondents, before they were asked the question about *Desert Island Discs*, were also asked another question which was intended to prime the salience of inequality. Here is the question:

> Nearly 90 percent of the people in *Who's Who* think that *both* the income gap and the wealth gap between rich and poor are too large. We also know that income inequality has gone up since the late 1970s and that the very richest households (for example, the top 1 percent) have captured a larger share of national income over time. In addition, the people in *Who's Who* are very affluent. Over 33 percent of *Who's Who* entrants are in the top 1 percent of the wealth distribution and over 16 percent are in the top 1 percent of the income distribution. Given this, how worried are you about some of the (potential) negative effects of inequality listed below?

The effects listed were the influence of the rich on politics, the number of children living in poverty, and the health effects of higher inequality. This question served three purposes. It reminded our respondents that 1) inequality had gone up, 2) they were likely to be beneficiaries of that rising inequality, and 3) some people believed that the rise in inequality was harming society. In other words, this question could be viewed as a status threat to elites. The other half of respondents did not receive this question and just answered the questions about *Desert Island Discs*. We used this experiment therefore to see whether members of *Who's Who* would alter their cultural self-presentation when primed about high inequality and their potential connection to it.

When inequality becomes more salient, as Figure 3.8 shows, people *do* become 8 percent less likely to say that their favourite track was a piece of classical music and they become less likely to choose a serious, big, highbrow book—by about 8 percent. On top of this, we see changes in how they talk about their tastes. Those exposed to this inequality question were less likely to aestheticize their music track when giving their reasons for choosing it and potentially—although the data are less clear here—more likely to explain their taste in terms of nostalgia.

This experiment provides support for our speculation that rising inequality may have contributed to the insecurity of elites. Certainly, in this quite stylised and seemingly low-stakes setting we see meaningful and consistent movement in how elites present their tastes. Now, it is important to be clear about our argument here. We are not claiming that high inequality

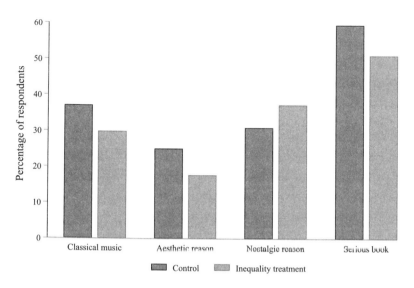

3.8 Cultural preferences shift when inequality becomes more salient.

Note: The *p*-value for the tests of statistical significance is: 0.07 for "classical music," 0.034 for "aesthetic reason," 0.113 for "nostalgic reason," and 0.040 for "serious book," which includes texts by the likes of Shakespeare, Tolstoy, and Dostoevsky. Experiment was conducted with 581 people.

will always lead to this kind of insecurity. As we explored in Chapter 2, there is little evidence that elites at the end of the nineteenth century (another period when inequality was very high) were all that concerned about seeming "down-to-earth" or ordinary. Rather, our claim is that against a backdrop of the decline of deference and the spread of a liberal conception of equality, rising economic inequality alters the sense of security that elites feel about their position in society.[46]

Ordinary Elite Distinction

In this chapter, we have revealed three distinct stages of elite culture in the United Kingdom over the past 125 years. First, a dominant mode of aristocratic practice forged around the leisure possibilities afforded by landed estates (shooting, hunting, riding, polo, sailing), where elites achieved distinction via the emulation of lower, aspirational social groups, who deferred to their authority as cultural paragons. We then showed how this mode was threatened at the turn of the twentieth century. Nouveau riche industrialists began to buy their way into high society, and existing aristocratic elites, battling economic upheaval, were unable to guard against this pecuniary emulation. Next, we showed how, in the context of this threat, a new generation of elites—influenced in particular by the Bloomsbury Group—developed a new mode of elite distinction. Positioning itself against the philistinism of aristocratic modes, this new cohort championed a set of more urban "high" cultural forms (theatre, ballet, classical music, abstract art) that would define elite culture in the 1920s, 1930s, and 1940s. This new highbrow mode was successful in delivering distinction, albeit via a different mechanism. Rather than relying on an ascribed cultural legitimacy, as in the emulation model, highbrow elites instead focused on generating a widespread misrecognition, via the state and allied institutions such as the BBC, of the inherent value of their own tastes and recreations. Again, this mode of elite culture was eventually questioned. Beginning in the 1950s, and accelerating in the 1960s and 1970s, the supremacy of highbrow culture was threatened by generational change and shifts within the art-world that challenged the highbrow aesthetic and precipitated a decline in snobbery and deference to elites.

The final part of our analysis explained how elites adapted to these threats, diversifying their cultural profiles and increasingly blending highbrow (and some aristocratic) recreations with popular culture and a range of everyday practices, such as spending time with family, friends, and pets. We see this as pursuing dual aims. First, it continues to be distinction-seeking, with tastes still tilting towards critically acclaimed artists. Second, the growing expression of everyday recreations, we argue, also signals something beyond distinction, and linked to the arguments about elite identity introduced in Chapter 2. Specifically, we find a contemporary elite that publicly emphasises everyday cultural practice as part of a wider effort to project ordinariness and authenticity, and forge cultural connection with others in society.

This is partly, we believe, about plugging an insecurity that elites feel vis-à-vis the wider public. As many studies demonstrate, and as we have found in our experiments in Chapter 2, non-elites and working-class groups often distinguish between elites who they see as "down-to-earth" and those they see as "out-of-touch"—with the former valued over the latter. It is thus not so much that elites are viewed with suspicion because they are elite: rather, it is perceived snobbishness that rouses negative reactions. So it is possible to see the public expression of everyday preferences as a means of accentuating cultural connection and ordinariness while retaining the legitimate culture traditionally tied to elite distinction. In other words, ordinary self-presentation is effective in securing distinction because it means that actual cultural boundaries existing between elites and others are not questioned, as those in lower-class positions no longer see the highbrow elements of the elite taste palette as status-seeking. Thus, Sharon Horgan and Kate Moss may play legitimate music on *Desert Island Discs,* which may be recognisable to audiences sensitive to such signals, but the fact that they explain such preferences through the lens of their own lived experience potentially transforms the way such tastes are understood.

This insecurity that elites feel is potentially connected to rising inequality. Because we no longer live in a society in which elites are simply assumed to be deserving of their positions because of birth, those who occupy these positions now feel a greater pressure to legitimate the fact that they are in positions of power. This shows up in our experiment where we prime elites about the salience of inequality. That is, when our respondents are reminded that they are the beneficiaries of rising inequality, they become less likely to deploy highbrow taste. Elites recognise that how they present themselves in public *matters.*

Looking across this and Chapter 2, what is most significant is the way in which these contemporary claims to ordinariness are premised on a particular conception of change over time. Whether it is distancing oneself from caricatured notions of ascribed privilege, old-school nepotism, or highbrow snobbery, today's elite presents itself as meaningfully different from elites in the past; more meritocratic, more tolerant, more normal.

But is that really true? In the next section we will hold these progressive narratives to account. Here we draw on our unique longitudinal data to interrogate empirically whether Britain has really opened up in this way. Specifically, we examine the three main ways Britain has traditionally made its elites: via elite backgrounds, elite schools, and elite universities. Have these channels of elite reproduction changed over the last 125 years?

PART TWO

How to Make an Elite

4

Silver Spoons

Shortly before David Cameron became prime minister, there was a tricky moment in a *Times* interview where he was stumped by a question about how many properties he owned. "Don't make me sound like a prat for not knowing how many houses I've got!" he implored the interviewer.[1] Downplaying his vast family fortune, and its aristocratic roots—his mother was the daughter of a baronet and his family has remained in the top 1 percent of the wealth distribution for at least three generations—was always a key political strategy for Cameron. Like many prominent British politicians that hail from wealthy extended families—Boris Johnson, Tony Benn, and Jacob Rees Mogg, to name but a few—he was always keen to distance himself from the historical caricature of ascribed elite privilege. Such efforts are often successful. Wealth is largely hidden from public view and tends to go unspoken in everyday life.[2]

One upshot of this is that we know fairly little about the relationship between family wealth and recruitment to Britain's most powerful and influential positions. The propulsive power of an elite background is often assumed in Britain, but solid evidence-based investigations are scarce.[3] Perhaps the most relevant touchpoint is the work of Erzsébet Bukodi and John Goldthorpe, whose recent research examines the changing class origins of Britain's scientific elite—finding that upward mobility has declined in recent decades, with top scientists from working-class backgrounds now almost completely nonexistent.[4] While this is undoubtedly revealing, one of the limitations of Bukodi and Goldthorpe's work is that they rely on broad class categories based on parental occupation. Thus, while their analysis shows the increasing importance of coming from a professional upper-middle-class background, it tells us little about the particular, pro-pulsive power of an *elite background.*

This is why we turn in this chapter to the question of parental wealth. It allows us to identify more extreme forms of privilege, and to look at the propulsive power of those like Cameron who hail from spectacularly wealthy families. To do this we've dug deep into Britain's probate archive—the of-ficial record of someone's financial estate when they die. (We explain *how* we did this in the Methodological Appendix.) Specifically, we track down the wealth-at-death of parents of 70,000 people in *Who's Who,* compare this to the wealth-at-death of other people in the United Kingdom who died at a similar time, and then examine how the chances of reaching the British elite have changed over the course of the twentieth century if you were born into a family at the top of the wealth distribution. Finally, while the transfer of privilege from parents to children (particularly fathers to sons) has long influenced access to elite positions, as the work of the economic historian Gregory Clark has shown, we extend our analysis beyond the immediate children of the wealthy to examine how wealth feeds into a wider, extended-family project of elite reproduction.[5] Here specifically we look at how family wealth may be implicated in the elite trajectories of grandchildren, sons- and daughters-in-law, and nieces and nephews. This perspective, as Shay O'Brien argues in her work on the Texas elite during the oil rush, disrupts the standard intergenerational way of thinking about elite repro-duction, and allows us to see how wealth can often scaffold a complex multigenerational web of relationships.[6]

The Great Equalization

In the late nineteenth century, wealth was still a key gateway to elite posi-tions in Britain. As late as 1871, if you wanted to be a lieutenant colonel in the army you could simply pay for the privilege—about half a million pounds (in today's money).[7] Similarly, family money was often central to success in big business. And yet a cursory glance at the profound changes that have taken place in British society over the last 150 years would lead most to suspect that there has been a sizeable shift in the link between wealth and elite reproduction.

Some might point to the collapse of the aristocracy and the way this has undermined the financial position of land-holding elites and loosened their grip on society's pivotal positions.[8] Others might highlight the expansion of voting rights and how this weakened the smooth transition between property and political power, so that wealth became a less certain mechanism through which you could acquire a seat in parliament.[9] Still others might point to a range of other societal-level shifts that potentially radically reconfigured Britain's traditional channels of elite recruitment: the erosion of empire and the way this closed off well-worn routes into the elite, particularly via the military; the rise of the joint-stock company and the concomitant managerial revolution, which may have pushed organizational power away from wealthy families and into the hands of managers and executives; and the financialization of the economy and the way this shifted economic power again, this time towards bankers and other financial intermediaries.[10]

One might reasonably expect all of these processes to have contributed to the fracturing of traditional forms of elite power—without even mentioning the destruction of wealth during the World Wars, the creation of the welfare state, and the oil crisis of the 1970s.[11] We certainly know that together these changes did lead to a profound restructuring of the wealth *distribution* in Britain. Known as the "great equalisation," the overall share of national wealth taken by the top 1 percent of wealth holders in Britain declined precipitously from 70 percent in 1900 to less than 20 percent by 1980, and there is only tentative evidence of a modest rise since then.[12] When viewed through this lens, the question appears less *has* the link between wealth and elite recruitment weakened, and more by *how much?*

Blue Blood

Our analysis disrupts these expectations. Figure 4.1 shows how the proportion of the British elite who hail from the top echelons of the wealth distribution has changed over time. It reveals two important facts. First, those from elite backgrounds have historically, and continue today, to be strongly over-represented in the contemporary British elite; over half of current members of *Who's Who* come from families in the top 10 percent of the wealth distribution, and over 20 percent or one in five are from the top 1 percent of the distribution. Notably, this has not changed much at all in the last few decades. Nearly one quarter of new entrants to *Who's Who* in the 1980s and the 1990s had parents in the top 1 percent, and this was still true among those entering elite positions since the turn of the century. This is not driven by gender; men currently in *Who's Who* are equally as likely as

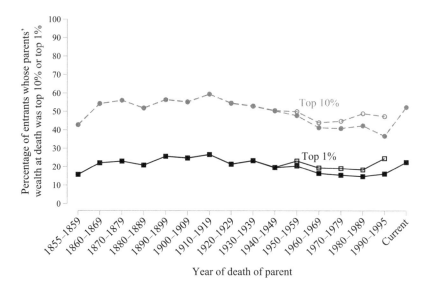

4.1 The modest decline in elite reproduction.

Note: The lines with solid squares and circles represent the raw unadjusted proportion of the people in *Who's Who* whose parent's wealth at death was in the top 10% or the top 1% of the wealth distribution. The lines with the hollow squares and circles represent the same proportions, but are adjusted for hidden wealth. We do not report estimates of hidden wealth for people currently in *Who's Who* because we do not have reliable data on the amount of wealth that is hidden after the 1990s.

women to be born to parents who are in the top 1 percent (both around 20 percent). We can also see the power of elite reproduction in other ways. Of the current elite, 76 percent come from families where one or more parents were doing professional or managerial work (compared to 37 percent in the population as a whole) and at least 15.5 percent had a parent who received an honour such as a knighthood or an OBE.

The propulsive power of wealth comes even further into focus when we compare the likelihood that the wealthy will reach different kinds of elite positions. Being born into wealth may increase your chances of reaching the elite, but this varies depending on the field you enter.[13] In Figure 4.2 we show the proportion of people in the elite born into the top 1 percent who have made their careers in different occupational domains. Unsurprisingly, people in the aristocracy or those whose influence is connected to charitable work and philanthropy—who we label "society" elites—are very likely to come from money. Those in the military, sport, and law are also comparatively more likely to come from wealthy backgrounds, whereas

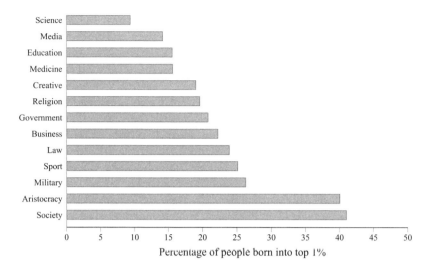

4.2 The scientific, media, education, and medical elite are less likely to come from elite backgrounds.

those in the sciences, media, and education are notably less connected to wealth.[14]

Second, and returning to Figure 4.1, the relationship between wealth and elite recruitment actually changed far less over the course of the twentieth century than we might expect considering the "great equalisation" outlined above. Figure 4.1 shows that the ability of those born into the top 1 percent of the wealth distribution to reach elite positions has only declined modestly over time (albeit with a larger decline for the top 10 percent).

This relative stability is further underlined when we try to account for hidden wealth, which can take both legal (tax-exempt trusts or inter vivos bequests) and illegal forms (tax evasion). As the economic historian Neil Cummins has shown, the amount of wealth hidden from probate records increased dramatically after 1950, largely because of a substantial rise in inheritance taxes which prompted wealthy families to put more of their assets into vehicles untouched by the tax office. For the very wealthy, such as those in the top 1 percent, around 60 percent of their wealth suddenly disappeared from official records, whereas around 30 percent of wealth was hidden for those in the top 10 percent. Such large discrepancies in the ability to hide wealth from tax officers could create a challenge for our estimates, making some families in the top 1 percent appear as though they are only in the top 10 percent. To account for this, in Figure 4.1 we distinguish two lines after 1950 for those born in the top 10 percent and top 1 percent of the wealth distribution—the solid squares or circles are the raw data, while the hollow squares or circles are adjusted for hidden wealth. Once we account for hidden wealth in this way, we see that even this modest decline in the power of coming from a wealthy background largely disappears.

In other words, despite the changes we know took place in Britain's wealth distribution over the twentieth century, which shuffled top shares away from the 1 percent to a broader upper middle class, this does not seem to have dented the ability of wealthy families to propel their offspring into the most powerful and influential positions.

Distance from Necessity

How do we make sense of this? Well, it clearly suggests that there is something distinctive, even propulsive, about growing up in a *wealthy* family.[15] Some of this, of course, is a reflection of what money can buy, such as elite schooling (which we explore in Chapter 5) or certain types of activities like expensive holidays and rarefied sports (as we saw in Chapter 3). But many have argued that wealth also inculcates a more fundamental sense of *confidence* about one's ability to have an impact in the world.[16] This self-assurance repeatedly came through in our interviews too. Those from wealthy backgrounds often exuded a sense of certainty about their ability to progress, and this appeared to have been decisive in helping them get ahead. This insight is supported by academic literature—particularly in social psychology, where a number of studies have found a relationship between class privilege and overconfidence, narcissism, rule-breaking, and entitlement.[17]

Yet such work fails to explain why and how this relationship exists. Confidence may be the overarching holding term that people reach for when they observe those from wealthy backgrounds, but what behaviours are they seeing and what produces them? A useful touchstone here, we think, is the theory of sociologist Pierre Bourdieu and in particular his concept of "distance from necessity." Bourdieu argued that material affluence affords people a certain distance from economic necessity that is then reflected in the way they bring up and socialise their children.[18] In particular, those who have time and space "freed from economic urgency" tend to approach raising their children as a project in what Annette Lareau calls "concerted cultivation"—providing extensive support with homework, carefully curating a roster of extra-curricular activities, and inculcating a propensity for "symbolic mastery"—that is, a certain mode of using language, including an elaborate vocabulary and "correct" grammar, as well as more generally an ease and familiarity with artistic abstraction and theoretical ideas.[19]

Most sociological work looking at the legacy of family wealth has focused on people's early lives.[20] This is far from surprising. Not only is it much harder to trace the direct effects of parental wealth as people get older and their lives become more complex, but it also remains a taboo subject. We certainly found in our interviews that wealth was difficult to talk about. People were distinctly uncomfortable discussing their family's wealth, seeking to play down its impact, even when we knew from probate records that it likely played an important role in their lives.

Still, a number of our interviewees were unusually candid. And it is in these accounts where it is possible to discern glimpses of the ways in which extreme distance from necessity shapes elite trajectories. For some this was about being immersed in a very distinct family milieu. Michael (born 1935–1940), who had enjoyed a long and successful career in both academia and politics, and was still active politically, provided a telling example. He described how the development of his identity was intimately bound up with early experiences in his family's several grand homes, exploring the abundance of antiques and paintings, and learning about the decorated lives of his extended family (his relatives were celebrated figures in business, politics, law, art, and literature). He explained:

> My family background is sort of littered with these rather interesting people . . . So I was brought up with the feeling that I was definitely special and—I dare say it sounds really bad to say, I felt very superior . . . I mean, my grandmother was a great antiques collector and had beautiful paintings and so on and had this amazing huge Georgian Regency house, ten bedrooms and so on. So I just assumed that this was, I was definitely—Yes, superior doesn't sound exactly the right word, but I definitely felt special.

For Michael and others like him, growing up in a very wealthy family was not just a matter of benefitting from the material comfort offered by their *own* upbringing, it was a principle that felt wider and bigger, that flanked successive generations of their extended family. It generated a feeling of visceral distinction, a sense of what Michael describes here as feeling fundamentally "special."

Parental wealth doesn't just produce a feeling of distinction. It generates an orientation to the future, particularly in terms of a willingness to take risks. We were struck by the deep sense of assurance that those from wealthy backgrounds recalled feeling when eyeing their future lives and careers. As Robert (academic, 1955–1960) recalls of his adolescent self, "there was just an expectation that things would work out fine." This sense of possibility, in turn, shaped particular orientations to risk. Take Stephen, a successful CEO in his sixties (1955–1960). Stephen had grown up in a very wealthy family, with his father continuing a prosperous manufacturing business started by his grandfather. The family lived in a six-bedroom house in London, had a second home, and Stephen and all his siblings were privately educated. Concerted cultivation was a key theme in his childhood: he was encouraged to study the oboe, played rugby and cricket, and starred in various school plays. Despite this, Stephen described himself as the "black sheep" of the family, a "rebel" that broke the mould of his fairly conservative family:

> We were living in a time when there was the kind of, you know, post 1960s environment. So, you know, there was drugs. We did a lot of stealing and I drove my mother's car from the age of about 14. I used to steal it at night when my parents were asleep. I'd push it out of the driveway and then drive around. So, I kind of was always taking risks . . . And there was always huge sums of money because my dad had a wallet stuffed full of notes that we just used to liberally help ourselves to. You know, it just used to finance everything. And sometimes I used to steal my mum's credit card, you know. We used to just use it to buy whatever we wanted on the credit card. And I think that that was like—the extraordinary thing about that was that there was so much money it wasn't missed.

What is interesting here is that parental wealth both facilitated Stephen's risk-taking and acted as an important psychological source of insulation should anything go wrong. He went on to university where he became involved in student activism, at one point even taking a year out of his degree to work for a charity. After getting his degree his passion for activism continued. He travelled internationally for several years, working on various social justice campaigns. Yet this activism was contingent on parental support—"basically my father financed my entire time," Stephen acknowledged. "I hadn't really thought about a job or earning money."

Stephen eventually began working for pay in his late twenties, eventually starting in a junior position in the charitable organisation he now leads as CEO. From here his ascent was rapid, and he has remained in the top job for over a decade. Asked to account for his success, Stephen returns to the theme of risk-taking:

> I suppose I was relatively successful at running an organisation. And it's a weird organisation because you're taking a lot of risks, you know, in terms of all the legal risks, threats. And, you know, you are ultimately, as CEO, responsible if anything goes wrong. But I was sort of comfortable with taking risks because I'd sort of done it going right back to my childhood . . . Like I always thought that actually the best people to run these sort of organisations would actually be criminals (laughs), because when you rob a bank you must think, okay, I'm going to get rich from robbing a bank if it works but you've also got to weigh that it's eight to ten years in prison if I get caught, and the chances of getting caught are quite high. So, you've got to be prepared to take quite high risks, and prepared to take the punishment if it goes wrong.

What's intriguing in this account is not just the emphasis Stephen puts on risk-taking but also how he traces this capacity directly back to his upbringing, where a financial security blanket acted to encourage him to experiment.

This kind of fearlessness was echoed by a number of people we spoke to from wealthy backgrounds. Many of the men and women we interviewed underlined the fact that their career success had been contingent on their willingness to be "disruptive" in the pursuit of challenging established orthodoxies. Amanda, for example, a journalist and activist (1960–1965) explained that the key to her most important achievements had been a "messianic conviction" that she was capable of "changing people's minds." It was, she said, "contagious." Yet she also acknowledged that forging her reputation as a disrupter had been highly contingent on access to the "bank of Mum and Dad":

> Because if it all went tits up I think, you know, there is an economic security blanket. So for example, I was working at Granada television. I was quite young, I was working as a researcher and I wanted to break off and be a freelance writer. And my mother had a flat where our nanny used to live, and each of us as children when we grew up, we had a spell living in the flat, and I didn't have to pay any rent. So that was enormously important.

For Stephen, Amanda, and others born in the 1950s or 1960s, recruitment to elite positions, and success once there, was contingent on developing a disposition for risk-taking that itself was only made possible by the insulation that flowed from an upbringing lived at an extreme distance from economic necessity. This may seem a little abstract. But we would argue that such comfort with risk can have a direct bearing on one's ability to reach positions of power and influence. It can guide, as a range of sociologists have shown, the selection decisions people make in their careers, allowing some to opt for riskier but ultimately more lucrative or prestigious pathways.[21] It is also a disposition that is often rewarded by gatekeepers in the job market.[22] Freed from any economic necessity, then, and armed with a confidence to take risks, the odds of success are significantly stacked in favour of the wealthy.

Family Fortunes

So far, we have discussed elite origins as a function of the relationship between parents and children. But this is a very limited way of understanding social background.[23] In reality, a multitude of different family members contribute to the way we're brought up.[24] This might be direct, like the influence of siblings, grandparents, and a whole web of other extended family members, or indirect, through the values brought to bear on our upbringing.[25]

This is particularly important in terms of elites because reaching positions of influence is rare even for those born into power and privilege. Elite reproduction is perhaps better understood, therefore, as an extended, multigenerational family project, which can easily skip a generation but still show up in the trajectories of nieces, cousins, or grandchildren. This broader view also helps us to see the pivotal role that elite women have often played in securing the trajectories of their children.[26] Women born to elite parents may not have ended up in *Who's Who* themselves—particularly in the past—but many will have married someone included in the directory or have had a child who will make their way into *Who's Who*.[27]

One way to apprehend elite reproduction through this broader lens is to think about extended family *networks*.[28] Imagine, for example, that there are two societies with very different ways of assigning elite positions. In the first, positions are allocated at random; that is, elites are simply picked arbitrarily from the census. Now imagine that we could trace the genealogy of those elites, following their children and grandchildren and looking at their parents and grandparents. In that society, it would be incredibly unlikely that you would find people in an elite person's extended family who had also achieved elite status. Now imagine a society in which positions of power and influence are closely connected to who your family was, the amount of money they have, or their connections to other elites. In this society, if you were to trace the genealogy of any given member of the elite, you would expect to find many other family members in positions of authority. In other words, familial networks tell us something important about the degree to which elite reproduction moves through family ties, even when it is not directly transmitted from parent to child.

To get a handle on this question, we constructed two networks, one from *Who's Who* and one from a genealogical website (WikiTree). For each we took a random sample of around 7,000 people born in the United Kingdom since 1800. We then collected data on the immediate relatives of each of these 7,000 people. Armed with that genealogical data we can see that around 6 percent of the 7,000 people taken at random from WikiTree were related to each other (that is, they had a common ancestor or descendant). Whereas, over 60 percent of the 7,000 people sampled from *Who's Who* were connected to someone else in that sample via a shared relative. In other words, the people in our *Who's Who* sample were ten times more likely to be connected to each other than the people listed in general genealogical data. This is a very high level of interconnectedness relative to what we would expect if elite positions were just given out by chance.

There is a second key take away from the family trees we constructed for the people in *Who's Who*. And this is that the structure of these elite connections is complex. Most don't involve a straightforward transmission of privilege from parent to child (although there is, as we will see below, some of that going on). Figure 4.3 visualises one of these family trees. We chose this kinship network because it has an above-average number of ties to other people in *Who's Who* (but is in no way extreme or unusual). To see the complexity in how privilege is transmitted, we need to focus on the different lines in the graph. Here a black line between two dots indicates a

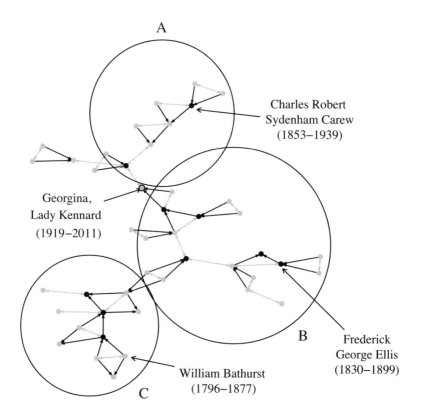

4.3 Elite networks over the last 200 years.

Note: Black dots are people in the random sample of 7,000 people from *Who's Who* (these are the "egos" of the network). Black lines are parent–child relationships. Grey lines are marriage relationships. We collected genealogical data on each ego (the 7,000 people sampled at random from *Who's Who*) and observed whether they were related to any of the other egos in that sample through their family trees. This allowed us to calculate the number of ties that each ego had to other egos. The network in this figure represented the 75th percentile of the number of ties (ten egos for the *Who's Who* network) across all 7,000 people. They were, then, more connected than the average person, but this was not the most densely connected network in this sample.

parent–child relationship, and a grey line a marriage. We have overlaid onto this graph three circles to draw attention to three different parts of the network.

Look at circle A and the people within it. Here (at the outer edge) we have a marriage (a grey line between two dots) that produced a child (black lines) who was in *Who's Who* (the black dots). This person is Charles Robert Sydenham Carew (1853–1939). Charles was educated at St. John's College, Cambridge, and was a justice of the peace and a Conservative politician. Charles married (grey line) Muriel Mary, the daughter of Sir John Heathcoat-Amory, a baronet, in 1891 and they had five children. One of those children (two black lines), Peter Gawen Carew (1894–1967), is included in this network but was not in *Who's Who*. Peter attended Winchester College and then Trinity College, Cambridge, before becoming a captain in the Royal 1st Devon Yeomanry. He and his wife, Ruth Chamberlain, had one child, Nichola (1930–2016), who was not in *Who's Who* but did marry someone who was—George Arnold Ford Kennard (1915–1999), a baronet educated at Eton who also served in the military.

Charles Carew's offspring and descendants, then, did not all reach positions of power. There was no simple elite reproduction from parent to child. But at the same time, the family remained intimately connected to the British elite, attending elite schools, and marrying into elite families.

Now let's look at Circle B. We start again with a marriage that produced a child, Frederick George Ellis (1830–1899), 7th Baron Howard de Walden and 3rd Baron of Seaford. Frederick attended Eton and then Trinity College, Cambridge, and helped his father manage their sugar plantations in Jamaica, attempting to implement modern technologies. These innovations failed and the estates became heavily indebted, eventually being sold off in 1912 to pay for those debts. Despite the loss of the family estate, Frederick's marriage to Blanche Holden (1856–1911)—twenty-five years his junior—ensured that his family's connection to the elite continued. Blanche and Frederick had a son, Thomas Evelyn (1880–1946), who was in *Who's Who,* but it was not a happy marriage. In 1893 Blanche sued for divorce and the baron countersued. He claimed "undue intimacy" with another man, while she claimed he was violent, abusive, and would return home drunk and "vomit in the bed." Once this cause célèbre had been resolved, Blanche married Henry Lopes (1865–1922), 2nd Baron Ludlow in 1903, another Eton graduate who went to Oxford and later became a barrister before joining the House of Lords. Blanche died in 1911, and Baron Ludlow remarried. Alice Mankiewicz (1862–1945), his new wife, had also been married before, to Sir Julius Charles Wernher, 1st Baronet. Their son, Major-General Sir Harold Augustus Wernher (1893–1973), 3rd Baronet, was also in *Who's Who*. Indeed, Sir Harold's daughter Georgina (Lady Kennard) almost brings us up to the present day. She died only in 2011 and was reputedly "one of the best connected women in the country."[29] Indeed, one can see why. Georgina (highlighted in Figure 4.3) was the linchpin between these two powerful families.

Through the middle of the last century, marriage practices both reflected and created the tight social worlds in which the British elite were operating and clearly played a role in generating dense kinship ties within the elite.[30]

The last perspective on this elite network can be gleaned from circle C. Here we have an interesting example of how the formation of an aristocratic line occurred from a position within the landed gentry. Again, we start with a couple, William Bathurst (1796–1877) and his wife Mary Rhodes (1793–1862), who had two children. William was an Anglican clergyman and noted hymnist who was himself the son of a reverend. He went to Winchester (a Clarendon School) and then Christ Church, Oxford. He was given a plum clerical position by an aristocratic uncle and eventually inherited his father's estate. One of Mary and William's children, Charles Bathurst (1836–1907), ended up in *Who's Who*. He was a justice of the peace and according to the "career" section in his *Who's Who* bio "owned 4,098 acres." His son, Charles (1867–1958), went to Sherborne, Eton, and then Oxford, before becoming a lawyer and entering politics as a Conservative and becoming governor-general of New Zealand. He was raised to the peerage as Baron Bledisloe, before becoming a viscount. The family was aristocratic and well established—note the aristocratic patronage which enabled William to get his first major job—but it was really Charles who secured the families' position within the elite. His son Benjamin (1899–1979—Eton and then Magdalen College, Oxford) was succeeded by his son Christopher (1934–2009—Eton and then Trinity College, Oxford), who was succeeded by his son Rupert (1964—Eton), a portrait artist who is also in *Who's Who*. This section of the network reinforces the way connections and family ties enabled a family to secure a more solid foothold in the British elite. It is true that this family eventually came to look exactly like the stereotype—father to son transmission—but its rise to prominence is predicated on other connections—that of an aristocratic uncle who bestowed a favour on William Bathurst (his nephew).

These familial networks provide a strong impressionistic sense of the importance of a diverse range of family ties in processes of elite reproduction. Not only fathers aided their sons but also grandparents, stepparents, and even aunts and uncles. These anecdotes are illuminating, but we also wanted to analyse these relationships more systematically. To do this, we first picked at random just over 100 people who were included in the first few editions of *Whos' Who* and then traced their family trees, collecting data on their "close" relations, namely parents, siblings, spouses, nieces and nephews, children, grandchildren, and sometimes great grandchildren. We also checked to see whether any of those families' members were included in *Who's Who*. We start with people in the early editions for two reasons. We want to uncover how influence (and wealth) flows down family trees, and so it makes sense to start with people in *Who's Who* and then see what happens to their descendants. At the same time, to do this analysis we rely on genealogical records, and these are far more patchy for people who are still living, which means it would be much less accurate to trace these ties in the other direction. We stopped collecting family trees after we reached 105 families because collecting new data was making a negligible difference to the overall estimates we were generating.

What we found was quite striking. Of the families we traced, 57 percent had descendants in *Who's Who* and often it was more than one (one person had ten). These 105 families had, on average, twenty-three "close" relations and around 6 percent of those relations were in *Who's Who*. This might seem quite low. But it is worth remembering how rare it is to get into *Who's Who* at all. Only 0.05 percent of the population would ever get into *Who's Who* if its members were spread across the population evenly. This means that people in *Who's Who* at the beginning of the twentieth century were 120 times more likely to see their descendants reach these elite positions than everyone else in the population. This is a staggeringly high number.

Colonial Ties

We should not assume, however, that all elite families had the same power to ensure their descendants reached elite positions. All of these 105 families were white, and their children would not have faced the same barriers as the children and grandchildren of elites of colour. Now, there were not many people of colour in elite positions in Britain at the end of the nineteenth century and the early twentieth century, as we explore in Chapter 9, but there were some. We tracked down the families of twenty-five people of colour, following the same procedure we used for the 105 white families. The vast majority of these elites of colour were in *Who's Who,* but we did supplement our analysis by looking at the *Oxford Dictionary of National Biography* and the list of 100 Great Black Britons, in part because there were so few minoritized elites in *Who's Who.*[31]

People of colour were able to help their descendants reach elite positions; yet this happened much less often than it did for their white counterparts. Around 20 percent of the elites of colour had a descendent who was also in *Who's Who,* a figure that is much higher than we would expect if elite positions were randomly distributed through the population (0.05 percent). At the same time, 20 percent is only one third of the rate of elite reproduction that we saw for white families (57 percent). Or, looking at this another way, only 3 percent of the close relatives of the people of colour were in the elite, whereas for white families it was 6 percent.

Still, the rates of elite reproduction among people of colour are higher than we expected, and digging into these family trees we can see some patterns that help us understand what made these families exceptional. One crucial factor seems to have been relations with the imperial establishment. One family (and the family with the highest degree of elite reproduction) was actually an aristocratic family. Satyendra Prasanna Sinha (1863–1928) was a British Indian lawyer and statesman who was the first Indian to enter the Viceroy's Executive Council (or the cabinet of the Government of India) and to become a King's Counsel. In 1919, he was appointed under-secretary of state for India and was, for his service, raised to the peerage of Baron Sinha of Raipur. He was the first and only Indian ever to be granted a hereditary peerage, a tradition continuing through today, with the 6th Baron Sinha (although not without some contestation along the way).[32] This family was able to incorporate themselves into the very heart of the British elite and have remained there ever since through the same mechanisms (for example, inheritance of titles) that allow some white families to remain in the elite. The other families that were more successful at getting their descendants into *Who's Who* were, likewise, either part of the colonial service or ran firms that were crucial to the imperial project (for example, Tata).

Not all people of colour in elite positions worked with the empire, however. Some adopted an oppositional stance. But these families appear to have been far less successful at ensuring their children reached elite positions in the United Kingdom. The one exception was Joseph Ephraim Casely-Hayford (1866–1930), a Ghanaian lawyer who passed the bar in the United Kingdom and became the head of an anti-colonial organisation in the Gold Coast after he established a legal practice there. His descendants—primarily through his son Victor (a lawyer and accountant)—include a number of prominent people in contemporary Britain, including Augustus Casely-Hayford (art historian and broadcaster), Joseph Casely-Hayford (designer), and Margaret Casely-Heyford (lawyer and now Chancellor of Coventry University). People of colour could, then, achieve elite reproduction, but it was partly contingent on their degree of cooperation with, or resistance to, the colonial state.

Zooming out, the key message we think this analysis underlines is that the British elite may not be reproducing itself generation to generation in the straightforward mechanical way that is sometimes caricatured, but are often orbiting power and influence in tight familial networks that create a web of relations capable of providing pathways into the elite.

How Money Talks

What role is wealth playing in this extended-family project of elite reproduction? It is, as you might imagine, critical. Recall the 105 elite individuals we discussed above. Some were in the top 1 percent of the wealth distribution when they died and around 7.8 percent of their descendants were in *Who's Who*. Among families where the original person was *not* in the top 10 percent of the wealth distribution, this figure drops to only 2.8 percent.

So why is this? How precisely does wealth lubricate elite reproduction in wealthy extended families? To interrogate these mechanisms, we dug further into the family histories of some of these 100 families. And here we structured our analysis to capture both "typical" *and* "deviant" cases.

Edward Fleet Alford (1850–1905) is a typical case: a successful businessman and Knight of the Realm whose elite trajectory was intimately bound up with wealth. He ended his life very wealthy, leaving a probate of £58,692 (or £5.7m in today's money). But Edward was not a self-made man. His father, the Right Rev. Charles Alford (also in *Who's Who*) was a major landholder in Somerset, in part because he had married into the Sydenham family. Edward's brother Josiah and his nephew Charles both ended up in *Who's Who* too, largely because of their positions in the clergy. We do not know where Edward went to school, but we do know that his great-great-grandfather, his great-grandfather, his grandfather, his father, his brother, and his nephew all went to either Oxford or Cambridge, and his father went to St Paul's School in London. The cost of attending these schools and universities was largely indicative of sustained affluence as a family across the generations. In short, we see how positions of power facilitated both the acquisition of wealth, the purchase of elite education (something we touch on in Chapter 5), and access to elite networks.

Not everyone, however, who died wealthy saw their descendants show up in *Who's Who* (our deviant case). Alexander Ure, a lawyer and lecturer, was appointed solicitor-general and then Lord Advocate, and served for a time as a Liberal MP. Eventually, he became Lord Justice General for Scotland and was raised to be the 1st Baron of Strathclyde. Yet, despite leaving a probate of £150,180 when he died in 1928 (£7.5m in today's money), Ure has no close family relations in *Who's Who*. What happened? Well Alexander's family was slightly different from Edward Fleet's. Alexander's grandfather was a baker who started a business which Alexander's father, John Ure, eventually took over. John became a prominent local businessman and was even appointed Lord Provost of Glasgow, but Alexander's father did not capitalise on his wealth and position. His brothers all stayed within the family business as flour merchants, and none of them went to university. The sole exception was Alexander. There was also a distinct lack of elite marriages. All the brothers, including Alexander, married women who were the daughters of local middle-class businessmen. Alexander himself had no male descendants. His only child, a daughter, died before he did, ending the generational succession to the title he had acquired. Despite Alexander's wealth, his family was not embedded in elite networks, and so they dropped out of *Who's Who*. Individual wealth and status were not able to compensate for the absence of a wider elite network.

The role wealth plays in elite reproduction is also revealed by examining the elites of colour we discussed earlier. Only 40 percent of these minoritized elites reported any wealth in the probate data. This figure was around 80 percent for our white elites. Now this may partly be because some of these individuals died outside of the United Kingdom and had no affairs to settle here. But even if we look at those who did leave wealth in the United Kingdom, none of the elites of colour were in the top 1 percent. In contrast, around 50 percent of the white families we traced were in the top

1 percent of probate distribution. Another reason, then, why people of colour have been less able to ensure elite reproduction is because they had fewer economic resources than the other elites in their milieu. The exclusion of people of colour from acquiring wealth remains a challenge across high-income contexts, one that likely weakens their ability to help their kids reach elite positions.[33]

What about families where the original person in *Who's Who* appears to have died with very little wealth but then saw very high levels of elite reproduction among their descendants? Strikingly, we could find no such cases in our research. There were one or two instances where we originally thought this may be the case—that is, where we could not find a probate record for the individual—but further analysis revealed that the person actually came from families that had been very wealthy at some point in the past. This is important. It suggests that our analysis of elite reproduction among the wealthy may underestimate its importance. In other words, there are probably a number of false negatives in our data—wealthy people whose probate records, for whatever reason, we have been unable to find.

Wealth as World-Making

Britain has experienced a profound equalisation of wealth since the turn of the twentieth century. And yet this has only modestly dented the ability of Britain's most wealthy families to propel their children into the British elite. Of course, this kind of elite origin is no *guarantee* of success. But our results underline that growing up surrounded by this extreme material affluence has provided a remarkably persistent propulsive power. The children of the wealthy are able to make mistakes, weather false starts, and take risks, all free from the spectre of economic insecurity. More broadly, our analysis indicates that wealth is not just an economic resource; it creates an extreme distance from necessity that fundamentally structures how people experience the world. It supports multigenerational projects of elite reproduction encompassing nieces, nephews, grandchildren, and cousins. The totalising, shapeshifting, and often hidden qualities of wealth are, we would argue, key in understanding why wealth has been such a persistent and effective force in propelling people into Britain's elite.

The equalization of wealth inequality was not unique to the United Kingdom. Between 1914 and 1986, the share of wealth owned by the top

1 percent fell by around 50 percent in Germany, 70 percent in the Netherlands, 45 percent in the United States, and 70 percent in France.[34] And like the United Kingdom, these dramatic reductions in wealth inequality did not lead to major changes in rates of social mobility in these countries.[35] Of course, access to elite positions is not the same as general occupational social mobility, but it seems unlikely that elite positions would have become far more open without also seeing a greater degree of openness within professional occupations more broadly. After all, most elites are recruited from within these professional occupations. The United Kingdom's experience of elite reproduction is unlike these other countries in many ways, but on these two big issues (wealth inequality and trends in social mobility) it is not distinct at all. In this respect, the persistent propulsive power of wealth in the United Kingdom may well be indicative of similar trends in a range of other high-income countries.

Yet one of the problems in trying to pin down the specific propulsive power of wealth is that it is intertwined with other channels of elite recruitment.[36] In particular it is often invested into education via private schools and elite universities. This is especially salient because in places where there have been modest changes in social mobility over the twentieth century, these changes have largely been associated with major educational reforms which expanded access to education (for example, in Germany and the United Kingdom).[37] In Chapters 5 and 6 we seek to unpack the complex relationships between these elite-making channels, beginning with Britain's most prestigious private schools in Chapter 5 and then moving on, in Chapter 6, to look at Oxford and Cambridge universities.

5

Old Boys

In 1861, amid complaints about the management of Eton College, a Royal Commission chaired by the Earl of Clarendon was established to investigate the state of nine leading schools in England: Charterhouse, Harrow, Merchant Taylor's, Rugby, Shrewsbury, St Paul's, Westminster, Winchester, and Eton. The subsequently released *Clarendon Report* outlined a number of problems with the schools—such as poor governance and dysfunctional relationships between the headmaster and his assistants—and recommended that the scholarship places offered to poor local boys should be eradicated because these boys "lowered the social tone."[1] Maintaining the right "tone" mattered because these were, the report noted, Britain's "Great Schools," defining institutions that prepared their old boys to take up positions of power across politics, law, business, culture, and the military:

> It is not easy to estimate the degree in which the English people are indebted to these schools for the qualities on which they pique themselves most—for their capacity to govern others and control themselves, their aptitude for combining freedom with order, their public spirit, their vigour and manliness of character, their strong but not slavish respect for public opinion, their love of healthy sports and exercise. These schools have been the chief nurseries of our statesmen; in them, and in schools modelled after them, men of all the various classes that make up English society, destined for every profession and career, have been brought up on a footing of social equality.[2]

Fast forward 160 years and the Clarendon Schools remain "the chief nurseries of our statesmen." They may now be attended by as little as

0.19 percent of all 13-to-18-year-olds, but remarkably they have educated 67 percent of all prime ministers (including most recently, Winchester alumni Rishi Sunak). They have also educated 53 percent of all Great Officers of State (prime minister, home secretary, foreign secretary, and chancellor of the Exchequer), 23 percent of whom have attended just one of these schools: Eton College.[3]

Private schooling has long been the subject of fierce public debate in Britain, and in recent years a steady stream of books by journalists and former students has spotlighted how such schools perpetuate privilege and at times leave a residue of psychological trauma.[4] Sociologists, meanwhile, have pointed to how they inhibit social mobility and act as key vehicles of class reproduction.[5] The focus here is almost always on private education *as a whole.* Yet as the *Clarendon Report* made clear more than a century ago, not all private schools are made equal. Among the 2,600 independent schools that exist today, for example, there are huge variations in prestige. Eton, Harrow, Winchester, St Paul's, and the other Clarendon Schools have traditionally sat at the top of that hierarchy, followed by a wider group of around 200 mostly single-sex public schools that modelled themselves on the Clarendon Schools, and that have been longstanding members of what until recently was called the Headmasters' and Headmistresses' Conference (HMC). Also key are the 200 or so leading elite *girls* schools of the Girls' Schools Association (GSA).

Although we know these schools continue to produce many successful high-profile alumni, we know fairly little about their propulsive power more generally and how this has changed over time. With this in mind, our starting point for this chapter is the simple observation that the relationship between schooling and the British elite requires a very precise lens. To provide this, we turned again to *Who's Who,* which asks its entrants to list the school they attended (rather than the *type* of school, as most surveys do). This means we can analyse the specific power of both the Clarendon Schools, as well as HMC and GSA schools.

We begin by exploring the degree to which the Clarendon and HMC schools have been able to propel their old boys into different areas of the British elite over the last 125 years. Taken together, our results indicate that the power of these elite schools has declined significantly, driven partly by the weakening representation of the military and religion within the elite and the rise of women in the labour force. Yet the most dramatic declines followed key educational reforms in 1918 and 1944.

Notwithstanding these changes, public schools remain extraordinarily powerful channels of elite formation. Even among the elite today, the alumni of the nine Clarendon Schools are fifty-two times more likely to reach the British elite than those who attended any other school. Tellingly, they are particularly over-represented in the wealth elite. Drawing on the experiences of old boys, we find that this could at least partially be explained by the ways in which such schools nurture and amplify ideas of exceptionalism that these men carry with them into their careers.[6]

Finally, we disrupt the traditional focus on boys elite schools to interrogate the power of old girls. Here we show that girls schools have also been powerful engines of inequality. Specifically, the alumni of twelve top girls schools have been around twenty times more likely than other women to reach elite positions. Yet significantly, such schools have also consistently been less propulsive than their male-only counterparts. We argue this is rooted in the ambivalent aims of girls elite education, where there has been a longstanding tension between promoting academic achievement and upholding traditional gender norms.

The Decline of the Old Boy

We begin by exploring the changing educational composition of *Who's Who* across birth cohorts born between 1830 and 1979. Specifically, in Figure 5.1, we plot the proportion of entrants in each cohort who report attending a Clarendon, HMC, private, or other type of school. Notably, there is a clear downward trend over time. Among those born in the 1840s, approximately 20 percent of the members of *Who's Who* had attended one of these nine schools. That figure has dropped to 8 percent among the most recent birth cohort. Compare this with all HMC schools (the Clarendon plus other HMC schools): during the Victorian era, as private boarding schools expanded in number and size, they educated a larger share of the elite. This influence peaked among individuals born between 1905 and 1914, when around 50 percent of those included in *Who's Who* had attended an HMC school. After this there was a noteworthy fall among those born between 1910 and 1950, which has stabilised since at 31 to 32 percent of all entrants.

This means that someone born in 1847 who attended one of the nine Clarendon Schools was approximately 220 times more likely to end up in *Who's Who* than someone born in the same year who did not attend one of

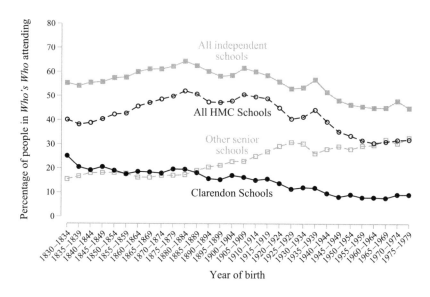

5.1 Clarendon Schools became less dominant over time.

these schools. If we move forward to our last cohort (those born between 1975 and 1979), we see a significant decline: someone born in 1977 who attended a Clarendon School is approximately forty-nine times more likely to end up in *Who's Who.*

One driver of this downward trend, according to our analysis, is changes in the makeup of the British elite, particularly the decline of military and religious elites and the increasing significance of women and foreign-born elites.[7] The representation of the military elite in *Who's Who* fell precipitously throughout the twentieth century, in tandem with the decline of the British Empire. This is significant because military elites traditionally had a well-established connection with Clarendon Schools.[8] Similarly, the secularization of British society coincides with substantial declines in the number of religious leaders in *Who's Who,* another sector with long-standing links to Clarendon Schools.[9] At the same time, our analysis also shows a sharp increase in the number of women and foreign-born entrants (see Figure 8.1 in Chapter 8), who represented a new source of competition for Clarendon alumni seeking elite positions.[10]

Another powerful driver of elite school decline has been educational reform. Over the past 140 years, the structure of British education has shifted significantly from a voluntary system combining fees and charitable institutions to a compulsory system that is largely state-funded with a small fee-paying sector. This transition began in earnest with the 1890 Elementary Education Act, which reduced fees for state elementary schools, and was extended under the Fisher Act of 1918 and then the Education Act of 1944, which raised the compulsory school leaving age to 15 (later 16) and abolished all fees. These reforms also introduced a standardised qualification, the School Certificate, which became the first unified secondary school examination system, and differentiated credentials by providing subject-specific grades.[11]

We conducted a series of what are called "structural break tests" to examine when sharp changes or "breaks" in the power of elite schools emerge, and whether their timing coincides with these key educational reforms.[12] The results for Clarendon Schools, which can be seen in Figure 5.2, show that significant changes or structural breaks matched the timing of at least two main education reforms (allowing time for their implementation). Alumni

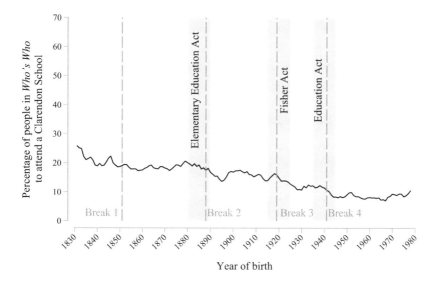

5.2 Educational reforms undermined the propulsive power of elite schools.

Note: Vertical dashed lines represent the results of our structural breaks analysis, which detects when a time series experiences a significant shift from the trend. The shaded grey areas represent cohorts affected by the different educational reforms. We can see that the structural breaks occur in and around those education reforms. We have conducted this analysis for the other types of schools and have found similar results, particularly for the later reforms. These are available in the online appendix: https://github.com/asreeves /born-to-rule.

of all three types of private schools experienced substantial declines in elite recruitment following the introduction of the 1918 Fisher Act and the 1944 Education Act.[13]

Why did these reforms make such a difference? To understand this, it is first important to return to the beginning of the period we examine. In the first few decades of the twentieth century, elite schools acted as unquestioned symbols of status and academic ability.[14] This meant that old boys were often able to move seamlessly from school, to university, to elite job in a fairly predictable and unimpeded manner. The educational reforms dented that pathway, ultimately forcing the schools to reinvent themselves to preserve their edge.

The testimonies of some of our early interviewees confirm this gilded pathway. George Baring, whose father ran Barings Bank and who went on to become governor of the Bank of England, attended Eton in the early 1930s. While at Eton he joined the Officers' Training Corps (OTC), which involved "basic training" and "simple military exams" but was largely considered a "bit of a joke affair among the boys." Yet when George finished school and started forging a career, he discovered "that the exams I'd passed in the OTC at Eton, qualified me to become a Second Lieutenant in the Army, without going to Sandhurst or anything. And so that proved to be fairly useful." Similarly, Jeremy Morse, chairman of Lloyds Bank between 1977 and 1992, explained how the signalling power of his Winchester education had been key to securing his first job in banking in the late 1940s:

> I had, some time before, decided that I was going to go into banking. That arose because when I was about 16, somebody who had known my father when he was a Solicitor, in fact, the Senior Partner in Childs Bank, where my father's firm of Solicitors had their accounts. He had approached my father, hearing that I was doing well at Winchester, and said, "Would your boy like to think about coming into the Bank?"

The Education Act of 1944 dented the ability of schools like Eton and Winchester to effortlessly propel old boys like George Baring and Jeremy Morse into elite environments like the City and the senior armed forces. At the simplest level, this was because it increased the pool of candidates able to compete for top positions. Beyond this, it also introduced a set of standardised academic credentials in the form of the School Certificate, which included specific letter grades, in an effort to level the academic playing field across the country. This didn't completely eradicate school-level effects: an *A* from Eton likely remained more powerful than an *A* from elsewhere. However, the process of grade standardization certainly made academic achievement more comparable across schools, such that the Clarendon Schools and other HMC schools could no longer rely solely on being status markers.

Levelling the playing field in this way soon revealed that these Clarendon Schools were not producing the best students in the country. Far from it. In the early 1960s, the *Times* found that Eton, Harrow, and Charterhouse were performing badly on these standardised tests compared to other schools, and an internal memo sent around Westminster School revealed that average marks in key subjects were below the national average.[15] No longer able to rest on their laurels, the schools now had to pivot towards becoming incubators of educational excellence.

This echoes the findings of sociologist Shamus Khan, who charts a similar process of adaptation within elite private schools in the United States. He argues that elite schools have successfully maintained their advantage by enacting a rhetorical sleight of hand: skillfully repositioning themselves not as upholders of ascribed social advantage, but as sites of meritocracy, admitting students based on individual educational excellence and propelling them on the same premise. This "ruse of elite rhetoric" obscures the ways in which these schools continue to reward privilege, he notes, "making differences in outcome appear a product of who people are rather than a product of the conditions of their making."[16]

We agree that deploying the rhetoric of meritocracy successfully masks many of the contemporary functions of elite schools, but it is also clear that adaptation to radical social change has not been seamless in the United Kingdom, and has led to a meaningful decline in the relative power of elite secondary schools. And unlike Khan, who situates this change in the context of the political movements of the 1960s, we trace the meritocratic turn in Britain's elite schools to the impact of much earlier educational reforms, and specifically the way they expanded access to the credentials needed to oil elite trajectories.

While most, at least in recent decades, have been very adept at negotiating this transformation, their relative power is still far weaker in this more competitive era than when the school itself acted as an unquestioned proxy for status.[17]

The Persistence of the Old Boy

It is important not to overstate this story of declining influence. Our results also show very starkly that public schools remain extraordinarily powerful channels of elite formation. Indeed, considering the radical changes to British society that occurred during the twentieth century, a reasonable take-away from Figure 5.1 would be that there has actually been remarkable continuity in the force of Britain's elite schools. Even now, at their lowest ebb, the nine small Clarendon Schools, representing less than 1 in every 500 pupils, still produced nearly 1 in 10 of all *Who's Who* entrants.

The persistence is further illustrated in Figure 5.3, which examines the educational backgrounds of the people added to *Who's Who* since 1986, splitting them into seven distinct periods. The figure shows the proportion of new entrants from the Clarendon Schools, all HMC schools, and all private schools together. We have already seen that the proportion of alumni from these schools has declined somewhat, and this is showing up here too. Yet what we see is that over the past twenty-two years, the proportion of new entrants from these elite schools has remained surprisingly constant, at around 8 percent for Clarendon Schools and around 30 percent for other

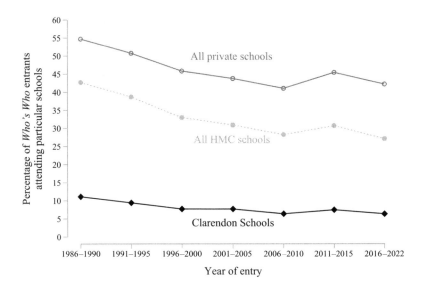

5.3 The persistence of the old boy.

HMC schools. This suggests, then, that the decline in the power of elite schools has largely stalled.

Finally, it is important to contextualize the profound *relative* advantage still enjoyed by the alumni of these elite schools. Even among today's elite, alumni of the nine Clarendon Schools are fifty-two times more likely to reach these positions than those who attended any other type of school. Even alumni of the other HMC schools—our weaker definition of elite schooling—are twenty-eight times more likely to be a member of *Who's Who*.

Talent Meritocrats

Britain's elite schools, then, may be less powerful today than in their heyday, but they remain profoundly over-represented in the educational profiles of the British elite. This invites an immediate question: is it really schooling that propels these individuals forward? Is there something happening on these campuses that is so transformative no other school can emulate its impact? Or could other factors, like the wealth and privilege we explored in Chapter 4, be at work?

If we want to know whether these schools have a propulsive power independent of wealth, we would need to know the wealth distribution of the students of Clarendon Schools. This is not a piece of information that is publicly available, but public records suggest around 15 percent of students at these schools receive means-tested support.[18] It is very likely that these students are not in the top 1 percent and it is probably true that the proportion of students who are not in the top 1 percent is even higher. So, let's assume that 70 percent of students who attend these nine schools are from the top 1 percent of the wealth distribution. Even in this conservative hypothetical scenario (the proportion of students born into the top 1 percent is probably lower than 70 percent), attending a Clarendon School still confers a clear advantage; students from the top 1 percent are still ~6 times more likely to reach *Who's Who* than those also born into the top 1 percent who did not attend one of these schools.

We can also consider this from another direction. There are students who attend these schools but do not come from elite backgrounds. To understand how the schools affect their chances of reaching the elite we can invert our hypothetical scenario. If we assume that 95 percent of students at these schools do not come from the top 1 percent (another conservative estimate but this time from the other direction), then these less affluent students would be twelve times more likely to reach the elite than kids who were born into the top 1 percent but did not go to these schools.

So, the alumni of elite schools are different. But why? Are these schools recruiting more able students? Or have these schools landed on a uniquely successful mixture of school culture, pedagogical excellence, and extracurricular activities that trains their students better than other schools? Or do they confer something more intangible that helps their students get ahead? Perhaps the most provocative account in recent years comes from the journalist Robert Verkaik in his book *Posh Boys*.[19] He argues that such schools cultivate "inflated egos," a "pathological willingness to risk everything," and are synonymous with the inculcation of a deep sense of "entitlement."[20] But can behavioural traits like entitlement really be discerned when we dig into the narratives of Clarendon alumni? If so, what do they look like in practice?

We conducted twenty-four interviews with alumni of Clarendon Schools, and these differed in subtle but important ways from our other interviewees. What we were struck by was the distinct way these men tended to understand themselves and their career success. They presented themselves as individuals who had achieved in life chiefly because of their exceptional abilities.

Now it is worth noting that nearly everyone we spoke to conceived of their career success as meritocratically achieved. Yet the package of attributes highlighted varied strongly across interviewees—particularly when it came to the relative value attributed to talent versus hard work. Among old boys, while there was usually some acknowledgment of hard work somewhere along the career narrative, this was often mentioned only fleetingly, as a taken-for-granted prerequisite rather than a decisive factor. Instead, what was striking was a tendency to foreground one's own unique and innate (rather than learned) talents. These talents tended to be expressed in three ways; 1) unique personality traits—with a special emphasis on creativity or risk taking, 2) the possession of innately "good judgment," and 3) "natural" aptitude, intelligence, or academic ability.

Almost all old boys mentioned possessing unique traits. Many underlined that they were "risk-takers" (Keith, law, born 1945–1950), unafraid to "think outside the box" (Robert, academics / politics, 1955–1960), or original and creative thinkers who had acted as disruptive entrepreneurs in their field. Peter, for example, an academic (1945–1950) who had been a close advisor to a recent prime minister, emphasised his importance as a creative thinker:

> When I was invited into Number 10 [Downing St] I wasn't actually very good at the day-by-day part of the job, and when I stepped out I had this leaving interview with [former Prime Minister] and I said I didn't think I'd done very well and he said, "No, you were a Rolls Royce in a Land Rover job." Which is a nice thing to say . . . Because . . . I was bad at the politics, I was briefed against, I wasn't firm enough with the Prime Minister, and I could often see the other side of the argument . . . So I think in the end ultimately probably my ideas were more influential or my thinking was more influential than my actual direct involvement in Number 10.

A second way talent manifested itself was via the idea that one's career success had revolved around the possession of "good judgment." Here many described how knowledge in their area was often tacit and hard to codify and therefore expertise was hard to verbalise or explicitly teach. Under these conditions, some stressed that their abilities were best characterised as an instinctive sense or acumen:

> It is essentially judgement. By and large you have to have a sound factual basis for anything you say but . . . but the judgement is whether it is so legally weak that it is improper to go ahead . . . and I think what I was good at was telling [government ministers] "This is the boundary of what you can do . . ." If it had been a purely legal expert decision they would have given it to a technocrat but they want you to make a political decision. So I certainly had much more than some of my colleagues a political sense. (Roger, civil service, 1945–1950)

The final manifestation of talent in these narratives came through the more blunt claim to a kind of natural intelligence. Sometimes this was hinted at indirectly and referenced via exceptional academic achievement— of demonstrating "natural aptitude" (Terence, business, 1950–1955), or what Heba (academic/political advisory, 1960–1965) somewhat modestly describes as "above-average intelligence." In other instances, references to intelligence were more explicit:

> Mind you there are two kinds of intelligence. There are some very intelligent people who complicate things enormously [laughs]. And then there's *simplifying intelligence* which tries to produce what is the point in as simple and straightforward a way as possible. People have said that I'm good at that, and obviously I think I partly got that genetically from the lawyers on my mother's side of the family. (Graham, finance, 1940–1944)

It is important to say that we are not arguing that people like Graham are somehow "wrong" about their talents. The accounts of old boys clearly constituted honest reflections on being successful. We neither want nor have the ability to interrogate the validity of any of these individual claims. What we are interested in is rather how these people see themselves, and whether there are certain reoccurring themes in their self-understanding. And what is striking to us in these narratives about intelligence, judgment, and aptitude, is that such traits were not presented as accumulated via experience or intentional self-fashioning. They are seen as unique or innate to the individual.

Scaffolding Specialness

Old boys, then, tend to see themselves as exceptional. But what's this got to do with their schooling? Our analysis suggests that elite schools play a key role as amplifiers of these natural talent narratives—promoting, nurturing, and inculcating a sense of one's exceptionalism. They do so by performing what education scholar Mitchell Stevens and his colleagues see as three key functions; they are sieves, temples, and incubators.[21]

First, elite schools are sieves in that they sift for certain students based on class background, financial resources, and academic ability. This type of selection often breeds a sense of intellectual exceptionalism. Many interviewees explained, for example, how they were continually reminded at school that they were what Kevin (business, 1955–1960) calls a "select bunch." And once in, most of these schools aggressively screen based on academic ability. At Eton and many other Clarendon Schools, a small number of boys receive "scholarships" based on ability and are then separated into a "scholars" house, replete with separate dormitories, traditions, and customs. Many interviewees described how the experience of being a "scholar" had further entrenched a sense of their intellectual distinction. As Sidney, a business executive and "scholar" at Eton (1930–1935), reflected:

> I think the emphasis was on the brain rather than on feelings or anything like that. We [scholars] were expected to run the world. Or anyhow run the UK . . . I think it was just an assumption. That's what we would be doing.

Connected to this, elite schools are also temples that provide their students with rare but highly valued forms of knowledge. This was traditionally achieved via a distinct academic curriculum, including subjects such as Latin and Greek and a wide range of modern languages that are not taught elsewhere, or rarefied extracurricular activities and sports, such as debating, rowing, lacrosse, rugby, cricket, and so on. These distinct aspects of the schools can still be found today. However, the old boys we spoke to, particularly younger ones, foregrounded more subtle dimensions of their experience. Much like Shamus Khan describes elite US boarding school students in *Privilege,* they emphasised that rather than prescribing certain forms of classical or highbrow knowledge, elite schools now encouraged more general knowledge or "habits of thought," as the Eton website boasts, over subject-specific expertise.[22] As part of this pedagogical strategy, many also described how they were afforded a distinct freedom to explore their own intellectual passions (whatever these might be) and, once identified, were explicitly encouraged to develop and nurture such interests:

> It was a great sense of sort of freedom and civilisation actually . . . you were at liberty to go and do what you wanted and that was encouraged in the sense of developing your interests. (Graham, finance, 1940–1945)

> So what was distinctive about it was that they really cared about how people thought, about cultivating the mind. (William, journalism, 1950–1955)

In many ways these accounts echo previous work on elite schools, such as Khan's and that of education scholars Claire Maxwell, Emma Taylor, Max

Persson, and Ruben Gaztambide-Fernandez, who all emphasise how such schools cultivate a sense of "ease" and familiarity with a broad range of subjects—classic and contemporary, highbrow and popular.[23] Yet what is also evident here is how such schools actively nurture and scaffold a belief in one's own *unique* capabilities. Very often this appeared to centre around cultivating a particular intellectual orientation—fostering original, daring, or creative thought:

> They did encourage and champion free thinking . . . they liked people who I guess were different or, not different, but kind of thought differently. They encouraged uniqueness in a way that, you know, I think was quite special for a school. (Pepita, academic / policy advisory, 1965–1970—went to a Clarendon School after it had transitioned to co-ed)

Strongly connected to their temple-like qualities, elite schools are also *incubators* where distinct identities coalesce and take shape. They are "miniature closed societies," as Bourdieu put it, where prolonged and intense contact with classmates generates a distinct elite identity that has long-lasting effects on embodiment, attitudes, taste, and lifestyle.[24] Certainly, among those we spoke to, there was a strong sense that their schooling had left a profound, even indelible, mark on their identity.

Some reflected that their schooling had provided them with a particular assurance or certainty about their singular ability to have an impact in the world. An exchange with Peter, an academic who had been to Eton, was telling. Despite coming from a fairly privileged background, Peter said that when he thinks about his early life, it is his school rather than home life that loomed large. He explained: "When I'm asked questions about my childhood I almost invariably refer to school, my instinct is to refer to school." As we delved into why this was, he paused for some seconds before continuing:

> *Peter:* I think [Eton] did give me, yes, a sense of confidence in dealing with the outside world . . . so it both was an advantage in terms of reputation but also an advantage in terms of confidence and ability to talk, to articulate, have confidence in one's own abilities.

> *Interviewer:* I'm interested in your sense of the future when you were there . . .

Peter: A sense of entitlement?

Interviewer: No, not necessarily entitlement, more a sense of . . .

Peter: . . . Groomed to be a part of the elite? Yes is the answer, yes I did feel that. I did feel that I knew, I thought I would do well in whatever I chose and I would get to the top. So I was not only ambitious but I also had the confidence to feel that I would fulfil those ambitions.

What is interesting here is the way in which Peter is both conscious of the charge of entitlement that others might impute to his schooling, but is also keen to explain more precisely the power of the school in boosting what might be called his "locus of control"—the sense that he could ultimately control his own destiny.

The influence of this type of elite schooling is arguably brought more sharply into focus when we consider the educational narratives of those who were educated in the state sector, particularly those from equally advantaged backgrounds. Schooling is noticeably muted in these elite narratives. In some cases, this is signaled by the conspicuous absence of schooling in accounts of early life: in others it is mentioned only in passing and often in fairly negative terms as "bog-standard" (Mark, policy, 1965–1970), "failing" (Christopher, civil service, 1980–1985), or "pretty shitty" (Paul, politics, 1955–1960).

Notably, it is often among interviewees educated in the state sector, particularly among women, people of different ethnic or racial backgrounds and those from working-class backgrounds, that hard work (rather than talent) was foregrounded as the decisive driver of academic success. Cerys, for example, an Asian British lawyer (1965–1969), spoke at length about the work ethic he developed at school:

I enjoyed school, but I very much had an attitude of, I knew I wanted to become a vet initially, and I'm now a lawyer but I really wanted to become a vet, so I always saw school as a bit like the place I got my ticket to go to what I wanted to do next. And so I had a very . . . I think of it now as ruthless, but at the time I didn't think of it like that, it just seemed to me it was obvious, if I was going to school I was there to get exams, and so that was the deal. I went to school because I needed the exams to get to where I needed to go, that's what I thought of.

Ian, a banker from a working-class background in the North of England, was similarly clear about the decisive role that hard work (rather than talent) had played in his success:

You know I'd always come in the top few of my class but that wasn't natural. Oh my gosh I would sit down and it wouldn't come naturally, that came through brute hard work. It was just brutal. It was, I just ground it through and nothing came to me easily. Nothing's ever come to me easily, nothing, nothing. Just ground, just ground it out you know really like a meat grinder. And I still do in a way.

Is There an Old Girls Network?

While all-male private schools remain powerful training grounds for future leaders, the scholarly (and wider public) preoccupation with this old boys network has often overshadowed and stymied inquiry into other equally important channels of elite recruitment. In particular—what about the "old girl"? Does a similar "old girls" network exist for women? Certainly, women's presence in the British elite has grown considerably in the past century. As we explore in Chapter 8, until the 1980s less than 5 percent of the British elite were women. This figure has now risen to 18 percent, and women make up around one third of new entrants to *Who's Who*.

It is also true that there has long existed a range of expensive, prestigious, and well-known fee-paying schools for young women in Britain.[25] Yet we know fairly little about the propulsive power of these schools. Again, *Who's Who* is an invaluable resource, providing data on the individual schools attended by women entrants. Our analysis distinguishes two types of elite girls schools. Although there is no clear-cut equivalent to the Clarendon Schools among elite girls schools, the historian Janet Howarth suggests that one way to identify elite girls schools is to look at their success at sending their alumni to Oxford and Cambridge.[26] Following this logic, we identified twelve girls schools that have been most successful at sending their students to Oxford and Cambridge, relative to when they opened and to their size. These are: Cheltenham Ladies College, North London Collegiate School, St Paul's School for Girls, Oxford High School for Girls, Queen's College on Harley Street, St Leonard's in St Andrews, Clifton High School for Girls, King Edward VI High School for Girls in Birmingham, Roedean, Godolphin and Latymer School, Wycombe Abbey, and the Benenden

School.[27] The reason we alight on twelve is that we wanted to identify a group of girls schools that educate a similar number of students to the nine male Clarendon Schools. We also examined a second tier of elite girls schools, based on ~200 schools represented by the GSA. This is a prestigious grouping of elite girls schools, educating approximately 2 percent of all girls, and comparable to the boys schools that make up the Headmasters' and Headmistresses' Conference (HMC).

Figure 5.4 shows that elite schooling was fairly uncommon among the women included in the early editions of *Who's Who*. This is partly because very few young women attended school in the early and middle parts of the nineteenth century; most were educated at home by governesses or tutors.[28] From 1870 onwards, Britain witnessed an explosion of girls' schooling, and many of the elite girls schools we focus on were founded in this period, including North London Collegiate School and Cheltenham Ladies College.[29] These newer institutions turned out to be far more successful at propelling their alumni than many of the more venerable girls schools, some of which had been around for centuries.

Yet despite the explosion in girls' schooling, there is no period in which these schools matched the performance of their male counterparts. Even

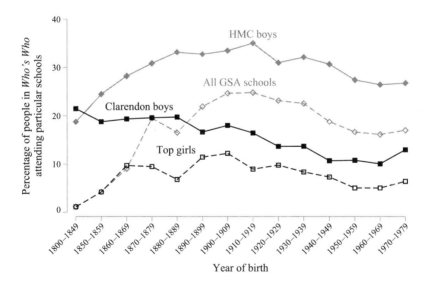

5.4 Elite girls schools were less powerful than elite boys schools.
Note: The proportion of women attending elite girls schools is calculated as a proportion of all women in *Who's Who* born in the same birth cohort, and the same is done for men.

at the peak of their propulsive power, among those born around the turn of the twentieth century, the percentage of female entrants attending an elite girls school (12 percent) was still significantly lower than that of male entrants attending a Clarendon School (17 percent). Likewise, while the GSA schools educated around 25 percent of women entrants to *Who's Who* born in the first decade of the twentieth century, the HMC schools educated over a third (34 percent) of men.

This difference is not explained by the background of sexism against which these schools were operating because we are comparing the alumni of girls schools with other girls. Nor does it imply that these girls schools were weak. On the contrary, we estimate that across the period of our analysis, a woman who attended one of the twelve most elite girls schools was approximately twenty times more likely to end up in *Who's Who* than one who had attended any other type of school. Old girls, in short, have long enjoyed a tremendous advantage over other young women in reaching positions of influence.

This is not surprising. Sociologists of elite girls schools such as Claire Maxwell and Joan Forbes have shown that such schools act as distinct *incubators* of elite identities—particularly dispositions of "assuredness," "surety," and "ease"—that are clearly central in shaping young women's desire, expectation, and confidence to push for elite positions.[30] Equally, these schools have also increasingly become recognised as *temples* that inculcate the right kind of rarefied curriculum that is highly valued in the employment market. In important ways these schools have continued to model much of their pedagogical offering on the Clarendon Schools, promising their students the same kind of traditional English education emphasising both academic excellence and the development of the "whole person" via sports and extra-curricular activities.[31]

However, it is important to reiterate that elite girls schools have remained far *less successful* than top boys schools when it comes to elite recruitment. To make sense of this, we return to the history of girls schools and to scholarship indicating that the functions of elite schools—as sieves, incubators, and temples—operated quite differently for girls and boys for most of the twentieth century.

As sieves, elite girls schools were less likely, particularly in the earliest years, to recruit students from Britain's most wealthy and aristocratic families.[32] For much of the nineteenth century, many elite women didn't even attend school because they were educated at home by private tutors, and those that did tended to go to boarding schools that functioned as finishing schools and focused on cultivating "ladies of leisure" skilled in reading, writing, singing, dancing, needlework, and household management.[33] As Uncle Matthew worries in Nancy Mitford's classic 1945 novel *The Pursuit of Love,* going to a "middle-class establishment" (as one of these girls schools was condescendingly thought to be) may well fill his niece's head with "information," but it is not "worth losing every ounce of feminine charm to find that out."[34]

Elite girls schools were also much less reliable status signals. This was partly driven by a number of structural barriers that prevented them from developing the same level of social and cultural power as their male counterparts. While the most prestigious boys schools evolved from medieval collegiate foundations, ancient grammar schools, or were set up by public trusts, girls schools often began as small, fee-paying establishments or were day schools catering to local students.[35] As a result, girls schools tended to suffer from financial precarity. Unlike the most elite boys schools, they could not rely upon alumnae to build their endowment, and even where sister schools of existing boys schools were set up, like St Paul's and Merchant Taylor's, they were often given a much smaller percentage of existing endowments.[36]

Girls schools thus lacked the legacy, economic power, and social prestige of boys schools. They also lacked the same cultural coherence as "incubators" of common elite identities and "temples" of legitimate knowledge. This was because, from their inception, elite girls schools had a more complex, and often ambivalent, set of aims and objectives which required them to deliver both educational excellence and gendered social reproduction—the bind of what the education scholar Sara Delamont has called "double conformity."[37]

Perhaps most important, then, in understanding why girls schools were less successful in propelling their alumni was that most remained at least somewhat ambivalent about the goal of (occupational) propulsion in the first place.[38] In the latter part of the nineteenth century, when many of the most successful girls schools were founded, proto-feminists frequently advocated for women's education, but they often did so in terms which adhered to the gender politics of the time, arguing that education would make women better partners and mothers.[39] This enduring ambivalence—between pursuing educational attainment and producing an "appropriate" femininity—ensured that these schools were never able to prepare their alumni for positions of power and public prominence in the same unabashed way as the Clarendon Schools.[40]

Eton and Then Oxford

Recent decades have seen both a decline and a persistence in the ability of elite schools to propel their students into the British elite. Yet it remains unclear precisely *how* this takes place. Is elite school attendance alone sufficient, or does the power of these schools to propel pupils into the elite lie more in their ability to place alumni into other elite institutions that will then have the more decisive impact?

In Chapter 6 we will explore this question via the most established pathway connecting elite schools with elite destinations—the intermediary of Britain's most prestigious universities. Here we show that while elite schools may for some students be a crucial institutional starting point, their ability to propel themselves to positions of power and influence is strongly mediated by their connections to elite universities. This, we argue, rests on the hub function performed by elite universities, where students from elite schools use elite universities to further cultivate networks and incubate worldviews that were initially established at school. It is precisely this dual incubation that provides distinct cumulative advantages later in life. As C. Wright Mills famously remarked, there are "two Harvards": one for a closely networked set of "old boys" and one for everyone else.[41]

6

Bright Young Things

It was a bit of a surprise to everyone when Sir Peter Daniell (1909–2002)—later senior government broker for bonds and gilts—"went up" to Trinity College, Oxford. The year was 1927 and he was a recent graduate of Eton (like his father and grandfather before him). The problem was that Peter was not, by his own admission, an especially strong student. The Daniell family, unperturbed, reached out to a cousin who had been to Trinity. He relayed that he would "obviously, put in a word" and Peter duly got a place. Trinity proved to be a "wonderful" experience. While some Eton graduates "never knew anybody but Etonians the whole way through [their] Oxford careers," Trinity was different. It recruited from a much wider range of schools. Aside from ten Etonians, as Peter recalled, Trinity had "8 Rugbyans, 8 Wykhamists, 5 from Marlborough, 4 from Tonbridge." There were even a few students who had not been to one of these elite schools (they had a "slightly different accent and that sort of thing, affected one a bit") but, happily, "on the whole they were rather carefully chosen."

Peter Daniell had a rich social life at Oxford. He received an allowance from his parents of around £300 per year (~£15,500 per year in today's money), which covered his expenses and allowed him to play golf and join a dining club, the Gridiron, whose later members would include Boris Johnson, David Cameron, and George Osborne. He didn't recall exactly how he ended up joining because it all seemed rather casual ("oh come on old boy, you must join the Grid").

He did have regrets, though. "I mean I had a wonderful time, absolutely marvellous time," but "I'm ashamed of my academic side at Oxford . . . didn't read very much." His essays were "bloody awful" and he ended up with a "pretty ropey third." But then again, as he explained, nobody really cared. The feeling was that "one probably would get a job" regardless. And he was right. He moved seamlessly into a job at his father's firm and was soon made a partner.

Sir Daniell's experience of Oxford in the inter-war period verges on the cliché. But this does not mean it was unusual. As we shall see in this chapter, stories of this kind were commonplace among those who attended Oxford and Cambridge (Oxbridge) before World War II. This was the era of the "bright young things" who became "notorious in the 1920s tabloid press for their decadent parties, riotous practical jokes and hedonistic behavior," and who were captured brilliantly in the novels of Evelyn Waugh, Anthony Powell, and Nancy Mitford.[1]

One hundred years on, Britain's two most elite universities have changed enormously.[2] The days when a quiet word from a family member would help you get into your chosen college have vanished. Even a cursory glance at the admissions data suggests that the gendered and ethnic composition of both universities has shifted dramatically.[3] Today, there are more women than men attending Oxbridge and the ethnic composition of new entrants is largely representative of the underlying population. The place of Oxford and Cambridge in the wider ecosystem of higher education has shifted too. It was once true that almost all university graduates attended one of these two ancient universities, and as late as 1860 nearly three in four university students were at Oxford and Cambridge.[4] Today, by contrast, they compete with several hundred other institutions.

In this chapter we examine whether these changes—both cultural and institutional—have altered the power of Oxford and Cambridge as channels of elite reproduction. We also unpack *how* Oxbridge operates. Do those who enter from elite families or boarding schools have a particular advantage in securing positions of power and influence?

The Puzzling Persistence of Oxbridge

Two basic facts should orient how we think about the roles Oxford and Cambridge have played in elite reproduction over the last 200 years. The first, starkly illustrated in Figure 6.1, is that the proportion of people in the British elite drawn from these two universities has remained high and largely stable over time, albeit with perhaps a slight increase from around 30 percent among those born in the second half of the nineteenth century to around

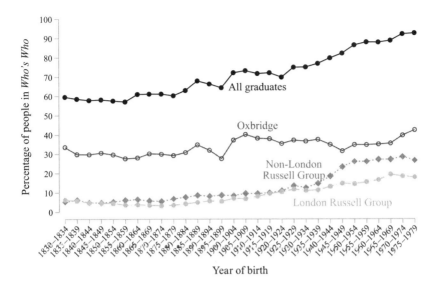

6.1 University attendance among people in the elite.

37 percent for the most recent graduates for whom we have data. Notably, both universities are approximately equally propulsive but there are slight differences in the elite sectors where their graduates end up. Oxford alumni are more often found in government and the media, while Cambridge alumni are more likely to end up in prominent positions in science and medicine.

The second is that the proportion of all university students attending Oxford and Cambridge has fallen dramatically during the same period.[5] In 1861, there were around 3,400 university students in Great Britain, representing only ~0.2 percent of young men and women of university age. Around 71 percent of these 3,400 students went to either Oxford or Cambridge. Today there are around 1.6 million full-time undergraduates attending university and only 1.3 percent of these are at Oxford or Cambridge.[6] As Figure 6.1 shows, this dramatic expansion in higher education had some impact on the processes of elite formation. Not only has the proportion of all graduates within the elite risen over time but the Russell Group universities, a collection of twenty-four research intensive universities including Durham, Edinburgh, London School of Economics, and King's College London, have emerged as significant channels of elite recruitment.[7]

This expansion casts the stability of Oxbridge's propulsive power in a different light. Even as the pool of competing graduates has mushroomed, Oxbridge has retained a remarkable stranglehold on elite recruitment. Yet Figure 6.1 also hides an important change story in the relative power of an Oxbridge education. To understand this, in Figure 6.2 we compare the proportion of people reaching the elite after attending different universities compared to the proportion of people reaching the elite among those who never went to university.[8]

Two things are worth highlighting here. First, Figure 6.2 shows the increasing propulsive power of other prestigious universities in Britain, especially the London-based universities (London School of Economics, King's College London, University College London, Queen Mary, and Imperial) that, with Oxford and Cambridge, make up what is often referred to as the "Golden Triangle."[9] From the inter-war period onwards the alumni of these London elite universities (that are now in the Russell Group) begin to have a higher likelihood of reaching the British elite than the average university graduate. Among those born in the late 1960s, around 1.12 percent of the alumni of these elite London-based universities were

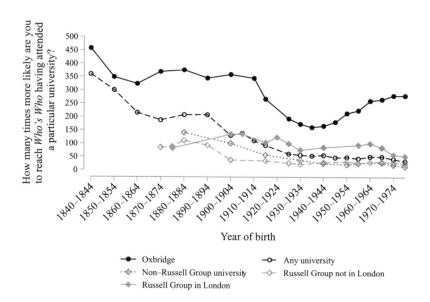

6.2 The decline and return of Oxbridge.

Note: Risk ratios of reaching *Who's Who* comparing the alumni of different clusters of universities with the total number of births in that cohort.

reaching the elite (compared to 0.011 percent among non-graduates). This means they were around 100 times more likely to reach elite positions. University graduates in general born in the same cohort were fifty times more likely higher than non-graduates to reach the elite. Thus, alumni of elite London universities were almost twice as likely to reach the elite than graduates in general. Equally, these London universities are now more than three times as likely to see their alumni reach the elite than Russell Group universities based outside London like Durham and Edinburgh.

Second, although Oxbridge has long operated on a different plane from other universities, Figure 6.2 shows that its advantage in terms of elite recruitment has fluctuated in important ways over time. Specifically, the propulsive power of Oxbridge declined sharply among those born in the initial decades of the twentieth century—albeit from a very high base—before rising again in more recent cohorts. To unpack this story, we draw on both historical accounts and our own interviews.

The Rise, Fall, and Rise Again of Oxbridge

Until the middle of the nineteenth century Oxford and Cambridge were dominated by "a small, homogenous, elite" that actively resisted efforts to provide training to a growing professional class.[10] Gradually, though, this position became untenable as this expanding middle class put pressure on both universities to accept their children and teach them something useful.[11]

It was during this period that a compromise was forged between the demands of the newly wealthy and the values of the old universities, originally created as theological academies whose function was to train the clergy.[12] A series of reforms in the mid-nineteenth century changed the governance structures and expanded the curriculum at Oxford and Cambridge but both universities retained the pedagogical structure and broader values that had dominated classical education for centuries.[13] Curricular compromises blended the education of a gentleman with a new desire to offer more concrete forms of professional training. In the shadow of these reforms, the universities became vehicles for civilising the new bourgeoisie, and forging it into a single elite.

Throughout the nineteenth and beginning of the twentieth century, Oxford and Cambridge had an incredibly close relationship with the British elite. Graduates were somewhat ludicrously 350 times more likely to end up in an elite position than those who did not attend university.

This was the Oxbridge that Peter Daniell entered in 1927, when entrance examinations were qualifying rather than competitive and attendance at the right schools or having family connections clearly influenced admission. Daniell's experience, our interviews suggest, was not exceptional. David Steel (born 1916, finance), for example, who attended Oxford in the mid-1930s, failed the scholarship exam but was still offered a "closed" (or reserved) place for students from Rugby School, where he had been a student. Elite networks were crucial in this process.[14] Steel went to University College, Oxford, where his grandfather, father, and brother had all gone. Such connections were often particularly important at the critical interview stage. Hugh Casson (1910, architecture) recalls that success in the interview could depend entirely on who you knew. It was not just family members, it could also rest on where you went to school and whether you were taught by a former student: "If you were old Allyson's boy . . . 'Oh yes, I remember Allyson. Yes, yes, let's have him'." School connections mattered in other ways too.[15] Anthony Mallinson (1923, finance), for example, did not even have to sit an entrance exam for Gonville & Caius College, Cambridge, because his "school certificate" (the most basic qualification one needed) and a recommendation from the Headmaster at Marlborough College, who had a connection there, were enough to "get [him] in." In these stories, then, we see the "sieve" function of elite universities operating in a similar way to elite schools, ensuring a degree of social closure over who can attend.[16]

Other features of this period are also salient. We have already heard how Peter Daniell regretted not working harder, but he was not alone. Chad Varah (1911, religion) also recalled he "didn't do much work" at Oxford and Michael Strachan (business, 1919) admitted that when he returned to Cambridge after World War II, he didn't "work terribly hard." The absence of work ethic aligned with how little academic performance mattered. The class of one's degree was, according to Anthony Mallison, "absolutely meaningless."

Undergirding this intensely relaxed approach to their studies was a sense of confidence about the future, which was often intertwined with the power of family connections.[17] We met George Baring (1918, finance) in Chapter 5, who eventually became governor of the Bank of England. Baring dropped out of Cambridge after just one year. He originally went "because father thought that I should try and make a career in the City . . . so he thought it would be a good idea to study law at Cambridge." The problem was that "the first two years of law at Cambridge was Roman law, and mostly in Latin!" This was not a good fit for Baring:

> So I went to my tutor . . . and said, do you think I could possibly learn some economics, or something like that, because I'm not very interested in how Justinian freed the slaves in Rome, it doesn't seem to be of very practical value to me. And he said, "No, you can't change. You must go on with it." So I said, "Well, in that case, I'm leaving." So he said, "Have you told your father?" I said "Yes, I have." So he got up, "Well, goodbye. It's been nice knowing you." And so we parted company. And I left Cambridge after a year. And, actually, I went to work in the City as an office boy at the family bank, which was much more useful.

These accounts are representative of what the historian Noel Annan called "the generation that made post-war Britain."[18] These men were distinct, for Annan, in part because of the "public school manners" that guided their style and informed who was "in." But these manners were not entirely inculcated at school.[19] They were reinforced by the culture circulating within Oxford and Cambridge during these decades. What Annan doesn't draw out is that this culture (including its orientation towards academic study) may have been a luxury afforded to men rather than women. Oxford formally allowed women to graduate in 1920, while Cambridge did not accept women until after WWII, and so very few elite women in this period attended these institutions. This is reflected in our data too. Only three of our interviewees born before 1930 are women and two of them went to Oxford. Their time at university was very different to the men described above. None recounted a sense of confidence about their future, or a lax work ethic. In fact, Josephine Barnes, later the first female president of the British Medical Association (born 1912) recalled the exact opposite. "One worked jolly hard," she recounted of her time at Lady Margaret Hall at Oxford. It seems noteworthy that the only Oxbridge graduate born before 1930 that we interviewed who said explicitly that they had worked hard was a woman. But this was about to change.

Those born in the 1930s and early 1940s, entering Oxbridge in the mid-1950s and 1960s, faced a very different reality. Other universities were starting to emerge and Oxbridge's grip on the elite began to weaken. As Sampson outlined in his *Anatomy of Britain,* in the early 1960s, "the old privileged values of aristocracy, public schools and Oxbridge" still dominated government and public life but they were beginning to be challenged.[20] Oxbridge students in this period, our data suggests, were caught between these two worlds.

Many approached Oxford and Cambridge with the same sense of entitlement as previous generations—enjoying themselves and not working particularly hard. Hugh Peppiatt's narrative is particularly interesting here. Born in 1930, he was part of that first post-war generation of Oxbridge matriculants. He had "happy days at Oxford" and recalled a "hedonist phase of life" where he spent too much time "in the boozer, on the golf course, and on the river." Indeed, Peppiatt nearly lost his scholarship for his "failure to work hard" (something noted by a few of our interviewees). Much like the generations that preceded him, this absence of effort was rooted in the sense that, as he put it, "coming from . . . privileged backgrounds, with . . . enough money" meant that "everything was open to you . . . Those of us who had, as good a training as you had at Winchester, frankly could get by on a minimum of work."

The problem with this orientation, though, is that recruitment processes at Oxbridge were starting to change and the culture of workplaces was shifting too.[21] Soon "Latin and History scholars" would no longer be running government departments and, as Sampson noted, "the cult of the amateur" was on the way out.[22]

Peppiatt was not oblivious to these changes. In fact, he recalled that they occurred "very, very quickly" after he was there, sometime around the "late fifties and early sixties." This was made clear to him when he returned to Oxford a few years after his graduation and found the hedonistic culture transformed. While there, Peppiatt spoke with one of the scouts (the staff who help look after the college):

> I said, "how is everything, Basil?" Now, Basil Bridgewater, says to me, he says, "Ah," so he said, "It's all changed. It's all changed." I said, "What do you mean?" I said to Basil, "No, no bottles about?" "Sir, there are hundreds of bottles, but they're all milk bottles!"'

Peppiatt's observations fit with a wider set of reforms that were rippling through Oxford and Cambridge.[23] The Latin language requirement for science students was removed in 1960, then, in 1962, Oxford effectively closed the separate admissions door for "gentleman," and finally by 1966 the admissions process was altered so that private school students with three years of sixth-form training were given a different test from state school students with only two years.[24] Together, these reforms had a dramatic impact both on admissions and the experience of Oxford students.[25] Between 1962 and 1966, the number of state school admissions increased from around 30 percent to 40 percent.[26] More broadly, it was in this period, according to the sociologist Joseph Soares, that Oxford and Cambridge transformed themselves from humanities-focussed finishing schools for the upper classes to world-leading science universities for the middle classes.[27] In so doing, "those not-very-academic sons of wealthy gentleman were bumped aside by meritocratic scholars, often from middle- or working-class backgrounds."[28] As Soares notes, as late as the 1950s (just after Peppiatt was there), nearly half of the peerage's eldest sons of university age were at Oxford or Cambridge. After these reforms (in the 1960s and early 1970s), this number was only 20 percent[29] Now, Soares may overstate the degree to which Oxford truly opened up to the working classes, but there is a very real sense that these universities did become less exclusive and more merit-based during the 1960s.[30]

Beyond university walls, patterns of occupational recruitment were changing too. When Peppiatt left Oxford, he was recruited into a prestigious law firm (Freshfields) where his father was a partner. In the late 1950s and early 1960s, he became responsible for hiring people out of university. He recalls that by the early 1960s firms across the city had started to recruit in ways that undermined nepotism and replaced it with an emphasis on credentials and performance:

Freshfields had fallen behind in size, and had relied on the traditional methods of people coming knocking on the door, and the, the someone at the Club, or the school saying, "Could you take my boy?" And, of course, it was soon found that was an extremely inadequate way to recruit.

The End of Certainty

All of this had a profound impact on how the people we interviewed spoke about their time at Oxford and Cambridge. Most clearly, we see a break between those born before the 1940s and those born after. Many of those born before 1940 explicitly said that they either did not work while they were at university or that they did not perform very well in their exams. This was almost never said by our interviewees born after 1940. Likewise, some of our interviewees born before 1940 said they did not pass the entrance exam to Oxbridge but managed to get in anyway (often through one of these informal routes left open to the alumni of favoured schools or the sons of "gentleman"). Only one person born after 1940 admitted they failed the entrance exam; and unlike the earlier students they went to university somewhere else.

One of the other striking differences is that later cohorts spoke about how much they got out of Oxford and Cambridge intellectually. When Linda (1950–1954, writer) went to Cambridge in the 1970s, for example, one of the things she thought was fantastic was that she learnt "how to work on my own and to be excited by that." Similarly, Cerys (1965–1969, law), who went to Cambridge after attending a comprehensive school, recalled how she was taught "how to think, rather than to memorise by rote . . . it wasn't enough to just learn the pages of the science, you had to be able to think well."

What one hears between the lines in these later narratives, is the end of certainty, the sense that an elite destination was no longer guaranteed. These women and others like them conveyed that if they had not worked hard at Oxbridge, then their lives may have taken a different, less prestigious path. We should be clear. It is not that Oxbridge became a meritocracy overnight, as some have claimed.[31] Rather, competition made it substantially more difficult to get into these universities and then to get jobs that would put graduates on an elite trajectory. The number of students taking A level exams rose from around 100,000 in 1951 to more than 600,000 in the mid-1980s, with the participation rate at university rising from 5 percent in 1960 to 15 percent in 1970, and then staying at roughly this level until the mid-1980s.[32] This rise in the number of people taking A levels corresponded to a significant increase in the number of applicants, as more and more middle- and working-class parents focused on their children's education and realised their kids could benefit from attending university.[33] This put upward pressure on the academic credentials required to get into Oxbridge. In 1965, only ~27 percent of those admitted to Oxford had top A level grades in two or more subjects. By the mid-1980s, ~82 percent had top grades in at least three subjects.[34] Bear in mind that this is not grade inflation because the proportion of candidates achieving As at A level never rose above 10 percent.[35] Elite schools, as we discussed in Chapter 6, recognised these winds of change, and responded accordingly, ramping up efforts to ensure their pupils received the necessary grades.[36]

Another manifestation of these wider changes was the improved performance of Oxbridge students in these decades.[37] From the beginning of the twentieth century up until the mid-1950s (the eras of Daniell and Peppiatt), the proportion of Oxford students receiving a low-achieving "Third class" degree remained stable at around 30 percent. From the late 1950s onwards, this declined steadily. By the end of the 1980s, only 5 percent of students were receiving a Third. Again, according to Brockliss, this is symptomatic of a real change in the quality of the work being done by Oxford students.[38] After all, the exam structure did not change, and for much of this period it was the same people marking those exams.

This shift towards a more formalised academic meritocracy helps explain, at least to some extent, the fluctuating fortunes of Oxbridge graduates in the second half of the twentieth century. While the generation following Peppiatt's, who approached Oxbridge with the same gentlemanly ethos of the past, may have found their credentials were now no longer a ticket to success, those that followed were quick to adapt. And so were Oxford and Cambridge as institutions. The relative fortunes of graduates born after WWII dramatically increased once more. The last cohorts for which we have reliable data (those born in the 1960s and 1970s) were over 250 times more likely to reach the British elite than those who never went to university.

The Two Oxbridges

So far, our analysis has assumed that Oxford and Cambridge universities are singular institutions. Yet as Daniell's experience has already illustrated, there have always been important social divisions *within* these elite universities. To echo C. Wright Mills's famous remark about another elite university on the other side of the Atlantic; there are "two Oxbridges": one for a closely networked set of "old boys" and one for everyone else.[39] Much has changed of course since Mills wrote *The Power Elite,* but recent research has reinforced his conclusions.[40] In *The Privileged Poor,* education scholar Anthony Jack has spotlighted the experience of what he calls "the doubly disadvantaged" at elite US universities, those from very poor backgrounds who often experience alienation and social exclusion during their studies.[41] This raises a critical question: does everyone attending Oxbridge have an equal chance of getting into positions of power and influence? Or do old boys from specific schools have a better chance?

We know that there is a close link between elite schools and elite universities among those who reach the British elite. The majority of Clarendon School alumni in *Who's Who* also attended Oxbridge, even in more recent birth cohorts, whereas alumni from other schools were far more likely to have gone to other universities.[42]

But again, we need to situate these results in a broader context to get a more accurate picture of how these "two Oxbridges" might play out. In Table 6.1, we look at individuals who were included in *Who's Who* in the first decade of the twentieth century. It shows that Clarendon alumni who went to Oxford or Cambridge were twice as likely to be included in *Who's Who* as Oxbridge graduates who had not attended a Clarendon school. In fact, attending an elite school significantly outweighed the power of attending an elite university at this point in history. Clarendon school alumni who did not ever go to Oxbridge were almost twice as likely to reach the elite than Oxbridge alumni who had never been to a Clarendon School.

Moving forward to today, Table 6.1 shows that the force of these institutional channels has declined somewhat, as elites are now frequently drawn from other schools and universities. Yet Clarendon School alumni who pass through Oxbridge continue to be approximately 1.4 times (7 divided by 5) as likely to reach the elite as Oxbridge graduates without the good fortune to have attended a Clarendon School. This shows the enduring *cumulative* advantages that flows from following this particular elite pathway.

Table 6.1 The Association between Clarendon Schools, Oxbridge, and the Elite

Different Groups	1900	Now
A: Proportion of Oxbridge alumni who attended a Clarendon School reaching *Who's Who*	21%	7%
B: Proportion of Oxbridge alumni who did not attend Clarendon School reaching *Who's Who*	10%	5%

Note: For 1900, we drew on a sample of *Who's Who* members who died after 1900—and were thus still included in the dictionary—but were born before 1865 and were therefore at least age 35 in 1900. We use published data sources to estimate that in 1900, 0.3 percent of the adult population (age 35 and over) attended Oxbridge and 0.25 percent of Oxbridge alumni attended a Clarendon School. Among the current cohort, 0.66 percent attended Oxbridge and 0.17 percent attended a Clarendon School. These data triangulate with other published statistics on how many Clarendon students attend Oxbridge. For more details, see the Methodological Appendix.

This split in outcomes may not be entirely attributable to the school, however. It may be more an issue of social origin.[43] After all, we know from Chapter 4 that those from wealthy backgrounds are more likely to reach the elite and are also more likely to attend these elite schools. We therefore need to consider the social origin of elites who attended Oxbridge. Our data on parental wealth gives us some clues. We know the proportion of people in *Who's Who* that went to Oxbridge and were born into the top 1 percent, for example. But to fully unpack these relationships we need to know the proportion of *all* Oxbridge students that come from the top 1 percent.[44] We do know, thanks to a Freedom of Information request, that the parental income of the 99th percentile of students at Oxford in 2020 (that is, the richest 1 percent of Oxford students) was around £100,000 per year, which suggests, perhaps surprisingly, that the kids of the very richest families are slightly under-represented at Oxford.[45] Now, wealth is not the same as income, but the wealthy do typically have higher incomes and so we use the data from this Freedom of Information request as a benchmark to understand the relationship between wealth, Oxbridge attendance, and entry into *Who's Who*. To do this, then, we imagined a scenario where 5 percent of the students at Oxbridge came from the top 1 percent of the wealth distribution.

Now, if this were accurate, around 11.5 percent of Oxbridge alumni born into the top 1 percent ended up in *Who's Who*. For those Oxbridge alumni who were not born into the top 1 percent, it was only 2.5 percent. This implies that coming from a very rich family means you are around five times (11.5 divided by 2.5) more likely to reach the elite than other Oxbridge alumni, even in a situation where we conservatively assume that there is a larger number of rich people at Oxbridge than we see in the Freedom of Information request. Coming from wealth and attending Oxbridge clearly seem to interact. The very rich who also get into Oxbridge are much more likely to end up in the elite than those who just get into Oxbridge. Now this is only a hypothetical scenario and this estimate of the advantage experienced by rich kids would go down if we assumed more students at Oxbridge were in the top 1 percent. But, to make this advantage disappear entirely we would need to believe that 20 percent of Oxbridge students come from the top 1 percent. Given what we know about the income distribution of Oxbridge students today, this is not impossible, but it is very unlikely. In other words, there are good reasons to think that coming from a wealthy background strongly accentuates the benefits of attending Oxbridge.

Stains and Socialites

Being born into wealth or attending an elite school confers additional advantages on Oxbridge students, but it is unclear what precisely it is about these backgrounds that makes a difference. It could be that wealth or schooling provides additional benefits entirely unrelated to the university experience. Now, we cannot rule this out but it would be less likely to be true if those from privileged backgrounds did not also spend their time together, become friends with one another, and later scaffold one another's careers. In other words, one way that wealth or schooling may interact with certain elite institutions is through the "hub" function of elite universities. If, as Mills suggests, there is not one hub within an elite university but multiple hubs, then these sub-groups could play an important propulsive role in building networks that may be beneficial in the future.[46]

Among the Oxbridge graduates we interviewed who were born before 1940, it is telling that there is almost no one who was not from a middle- or upper-class background and did not attend a public school. This absence alone is evidence of the clear forms of social exclusion that structured the admissions process at the turn of the twentieth century. Recall that Sir Peter Daniell (albeit likely with some exaggeration) had a friend who barely met anyone who had not attended "Eton." Daniell also recalled one particularly influential Oxford don, Philip Landon:

> He was a snob and he very much cultivated the Etonian clique . . .
> had a tremendous influence on what one did and things like that. And
> I used to go and play bridge in his rooms and things like that, you
> know. And one got to know him very well.

Landon was actively creating two Oxfords, one for Etonians and one for everyone else. This is symptomatic of how Oxford and Cambridge in this early period served to reinforce elite networks. Informal societies were curated to build ties with others who were from the same social circle.

Layered on top of this there were social clubs, whose membership was often predicated on "recommendation and election."[47] These were central to the narratives of our interviewees who attended Clarendon schools. All but one spoke of the societies they joined, the sports they played, and the highbrow culture they either consumed or participated in (theatre, cricket, golf, and so on). For those who did not go to these schools, the clubs, societies, and sports were much less present in accounts, and those from less privileged backgrounds in particular often expressed a sense of being on the outside of these cliques.

Yet according to our interviewees, the shifting composition of Oxbridge through the twentieth century partially disrupted these networks and altered patterns of friendship. When Hugh Peppiatt attended Oxford, he largely made friends with people connected to his school (Winchester College) and these networks formed the basis of "his professional and social life" ever since. But, on his return in the early 1960s, he noted that such co-alescing around the "old school tie" had now been "totally dismantled."

While Peppiatt is probably correct that the boundaries around this network of old boys became more porous after the 1960s, it was never totally dismantled. In the 1980s, for example, the journalist Toby Young drew the distinction between "stains," the hard-working, upwardly mobile children of professionals, and "socialites," the alumni of schools like Eton and Westminster.[48] The "smart set" (the "socialites") were "either very rich, very upper-class, or both." For the "stains," Oxbridge was often a very different experience. Deepak is an Indian British lawyer who was born in the early 1960s. His father, who was a legal advisor, moved to the United Kingdom in the late 1960s. Deepak went to a state school and recalls initial feelings of real "culture shock" on arriving at Oxbridge:

> Because . . . it was . . . very public school-y . . . quite exclusive and quite cliquey . . . and I didn't have that kind of natural confidence, which I think a lot of the public school applicants kind of had naturally. And so, I kind of felt a bit overwhelmed . . . [but then] I started making more friends, including friends from public schools, which got me into kind of a wider friend circle within [Oxbridge], particularly St Paul's; I made a very good friend from St Paul's who kind of introduced me to his friend circle.

Deepak's experience is telling. It illustrates the insecurity and anxiety that often went hand-in-hand with feeling that one was on the outside of these kinds of "socialite" networks, particularly for students of colour. Indeed, as the work of education scholars such as Kalwant Bhopal and Diane Reay have shown, students from less privileged and / or ethnic minority backgrounds often experience feelings of alienation and isolation at these universities.[49] But Deepak's experience also illustrates that these cliques were not an entirely closed shop. Gaining entry could be a gateway to a very different experience of university life.

Alongside class-based forms of exclusion, there was, as Deepak knew all too well, the question of race. Racism was certainly a problem at Oxford and Cambridge, though students came to understand that some colleges were worse than others.[50] Trinity College, Oxford, had a particularly bad reputation. When P. T. Rajan applied to Trinity in 1912, even though he had attended the Leys School (an elite public school in Cambridge), the college president, Herbert Blakiston, wrote to his headmaster: "We have not had an Indian at this college for nearly twenty years, and are not anxious to encourage Indian students to come to Oxford."[51] Rajan eventually went to Jesus College and later became Chief Minister of Madras Presidency. Around this same period, students at Trinity were so incensed by their neighbouring college's willingness to admit Black and brown students that they developed a racist chant they would shout outside the college on drunken evenings.[52] Years later, there was still a residue of these attitudes. The experience of Anne, a Black British cultural professional (1950–1954), is revealing here, particularly because her mother—also a woman of colour—attended Oxbridge too:

> My parents had met [at Oxbridge] and they absolutely loved it, so I had a slightly rose-tinted view of the whole thing. I arrived in the 70s after the Windrush. So I walked into the kind of prejudice that my mother never sort of met. She was met by a lot of curiosity, but not the same sort of overt racism . . . They thought my mother was Haile Selassie's daughter and she kept having to insist on paying for things, because they kept putting it on a credit account, she says, "No, I'm not that Black woman I'm the other one, can I pay please." So she was treated very differently, whereas I actually had friends who said to me, "don't come to my room while my parents are here, because they don't like coloureds." "They don't like West Indians." So it was, yeah, it was a strange, fairly brutal situation.

Racism clearly continued to structure the experience of some students, highlighting their otherness in a world dominated by whiteness. This potentially helps explain why students of colour were less likely than white students (despite attending Oxford and Cambridge) to end up in the British elite. For example, when we use our survey data to estimate the chances of reaching the elite among those who attended Oxford or Cambridge, we find that white alumni were nearly twice as likely than students of colour to reach elite positions.

Anne's experience of Oxbridge as a Black woman was shaped by both her race and her sex. She recalls her supervisor engaging her in sexually explicit conversations in part because he "really like[d] Black women":

> And I was being supervised alone, they sent me alone to be in this man's office. So at 18 I'm going, "Oh my God" . . . But it was, yeah . . . he said to me, "We don't need to cover the curriculum, you're far too bright for that, we'll just talk about this that and the other." And then says, "What are the Jamaican swear words?," knowing fully well that they all describe female genitalia . . . He was a nasty piece of work.

Anne was not alone. Many women told us about the sexism they experienced at university. Some were sexually harassed by staff and fellow students, while others had their academic ideas stolen by senior faculty.

Women have also consistently been less able to capitalise on their Oxbridge education. Table 6.2 shows that among those born at the beginning of the twentieth century and attending Oxbridge in the 1920s and 1930s, men were four times more likely than women to reach elite positions. Among current entrants, this gender gap has narrowed but not fully. Men who attended Oxbridge were still 1.5 times more likely (5.6 divided by 3.8) than the women in their cohort to reach elite positions.

It may be too simplistic to say that there are only two Oxfords or two Cambridges. A wide range of friendship groups have always existed within

Table 6.2 The Association between Gender, Oxbridge, and the Elite

Different Groups	Born 1900–1920	Now
A: Proportion of Oxbridge men reaching *Who's Who*	11.1%	5.6%
B: Proportion of Oxbridge women reaching *Who's Who*	2.7%	3.8%

Note: For the 1900–1920 cohort, we drew on a sample of *Who's Who* members who were born in those years. We use published data sources to establish the proportion of women attending Oxbridge. Around 18 percent of students at Oxford were women in 1921 and around 8.5 percent of Cambridge's student population in 1932. We assume that this was ~5 percent in 1921. Data on the proportion of women at Oxbridge is available from the Oxford and Cambridge admissions statistics. For more details, see the Methodological Appendix.

universities. Yet this idea is still useful, we would argue, because it focusses attention on the fact that there has long been a social *centre* at these universities that has largely been occupied by white young men from very privileged backgrounds.[53] These socialite hubs are important for our analysis because they almost certainly contribute to the increased likelihood that wealthy, public school–educated Oxbridge alumni eventually reach positions of power and influence. This does not mean that all privileged white young men have an easy time at Oxford and Cambridge, or that they are guaranteed to get into the elite. Nor does it mean that these networks are entirely rigid. But it does suggest that the historical dominance of these groups has created a durable set of norms and practices at Oxbridge, often institutionalised via particular social clubs or societies, that contribute to the foundation of abiding friendships that persist long after university and often provide tangible sources of social capital later in life.

Family- to School-Mediated Reproduction

There are far fewer people like Sir Peter Daniell at Oxford today. Oxford and Cambridge have dramatically reformed their admissions procedures in recent decades and broader cultural changes have eroded the sense of ease and certainty that old boys like Daniell once felt about their gilded passage into and through these institutions. But this does not mean that the power of Britain's elite universities has somehow disappeared. The "bright young things" of the 1920s have merely morphed into something different.

The sociologist Pierre Bourdieu connected these trends to what he described in *The State Nobility* as a transition from "family-mediated" elite reproduction to "school-mediated" reproduction.[54] In Peter Daniell's story, his family was essential to his trajectory. Attending Oxford or Cambridge seemed almost irrelevant to his career. Oxbridge was something equivalent to the "grand tour," a fun, civilising experience but certainly not high-stakes.[55] And any future career was not hampered by a "gentleman's third." In fact, spending too much time in the library may have even been a hinderance to your career.

Later in life, Daniell was asked by an interviewer whether it might be "rather frowned on" that he had found a place as a partner in an important finance firm because his father was already a senior official there. He responded that he thought modern, meritocratic attitudes were "damned stupid" and that nepotism "doesn't do any harm at all."[56] This is illuminating. At a basic level, he was giving his unqualified support for the family-mediated mode of elite reproduction that had scaffolded his own career. But his remarks are shocking to contemporary sensibilities. The fact that it is almost inconceivable that any influential person would say something like this today, in public at least, is indicative of the dramatic cultural shift that has taken place since he graduated in the 1930s.

Under the school-mediated mode, your grades really do matter. Your ability to get into an elite university is viewed as an important signal of talent or merit. Now, crucially for Bourdieu, the school-mediated mode is not a meritocracy. Rather, it is a form of obfuscation. The qualifications, he argues, are really a shroud placed over class privilege. This mode of elite reproduction rests less on the parental transfer of economic capital and more on the transfer of pedagogical resources, or cultural capital, which can then be cashed in for meritocratically legitimated credentials.

But critically, and echoing the changes we observe, Bourdieu concedes that this mode of elite reproduction can be "less effective," as not all economically advantaged pupils will be educationally successful. Nevertheless, "this academic transfer compensates for its lesser reproductive return through an increased effectiveness in its concealment of the work of reproduction."[57]

One aspect of our results complicates this story. Yes, the transition to the school-mediated mode was somewhat "less effective" in the sense that there was a decline in the power of Oxbridge, particularly for those from privileged elite-school backgrounds. But this decline was temporary. It seems primarily linked to cohorts who were inadvertently trapped in the transition between these two modes. They approached the world as if it were family-mediated, but that world had started to crumble and a new school-mediated world had emerged, full of the kind of hard-working young people that Toby Young called "stains."[58] Elite families, schools, and other institutions, however, eventually responded. And when they did, they were highly effective, leaning into this school-mediated mode, and aggressively channeling their resources into whatever pedagogical or extra-curricular project would give their children the greatest chance of getting into the right university and reaching the elite.

PART THREE

Why Elite Reproduction Matters

7

How Elites Think

So far, we have shown that while the British elite tends to see itself as ordinary and meritocratic (especially compared to elites in the past), the cold empirical reality tells a different story. While there has certainly been some opening up over time in terms of social background and elite schooling, those who begin life from an elite starting point tend to retain profound advantages later in life. But why does this gap between how elites see themselves and what we know about them matter? Why should we care where our elites come from?

Our answer in this chapter is that how elites are formed has important implications for the politics we get. More specifically, we show that elites from privileged backgrounds tend to lean in different directions to the rest of the elite on key policy questions and certain socio-cultural attitudes. But our interest in the political preferences and behaviour of elites stretches beyond the question of elite reproduction. In fact, it brings us to some of the deeper theoretical issues we grappled with in Chapter 1. Specifically, is our British elite important only as a nominal category of influential office-holders? Or is it a real, active social group?

Recall that for two of the foundational elite theorists, Karl Marx and C. Wright Mills, ideological unity is a pivotal feature of what makes elites worthy of our scrutiny. Both argued that elites have a distinct way of approaching the world, and this cognitive unity emerges in large part from their shared social position. For Marx, this is grounded in their economic position as owners of capital, while for Mills the "structural coincidence of their interests" and their "psychological affinities" are grounded in their biographies, their class origins, their passage through particular elite schools and universities, and their memberships in particular clubs and associations.[1] This commonality, he argued, "tends to make members of the power elite more readily understood and trusted by one another" and more likely to "sympathize with one another's point of view." It makes them more likely, in short, "to say to one another: he is, of course, one of us."[2]

These issues continue to inform public debate. Owen Jones's revival of the idea of "the establishment," for example, was arguably particularly influential because of his claim that this group was bound together "by common economic interests and a shared set of mentalities" oriented around "protecting the concentration of wealth in very few hands."[3] Meanwhile, from the right, Matthew Goodwin argues strongly that his "new elite" are "united, more than anything, by their liberal cosmopolitan if not radically progressive beliefs."[4]

Such assertions of ideological unity may be appealing, but they are rarely empirically grounded.[5] There is very little research that has both identified a broad elite group across many sectors of society and systematically interrogated how these people think. The evidence we do have is mostly from the United States, or based on particular groups such as politicians or billionaires.[6] We draw, by contrast, on survey data that directly taps the political views of both our overall British elite—which cuts across a number of domains—and of the wealth elite that sits within it. And it is here that we see the analytical value of delineating this elite-within-the-elite. As we shall see, the British wealth elite has a distinctive profile when it comes to policy preferences and social attitudes, and their access to positional *and* economic power grants them a unique ability to convert these beliefs into action.

Elites versus the People?

In the popular imagination, one of the most powerful preconceptions is that elites are out of step with the rest of the population. This accusation is often baked into the very formulation of terms like the "establishment" or the "new woke elite."[7] It is certainly key to the rhetoric of high-profile politicians. Take Suella Braverman, the former UK home secretary, who in May 2023 railed against an elite "who think they know best what is in the public's interest, even when that public is quite certain that they need something different."[8] Or Jeremy Corbyn, who criticised Theresa May's government for being "in the pockets of a super-rich elite."[9] Some research does support this kind of assertion. A series of studies conducted by Benjamin Page and his colleagues showed that American billionaires not only tend to have quite different policy preferences from others but are strongly invested in keeping these hidden from view.[10] These economic elites engage in a sort of "stealth politics"—seeking to influence policy in ways that reflect their own economic interests while flying under the radar of public scrutiny.[11]

But what about the contemporary British elite? The reality is that we know comparatively little about how Britain's influencers and power brokers think. While we frequently hear from certain elites like politicians and commentators, the vast majority never go "on the record" with their wider political preferences. And when they do, it is often on very specific issues related to their work (or identities), making it hard to infer their positions on other issues. So how do their policy preferences and social attitudes align with the UK population as a whole? And what about the very wealthy within their ranks—are they politically distinct?

To answer these questions, we asked all current members of *Who's Who* about their political attitudes and policy preferences. As we explained in Chapter 2, not everyone responded to our survey. Crucially, though, those that did were quite similar in profile to those who did not, suggesting that any bias that might have been introduced by the nonresponse of some groups is minimal (see the Methodological Appendix for more on this). We then compared this to nationally representative survey data (for example, the British Social Attitudes Survey or polls conducted by YouGov) where the same questions had been asked of the UK population. This gives us the ability to see whether our elites are similar to other people in the population as a whole.

We found that in several important policy areas the British elite are fairly closely aligned to the UK population. On issues of inequality, for example, elites are slightly more concerned about the scale of the problem. They are *more* likely to say that the income gap between rich and poor in Britain is "too large" (90 percent compared to 81 percent in the population at large) and more likely to say that they believe there is "quite a lot" of real poverty in Britain (82 percent among elites vs. 70 percent in the population). They are also more likely to advocate for raising taxes so that more money can be invested in "health, education, and social security" (70 percent vs. 56 percent)—although notably the wealth elite are much less supportive of tax and spend than other elites (Figure 7.1).

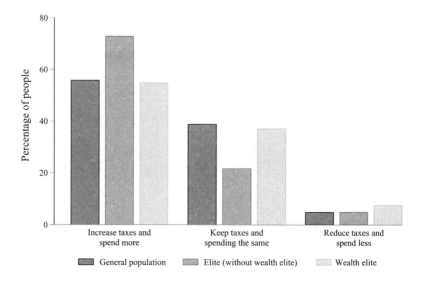

7.1 Elite are more willing to see taxes and government spending rise.

Education Meritocrats

Yet elites do not track the British population on every dimension of tax and spend. This is most clear when we separate out tax and spend preferences for education, health, and social security. These are all pillars of the welfare state, but they represent different orientations to what government should be prioritising, and just because you are in favour of one does not mean you will necessarily be in favour of others. Education, for instance, is commonly thought of as "investment spending" because it is concerned with longer-term returns (such as productivity and economic growth in the future), while social security spending is sometimes described as "consumption spending" because it is concerned with short-term goals (such as reducing poverty today).[12] To delve further into these questions, we asked respondents to identify their highest priority for additional government spending. Here, as Figure 7.2 shows, the distinctive interests of elites emerge in telling ways.

In particular, the British elite have a distinct belief in the power of education. Although nearly half of this group were themselves privately educated, education spending emerges as by far the most popular priority area for additional state funding. While only 20 percent of the British population think that additional spending on education should be the

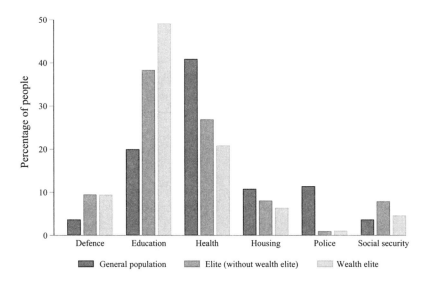

7.2 The wealth elite think education should be the "highest priority" of government. *Note:* We have removed the following options to simplify this figure: help for industry, overseas aid, public transport, roads, and none. The numbers were low for these preferences and there was little difference between groups.

government's highest priority, the figure among the elite is nearly 40 percent, rising to 50 percent among the wealth elite.

There are two ways to understand this preference for education spending. Ever since the expansion of the industrial workforce in the nineteenth century, business elites have put pressure on governments to spend more on education.[13] An educated workforce, by this logic, was seen as more productive (and thus more desirable). Others may favour education because they see it as an engine of social mobility. Despite powerful evidence to the contrary, selective "grammar" schools and private schools are often seen as important vehicles for increasing rates of upward mobility.[14] Wealth elites may therefore believe that education can break the link between origins and destinations, and so support particular investment in education.[15]

We found hints of this orientation in our survey data. The wealth elite were more likely than other elites to say that "merit" was important to their success, but they were also more likely to say that going to best schools was important for their success. Finally, this orientation to education policy fits with our qualitative data which reveals how some elites are keen to tell a meritocratic story of their success in order to seek legitimacy for their current position in society. Together, we start to get a picture of a wealth elite that sees the value of funding "great" schools in helping those with ability and talent, like themselves, to succeed.

The other area with striking differences is health. Where 40 percent of the general population think that health care spending should be the government's highest priority, only 20 percent of the wealth elite would agree.

Tax the Rich?

The British elite may agree with the British public that it would be a good thing to increase government spending but do they also agree on who should pay for this additional expenditure? The answer is a resounding no. Specifically, we asked respondents to choose which tax rises they would support. Some were progressive (the more you earn or have, the more you pay), such as a wealth tax or taxes on capital gains, others regressive (the less you earn, the more you pay as a proportion of your income), such as VAT (value-added tax) or an income tax levied on all earners.

If taxes are going to rise, as Figure 7.3 shows, most people in the United Kingdom want them to fall disproportionately on the rich. Over 40 percent are in favour of a new wealth tax and over 15 percent support higher capital

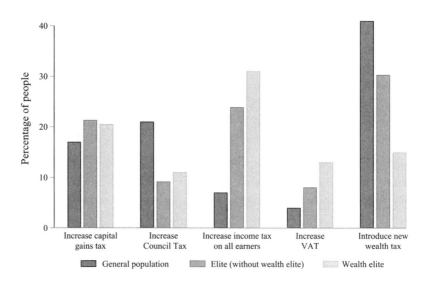

7.3 The wealth elite want taxes to rise on all earners and do not favour a new wealth tax.

gains tax. The wealth elite disagree. They want taxes to go up for everyone and are far less likely to support a new wealth tax (although many do support an increase in capital gains taxes).

We can combine these different tax policies by whether they involve "taxing the rich" or not. Doing this only further underlines the difference between the elite and the public: while around 80 percent of the population want tax rises to fall on the rich, this figure falls to 46 percent for the wealth elite.

When elites say they are in favour of higher taxes and more public sector spending, then, they do not mean the same thing as most Britons. They favour across the board tax hikes and spending on education, whereas the public wants tax rises to fall on the rich and spending to go to the National Health Service.

One other major difference between the elite and everyone else concerns their beliefs (see Figure 7.4) about what the overarching policy priorities of government should look like. The wealth elite want government to be focussed on education, in line with their spending priorities, but they are also keen to see politicians prioritise economic growth and (to a lesser extent) cutting poverty. The first two of these goals are much less salient for the population in general. Indeed, only 10 percent of the population want government to focus on improving economic growth or education. They

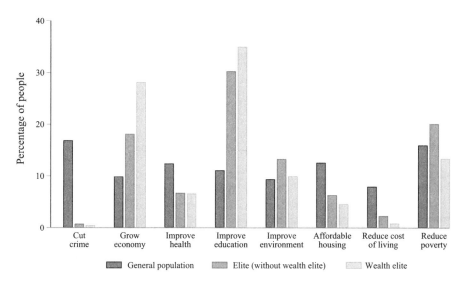

7.4 What should government be prioritising?

are far more concerned with reducing crime and poverty, ensuring housing is affordable, and improving the health care system.

One possible interpretation of these results is to say that they reveal the centrist political inclination of the British elite. Indeed, in some respects the policy preferences of the elite and wealth elite are reminiscent of the New Labour era. Tony Blair was happy to increase taxes and spend more but wanted this investment to go to education, economic growth, and cutting poverty.

Yet there are two issues with the way we've analysed political attitudes so far. First, we treat the elite as one coherent group. But a close look at Figure 7.4 makes it clear that there is wide attitudinal variation *within* the elite. Actually, few policy areas receive a clear majority of support among either the elite or the wealth elite. As Mills notes, there tend to be factions within the elite and ongoing contestation between them.[16] Second, our analysis has focused on responses to individual questions. Yet this potentially obscures the way political preferences may hang together as particular ideological orientations. To address these issues, next we attempt to draw out ideological configurations *within* the elite.

Are the Wealth Elite Ideologically Coherent?

We uncovered these ideological configurations within the British elite by conducting what social scientists call latent class analysis (LCA) on five key policy questions featured in Figure 7.5.[17] What this statistical technique does is uncover the dominant patterns that exist among responses to a specific set of questions. In effect, it can both tell us how many different ideological orientations there are within the elite and help us identify their nature.

As Figure 7.5 shows, the first three questions we focus on in this analysis examine policy priorities—they look at whether government should prioritise economic growth, preferences on tax and spend, and whether tax rises should fall on the rich. Alongside these, we focus on two attitudinal questions on race and empire that have emerged in recent years as highly divisive "culture war" issues. These asked respondents whether they "agree that Britain is a racist country" and whether they "think the countries that were colonised by Britain are better off or worse off for being colonized."[18]

164

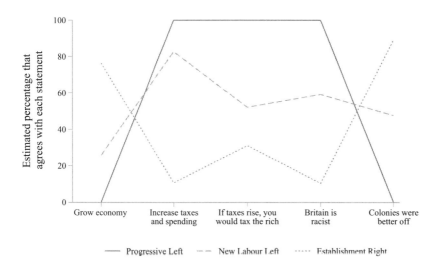

7.5 Three ideological orientations within the elite.

Note: The results reported in this graph are drawn from a latent class analysis. This type of analysis looks at the answers people gave to these questions and tries to discern (a) whether there are any common patterns across people, (b) groups those people together, and (c) calculates how many of our respondents fit into each group. We can then look at the features of these groups.

What emerges from this investigation is evidence of three distinct ideological formations within the British elite. The largest of these groups reflects the centrist, or marginally centre-left, orientation outlined earlier, what we label the "New Labour Left." These people are divided on culture war questions of racism and colonialism, as Figure 7.5 shows, but squarely in favour of higher taxes and more spending. They are less concerned about economic growth, however.

Our analysis also identified two further groups of roughly equal size but almost entirely opposed in ideological terms. On the political left we have a group convinced that government should *not* focus on growth but should increase taxes and spending, and that those taxes should be raised by taxing the rich. They are also certain that Britain is racist and that former colonies were *not* better off as a result of colonialism. We call them the "Progressive Left." And finally, there is an almost diametrically opposed group who think growth should be the key government priority. This group—who we call the "Establishment Right"—wants taxes and spending to stay the same, but if taxes do go up, they do not want those taxes levied on the rich.

Members of this group do not think Britain is a racist country and are more likely to believe the colonies were better off thanks to the British presence.

There are three further dimensions to draw out about these ideological formations. First, the Progressive Left orientation varies across occupations, as we see in Figure 7.6. The ideological centre of gravity among elites in the military, the aristocracy, and even sport tilts strongly to the Establishment Right, while elites in religion and the media are dominated by the Progressive Left. While the New Labour Left is well-represented in most occupations, it is an outright majority among scientists and in medicine.

Second, the Progressive Left orientation may be gaining ground over time within the elite. Although the Progressive Left and Establishment Right are approximately the same size among the contemporary elite, their *trajectories* look quite different. This is because, as Figure 7.7 demonstrates, support for these ideological configurations is closely linked to birth cohort. Among those born after 1959, the Progressive Left are marginally the biggest ideological grouping within the British elite. But this is not so much because the Establishment Right is shrinking—they have actually been relatively stable. The big change has been that the Progressive Left are replacing the New Labour Left within the elite, a change that echoes recent contestation within the Labour Party with different factions vying for control.

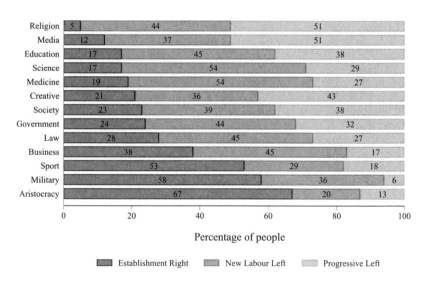

7.6 The ideological orientation of elite occupations.

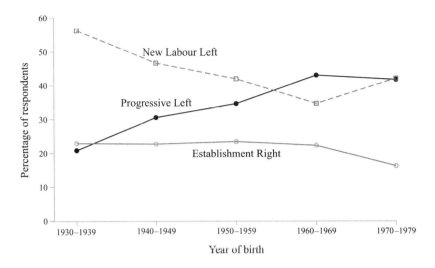

7.7 The rise of the Progressive Left.

But there are some important caveats, and a very significant one concerns the ideological orientation of the wealth elite. As you will recall, this group represents those who have both positional *and* economic power, and are therefore particularly important in any discussion of the potential political influence of the elite. The ideological orientation of this wealth elite differs in important respects from that of the elite more broadly, as Figure 7.8 shows. The Progressive Left represents only a small minority of the wealth elite—barely 20 percent. The Establishment Right, by contrast, represent nearly twice that, at 37 percent. While they do not necessarily represent the majority within the wealth elite, we would argue that the key takeaway is that this group's political centre of gravity tilts strongly to the right when compared to others in the British elite.

What does this analysis tell us? Well, we would argue that these trends shed light on a range of seemingly conflicting political narratives in the United Kingdom. The growing Progressive Left orientation among younger elites, for example, could explain some of the ire that has been directed at "woke elites" in recent years by those on the right *and* the centre left of the political spectrum. Those like Matthew Goodwin who argue the elite is increasingly dominated by radical and progressive values are not entirely wrong to draw attention to a growing number of people in influential positions tilting towards the Progressive Left.[19] However, our analysis also

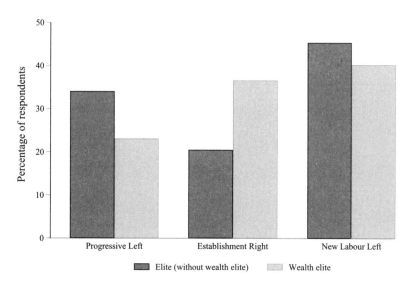

7.8 The wealth elite lean towards the right.

shows the limitations of this argument. The rise of the Progressive Left has not been driven by a decline in the Establishment Right, they have not declined in any meaningful way over this period. If anything, it is the New Labour Left that has lost out.

It is also not true that the rise of the Progressive Left has been concentrated in certain powerful sectors of the elite. Progressive Left attitudes only represent an outright majority in two relatively small sectors (religion and the media, with another smaller sector, the creative industries, following a bit further behind). Among the biggest fields in *Who's Who*—namely government, education, law, and business—it is the New Labour Left that are the largest single ideological group. And more importantly, this story about the dominance of the Progressive Left also fails to explain the orientations of those who hold more power *within* the elite. Our analysis shows that while there may be a shift to the left within the British elite as a whole, those within their ranks who hold both positional and economic power continue to tilt to the right.

How Elite Reproduction Matters

So far, we have demonstrated that the British elite is not entirely ideologically coherent. If anything, its prevailing character is politically centrist, although significantly the very wealthy within its ranks—the wealth elite—

tilt to the right in significant and telling ways. The question we will now turn to is how these ideological formations map onto the questions of elite reproduction we examined in Chapters 4, 5, and 6. In particular, are those recruited to elite positions through Britain's traditional and narrow channels of elite formation—privileged class backgrounds, boarding schools, Oxbridge—distinct in their attitudes and policy preferences?

We begin by looking at class origin. Here, as Figure 7.9 shows, we find clear attitudinal differences on a number of questions.[20] Those who say they come from a middle-class background are broadly more right-wing; they are much more concerned about economic growth and far less likely to want higher taxes and more spending on health, education, and social security than those who identify as coming from a working-class background. They also have different views on cultural issues—in particular, they are more likely to be proud of empire.

This finding is also reinforced when we examine whether those who identify as coming from different class backgrounds also align with different ideological orientations. Again, we find that those from more middle-class backgrounds are significantly more likely to align with the New Labour or Establishment Right orientation (Figure 7.10).

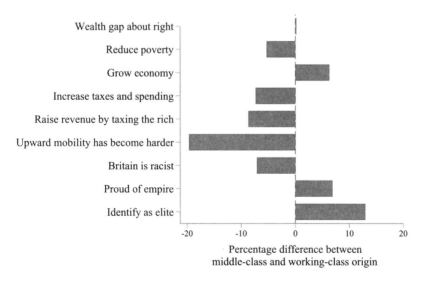

Percentage difference between
middle-class and working-class origin

7.9 Elites from working-class backgrounds are more left-wing.

Note: Higher numbers imply the middle class is more likely to agree. The *p*-value for these contrasts was less than 0.05 except for the wealth gap question and the question about whether government should reduce poverty.

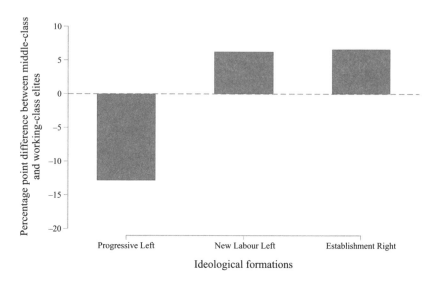

7.10 Those who identify as working-class are more likely to be found on the progressive left.

Note: The *p*-value for these contrasts was less than 0.05.

What about elite schooling? Recall that many scholars argue that when elites are drawn from narrow educational backgrounds, they are more likely to develop what sociologist John Scott calls a "a unity and cohesion of consciousness and action," which has profound implications for the exercise of power. Scott argues that the country's elite boarding schools have long functioned as "total institutions" that provide a very distinct shared experience that acts to maintain the "cohesion" and "solidity" of what he calls Britain's "upper circle." More recent evidence has underlined this link between schooling and ideological coherence, finding that those who have been privately educated in Britain are twice as likely to vote for the Conservative Party.[21]

Our interest here, though, remains the more elite form of private schooling, what are traditionally known in Britain—somewhat paradoxically—as "public schools." In Chapter 5 we showed that those educated at these expensive and prestigious private schools continue to be vastly overrepresented among the elite. While graduates of the nine Clarendon Schools represent just 0.17 percent of all secondary school students, they make up 8 percent of the current British elite, and although only 2.5 percent of all pupils are educated at one of the HMC schools, their alumni make up 30 percent of the elite.

In Figure 7.11 we aggregated data on the attitudes of this large group of elites educated at HMC schools. What we see is that graduates of Britain's public schools are less likely than other members of the elite to think government should prioritise poverty reduction and do not want taxes and public spending to rise. They are also more likely to say they are proud of empire. In short, attending these schools is associated with a rightward tilt on a range of policy and cultural issues.

These results are significant because they indicate that elite reproduction *matters*. Not only does it pose a glaring impediment to equality of opportunity but it may also impact the kinds of elites we get—both in the past and still today. Those from more privileged backgrounds who reach elite positions, to put it bluntly, tend to tilt towards the economic right and to be more culturally conservative, whereas those from working-class backgrounds orient the other way.

These results might be read as saying that if we increase the representation of the elite who hail from working-class backgrounds, it will tilt the ideological centre of gravity to the left and precipitate a progressive shift in

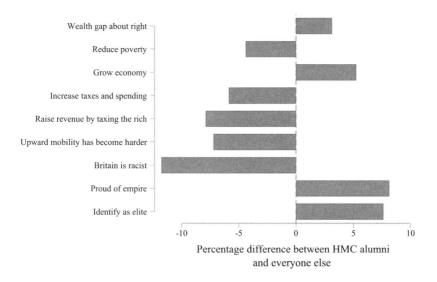

7.11 The alumni of British public schools are more conservative than other elites.
Note: Higher numbers imply HMC alumni are more likely to agree. The *p*-value for these contrasts was less than 0.05.

British politics. This may be correct, but we should be cautious about drawing this conclusion (not least because the politics of the working class in Britain are not unambiguously left-wing).[22]

One way to explore this issue is to examine particular types of upward mobility into elite positions, and to consider how this impacts people's political preferences. Now, by definition, anyone who enters the British elite from a working-class background has experienced fairly profound upward mobility. But what about those who have been upwardly mobile into the wealth elite? Do their preferences look more like those of other elites from working-class backgrounds or more like the attitudes of other members of the wealth elite? The answer is somewhere in-between. The data suggests that these people tend to be more right-wing than others from working-class backgrounds but less right-wing than those around them from more privileged backgrounds. Their attitudes still bear the residue of their more working-class origins, in other words, but they also assimilate to some extent—complicating any simplistic connection between class origin and attitudes.

Another confounding consideration, when drawing conclusions about political socialisation, is Oxbridge. Here we see a quite different relationship to political preferences. Oxbridge graduates—like university graduates more generally—tilt to the left politically and culturally.[23] They are less likely to think the wealth gap is about right and more likely to say that they want to see taxes rise and public spending increase.

From Attitudes to Action

Documenting the political dispositions of different substrata of the elite may partially help us understand the politics we get, but it would be unwise to assume that political preferences necessarily map onto behaviour. "Talk is cheap," as sociologists Colin Jerolmack and Shamus Khan famously wrote in 2015.[24] But capturing the political "behaviour" of the British elite is not a straightforward task. It isn't the kind of thing researchers can easily observe or record. Still, we do think several areas in our analysis shed light in this direction. One way to get beneath what people say to see what they might actually do is through survey experiments. For example, when two sociologists—who are often presumed to be left-wing—present you with policy options in a survey or interview you may feel some social pressure to come across as more progressive than you really are. Survey experiments can mitigate against this social desirability bias by manipulating aspects of the question to tap into underlying attitudes.

Elites, for example, may make decisions which, intentionally or not, exclude those from less privileged backgrounds. This may operate directly via outright class discrimination or indirectly by giving preferential treatment to people in one's own social network. We tried to test both mechanisms with brief vignette experiments. In one we explored whether elites would offer a lower starting salary to someone they knew came from a less privileged background. In the other we tested whether they would give preferential treatment to someone if they shared a mutual acquaintance. In both experiments, we found no clear evidence of class discrimination.

But there are other forms of bias that might be important when it comes to understanding political behaviour. One of these is "sunk cost bias."[25] A sunk cost is a cost that has already been incurred.[26] Economists would argue that sunk costs are already past and should not affect one's decision about whether to continue with an endeavour. For our purposes, we are interested in whether people would be willing to continue to put money into a government programme that is not working. In general, people (including politicians) are willing to invest more money into an existing failing policy if the sunk cost (the money already invested) is larger.[27]

We decided to explore this sunk cost bias in a slightly different way. We wanted to see whether there would be any variability in people's responses depending on the policy context. So, we came up with two scenarios of programs into which government had already invested a lot of money and for which ministers were now asking for more cash. In scenario 1, the policy was a reduction in capital gains tax. In scenario 2, the policy was an income support programme for people who were out of work. We picked these two policies because the capital gains tax policy has a degree of self-interest for the very rich, especially those who are in the wealth elite, whereas income support for people out of work is one of the tools of poverty reduction.

Most people (including our elites) were in favour of investing more money into these policies irrespective of what the policy actually is: this is what we would expect if sunk cost bias were present. But our elites differed from the other people we surveyed in how strongly sunk cost bias showed up when it was applied to specific policies. The general population were less likely to want to invest more money in the capital gains tax proposal (a difference of 5 percent points, $p = 0.027$). This gap was bigger among our elites, but it depended on whether you were part of the wealth elite or not. The richest people in *Who's Who* were around 10 percent *more* likely to favour keeping the capital gains tax low than the rest of the elite (63 percent versus 54 percent), but were around 10 percent *less* likely to support investing more in the poverty reduction policy (58 percent versus 67 percent). Sunk cost bias, then, is modulated by the policy context and varies in ways that are consistent with self-interest. In this respect, elites are not that dissimilar from everyone else. What makes them different is their economic position, which pulls them towards other priorities.

This experiment may help us see how being wealthy might influence how elites make decisions, but it does not shed any light on how the class background and upbringing of elites may affect their decision-making in the real world. To look at this we move to a setting where elites make very important decisions; the British Supreme Court. We draw on data compiled by political scientist Chris Hanretty who has explored, in his book *A Court of Specialists,* how judges on this court behave, and how in their judgments some favour more right-wing and others more left-wing outcomes.[28] We use these same data (generously provided by Hanretty) but look at how such outcomes map onto the class backgrounds of judges. Specifically, we look at whether the backgrounds of the judges who make up the decision-making panel for a particular case affect the likelihood of reaching what Hanretty calls a "left-outcome," decisions which, for example, favour economic underdogs over economic top dogs (such as employees in disputes with employers). We take data on 467 decisions made by the Supreme Court since it was established in 2009 and add to it the information we have collected from *Who's Who* and other sources, such as probate records. Judges whose parents' wealth at death was in the top 1 percent were defined as coming from a privileged background. They made up 16 percent of the judges in the sample and at least one of them sat on 40 percent of the cases. We find that the presence of at least one judge on a case from these kinds of privileged origins reduces the proportion of decisions that reach a left outcome from 59 percent to 48 percent. These findings are telling. They suggest that the class origins of elites do not just influence their political ideology of our elites but may also impact what they actually do when they have power.

Using Wealth to Wield Influence

Being born into wealth shapes your politics but so too does accumulating wealth in your own life. We have seen that the wealth elite skew towards the right. This matters because they also have more political influence than other groups. Our survey analysis shows, for example, that the wealth elite are more politically active than other elites. Over 60 percent have spent time with a politician (compared to 50 percent for other elites) and 60 percent have had the opportunity to discuss policy with a politician (compared to 54 percent among the non-wealth elite). They are also more likely to have donated to a political party (30 percent among the wealth elite compared to 22 percent among other elites).

The wealth elite may be more politically active, but how does their wealth inform their ability to wield power? Our interviews with thirty-eight members of the wealth elite are essential here because they help us see how wealth often undergirded, or provided a platform, from which these people could exert influence. Many were able to (semi-)retire in their fifties and early sixties and move into modestly paid or even unpaid non-executive board roles or "passion projects" that provided them with unique opportunities to push for change. Take Hugh, the CEO of a professional service firm who had recently retired and taken up a role as chairman of a university (born 1960–1965). This role, he explained, had allowed him to focus on number of "strategic" issues which he felt were "central to the future of British higher education," such as "academic freedom and freedom of speech." Rupert (1965–1970), who identified as "white other," had similarly retired early after thirty years as a corporate financier in the City. Since retiring he had become chairman of two high-profile FTSE250 companies and joined the board of an elite private school and a national charity. Wealth, as Rupert explained in this illuminating conversation with us, gave him the "financial security" to take on these roles, and a certain licence to express his views without fear of consequence:

Rupert: I don't think anyone is going to be terribly interested in what I say publicly but I should have no difficulty in doing that if I did. And back to one of the things earlier, one of the luxuries of my financial position is that if I do that then my world doesn't end.

Interviewer: Is there any realm that you are interested in that you are sort of actively working in?

Rupert: I would certainly . . . , having voted Conservative all my life on the basis that even Boris was better than Jeremy Corbyn . . . I would actively seek to make sure the Conservatives get re-elected [at the] next election.

Interviewer: And what does that look like for you?

Rupert: I think that, you know, talking to an extent to anybody who cares to listen, [and saying] that these people have got to get in . . . I was invited to some dinner where William Hague was speaking a month or so ago . . . And I would certainly actually speak up on those sort of occasions. Whether it does any good or not, I don't know.

Interviewer: Do you think it's ever been consequential in any way?

Rupert: On a micro level definitely. I mean I think again one of the pleasures of being a chairman of things is that in the end people listen to you, which is quite nice when you are in your sixties. And so yes that sort of level certainly what I say has influence on outcomes.

Amanda (media, 1965–1970) had similarly used her wealth and that of her husband, who was also in the wealth elite, to move from a full-time job in the media towards a "portfolio" career on the board of various charities and cultural organisations. This, she acknowledged, had given her a unique ability to exert influence in the areas she was passionate about, particularly state funding of the opera, theatre, and visual art:

I mean I earn very, very little now because all the stuff I do is voluntary. I mean I don't need to work . . . I am doing a report at the moment [about visual art] but my total fee for that will just be nothing, you know. And I am aware that, and this is going to make me sound like one of the elite, it's very prestigious, people who, decision makers will listen. And I will have a spin off article about it in the *New Statesmen* and the *Spectator*. And . . . it's a bit of a cultural asset to me. I can only do that because I am wealthy.

The point to underline here is that this unique capacity to influence is significant because the political orientation of this group is often quite distinct from other sections of the British elite. The wealth elite, in other words, not only tend to be more right-wing and culturally conservative, but their wealth furnishes them with an outsized ability to further their political agenda.

The View from the Top

Paul is a corporate consultant who has had a long and varied career touching on education, business, and politics (1955–1960). He grew up in a very poor, working-class family in the North of England and his politics, he explains, are fundamentally rooted in these early experiences. "There are certain things that sort of live with me from my childhood," he explains. Career-long interests in tackling educational and health inequality, for example, are "sort of in my DNA partly for familial reasons":

> So I feel very protective of people, I guess this is where the sense of social injustice, I can't stand that stuff, I can't stand the fact that you know a Black person would be treated different from a white person or a gay person would be treated different from a straight person, it just gets in my craw, it sort of ignites something that I find offensive and I find it offensive for a very personal reason, which I'm not Black and I'm not gay, but I can empathise.

This connection between background and social justice is not entirely straightforward for Paul, however, and has not produced an unambiguously socialist or radical left politics. Paul instead identifies with the centre left. He is both highly successful and very wealthy, and recognises that this upward mobility has informed and somewhat complicated his political identity:

> Of course if you were doing an academic exercise and marking my class basis today, I'm sort of you know I'm sort of top 1 percent or whatever. But that's not what it feels like . . . if you come from where I've come from and if you have the opportunity to do what I've done that's rooted in a very simple idea which is that you should probably want for others what you've had for yourself.

Paul's example underlines that what is at stake in thinking about elite reproduction is not just who gets to join the elite in Britain, but also how they think and behave—particularly as political actors. We have shown that not only are the political preferences of the British elite *as a whole* distinct from the UK population—particularly their belief in educational meritocracy and their resistance to shoulder a higher tax burden—but there are also key ideological divisions *within* the elite. Most strikingly in the context of Chapters 4, 5, and 6, elite reproduction really matters; those like Paul who enter from more humble backgrounds tilt to the left (although, like Paul, this orientation is often somewhat tempered when they join the *wealth* elite).

But elite reproduction is not just about social origin. Britain's elite has traditionally also been profoundly white and male. This is finally beginning to change. In Chapters 8 and 9, we explore what this might mean for the elites we get.

8

Radical Women

Britain's elite has always been, and remains today, dominated by men. Masculinity is in fact so tightly bound up with eliteness that the "old boy network" remains perhaps our most familiar byword for who runs Britain. And yet in many ways the most significant shift in the composition of the elite over the last 125 years is the number of women in formal positions of power and influence. Until the 1980s, less than 5 percent of the people in *Who's Who* were women. But this has changed considerably in the last few decades, and the rate of change may have even accelerated slightly in recent years. As Figure 8.1 shows, between 2016 and 2022 around one third of new entrants to *Who's Who* were women.

It is this profound change that we grapple with in this chapter. In particular, we wanted to understand in what ways—if at all—the rise of women in elite positions has altered the character of the British elite. The story we uncover points in several directions. In some respects the rise of women in positions of power may have profound implications. We show, for instance, that women elites tend to have distinct policy preferences and social attitudes that tilt significantly to the left. Compared to men in similar positions, they are much more concerned about inequality and poverty, less concerned about economic growth, more in favour of increasing spending on public services, and happier to increase taxes on the rich. Equally, they are also significantly more progressive on a number of culture wars issues—although notably not when it comes to trans rights.

What is less clear is why these gender differences exist. One possible explanation we consider is that these new elite women might be more

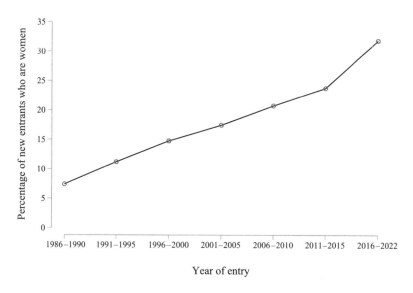

8.1 Women elites on the rise.

likely to come from poorer backgrounds.[1] One of the critiques of the feminist movements of the 1960s and 1970s, after all, was that its focus on gender equality and workplace discrimination (rather than a more radical politics) was driven by the fact that its main proponents were largely class-privileged white women.[2] Yet we do not find that the more recent influx of left-leaning women are more likely to come from working-class backgrounds.

We then turn to examine whether the progressive preferences of elite women translate into more radical political action. Here the picture is distinctly mixed. While we find some evidence that women are not as predisposed to bend the rules to their own advantage, at the same time they exhibit a similar behavioural bias towards the status quo. We also home in on the topic of gender equality to show that despite an almost universal rhetorical commitment to feminism, only recently has this precipitated widespread action among elite women to tackle gender inequality. In fact, many of the women we interviewed explained that they had opted to deploy a strategic, small *p* politics during their careers, calling into question the idea that the growing number of progressive women in the British elite will necessarily shift policymaking or drive national politics to the left.

Elite Women versus Women in the Elite

We should not confuse the absence of women in *Who's Who* with an absence of "elite women."[3] Women have historically played a central role in elite reproduction through their roles at the centre of elite social and familial networks and through myriad forms of domestic labour that ensured what the feminist thinker Silvia Fedirici famously termed "social reproduction."[4] Aristocratic women in the eighteenth and nineteenth centuries were prominent "confidantes, advisers, agents and partners" in the social politics of Westminster, as historian Elaine Chalus reminds us, where they managed parliamentary seats, organised debates, and got involved in campaigning.[5] Beyond the political realm, women have also long been key brokers of patronage, securing access for family members to plum positions in the civil service and religious orders, or by cultivating and socialising sons capable of becoming suitable "heirs."[6] It is also important to recognise that the creation of elite directories like *Who's Who* was a "social process" that was undoubtedly gendered.[7] After all, it wasn't until 1897, when Douglas Slade assumed the editorship, that women were included in *Who's Who* at all.[8]

Yet, although there have always been elite women, we would maintain that the increase of women in *Who's Who* is sociologically significant. This is because entrance to *Who's Who* is largely premised on widely recognised public and occupational achievement, so it captures women's growing involvement in an elite *professional public sphere* previously occupied almost entirely by men.

What, then, has driven this rise in the number of women in elite positions? We have seen big changes in how people view women and their place in society (as we discussed in Chapter 5), but it is not clear that these ideological changes were the precipitating factor that opened up formal positions of power and influence.[9] Changes to gender norms could have occurred *because* women achieved those positions of power.[10] The timing is intriguing. This rise of women into positions of power and influence did not occur in the 1960s and 1970s, when feminist movements challenged gender norms and the ideology of patriarchy.[11] Instead, the changes have been happening since the late 1980s. It was the women *born* in the 1950s, 1960s, and 1970s, in other words, who came of age against the backdrop of what is commonly called second-wave feminism, who were most successful at breaking the various glass ceilings.[12] These women saw important changes that steadily opened up opportunities for them to reach elite positions. First, this generation experienced a rapid rise in access to university (women were 23 percent of UK graduates in 1950, but that had almost doubled to 44 percent by 1990), including, eventually, elite universities.[13] Second, the demands and expectations placed on women in the domestic sphere have changed significantly, though in many respects not enough. Higher workplace participation among women coincided with declining fertility rates, technological shifts affected the gendered division of labour, and the formation of the welfare state, which offered avenues for the development of women's careers and, in some places, subsidised the costs of child care for pre-school children.[14] Third, formal measures to combat gender discrimination have allowed some women to progress who might have been held back in the past.[15]

All of these changes contributed to rising numbers of women in the British elite but gender parity is still a long way off. Men still strongly outnumber women in the current edition of *Who's Who*—82 percent to 18 percent. At the current rate of improvement, the number of women entering *Who's Who* will only reach 50 percent around 2050, and even this is in no way guaranteed.[16] Some argue that reaching gender parity is not necessarily essential for women to become politically powerful so long as there is a critical mass of women in key sites of power (for example, over 30 percent of politicians).[17] This bloc would then large enough to feel empowered to push for changes that "trickle down" to women at all levels of the firms or other organizations in which they work.[18] They point to evidence, for example, that in firms where there is a critical mass of women in influential positions there are smaller gender pay gaps and less workplace gender segregation.[19] But whether the presence of women leads to change is partly contingent on whether they actually bring with them a different political orientation, and this is what we unpack next.

How (Elite) Women Think

The growing numbers of women in the British elite could radically alter the political landscape if elite women tend to have distinct policy preferences and social attitudes. But do they? We tackled this by returning to the survey answers explored in Chapter 7.

We are not the first to look at this question. In a study jointly conducted with Esther Duflo, Raghabendra Chattopadhyay found that women politicians in India are more likely to prioritise legislation related to children and family, gender discrimination, and health care and social services.[20] There is also some evidence women will introduce different kinds of policy legislation to their male colleagues, focussing more on crime prevention, for instance, rather than punishment.[21] Lots of this research has focused narrowly on the United States or on politicians.[22] And so, we were eager to explore whether British women in various positions of power and influence also had distinct policy preferences. The short answer is yes. And the differences are quite profound. Returning to our survey data (which gave us around 600 responses from women, comprising about 20 percent of our sample), we found that elite women were different from elite men on almost every dimension.

Consider questions related to inequality, mapped out in Figure 8.2. Although small numbers of both groups agree that current income or wealth gaps are "about right," women are half as likely as men to agree with these statements.

These differences are also observable when we look at policy preferences, in Figure 8.3. This shows that women are much less concerned about economic growth and much more concerned about reducing poverty. Alongside this, a larger share of women (79 percent opposed to 68 percent) want government to invest in health, education, and social security and are more

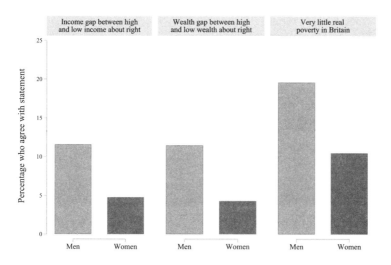

8.2 Women are more concerned about inequality.

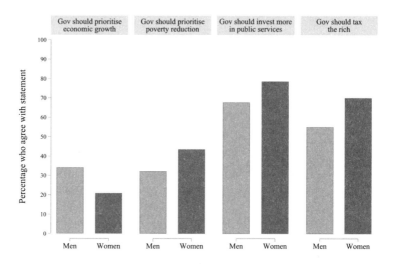

8.3 Women want more action on poverty reduction and are willing to tax the rich to get it.

willing to tax the rich to finance these additional expenditures. Elite women, these answers reveal, are much more likely to be on the political left than elite men.

But women's more progressive views are not only limited to economic inequality, as Figure 8.4 shows. They are also more left-leaning on a number of culture war issues. For example, women are more likely than men (by around 20 percentage points) to say that Britain remains a racist country and, linked with this, are much more ambivalent about the legacies of empire.

There is one area, however, where elite women are not distinct from elite men, and this is around the issue of trans rights. We asked our respondents whether they thought transgender people should be able to change the sex on their birth certificates. Around 30 percent of both men and women in our survey agreed that transgender people should be able to do this. This reflects very high-profile debates over trans rights and the fact that some women are concerned about what the push for trans rights will mean for broader debates about feminism, an issue the women in our sample feel strongly about.[23] Interestingly, in the British population in general men are more pro-trans rights than women (18 percent versus 12 percent).

The main takeaway from this data is that elite women have distinct policy preferences from elite men. This can be seen most clearly when we look at

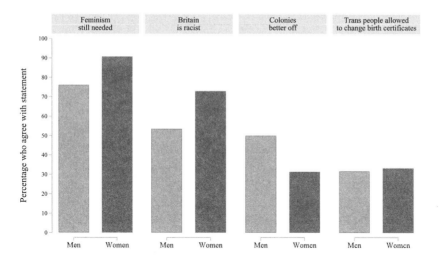

8.4 Gender and the culture wars.

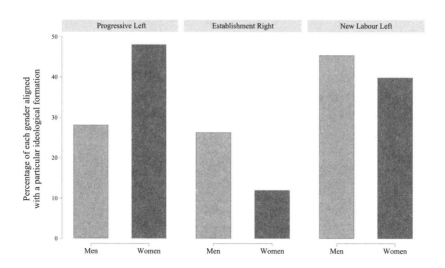

8.5 Women tend to be on the Progressive Left or New Labour Left.

gender differences across the different ideological formations we described in Chapter 7 (Figure 8.5).

Recall that the Progressive Left is less concerned about economic growth, wants more investment in public services, and is willing to tax the rich to achieve this goal. They also tend to think Britain is a racist country and typically do not think former colonies are better off as a result of being colonised. Strikingly, women are about 20 percentage points more likely to be found in this ideological grouping than men. By contrast, women are much less likely to be in the Establishment Right formation. Barely 1 in 10 women are found here compared to nearly 1 in 4 men.

These differences matter because if the proportion of women in the elite increases over time, as we expect it will, it could have profound effects on the attitudinal composition of the British elite.

The Economic Roots of Women's Progressive Politics

What explains women's more progressive views? Chapter 7 revealed that both class origins and current economic circumstances are strongly correlated with attitudes towards inequality and how to address it. Are elite women, then, more progressive politically simply because they are less likely to come from advantaged backgrounds, less likely to work in sectors like business or finance, or less likely to accumulate extreme wealth?

The answer to all these questions is essentially no. For starters, women and men in our data have fairly similar class backgrounds. About 26 percent of elite men and women in our sample say they come from working-class backgrounds. And when we look at what their parents did for a living, we see a fairly gender-neutral story; 82 percent of women come from families where their parents were doing professional work versus 75 percent of men. The same holds true when we examine *elite* origins. Around 17.5 percent of women in *Who's Who* had a parent who was also in *Who's Who,* whereas the figure for men is 16.5 percent. In sum, it is hard to argue that the women in our sample are more progressive because they come from less privileged backgrounds.[24]

Women may be more progressive because they are more likely to be found in sectors with a more left-leaning culture, such as the cultural and creative industries (CCIs) (see Figure 8.6).[25] Historically speaking, some industries have been more open to women's success than others, and it is true that museums, media, and the arts were sectors where women's contributions to public life have been more readily recognised. In the late 1980s, when women entered the elite they were commonly admitted because of their connection to the CCIs rather than because of their links with business. As time passed, the number of women entering all these fields increased but women remained more likely to enter the elite through the creative industries. Notwithstanding these differences, it is still true that

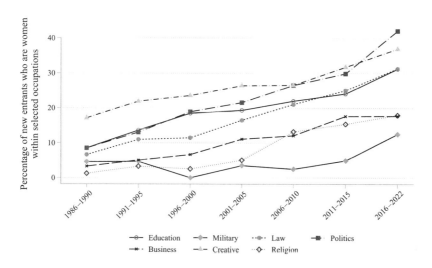

8.6 Women entrants have gone up in all fields over the last forty years.

even women working in traditionally more conservative fields such as business have different policy preferences. Among business elites, for example, men are still around three times as likely as women (23 percent vs 8 percent) to say they think the income gap between rich and poor is about right.

Finally, what about wealth? As noted in Chapter 7, one of the strongest predictors of political ideology within the elite is being rich. So another explanation for gender differences may be that women in the elite are simply less wealthy. It is true that the women in *Who's Who* were slightly less likely than men (both in the past and today) to be in the top 1 percent of the wealth distribution. But surprisingly, these differences are relatively modest (Figure 8.7). Around 24 percent of men in *Who's Who* have historically been in the top 1 percent, while the figure for women is around 20 percent. There are slightly larger gaps in income—60 percent of men are in the top 5 percent of the income distribution versus only 50 percent of women—but, again, these gaps are not large enough to generate significant differences in political attitudes.

We can also consider this question in a formal way by comparing men and women in the wealth elite to those who are not. In Figure 8.8, we show the proportion of men and women who support increasing taxes on the rich. About 60 percent of men who are *not* in the wealth elite are in favour of increasing taxes on the rich while about 70 percent of the corresponding women share this view. Interestingly, this gender difference is even more

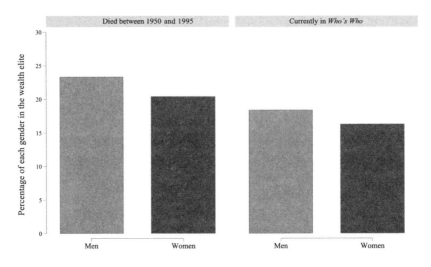

8.7 Women are less likely to be in the wealth elite.

8.8 Wealthy women are more likely than men to support higher taxes on the rich.

pronounced in the wealth elite; 40 percent of men are in favour of taxing the rich, whereas this rises to about 60 percent of women.

If demographic and economic differences do not explain political differences between elite men and women, what does? Answering this question definitively is beyond the scope of our analysis here, but our tentative hypothesis is that elite women hold different political views from elite men in much the same way that research has shown that women *in general* tend to be more progressive than men. There is long-running evidence, for example, that women are more supportive of equality, redistribution, and state intervention than men.[26] Elite women are potentially more progressive than elite men, then, for similar reasons that elites from working-class backgrounds are more progressive than elites from privileged backgrounds: while their destinations in life may be more assured, their experiences of marginalisation may make them more sensitive to forms of economic or social exclusion experienced by other groups. More specifically, women have historically experienced, and continue to experience today, more precarity and less autonomy, and these experiences may lead them to be more concerned about equality and redistribution. In fact, gender gaps on these issues can be larger in contexts where welfare provision is weaker.[27]

Who Is More Likely to Bend the Rules?

Elite women think differently from elite men in ways that can't be easily explained by their social origins, what they do for a living, or how wealthy they are. But just because women have different political orientations doesn't mean that they will behave differently once they achieve positions of power and influence. The relationship between attitudes and action, as we explored in Chapter 7, is incredibly complicated. Yet there are some ways we can get at this question.

A longstanding way that political scientists have tried to study behaviour is via survey questions that examine the ethics driving people's decision-making processes. In our study we tried to mirror these methods. Specifically, we asked respondents questions about situations in which there is some ambiguity about the rules. This can arise in a situation in which there is a norm which might be out of step with a particular law. Here we focussed on tax and social security (what British people sometimes call "benefits") loopholes.[28] These tend to receive extensive press coverage in the United Kingdom—both right-wing caricatures of "benefit cheats" and left-wing scrutiny of wealthy tax avoidance. We asked our respondents two questions (both copied from the British Social Attitudes survey):

Suppose someone used a loophole in the system to increase their benefit payments without breaking the law. What would your view of this be?

Suppose someone used a loophole in the system to reduce the amount of tax they pay without breaking the law. What would your view of this be?

We then gave respondents a scale which ranged from "Always wrong" to "Never wrong."

The first thing to say is that all-out rule-dodging (if we are to believe people's self-assessments) is actually not that common. Only around 20 percent of the elite think it is permissible to use loopholes to avoid paying taxes. At the same time, we do find that the wealth elite are more likely to bend the rules by using loopholes to avoid paying taxes. On average, members of the wealth elite are around 9 percentage points more likely to think this is permissible, around 50 percent more than other elites.

Crucially, gender plays a significant role here, as we see in Figure 8.9, Not only are elite women less likely to think it is permissible to use such loopholes to avoid paying taxes but the change associated with being in the wealth elite on the permissibility of these schemes is smaller for women too. More precisely, women in the wealth elite are far less likely than men to feel it is permissible to use tax loopholes. We also find similar results when it comes to using loopholes in the benefits system. Elite women are significantly more likely than elite men to believe that using loopholes to gain from the benefits system is wrong. Of course, making the leap from prospective behaviour in surveys like this to actual behaviour is somewhat perilous. But there at least signs here that elite women not only think dif-

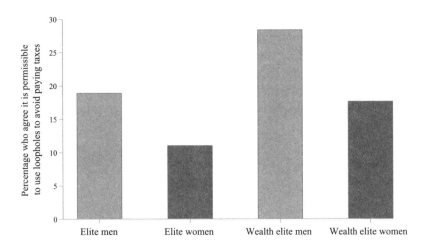

8.9 Affluent people are more likely to bend the rules, but women less so.

ferently to elite men, politically, but may also act differently—in terms of bending rules towards their own interests.

Varieties of Feminism

Survey questions are of course somewhat blunt instruments to get at questions of behaviour. Next, then, we return to our interviews and, specifically, conversations with elite women about the role of feminism in their lives and careers. Our survey data made it clear that attitudes towards feminism were one of the clearest areas where elite women differed most markedly from men. Strikingly, over 90 percent of the women we surveyed believe feminism is still needed in Britain today compared to 75 percent among elite men. These figures are both much higher than those in the British population as a whole (around 57 percent of women in the general population and 48 percent of men think feminism is still needed).[29]

We thought this would be a salient area to probe further in our interviews, in the hope of gaining insights into the extent to which these women's views had translated into actively pursuing, or advocating for, gender equality during their careers. Had they been agents for change?

Interviews revealed a complex picture. Almost all the women we spoke with, across all ages, said they had experienced sexism in some form over the course of their careers. They recounted being discounted, disempowered, harassed, and "groomed"; and they told us about having their work "stolen" by male colleagues, being misrecognised as secretaries, and being "touched up in pubs."

Yet although experiences of gender discrimination were almost universal, this didn't necessarily correspond to a common feminist political project. In fact, we observed a variety of views among our interviewees. This breadth makes it hard to draw a straight line between the almost universal attitudinal commitment to feminism and the active pursuit of gender equality.

While none of the women we spoke to rejected the basic idea that women and men are equal, how they understood this equality did vary. For Jean (born 1940–1944, business) equality is a "mindset," "it's about whether or not you think you are equal." Barbara (1940–1944, academic), saw men and women as equal but different. When asked whether she "believed in gender equality" she responded:

> Well I don't know. Equality, but I think that actually women, especially
> as I said if they have children, it's not identical, it's really different

191

paths should be carved out and I don't think men and women are the same and should be treated the same. I mean I think they should be treated pretty much the same if they're not having children . . . , but if they're having children they need to be treated differently, but given equal ability to flourish and fulfil their potential . . . I think it's a mixture of genes and environment, but biology shows that we're not the same. So I don't think they should be treated the same but I think they should be treated in a way that allows them to fulfil their full potential. Which is different.

Allied to this more ambivalent and qualified view, was the fact that a small group of women—who were largely born before the 1960s—did not see their careers as inflected by sexism. While these women accepted that opportunities had not necessarily been the same for them as for their male counterparts, this did not mean that they felt they had faced discrimination. "I didn't feel any sexism at all," Barbara told us (phrases like this were surprisingly common in these interviews, although it was often followed by some nuance alluding to a sexist experience). These women instead foregrounded their own agency as decisive; their drive, determination, and resilience. Success, for Jean, was about being "optimistic . . . about taking life by the scruff of the neck." Or, as Josephine Barnes (1912, medicine) put it when asked if she ever worried about going into a male-dominated field in the 1940s and 1950s: "I don't think I thought about that . . . we just got on with it."

Another way in which these variations of feminism emerged was in discussions about progress on gender equality. There were basically two positions here. Some women were largely positive. Fiona (1965–1979, entrepreneur), for example, hoped that the experience of the last few decades will show "more young women, women generally . . . that change is possible." Likewise, Dawn (1960–1964), who had had a successful career working in finance, when asked whether things have improved for women, responded: "Hugely, hugely is the answer, yes. And they've improved beyond, it may still seem like a struggle, but it's improved out of all recognition."

These stories of progress can be juxtaposed with those who were far less sanguine. Sometimes people say to Jacqueline (1955–1959), an Asian British lawyer, "Oh well, the diversity and the gender thing has changed," but she does not accept that. She responds: "no, it hasn't actually, not as much as it should have done." Likewise, Karen (law, 1960–64) observed, "I think we were a generation that just was treated far more respectfully than I regret to say my children's generation or even worse, the bit below them."

This concern about a lack of progress (or even a reversal, or degeneration in mores) comes through very strongly when elite women spoke about their kids. Margaret (1945–1949, artist) did not think gender equality had gotten any better and said that her daughter "still suffers even at work as a senior civil servant from this." When Patricia (1945–1949, academic) is asked "Do you think your daughter [will] have more opportunities than you?" She quickly responds, "No, no, I really don't. No, I really don't."

One reading of these divergent accounts is that they problematise the idea that the progressive attitudes of elite women necessarily translate into a common political agenda for change. As our data shows, a universal rhetorical commitment to feminism belies a set of fairly distinct political projects. The sense that things are getting better, for example, and that change is possible is arguably connected to a more incrementalist view of what it will take to bring about gender equality. Women who support this narrative of progress may feel that government initiatives mandating greater gender equality in the workplace, when combined with legislation banning gender discrimination, have the potential to move us towards a more equal world. In contrast, those who feel that despite well-intentioned efforts very little has changed, may be more sceptical of the capacity of organizational and even legislative efforts to bring about gender equality. Thus, while 90 percent of women in positions of power and influence agree that feminism is still needed in Britain, what it is needed for and what it should hope to achieve, is far less clear.

Feminist Awakenings

There is another way to make sense of these varied responses. And that is that, in recent years, something has shifted. What is interesting about many of the women who told us they didn't feel that they had experienced sexism, particularly the older women, is that in recent years they had begun to reassess their experiences:

> I think it probably was quite sexist, but I just didn't really notice it terribly. (Karen, law, 1960–1964)

At the time I don't think I was aware of it. (Fiona, education, 1965–1969)

I haven't until recently felt that being a woman was . . . any sort of disadvantage. (Christine, architecture, 1945–1949)

Crucial here are phrases like "until recently, "at the time," or "I didn't notice it." Sexism, these women seem to be saying, was always there but somehow was less visible because it was so acceptable at the time.

The invisibility of sexism seems to be linked with a muted connection to what has sometimes been called the second-wave feminist movement of the 1960s and 1970s.[30] In fact, most of the women we spoke to explicitly acknowledged that they had not played an active role in gender politics in earlier decades. Diane (1960–1964, academic) remembers, "I was actually quite apolitical at that (time), I hadn't really organised." Karen, when asked about her activism, responded, "I actually spent a shameful amount of my life trying to stay under the radar and fit in." Others acknowledged that feminism eventually became important to them intellectually, but this didn't necessarily lead them to do anything concrete about it. As June (1945–1949, academic) notes, "It was through the 80s that I got very involved . . . intellectually in feminism, though not in any action." Or as Linda (1950–1954), a novelist, recalls: "in my head, yes [feminism was important], but if I'm honest in practice, not really, no." It is not that these women were unaware of feminism or opposed to it. Some had made important contributions to the intellectual work around feminism. It just did not translate into concrete activism.

In some respects, the unintelligibility of sexism combined with this ambiguous relation to feminist politics could be viewed as somewhat surprising because these are women who grew up during or just after the feminist movements of the 1960s and 1970s. We might expect that they would be part of a feminist generation who absorbed the struggles that were happening around them and spent their careers fighting to overturn them. Yet this does not seem to be the case.

So, what, then, precipitated these more recent "feminist awakenings"?[31] They appear to be grounded in a contradiction between the ideals of gender equality promulgated in their homes and especially at their schools (particularly if they attended an elite girls school) and the grinding reality of daily life as a professional woman or working mother.[32] Those who attended elite girls schools, in particular, pointed to how these schools inculcated a strong initial sense that they could do whatever they wanted in life. As Zahra, who was Indian British (1965–1969, creative), recollects: "I think all of us who went to that school, my friends still would say, [developed] an inner confidence that we're brilliant." However, in the years since, many explained that they had gradually become disillusioned. And despite their apparent success, these women now looked back and saw much more clearly the sexism to which they had been exposed in the past. As Margaret, an artist who attended an elite girls school, articulated:

What made me very angry for far too long in my life has been the fact that at school I got the message that life had improved and women were as good as men and if you grasped the opportunity the world could be yours . . . And then gradually, gradually my experience . . . showed me that actually, no, things had not changed that much at all.

Of course, alongside these experiences, wider shifts in how we think about sexism have further catalysed this reassessment of the past. Very few spoke about #MeToo or the Everyday Sexism Project directly, but movements like these inevitably lurked in the background, surely contributing to both reevaluations of past experiences and motivations to become more active in gender politics, particularly at work.

Political with a Small *p*

While there may be some evidence that there is a link between elite women's progressive attitudes and a propensity for progressive action, especially in recent years, does this really hold true beyond the issue of gender equality? Here we are more cautious, even possibly sceptical. Part of this scepticism comes from the survey experiments we conducted. One form of bias we consider is "status quo" bias.[33] This is the idea that irrespective of your actual ideology, people have a preference for policy decisions that require little change. We used a question which has been used before in this type of research, which asks people to imagine they are a government minister who has to choose between two economic policies. One plan keeps growth high but also maintains a high deficit. The other has lower growth and a lower deficit. The only difference between the two scenarios is which one is presented as the status quo. That is, do you want to *keep* growth and the deficit high / low or do you want to do something different? Notably, our results showed no gender differences among the elite in either of these areas. That is, women may be increasingly replacing men in elite positions but we find little evidence that they are more likely than the men they are replacing to pursue changes that disrupt the status quo.

This scepticism as to their likely support for a broader agenda focussed on reducing inequality fits with historical accounts of women's critical role in ensuring elite reproduction.[34] It is unclear why women's influence on these processes would change simply because they now occupy formal positions of power rather than informal ones. Consider this conversation with Sharon, a businesswoman and long-term advocate for gender equality in the workplace, about her children's education:

Sharon: I failed to get any of them to go Oxford. [One son] did apply to Oxford, and he got all the way through to the end of the process, and then didn't get a place which was surprising because he's very good at interviewing. But he had Eton on his CV and I think unfortunately, that's a negative these days.

Interviewer: Oh, do you think so?

Sharon: I know so. I mean, they've gone from having about 100 Oxbridge places per annum, to about 40 over the last four or five years. And the intelligence the boys' have got is greater and not less. So yeah, I would have been better off sending him to a comprehensive, it's just how it is . . . I just think, unfortunately, they're just trying—which is a good thing in many ways. I mean, it's something I've advocated for a long time, it shouldn't be lots of public-school boys. But, not so good if it's your son.

This tension between seeking to open up previously closed educational institutions and the implications of that agenda when it comes to your own family members has always plagued progressive politics. Women may be more critical of inequality than men, in other words, but we should not necessarily expect them to be any different to men when it comes to actively seeking to ensure their own children get the best opportunities.

There is another reason why we should be cautious about expecting radical change simply because there are more women in elite positions. And this is that change is hard and even the women who are trying to change things are working against entrenched power. There are times when the women we interviewed spoke explicitly about pushing for change. But, what is striking about the experiences they recount is that the scope of their action is always rather local. This is perhaps best exemplified by Teresa (1955–1959), a broadcaster and the alumnus of an elite girls school, who describes herself as "political with a small *p*." For Teresa, there are two facets to this orientation. On the one hand, it is about being "independent," and even to some extent "totally politically independent." Indeed most of the women we talked to said they had deliberately refrained from bringing their personal politics into their work. As Patricia noted, "I think we were all kind of desperately trying to manage to keep our heads above water." This is understandable. Many of these women were dealing with far less linear elite trajectories than their male counterparts while doing more than their fair share of the work at home. Avoiding being overtly political was a crucial survival strategy.

On the other hand, being "political with a small *p*," Teresa notes, "means knowing the right words to say at the right time." It is the ability to push for change without pushing so far you lose people in the process. She believes you need "people like us, slightly pushing, making sure that the government, and ministers, and politicians understand what it can do and then somehow dealing with the antis." Other women talk about similar strategies. Doreen (1945–1949), an academic, reflected on how she had used humour to push back on a particular policy at work. "I don't actually find that aggression works," she explained. "It is much better to be unthreatening and concise." Teresa concurred: "convincing people that there is a way forward and bringing the right people on, I think that's political with a small *p*."

We want to be careful here. These women were clearly making strategic calculations about how to bring about change in sexist environments. And yet what is striking is that pursuing politics with a small *p* tends to mean aiming for small and local improvements. If women tend to pursue this approach, it suggests that even if the number of women in the elite increases, and therefore attitudes shift in more progressive directions, this may not meaningfully change the policy agenda.

Tipping the Scales

Elite women, like British women in general, have distinct political views. They tend to be more progressive, are more worried about economic inequalities, and want government to take a larger role in addressing those inequalities. On top of this, women appear to be less comfortable with using formally acceptable but morally questionable avenues to enrich themselves. As the number of women in the elite continues to grow, these political differences could become increasingly important, potentially shifting the centre of gravity among elites.[35]

Whether this will produce meaningful policy change is less clear. This is partly because being in favour of something and acting to accomplish it are two different things. But it is also a reflection of the duality of the experiences of many women. Most we spoke to conceded that they had experienced sexism at various points in their lives, both the blatant and subtle kinds, and this fact had clearly become more salient to them in recent years. And yet they are also women who made it. They have been successful and their stories are inevitably informed by what has been called "survivorship bias." This could inform their politics in two important ways.

The first is that they have become relatively economically privileged, and may have acquired a vested interest in policies that would not dismantle their own position. As we have shown, while rich elite women are more progressive than rich elite men, being in the wealth elite is still associated with slightly less progressive views. In this way, the structural disadvantages that women experience are likely to be modulated by their own success.

The second way survivorship bias is important is that a nontrivial number of the women we spoke to did not view their trajectories as fundamentally shaped by sexism. In this respect, they may be unlike others whose sexist experiences derailed their career path. There is a possibility, then, that the women who remain are those who are more comfortable with the status quo and who may therefore be less inclined to push for change.

What militates against this interpretation is the fact that while this may have been true of these women at one point in time it has become harder to sustain this reading in recent years, as the widespread efforts to expose sexual harassment in the workplace has invited many women to see their trajectories in a new way.[36] Many that we spoke to said that they were now more aware of the sexism they had experienced and more aware of and frustrated by the experiences of their daughters. In this way, survivorship bias may actually become a driver for change.

These developments have led some to wonder if "critical mass" theories of gender equality can really be considered correct.[37] Critical mass theory, outlined earlier, holds that women will be more able to push for change when they form a significant bloc of influential people. If progress continues, the coming years will reveal whether, as more women reach positions of influence, political attitudes will translate into political action.

9

Centring Race and Empire

"A model for other white-majority countries."[1] This was the conclusion of the UK government's high-profile Commission on Racial and Ethnic Disparities when it published its final report in 2021. Britain has made, the report went on to claim, particular progress on racial equality in the elite professions where "issues around race and racism are becoming less important and, in some cases, are not a significant factor in explaining disparities."[2] A cursory glance at the British political establishment seemed to support these findings. In 2023, the Conservative cabinet was the most ethnically diverse in British history.[3] The prime minister (Rishi Sunak), the foreign secretary (James Cleverly), the home secretary (Suella Braverman), and the minister for women and equalities (Kemi Badenoch) were all of Asian or Black heritage. On top of this, the first minister of Scotland, Humza Yousaf, and the mayor of London, Sadiq Khan, were also both Pakistani British.

But these high-profile examples by no means tell the whole story. Our analysis of *Who's Who* suggests a very different account of racial equality and the British elite. We found that the number of people of colour in the British elite is far lower than we would expect if our leaders were selected at random from the population. If we estimate ethnicity based on names, as Figure 9.1 makes clear, then over 96.8 percent of the people in *Who's Who* are white, which includes "White British" but is also made up of people classified in the census as "White Irish" and "White Other." Only 1.81 percent are classified as Black or Asian. By comparison, around 8.2 percent of Britons in a similar age group as those in *Who's Who* (50 and above) are Black (3 percent) or Asian (5.3 percent). This disparity is considerable. Put

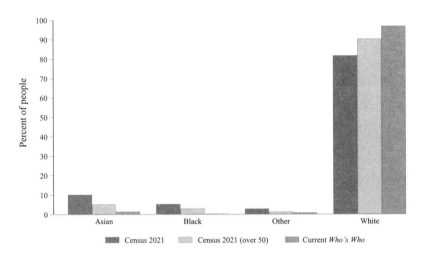

9.1 People of colour are under-represented in the British elite.

Note: The ethnic composition of the UK population changes considerably among younger age groups. We compare the elite to those over the age of 50 because most of the people in the elite are over the age of 50. Unlike the analyses below, these estimates are derived from Onomap, which is an algorithm that uses names to predict ethnicity based on data from the census. Other ethnicity includes "Arab" and a catch-all category called "Other" as well as mixed or multiple ethnicities that are combined with the "Other" ethnicities.

another way, the proportion of Black and Asian elites would need to be 4.5 times higher to be nationally representative of Britons in that same age group.

This does not mean that there has been *no* progress on ethnic diversity. The representation of people of colour within the British elite *has* increased, particularly among those born after 1950. Some argue that the influence of Black and Asian elites is already being felt through the rise of a "new British politics" dominated by "radical progressive" views on race and empire. But those making this case have a tendency, as Nirmal Puwar has pointed out, to read politics off of skin colour and overlook the considerable diversity of political viewpoints among people of colour.[4]

Such work also ignores the pace of change, as Figure 9.2 illustrates. All minoritized groups are starting off from a very low level of representation. There were—according to our estimates—almost no women of colour included in *Who's Who* in the late 1980s and early 1990s, and only 1.2 percent in the most recent editions. At the current rate, it will take Britain another fifty years for Black and Asian elites to constitute a nationally representative

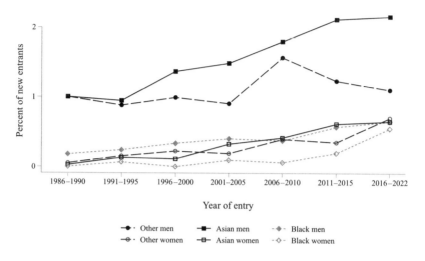

9.2 The slow progress towards ethnic diversity.

Note: Unlike the analyses below, these estimates are derived from Onomap, which is an algorithm that uses names to predict ethnicity based on data from the census.

proportion of new entrants to *Who's Who.* We remain, in short, a very long way from achieving even a quite superficial form of racial equality.

Our aim in this chapter is to think through the likely political implications of greater ethnic diversity among the British elite. First, we consider whether different ethnic groups have distinct political orientations. Is there evidence, for example, that Black or Asian elites share the same political views as their white counterparts when it comes to questions of inequality or taxation? And do these policy preferences change when these people enter the wealth elite? Second, we examine the explicitly racial dimensions of these political preferences. We show in particular how the attitudes of elites on issues of race have been shaped by their own (and their extended families') experiences of racism and colonialism, and how this has often driven them to pursue a distinct politics of race.

Who Counts as "White"?

When someone completes the census, they are asked to describe their ethnicity. A long list of options follow, including "White," "Asian, Asian British or Asian Welsh," "Black, Black British, Black Welsh, Caribbean or African," "Mixed or Multiple ethnic groups," and "Other ethnic group." This list may feel obvious today but it is actually the product of relatively recent efforts to produce a set of categories that reflect the varied experiences and backgrounds of those living in the United Kingdom.[5] The first time the UK census included any measure of ethnicity was 1991.[6] Before this, data was collected on the basis of country of origin, as the government was more interested in tracking migration into Britain rather than capturing people's ethnic identity. Racial and ethnic categories have been updated at almost every census since, becoming ever more varied. "White Irish" was only added in 2001 and "Roma" only in 2021.[7]

Reflecting on this history, it is worth considering what it means when someone describes themselves as "White British" or "Black British." Just as the categories used to capture ethnicity have changed over time, so too can ethnic identities. For example, researchers have found that around 4 percent of people chose a different ethnic identity in 2011 from the one they had chosen just ten years earlier in 2001.[8] Alongside this fluidity of ethnic categories and ethnic identities, there is also a long and complicated history surrounding the degree to which certain ethnic groups are considered white.[9] In the past, Irish, Jewish, and Italians (among other groups) have faced discrimination in the United Kingdom because they were not seen as fully white and had a lower standing in an imagined racial hierarchy.[10] These racial hierarchies have changed over time and some of these groups (to differing degrees) have been brought under the umbrella of "white." But what it means to be white is not a fixed category, even if it is commonly and uncritically accepted as natural and durable.[11]

This complex history is important because being white has historically brought with it a number of social and economic advantages, albeit unequally distributed across class.[12] Len Johnson became the "uncrowned champion" of British boxing in 1928 because the only valid challengers had to have "two white parents." Until World War II, some parts of the armed forces excluded recruits who were not of "pure European descent" and throughout the early part of the twentieth century people of colour were refused positions in the medical profession on account of their race.[13] Exclusionary institutions also stopped persecuted Jews from entering the United Kingdom from Eastern Europe.

This raises an important question about how we interrogate and measure ethnicity in our analysis, especially in a historical context where the notions of what it means to be white have both changed over time and been subject to constant contestation. This difficulty is exacerbated in our analysis by the fact that *Who's Who* has never asked entrants to report their ethnicity.[14] Given these challenges, readers might reasonably ask why we try to analyse these kinds of questions at all? Our response mirrors something Sara Ahmed argued over a decade ago, namely, that to proceed in an analysis of race "as if the categories do not matter because they should not matter would be to fail to show how the categories continue to ground" the lives of those subject to such categories.[15] In other words, we think it is better to attempt to analyse the racial composition of the British elite, even when the methods used have problems, than allow this kind of topic to remain untouched.[16] Indeed, we are of the view that failing to address these questions is likely to result in important racial inequalities remaining hidden from public view.

We drew on two types of data on ethnicity in our research. First, we analysed data from the survey we sent out in spring 2022, in which we asked all 3,160 respondents to identify their ethnicity and locate themselves using the categories used by the census ("White," "Asian or Asian British," Black African, Black Caribbean, Black British," "Mixed / multiple ethnic groups," and "Other ethnic group"). Second, to better understand the trends among those who did not complete our survey or who were in *Who's Who* in the past, we use Onomap, an algorithm which uses census data to estimate the correlation between someone's name and their self-identified ethnicity.[17] The algorithm takes the names in *Who's Who* and probabilistically assigns these individuals to one of the ethnic categories in the census.

There are a number of problems with this algorithmic approach. One is simply accuracy.[18] These kinds of algorithms are known to lack precision when it comes to predicting ethnicity for people of Black Caribbean heritage. This is partly because colonialism led to a widespread anglicisation of names in these regions, and partly because these algorithms sometimes struggle to accurately discern people of mixed or multiple ethnic heritage.[19] It is also important to note that we are primarily using this algorithm to *estimate the proportion* of people who might have been elites of colour.[20] We are not using this data to identify the ethnicity of *specific* people. There are times when we will discuss specific individuals, but in these instances, this is because they have self-identified as belonging to a particular ethnicity.

Another limitation of our analysis is that we only distinguish between three broadly configured racial or ethnic groups. The first is white elites. Within *Who's Who,* and British society more broadly, this is the normative, default racialised category against which others are compared. Almost all the people in this group are British.[21] The second group is made up of those who have traditionally been viewed as people of colour. These are individuals who very likely experience being racialised in some way, often (but not always) because of phenotypic differences. More precisely, we grouped together individuals who identified as Black, Mixed or Multiple ethnicities, and Asian or whose names are the same as people who identify as Black and Asian. We do not always know the nationality of these individuals but the vast majority were either born in the United Kingdom or in former colonies where (up until recently) they would have been British citizens.[22] So, unless we have explicit information to the contrary, we assume that the people in this category are British citizens.[23] We call this group "Asian and Black." We are aware that aggregating in this way is problematic, but the small number of people in each sub-category prohibits us from capturing more granular differences between specific ethnic-racial communities, such as Pakistani British elites, Bangladeshi British elites, or mixed / multiple elites.[24]

The third group, who we label "Other ethnicities," are largely made up of people potentially viewed as white but whose whiteness has been contested and unsettled. In the census, this group frequently would include "Arab," "Hispanic," or "Kurdish." But in our data, the people in this group are somewhat different. There are some Iranians (as we might expect based on the way the census would code these groups), but there are also a number of Jewish and Irish people, as well as Eastern Europeans. Those who identify as "Other," then, largely belong to groups that have been, or still are, subject to discrimination. These groups are important because, while they still often face racial discrimination, they have over time (to differing degrees) become more proximate to notions of whiteness.[25] We call this group "Other ethnicities" because it does include people who may not identify as white. We avoid the term "British" here as this group also includes people born in other countries, and so we are less certain about citizenship.

Now that we have defined these three ethnic groups, we can dissect their educational and gender composition in more detail. Of the current white elite, 29 percent attended an elite HMC "public" school, whereas this figure drops to 22 percent for those of Other ethnicities and to 15 percent among Asian and Black elites. Oxbridge, in contrast, seems equally important for all—over 40 percent of those in all three groups are graduates. Finally, women are over-represented among elites of colour and Other ethnicities;

19 percent of the white elite are women, whereas 29 percent of the Asian and Black elite and 35 percent of those of Other ethnicities are women.

Being White and on the Right

We have seen that Britain's elite is (slowly) becoming more ethnically diverse. But, like the shifts in gender we considered in Chapter 8, what implications might this have for its political orientation? In considering this question, we need to tread carefully. Our survey, while large, still has only a relatively small number of individuals who identify as Asian/Black ($n = 76$) or Other ($n = 32$).

Despite this caveat, we do see some striking differences in political orientations between our three racial-ethnic groups. Across the ideological formations discussed in Chapters 7 and 8, for example, both the Asian and the Black respondents are far more likely to agree with positions that align with the Progressive Left formation and less likely to take positions associated with the Establishment Right (see Figure 9.3). In contrast, those in the "Other" category sit between the white population and Asian and Black elites.

Digging into more specific policy preferences, we see that elites of colour are slightly more progressive on issues related to inequality. But these differences are modest and less pronounced than those between men and women. Similarly, when it comes to government priorities, there are again

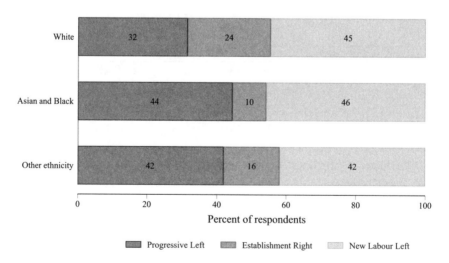

9.3 Elites of colour are more likely to be aligned with the Progressive Left.

modest differences between these groups. Elites of colour are slightly less supportive of government prioritising economic growth, slightly more concerned about poverty, and mildly more supportive of additional government spending.

One way to think about these differences in political attitudes is to wonder if they might be linked to differences in class origins. As we saw in Chapter 7, family background often impacts political ideology. If Black and Asian elites are more likely to come from working-class origins, might their family background explain these differences in political views? Interestingly, we found the opposite to be true. Asian and Black elites and "Other" elites are, as Figure 9.4 shows, more likely than other elites to come from middle-class families where their parents had professional or managerial jobs, although differences with the white majority are small.

This is exactly the reverse of what we would expect based on the attitudes data. That is, Asian and Black elites are slightly more progressive politically, but their class origins are more advantaged. "Other" elites are less progressive than other elites of colour but come from more advantaged origins.

Another way to think about these differences in political orientation is to consider how they differ between the wealth elite and everyone else. This matters because we might anticipate that current class or economic position is a more important driver of political attitudes than ethnicity. Interestingly,

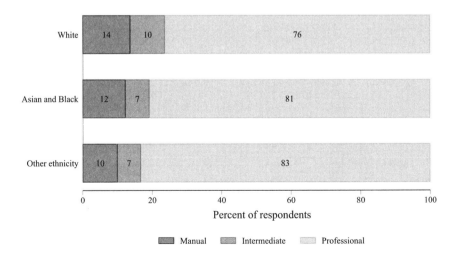

9.4 Class origins (parental occupation) of different ethnic groups.

among the people in *Who's Who* today, members of all three ethnic groups have a similar chance of being in the wealth elite (~20 percent). If anything, the share of Black and Asian elites who are also in the wealth elite is larger than it is for white elites (although it is important to remember here that Asian and Black elites are a very small group in the elite as a whole).[26] Given that a similar proportion of each ethnic group are found in the wealth elite, does being in that very wealthy group have a uniform impact on attitudes?

No, it does not. Look at Figure 9.5. On the left-hand side we show data on a central issue to progressive politics. Do you want government to increase taxes and spend more on key public services, such as health, education, and social security? In general, the wealth elite is less supportive of this idea. But as we can see, this depends on ethnicity. Very wealthy elites of colour are not that different in their position from other elites of colour on this question. In contrast, very wealthy white elites are far less likely to be in favour of seeing the government increase taxes and spending.

Turning to a different question, we see even larger differences. People of colour in the wealth elite are actually more likely to say that they believe government should be prioritising poverty reduction than other elites of

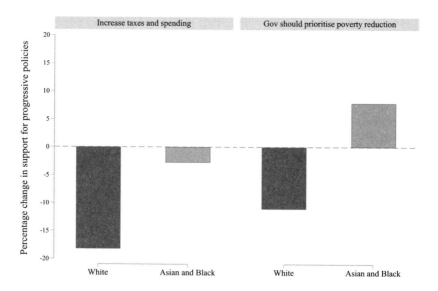

9.5 People of colour are not like other members of the wealth elite.

Note: We are comparing the wealth elite to the rest of the elite. We have removed "other ethnicity" from this graph because the numbers were too small to meaningfully compare.

colour. In contrast, very wealthy white elites are far less likely to be in favour of prioritising poverty reduction. On these questions, then, there is some evidence that Asian and Black elites are resistant to the impact of wealth on their political attitudes. Ethnic identity, then, may be informing their political commitments.

The Politics of Race and Empire

Black and Asian elites are thus slightly more progressive on issues related to inequality. We might anticipate that there would be bigger differences on issues related to race and empire. At a basic level, as Figure 9.6 shows, this assumption holds. Asian and Black elites are slightly more likely to think that Britain is racist and much less likely to think former colonies were better off thanks to British rule. They are also more likely to think that feminism is still needed and more supportive of trans rights.

The "Other" group, by contrast, is more conservative on these issues and sits closer to white elites than elites of colour. At first glance this might seem puzzling as many people in the "Other" group are likely to have themselves been subject to discrimination and come from countries subject to colonial oppression. Yet this aligns with research exploring the development of whiteness over time.[27] In his book on the United States, *How the Irish Became White,* Noel Ignatiev argues that this group of marginalised whites adopted

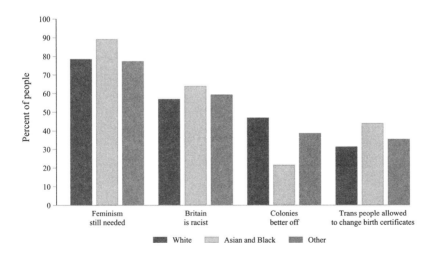

9.6 Elites of colour are more critical of empire and are more likely to think that Britain is still racist.

the racial politics of the patrician whites in order to receive the "public and psychological wage" of whiteness, originally described by African American scholar W. E. B. Du Bois.[28] This political alignment, for Ignatiev, was a crucial aspect of their inclusion under the umbrella of whiteness.[29] Now, obviously, we cannot see change over time in our data, nor can we discern the subtleties that exist within the "Other" group, which does contain peoples whose experience of and proximity to whiteness varies. Nonetheless, it is striking to note the intermediate position that emerges around the issues of racial politics for the "Other" ethnic categories.

Again, does being part of the wealth elite change your position on these questions? We already know that the wealth elite are, in general, less likely to think Britain is racist, more likely to think former colonies were better off, and more likely to think empire is something to be proud of. But does this vary by ethnic group? White respondents in the wealth elite are less progressive on these issues, but then so too are Asian and Black members of the wealth elite (see Figure 9.7). The difference between the wealth elite and the rest of the elite is similar for white, Asian, and Black elites. Asian and Black members of the wealth elite are more likely to think that colonies are better off than other Asian and Black elites. In this way, they

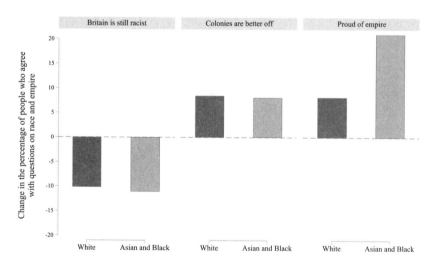

9.7 Elites of colour are not different from other wealth elites on race and empire.
Note: We are comparing the wealth elite to the rest of the elite. We have removed "other ethnicity" from this graph because the numbers were too small to be meaningful.

are not entirely rejecting the racial politics of the white majority wealth elite.

In sum, our survey data suggests that the expanding number of Asian and Black people in the British elite does have the potential to effect political change, but the exact relationship between ethnicity and political views is complicated. We may see less of a clear-cut shift to the left, as we saw with women, and more of a mainstreaming of a critical, even radical, political agenda around topics of race and empire (albeit to differing to degrees depending on wealth). This was a key theme that emerged from our interviews with Asian and Black elites.

Living Racism as a Driver of Change

Racism loomed large in the personal narratives of the elites of colour we interviewed.[30] Nearly every one of them mentioned being the victim of some kind of racist discrimination or harassment at some point in their lives; many mentioned such experiences spontaneously and without prompt. Registering such discrimination is clearly important in its own right, especially in the context of the celebratory political narratives around race promulgated by recent UK governments. Yet these experiences are also noteworthy because they had sometimes been formative, serving as catalysts for the direction of careers.

For some, early life experiences of racism had been the clear driving force in their work. These people, who were often from working-class backgrounds, developed a strong sense of racial injustice when they were young, which had then motivated them to get involved in community activism and, later, to lead organisations dedicated to serving disadvantaged groups and furthering an explicitly anti-racist political agenda. Asif, for example, a British Pakistani lawyer (born 1965–1969), described how the incessant racist attacks he suffered while growing up in a white neighbourhood had been formational:

> I started getting a bit more political—community politics as opposed to party politics. There were various campaigns going on in the area where groups of Asian youths were arrested and prosecuted for criminal offences where they were defending themselves. And having grown up on the end of racist attacks—there was a sense that this is unjust.

Asif subsequently made a career as a specialist in anti-racist campaigning—
"I'm Mr Race. I'm Mr Racism," he told us—and later started an organisation that specialises in pushing for progressive change. A number of people
we spoke to, like Asif, positioned themselves as explicitly oppositional to
existing elites. Yes, they entered positions and spaces of power, but only on
the proviso that they could be a disruptive force that was challenging the
status quo, particularly on race. As Asif explained:

> Everything I've ever wanted to do was to be challenging what the es-
> tablishment represents and the things that it does. [. . .] I recognise
> that by being anti-establishment or [to] challenge the establishment,
> you need to be on an equal and opposite footing. So I want an anti-
> status. I suppose that's what I was trying to do. I thought, yeah, the
> more I am the establishment, the more the establishment's got to listen
> to me, the more I may be able to change things.

For others with careers in established professions like law and medicine,
or in large corporate businesses, the lived experience of racism had also informed their work, but only after they had reached positions of influence.
Here, many had tilted their work specifically towards issues of racial
justice—taking up leadership positions focussed on improving racial diversity or furthering racial equality more broadly. They often reflected on both
the opportunities and constraints of such roles.

Nasir, for example, a Pakistani British policy advisor (1950–1955), acknowledged that his racial identity had enabled him to be more radical in
driving change ("I have been able to argue some very controversial things
just because I'm brown"), but he conceded that this had come at a cost in
terms of his career ("I would say that I have suffered considerably for being
who I am and thinking what I did"). This type of role often acted to accentuate interviewees' sense of their difference within elite organisations.
As Anne (1950–1954, culture) explained, its "sad to say, but I'm the sort of
the go-to person for Black stuff for [the institution], because it feels safe.
They can say, 'Oh, a Black woman did it.'" Proposing controversial organ-
isational initiatives on race, she went on, was often exhausting and came at
an emotional cost. "I'm just not going to do anymore of this sort of Black
pain stuff. I can't do it." She was tired, she told us, of "always having to
retell the same stories."

Not all the people of colour we interviewed had this active orientation to race in their work. A significant minority of those we spoke to—mostly from privileged, private school backgrounds—did not mention race when speaking about their career, except latterly, reflecting on their influence as a role model. Although their careers had often included some diversity and inclusion work, it had not played any decisive role. Instead, these interviewees, like most we explored in detail in Chapter 2, positioned themselves as leaders who had achieved a distinctly meritocratic success. While they often acknowledged that racism existed elsewhere, they distanced themselves from that experience. Deepak (1960–1964, law) is typical in this respect. He described how his degree and the prestige of his barristers' chambers insulated him from racial discrimination:

> That background of having a first from [Oxbridge], being in a really good set of chambers, which then appears at the bottom of court documents and so on, it's a slight leg up. When you appear in court, judges will know to be in my chambers, you'd have to be pretty bright. I have a feeling that I've been slightly insulated from the kind of things that other ethnic minority [people], operating in different fields have experienced. [. . .] One has heard horror stories of female Black [members of the profession] being told by judges or court ushers and so on that they're sitting in the wrong place, assuming that they're a defendant [. . .]. I've never had any experiences like that. I operate in quite a rarefied sphere.

It is important to register, then, that not all Black and Asian interviewees we spoke to foregrounded an explicit political project to address racial inequality in their work, and even among those who did, there was often some tension regarding the nature of that project—particularly among those advocating for a more radical anti-racist agenda and those working more on improving racial diversity within the elite. Either way, the main point we think these narratives underline is that increasing the representation of elites of colour is likely to have some effect on the way race is thought about and discussed in elite spaces.

Yet it is hard to gauge the extent or character of this change, particularly as class and race seemed to intersect in how our interviewees pursued anti-racism. Recall that elites of colour are more likely to think Britain is racist, but the gaps here are not huge—possibly reflecting the fact that they are overwhelmingly recruited from middle-class backgrounds (which seems in our data to tilt people towards the political right). If this continues, the elite may be pulled towards a somewhat more progressive position on race but one potentially less radical than would be the case if elites of colour were drawn more from working-class backgrounds.

The Legacy of Empire

The issue on which we saw the largest differences between white elites and elites of colour was the thorny question of the legacy of empire.[31] Disagreements on this issue have been central in recent public debate, with some calling for a reassessment of Britain's cultural and institutional relationship to the imperial project. Colonial statues have been removed, buildings have been renamed, and many have called for a critical reading of empire to be integrated into the school history curriculum (including prominent efforts to decolonise university curricula).[32] Equally, the pushback to this has been just as fierce, with many insisting this is just the latest incursion of the "woke" political agenda.[33]

Our analysis gives us a number of illuminating angles on the relationship between empire and the British elite. First, our historical analysis of *Who's Who* demonstrates that there has always been a significant group of ethnic minorities in the British elite. As Figure 9.8 shows, around 2 percent of entrants have always been elites of colour or "Other" individuals—even among those born in the nineteenth century. Indeed, the high degree of stability is really the big story. "Elites of colour" have consistently been part of the elite over this whole period but at a low level. But this group has also seen some change. Among the youngest cohorts in our data, 4 percent are people of colour, increasing from 1 percent among those born between 1900 and 1909.

This stable presence of elites of colour might be surprising to some.[34] Certainly, it is at odds with the story of Britain that is commonly promulgated in the news and in British schools.[35] But as a number of historians have demonstrated, the presence of Black and Brown people in the United Kingdom has a long history and, perhaps more importantly, colonised peoples were in fact British citizens and many had senior positions in colonial institutions that warranted inclusion in *Who's Who*.[36] Take, for example, Lt-Gen. Shri Sir Harisinghji. Born to an elite military family, he

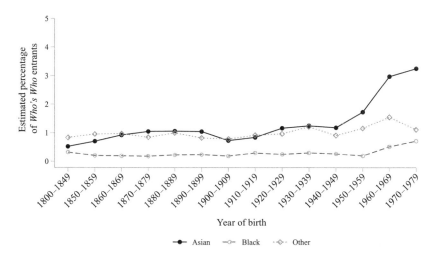

9.8 People of colour have been a small but fairly consistent proportion of the British elite over time.

became a lieutenant-general in the British Army and was a representative of India to the War Cabinet through the latter part of 1944. Or Sir Kanthiah Vaithianathan who went to the prestigious St Joseph's College, Colombo, and then to King's College London. He returned to his home country to work in the Ceylon Civil Service before becoming the first permanent secretary to the Ministry of External Affairs and Defence of an independent Ceylon (now known as Sri Lanka).

We have documented the scale of these links to empire for both the white and the people of colour in *Who's Who* by calculating the proportion of people who had worked in imperial institutions (like the Indian Civil Service). Among those born in the nineteenth century, around 10 percent of those in *Who's Who* had at some point in their careers worked for imperial institutions. The number is slightly higher for elites of colour, suggesting that imperial work was an important channel into the elite for Asian and Black elites. It also provided opportunities for their children and their grandchildren. Indeed, approximately 10 percent of the Asian and Black individuals born before 1940 in *Who's Who* also had a parent in *Who's Who*. This figure is only slightly higher among white entrants.

These connections to the imperial state informed how many of the elites we spoke to think about colonialism today. Here it is worth noting that at a high level, and despite the divisive nature of contemporary public discourse on empire, the most common response to the issue—irrespective of ethnic identity—was to acknowledge both the harms and the benefits wrought by the imperial project. Among many of the elites of colour we spoke with, this ambivalence was rooted in the fact that, as Nasir put it, "I am who I am because of the British Empire." This sense of identity was not straightforward and, as Nasir went on to explain, had many "layers." Thus, "the British came to India and took my ancestors'" empire away from them, subordinated them, and became the new rulers," Nasir explained. At the same time, "if the British had never come to India, I would never be here, I would never be British. So I'm glad to be British, I'm proud to be British. It's who I am."

White interviewees also articulated ambivalence about empire but their reflections tended to have a different tenor, especially those with family links to empire. These interviewees talked of having a "balanced" view of empire but this notion of balance had a defensive feel. They were willing to acknowledge the harms wrought by empire but did so in a depersonalised intellectual way, often via references to books they had read or particular historical moments. And when they spoke about their own family histories, they often emphasised the societal contributions of their ancestors and often explicitly distanced themselves from notions of harm. Thomas (1940–1944, civil servant), for example, insisted that his father was not "putting people in concentration camps" or "shooting protestors." As the director of education in Somaliland and Uganda, his parents had setup the "first girls school" in the country.

Another important difference in these accounts was their orientation to the past. Our white interviewees frequently tried to draw clear distinctions between the past and the present, arguing that it was wrong to interpret colonial history through the prism of modern values:

> You can't use the prism of now [to examine imperialism] any more than you can to the Roman Empire and say how Julius Caesar was, you know, a mass murdering rotter. We are the product of our ages. And there'll be a lot of what we're doing now that future generations say, "How could they have done that?" (sic). (Kevin, 1955–1959, creative).

In this way, there was often a kind of resignation about the immutability of colonial history (the "past is the past," we often heard). And this orientation seemed to be deployed to create a clear separation with the present, to alleviate any culpability. "I don't see why we should be held accountable," Martin (1955–1959, law) argued, "my being British is by happenstance."

In contrast, many of our interviewees of colour (though not all) felt the temporal closeness of empire. They spoke about how its influence lingers on and could be forthright about the political need for a wholescale decolonial political project, including, for some, reparations. As Ashura (1960–1964), a Black British academic whose parents lived through the colonial period in Africa, explained:

> You know there was a certain amount of unpleasantness, should we say, that went along with being the colonised . . . I want to see more radical change in the future because things haven't gone nearly far enough. I think the re-evaluation of the Empire has been long delayed; it's about time that it happened. And I think there's still a lot of sentimental claptrap about the Empire, and a failure to face up to its realities.

Empire has been central to processes of elite formation for white elites just as it has been for Asian and Black elites, and yet the distinct familial experiences of empire across these groups have shaped their perspectives on the imperial project. On this issue, then, changing the composition of the elite very well could impact prevailing attitudes towards empire.

Working towards Racial Justice

Born in the 1970s, Abeni grew up in an upper-middle-class neighbourhood in Nigeria. She was the third generation of graduates in her family and her parents were both successful medical consultants. She was privately educated, at first in Nigeria, before travelling to the United Kingdom to attend a selective, fee-paying boarding school. Despite having top grades and strong work experience, Abeni had to make 150 calls to get her first job in the legal profession, which she attributed to name discrimination. During this period, a recruiter told her that her chosen specialty was "too competitive for a Black woman." She reflected:

> That was the first time I was very, very aware that something wasn't fair. Until then, because I was born to privilege, if I'm honest, I hadn't thought about myself being Black, female, nothing.

She encountered discrimination again after taking a period of maternity leave. "That's the point at which I realised that enough was enough," she said. Over a couple of decades, she built a reputation in her sector advocating for diversity and inclusion. After the death of George Floyd, she recalled, "my whole network reached out to me."[37] She realised she could work more flexibly and earn more as a consultant focused on diversity and inclusion than in her salaried role as a lawyer so she started her own business, eventually becoming a partner in another firm alongside several non-executive roles in other companies.

Abeni's story speaks to many of the themes we have touched on in this chapter. While she had built a successful career in law, like many people of colour making their way in Britain, her career had been pockmarked with repeated experiences of racism. These experiences had a big impact on her politics and her career trajectory, motivating her to pivot towards making racial equality the focus of her professional practice. In this respect, Abeni was not alone. Experiences of discrimination informed the work of many of the people of colour we spoke to, who expressed strong concerns about the degree of racial justice in British society.

What is less clear, however, is what these concerns will mean in concrete policy terms. Even some of those most critical of empire registered ambivalence about removing statues and only a few directly called for reparations. The material politics of decolonisation still needs to be worked out, but the debate will become increasingly prominent as elites from all ethnicities are forced to confront the legacies of colonialism.[38]

Our results also point in intriguing directions for how we think about the relationship between what it means to be white in Britain today and political ideologies more broadly. We want to be careful about over-interpreting the data—we lack evidence pointing to change over time and have only a small number of respondents—but it is striking that people who self-identified as "Other" (and not "White") expressed political preferences that sit between the white majority and elites of colour. This is noteworthy because these are individuals who, in many cases, come from Jewish, Iranian, or Eastern European communities, some of which have experienced discrimination, racism, and even violence at the hands of the British state. And yet, these experiences do not seem to be structuring their responses to the ideology questions in quite the same way that these experiences have influenced our Asian and Black respondents. One way to ground these differences is, as we have alluded to throughout the chapter, in terms of whiteness.[39] Perhaps some of the groups gathered here aligned themselves (albeit not completely nor necessarily consciously) with the white majority as an act of self-preservation against a hostile white majority elite and perhaps this will change over time as we see important realignments within British politics.

Conclusion

Who Rules Britain?

Remember Henry, the corporate lawyer who we introduced at the start of this book? Like so many of our interviewees, Henry strongly rejected the suggestion that he was a member of the British elite. "Complete rubbish" were his exact words.

Now compare Henry with another corporate lawyer, Hugh Peppiatt, who forged a similarly successful career in the City fifty years earlier. These men may have shared similar professional trajectories, but the way they told their stories, the personas they project, were strikingly different.

Henry, in many ways, exemplifies the contemporary yearning for ordinariness; he plays down his privilege, stresses the meritocratic nature of his success, and belittles his influence. Hugh's self-presentation is noticeably different. He breezily recounts his privileged background ("We were very comfortably off. I mean, we had a full-time gardener . . . two maids . . . and, of course . . . a nanny"), delights in his sense of cultural distinction ("I was very, very widely read"), and is quite open about the less-than-meritocratic nature of his trajectory:

Well, then I went to Oxford, which, of course, all of us from what was really a privileged background, we all assumed that if we wanted to, we'd go to Oxford or Cambridge. In those days, there weren't many other universities, well, not ones that we counted—in no doubt a somewhat snobbish way . . . Coming from privileged backgrounds, with anyway enough money, and having been [to] Winchester . . . everything was open to you . . .

Hugh, in other words, exhibits an unapologetic upper-class identity. He is comfortable with, even proud of, his eliteness, and confidently (although not arrogantly) parades his influence.

For many we spoke to, these divergent personas are emblematic of a fundamental change that has taken place in Britain over the last century; from a stuffy, entitled upper class to a down-to-earth, dynamic meritocratic elite. Yet one of the key arguments in this book is that it is all too easy to read these shifts in self-presentation as manifestations of structural change. The reality, as we have shown, is that there is a lot more continuity when it comes to who gets into the elite, and how they get there, than these narratives suggest.

In fact, told another way, Henry and Hugh represent a story of succession. Although they may look and sound different, they directly mirror one another in important ways. Both were brought up in wealthy families; both attended prestigious boarding schools; and both went to Oxford or Cambridge.

Our key argument, then, is that when people like Henry present themselves as ordinary, when they downplay their economic power, when they deflect privilege, they are effectively masking the absence of genuine change and obscuring the very real differences in wealth and opportunity, power and influence, that continue to separate themselves from everyone else.

In this final chapter, we reiterate how we arrive at this conclusion, pulling out the main themes that emerge from our analysis and explaining why we think they should concern everyone living in contemporary Britain. Then we move to outline what policymakers might do about elites, outlining a set of practical policy steps to tackle the link between wealth and elite recruitment, reduce the power of elite schools, equalise Oxbridge, and redistribute power. We end by spelling out why we think our findings matter for scholars of elites.

The Struggle for Ordinariness

It might seem paradoxical but one basic message that emerges from this book is that the elite nowadays do not want to be elite. Or, perhaps more accurately, they do not want others to see them as such. Unlike their predecessors, who occupied influential positions throughout most of the twentieth century and who often luxuriated in a sense of social and cultural distinction, today's most influential people go to significant lengths to position themselves as regular, common, normal, and unspectacular. At some level this is hardly surprising. When the elite are invoked in British public life—by politicians, in the pub, in cultural circles, or in the media—the tone is invariably pejorative. Yet the expressions of ordinariness we uncover here reach far beyond simply resisting the charge of elitism. They are intimately intertwined with how people tell their life stories.

This often begins, as we describe in Chapter 2, with the elaborate, even tortured ways, that the elite dance around or downplay their class origins. Many of the people we spoke to deflected aspects of their upbringing that might signal eliteness—sometimes via "upward-orientated" comparison with more advantaged peers or sometimes by emphasising an extended family history of upward social mobility and meritocratic striving. It is telling, for example, that 43 percent of elites who told us in our survey that they are from working-class backgrounds actually come from professional, middle-class families. We are keen to stress, though, that such subjective understandings of social origin are not necessary cynically strategic, and often reflect real experiences of multigenerational upward mobility or real relational differences in advantage. Yet nonetheless such deflections of privilege reveal something important about the desire to tell an upward story, and to claim a meritocratic legitimacy for one's privileged destination in life.

Claims to ordinariness are also staked via expressions of taste and lifestyle, as we saw in Chapter 3. Here we draw on the fact that, since its inception, *Who's Who* has asked its entrants to describe their recreations, providing a unique window into the changing cultural lifestyles of the British elite and giving us insights into how they perform their cultural selves in public (*Who's Who* is, after all, a public document). Our results reveal that while highbrow culture dominated the cultural palette for most of the twentieth century, contemporary elites now perform a complex dance in relation to taste. Most retain a penchant for highbrow pursuits, but these are now increasingly blended with preferences for more popular or everyday activities such as watching football or films, or spending time with family, friends, and pets. Key to understanding this is the distinction between the private and the public. There is often a tension between the highbrow passions elites describe in anonymised interviews, or communicate in closed elite settings, and the more ordinary cultural pursuits they emphasise in public.

Finally, the quest for normality is forged by counterposing one's own life experience against a distinct vision of the past. Here the prevailing narrative is that the elite institutions our interviewees had traversed in their lifetimes—elite schools, universities, or firms—*used to be* closed or exclusive, but things have changed, and their success is evidence that such settings have become markedly more meritocratic over time.

It (Still) Pays to Be Privileged

There is, however, one central problem with elite narratives of ordinariness and opening up. They simply do not square with empirical reality. In fact, one of the main takeaways from our analysis is that it still profoundly pays to be privileged in Britain. Specifically, we provide the most detailed analysis ever of how Britain makes its elites, interrogating how the propulsive power of family wealth, elite private schools, and Oxford and Cambridge universities has changed over time. And the main picture our results paint, spanning 125 years of elite recruitment, is one of powerful continuity.

This is not to say there has been no change. Chapters 4 and 5 reveal that the propulsive power of a wealthy background and an elite education have been somewhat dented. This is perhaps most significant in the context of Britain's most elite boarding schools—the nine Clarendon Schools which today educate roughly half the number of the elite that they did at the end of the nineteenth century. While these schools once functioned as unimpeachable markers of status, today they must jostle for position in an increasingly complex and competitive school landscape. It is also true that there have been intriguing fluctuations in the fortunes of perhaps Britain's key institutional channels of elite formation: Oxford and Cambridge. These universities too, our analysis shows, struggled for a time to adapt to the shift to formal and competitive educational meritocracy.

Yet despite these changes, our results ultimately underline the maintenance of Britain's main channels of elite reproduction. Some of our statistics in this regard are fairly startling. Since the 1890s, if you hail from the top 1 percent of the wealth distribution, for example, you have consistently been about twenty times more likely to reach the British elite than others of your age. Similarly, and even with a notable decline in their power, the alumni of the nine Clarendon schools are still today fifty-two times more likely to reach the British elite than those who attend any other type of school. And the most recent Oxbridge graduates for whom we have reliable data—that is, those born in the 1960s and early 1970s—were over 250 times more likely to reach the British elite than others born at the same time who did not attend university.

It's worth underlining that this does not mean that the British elite is a closed shop. Some may even be surprised at the degree of openness, considering the historical caricatures of elite reproduction in Britain. Elites are rarely entirely closed and Britain is no exception.[1]

Our interpretation, nonetheless, is that these patterns of elite reproduction are deeply concerning and demand urgent political attention. Certainly, they provide a sobering corrective to those who believe that Britain is becoming, even slowly, a place where, as Theresa May proclaimed when she became prime minister in 2016, you can "go as far as your talents will take you."[2] This really matters. In recent years, key policymakers have shifted their focus away from elites and advocated for an emphasis on social mobility into lower tiers of the labour market.[3] We don't dispute the need for a broader focus. But at the same our results underline how pivotal it is that we continue to tackle the enduring social exclusivity of Britain's elites. Ignoring this simply leaves the most influential individuals dangerously unmoored from public scrutiny.

The Symbolic Market for Ordinariness

The reality of persistent elite reproduction also brings us back to ordinariness. Specifically, if contemporary claims to ordinariness do not reflect a meaningful opening up within the British elite, as many in this book claim, then what exactly do they reflect? Why do extraordinary people so yearn to be ordinary? The answer, we conclude, is that this represents a distinct strategy of impression management, an attempt, as sociologist Jo Littler has noted, to dissolve the very real economic, cultural, and social divisions that exist between elites and everyone else.[4] And, as our results in Chapter 2 and 3 suggest, there is a strong symbolic market for ordinariness; it carries a distinct cultural currency. Elites who successfully convince the general public that they have been risen from a humble background, or have mainstream cultural tastes, are viewed more favourably in a range of important ways.

But this does not necessarily explain why this performance of ordinariness is so marked among the contemporary British elite. Here our tentative argument is that this is connected to the rise in economic inequality that has taken place in recent decades, particularly at the top end of the distribution, and the growing focus on the damage that comes from this gaping divide. Put simply, as elites have pulled away economically, we suspect they have become increasingly insecure about their moral legitimacy in the eyes of the public, and sensitive to public concern that they are aloof, snobbish, and purely self-interested.[5] Our results support this hypothesis, demonstrating that when elites are reminded that they are the beneficiaries of rising inequality, they ramp up efforts to present themselves as culturally ordinary.

There are several reasons, we think, to be concerned about these findings. At a basic level, the illusion of solidarity forged by expressions of ordinariness is dangerous because it obscures very real class inequalities. If the public does not perceive or "feel" inequality, in other words, it may be less motivated to challenge its foundation.

This is also a story about meritocracy. Mindful of Britain's tarnished historical legacy of ascription and of a policy agenda that holds up the upwardly mobile as the "winners" of meritocracy, elites often instinctively reach back to extended family histories to tell an upward story. This, though, contributes to a "meritocratic hubris" among elites and further perpetuates a misplaced belief that resulting inequalities of outcome are fair.[6] If I am just like you and I made it, these elites seem to be saying, then anyone can make it.

While we are certainly not claiming that all expressions of ordinariness are intentionally intended to dupe, our results do suggest that there is often a gap between the private cultural lives of elites and how they choose to present themselves in public. We show, for example, that elites often continue to harbour snobbish sentiments that linger beneath the veneer of carefully chosen popular tastes, and project very different versions of themselves in settings where highbrow culture still has currency. Ordinariness, in short, is bound up with efforts to promulgate two modern myths: that Britain is a meritocracy and that it is culturally egalitarian. Neither, in our view, are entirely true.

Why Elite Reproduction Matters

The value of revealing persisting patterns in who reaches elite positions, as we have done in this book, is not just that it punctures claims to ordinariness and meritocratic legitimacy. It also tells us something fundamental about the elites we get—and specifically how they think and behave. Elite reproduction affects the politics we get in Britain. Our results suggest that the family you were born into, the school you attended, the university you studied at, all leave their mark on what you value, your way of being in the world, and even the kind of society that you want to live in. While scholars and commentators have long proposed a link between social composition and the exercise of power, the empirical evidence has always been thin, and even suggested no such relationship exists.[7] This might be our biggest contribution. In Chapter 7, we interrogate detailed survey data to show that elites drawn from privileged backgrounds have distinct policy preferences and socio-cultural attitudes. Notably, they tilt to the right compared to both other elites and to the UK population at large, whereas elites from working-class backgrounds orient the other way. In Chapters 8 and 9, we show that women and elites of colour also think differently. Women are notably more progressive politically, whereas elites of colour are more radical on the need to address problems of racism and promote decolonial thinking.

Finally, it is also in the realm of politics that we have shown the particular value of digging further to identify a distinct British wealth elite—those with outsized positional and economic power. In Chapter 7, we show that this group also skews significantly to the right politically. This is significant, we show, because these people are more politically active than other elites and able to deploy their wealth to accentuate their influence and power.

These results have potentially important implications—although what you make of them will depend strongly on your own political persuasion. Certainly, they suggest that what is at stake in tackling elite reproduction is not just a question of equality of opportunity. It is also centrally about the sort of politics we want. The story we tell here is not straightforward. It would be naïve to assume that greater diversity will automatically produce a radical reorientation of the ideological centre of the British elite.[8] Yet clearly there are ways in which women, working-class people, and people of colour think differently from the affluent white men, the "somatic norm" as Nirmal Puwar puts it, who have historically dominated the elite.[9] And therefore, as the British elite continue to become more diverse—in terms of gender and race at least—significant political change may be coming.

So What Do We Do about Elites?

Sociologists tend to be better at diagnosing problems than proposing concrete solutions. This is partly a matter of the kinds of findings our research generates. For example, our analysis may indicate that an emphasis on presenting one's self as ordinary obscures the true extent of class inequality, but what policy levers could easily address such complex aspects of identity and self-expression? And even in areas where policy solutions do come to mind and would be more appropriate, such as tackling the mechanisms of elite reproduction, it is worth remembering that there are no silver-bullet solutions. Yet despite these caveats, we believe there are policy options that could be leveraged to produce meaningful change in weakening the link between wealth and elite status, undermining the distortionary power of a handful of elite private schools, opening up access to Oxford and Cambridge, and redistributing power away from those who reach the top of particular professions. In what follows, we propose two ideas to tackle each of these areas—one modest, the other more radical.

Weakening the Link between Wealth and Elite Reproduction

Wealth plays a critical role in producing future elites but, as we have seen, the dramatic equalization of wealth throughout the first seventy years of the twentieth century had a rather modest impact on the relationship between being born into the top 1 percent and entrance into the elite. This is partly because the absolute value of the wealth held by the richest people in the past is not that dissimilar from the amounts held by the richest people today. In 1900, you needed to have about £1m (adjusted for inflation) to be in the top 1 percent of the wealth distribution. In 2000, you still needed roughly £1m. Now, the wealth threshold for the 1 percent did fluctuate in the interim, falling to around ~£600k for the decades just after WWII. Certainly, some of this decline was people hiding their wealth, but some of it did represent a genuine fall in the wealth held by the richest families, and therefore their ability to channel that wealth into the future trajectories of their children. It was in these same decades, as our analysis has shown, that the link between wealth and access to elite positions was at its weakest; suggesting that if we want to weaken the link between wealth and elite destinations, we need to compress the top end of the wealth distribution by bringing the top 1 percent and the 0.1 percent closer to the bottom 90 percent.

One way to do this is so obvious and realisable that it is bizarre it has not been done already. That is reforming Britain's system of property taxes (what are called Council Taxes). In the 1980s, Margaret Thatcher tried to replace Britain's more traditional property tax, based on a proportion of the value of your house, with a flat-rate charge applied to everyone. This highly regressive move prompted riots and eventually contributed to her resignation. The

Conservatives backed down and instead introduced the Council Tax, which was no longer a flat rate but was still highly regressive. The amount of Council Tax you owe is linked to the value of the property you live in, but this is based on the value in 1991, meaning wealthy people living in properties that have appreciated strongly in recent decades often pay a similar rate to homeowners or renters living in much poorer areas. The current system is so distorted that Buckingham Palace (worth around £1bn) is charged less in Council Tax (around £1,828 per year) than 46 percent of all households in England.[10] Following the late Tony Atkinson and the Mirrlees Review, we would recommend a "proportional, or progressive, property tax based on property assessments," basically a return to the form of taxation that existed before and which is similar to how property taxes are levied in the United States.[11] Setting this new tax at around 0.5 percent of property values could raise roughly the same amount of money as the existing Council Tax but do so in a way that falls more heavily on the very wealthy. This could even be more progressive at the top end of the property market, rising to 1.15 percent for very expensive properties (which is the average rate of the property tax in the United States).[12]

One reason why wealth secures elite status is because the wealthy can buy advantages for their children. When people think about addressing wealth inequality, they often turn to inheritance tax, but wealth is actively perpetuating privilege long before people inherit money. This leads us to our second, more radical idea: introduce an annual wealth tax, starting at £2m at a rate of 0.6 percent (not including mortgage debt), which would raise around £10bn per year.[13] Wealth taxes have become increasingly prominent in public debate and are supported by the majority of the UK population.[14] Tax economists also generally agree that societies should be taxing wealth accumulation.[15]

Sceptics point to the fact that wealth taxes have been tried before in countries such as France and Sweden but have largely been repealed since the 1990s. In particular, earlier efforts have not always raised much additional revenue because they have had multiple exemptions or had virtually no fiscal auditing.[16] Part of the reason they have been implemented in this rather toothless fashion is because, as the OECD (Organisation for Economic Co-operation and Development; a think tank for high-income countries) expressed in a 2018 report, policymakers worry wealth taxes will undermine efficiency, risk capital flight, and come with a high administrative burden.[17] There is a danger, in other words, that wealth taxes simply reduce the *appearance* of wealth inequality because the rich either relocate or hide their wealth offshore.[18] Yet evidence suggests that the number of people who move to avoid wealth taxes is negligible and fears about high administrative costs may also be exaggerated, particularly with the advent of digital trace data in recent years.[19] In short, we would push for a wealth tax that would minimise potential behavioural responses among the rich and which would, as Advani and Tarrant argue, "feature a broad base, equal treatment of asset classes, extensive use of third-party reporting, exit charges (or similar) to discourage migration, and robust enforcement procedures, and would be levied at the household level."[20] In practical terms, this means a wealth tax which treats all forms of wealth the same (except one's main residence), uses data provided to tax authorities by banks or other financial institutions, and which continues to tax emigrants for a minimum period after departure.

Wealth taxes are hard to administer but it is important to recognise that this is not the only reason why they have not been implemented. The wealthy tend to strongly resist such taxes, and sometimes do so very proactively.[21] We would argue that this resistance is partly premised on the fact that they know that holding onto their wealth will affect their lives and the lives of their children. In the context of our data, this makes it all the more important that societies try to reduce the gap between the top 1 percent and the bottom 90 percent.

Reduce the Propulsive Power of Private Schooling

One clear driver of elite reproduction is private schools. We think there are two ways Britain could dent the power of these schools. The first, more modest, approach would involve removing the unjustified VAT exemption private schools currently receive for fees.[22] This would automatically increase the costs of attending a fee-paying school without having to go into the complexities of deciding whether a school is a charity or not (removing the charitable status of private schools is another often-cited policy idea).[23]

Beyond this, we would advocate for restricting the proportion of privately educated students accepted to study at Russell Group universities to 10 percent, which is the proportion of people in the UK that have attended a private school at some point in their education.[24] If implemented, this would mean the proportion of privately educated students at Russell Group universities would fall by around 50 percent (currently 20 percent of students at these prestigious universities attended a private school). The impact on admissions would vary across institutions and would be especially large at places like Durham (38.4 percent privately educated), Edinburgh (35.5 percent), Exeter (34.5 percent), Imperial (34.2 percent), and University College London (32.4 percent). Oxford, LSE, and Cambridge would need to make big changes, too (all have around 30 percent).

But why would we want to make it harder for what many perceive as the best schools to send their students to elite universities? Well, even if we do accept that they are "better" (which is not entirely clear), their propulsive power far outstretches what they offer in terms of academic excellence. As we have shown, alumni of the Clarendon Schools remain fifty-two times more likely to reach elite positions than those attending other schools. Their stranglehold on elite recruitment, we believe, is perverse and makes a mockery of the idea that access to elite positions in Britain is meritocratically achieved.[25] Many of the British public agree. Around 50 percent think private schools "harm Britain" because "they reinforce privilege and social divisions, give children from better-off families an unfair advantage and undermine the state school system."[26] One of the reasons the UK cannot loosen the grip of these schools on elite positions is precisely because they are so successful at getting their alumni into elite universities. Access to elite positions today is rarely possible simply because you went to Eton. Attending an elite university has become increasingly important. This is especially true for Oxford and Cambridge but also applies to Russell Group universities. And private schools know it. Introducing this limit in their propulsive power will not eradicate parents' desire for private education, but it would probably dramatically quell demand and direct many parents back to the state sector.

Encouraging families who want private schooling into the state sector, by contrast, could have two advantageous spillover effects. The educational advantages children from affluent backgrounds often bring to schools could positively impact other students and, on top of this, affluent parents would be incentivised to advocate politically for investment in state schools rather than opting out.[27]

This is obviously a radical move and would run up against significant resistance. One crucial objection might come from elite universities. We know they care about widening participation but they want to achieve this goal while still recruiting the best and the brightest. Some may worry this reform would limit their ability to do so. In reality a reform like this is really shuffling students with similar attainment between largely comparable institutions. Some of the private school students now attending Nottingham would go to Essex, for example, while some of the state school students at Essex would go to Nottingham, and we are cautiously optimistic that Russell Group universities would not see a notable difference in "student quality." But even if the "quality" of admitted students declined, would this be a bad thing? It is undoubtedly thrilling to teach brilliant students, but universities are developmental institutions, places where students have their capacities expanded and improved. This reform would re-emphasise that transformative mission of elite universities. Finally, the worry about recruiting the best and the brightest is fundamentally a short-term issue, especially if parents themselves start rejecting private schools. By levelling the playing field in this way, we will start to see more clearly whether some of those students who flourished at private schools really were more able than their peers in the state sector.

This reform would not be a panacea for addressing educational inequality. We know that rich parents already "buy" school quality by purchasing homes in neighbourhoods that give their children a leg up.[28] Our proposal might intensify this process, and therefore would need to be complemented by policies which stop residential sorting from crowding-out low-income kids from good state schools.[29] Despite this, we would maintain that there is also a broader symbolic value to this reform, one which reinforces the intuition that the school you attended should not have a disproportionate impact on your life chances.[30]

Equalising Oxbridge

The status hierarchy that exists between British universities creates perversity throughout the whole of British higher education. Despite this, it is very unlikely that measures seeking to actively reformulate that hierarchy are going to be successful in the near future. In light of this, we propose two linked reforms.

After making notable changes in admissions procedures over the last few decades, Oxford and Cambridge are currently quite effective at making sure their incoming students reflect the demographic coordinates of applicants in terms of gender, ethnicity, and school type. What has improved the situation is the contextual information introduced to the admissions process regarding where applicants went to school, whether they were low income, and where they are from.[31] Yet these contextual datapoints can be rather blunt. Living in a given postcode is no guarantee that the applicant is poor or from a working-class background. Even the measure of low income (whether they were eligible for free school meals) is problematic because a third of eligible families do not use it given it is so stigmatised.[32] Plus, poverty has become less geographically concentrated over time and so these metrics are becoming less reliable when it comes to identifying less advantaged students.[33] To tackle this, the first reform we would propose is for these universities (and we hope others) to start measuring the applicant's socio-economic background (by parental occupation) and to then use this information in decisions about who gets interviewed in much the same way that priority is currently given to those who, for example, received free school meals. Without data on individuals, we simply cannot know whether Oxbridge interviews are putting some students at a disadvantage.[34]

Beyond better measurement, one big issue is who applies in the first place.[35] Only 12 percent of state school students in the North East who achieve three As or above in their A levels apply to Oxford or Cambridge. By contrast, for London, it is 43 percent.[36] These differences in application rates are a crucial component of geographical inequalities in the student body, as the admission rate of applicants from the North East is about the same as those from London. We therefore recommend removing the applications process to Oxbridge entirely for academically able students. Instead, we propose a system in which these two universities recruit from among the best-performing students in different parts of the country. This would involve putting the top 5 percent of students into a lottery and then allowing Oxford and Cambridge to randomly select students from this group.[37] This could even be combined with the admissions reform advocated above. It would simply require Oxbridge to split the lottery into two pools—one for the privately educated and one for everyone else—and then admit by random selection the number of students from each pool needed to meet their respective allocation (for example, 10 percent of places can go to private school alumni). This would both return Oxford to the kind of regionally sensitive admissions procedure that it used before the nineteenth century while also undermining the propulsive power of private schools.[38]

Redistribute Power

All of the reforms we have described so far have been concerned with addressing access to the elite. But a broader issue that flows from our analysis (especially our identification of the wealth elite) is who has power in Britain and whose voices matter. Our wealth elite certainly have more influence than those who have neither wealth nor position and if we care about ensuring that our politics is not unduly influenced by those in the wealth elite, then we need to find ways to directly incorporate a more diverse set of perspectives (including working-class voices) in decision-making. This requires rebalancing the power between the positional elite (including the wealth elite) and others in society. We suggest two (admittedly more radical) ways to achieve this goal.

First, we propose that workers be added to corporate boards.[39] Thomas Piketty has suggested that 50 percent of the seats on a firm's governing body be granted to workers. This is clearly ambitious, but any move in this direction would directly address the presence of working-class voices in these decision-making settings. Plus, ideally, we would want to see voting rights connected to capital investment altered so that it diminishes the power of large shareholders in major corporations. However, we stress that for these reforms to really be meaningful they need to be embedded in wider reforms which reinvigorate collective bargaining and give more power to workers.[40]

Second, we would replace the House of Lords with a randomly selected senate.[41] The political theorist Hélène Landemore has argued that democracies should operate through a form of "democratic reasoning" that is not dependent on "individual ability" and more concerned with "the cognitive diversity of the individuals taking part in the decision."[42] A senate designed in this way would make this is a reality. There has been scepticism that more egalitarian decision-making processes like these would work in practice, but it turns out that citizens do want to deliberate about policy *if* the possibility of meaningful deliberation is offered. In fact, it is those who are typically most turned off by standard party politics who want to deliberate in this deeper way.[43] Moreover, when meaningful space for discussion is offered, ordinary people are capable of high-quality deliberation in part because they are able to see through "elite manipulation" and overcome polarization.[44] There is even evidence that random selection produces good policy outcomes.[45] But beyond the instrumental argument, there is also the idea that democracies should work hard to ensure that everyone has the chance to become a politician, which is simply not practically true today. In any event, creating a mechanism that encourages the selection of political leaders who represent the views of the wider population has particular value in representative democracies and will only bolster the currently embattled legitimacy of democratic institutions.[46]

Conclusion

Why This Matters for Elite Studies

We have tried to write this book in a manner that appeals to a wide range of different readers. Yet we also want our results to inform academic debates about elites. It is to our contributions in these areas that we now turn. Non-academic readers can easily skip this section if they wish, but equally we hope all readers will stay with us. Academic discussions about elites can be dense but, ultimately, they address questions we think everyone invested in this area is interested in.

The Cultural Currency of Ordinariness

We are by no means the first scholars to argue that contemporary elites position themselves as ordinary.[47] There is a rich literature in this area. However, we move this work forward in two key ways. First, we use a longitudinal qualitative lens to show that this was not always the case. While others may have gestured in this direction, this is the first study that we know of that has empirically captured this shift in elite identity—both in terms of self-presentation and taste. Second, and perhaps more importantly, we address the question of why elite ordinariness actually *matters*. Specifically, we show that there is a symbolic "market" for ordinariness; that the general public are more likely to favour elites who they see as down-to-earth, upwardly mobile, or culturally ordinary. Again, this phenomenon has been detected in a few other pioneering qualitative and experimental studies, but we are the first to demonstrate that this "market" extends to a nationally representative sample of the UK population.[48] Our analysis is not without limitations. The vignettes we deploy are stylised and don't necessarily mirror social reality, and it is worth remembering that in real social interactions performances of ordinariness often fail and can even backfire as signals of phoniness or inauthenticity. Nonetheless, we think our analysis provides a useful empirical platform for others to further interrogate not just the phenomenon of elite disidentification, but how it can actively obscure divisions between elites and wider publics.

Reviving and Refining the Sociology of Elite Recruitment

We think our results also speak to current debates on social mobility and specifically the intergenerational reproduction of elites. Such work, known as the "sociology of elite recruitment," is experiencing a revival and we hope

235

this book can contribute to this current. Our main offering here is empirical.[49] Martialling a range of unusual and detailed longitudinal data sources, our results underline the fundamental maintenance of Britain's main channels of elite reproduction. To be clear, the power of certain elite schools has waned to a degree and the centrality of Oxford and Cambridge has ebbed and flowed. But at a very basic level the durable link between wealth and elite reproduction, as far as our data allows us to see it, undermines any strong claims that Britain's elite is—even slowly—becoming representative of the population it represents. Finally, in showing these trends, we demonstrate the power of a more *refined* approach to elite recruitment.[50] While large-scale studies of elite reproduction tend to rely on broad measures of social origin, such as parental occupation, type of schooling, or type of university, the data we deploy here allows us to mine down to more granular measures of *elite* origin; growing up in the *very top* of the wealth distribution, going to a *specific* elite private school, and attending a *particular* prestigious university.[51]

This type of data, in turn, allows us to see the profound importance of precise channels of elite recruitment and the cumulative advantages that accrue to those who pass through more than one. In the sociology of education, an extensive body of work documents how elite schools and universities act as incubators of social and cultural capital.[52] However, this literature sometimes neglects the potential duality of such institutions, whereby individuals entering from specific places—such as elite secondary schools—may be better situated to take advantage of opportunities once inside.[53] As our results indicate, Oxbridge may act as an elite switchboard for all, but their propulsive power is greatly enhanced if one is doubly consecrated by a Clarendon School.

Who Elites Are to What They Do

Our emphasis on how elites think, and what elites do, rather than simply who they are (what academics call "prosopography"), will—we hope— interest elite scholars in political sociology and political science. We think our data fills a conspicuous gap here; we don't know of any large-scale studies examining the policy preferences and social attitudes of the British elite as a whole, and only a handful of studies elsewhere in the world.[54]

Moreover, our substantive findings in this area also have implications. For a long time, scholars have hypothesised a connection between patterns of elite reproduction and particular political ideologies, but the evidence supporting this claim was weak.[55] In this book, we have shown that elites recruited from traditional, privileged channels do indeed have distinct preferences. Yet many unanswered questions remain. In particular we do not know whether the relationships we have documented between schooling or wealth and political ideology are stable over time.

The Sociology of Elites as a Sociology of Class

There is a risk that the current resurgence of sociological interest in elites takes place at the expense or erasure of a wider sociology of class. This risk manifests in two ways. First, there is arguably something inherently spectacular and alluring about elites. At times it feels like everyone—social scientists included—have a kind of prurient fascination with the wealthy, the influential, and the powerful. But this seduction can be a distraction from other kinds of intellectual work that is ethically more complicated (studying up is less ethically fraught than studying down the class hierarchy) but equally important.[56] Second, researching any group can lead to a kind of alignment with that group, and this is particularly acute when it comes to academics studying elites—especially two professors from prestigious universities.[57]

We want to be clear that we see the sociology of elites as most effective when it is embedded in, and in dialogue with, the sociology of class. This should play out in at least two ways. First, studying elites allows sociologists to return to a vision of class that explicitly considers the domination of the working class by an elite.[58] The middle classes may be more numerous and involved in processes of domination and exploitation, but their degree of power in these relations is arguably far weaker than the elite.[59] After all, in recent years it is elites who suppressed wages, who undermined trade unions, and who implemented cuts to social security, all decisions that fundamentally and often disproportionately affected the lives and the power of working-class people.[60] Second, studying elites historically also uncovers the way that social relations between elites and the class structure are far from stable.[61] Technological, economic, and political shifts have altered how elites relate to the working class. The decline of deference in the 1950s and 1960s produced a realignment within the class structure which has then been combined with greater inequality since the late 1970s to produce the symbolic market for ordinariness and the pressure to deflect privilege.[62]

These shifting class relations matter because they are a response to higher inequality without being a solution to it. This desire to appear ordinary, in other words, is politically salient because fostering cultural connection can very effectively mask the very real economic, cultural, and social divisions that separate elites from the rest of society.

Eton's Failure

On 13 June 2023, just days after Boris Johnson had resigned from parliament in the wake of the "Partygate" scandal, a short and brutally damning letter was published by the London *Times*.[63] Entitled "Eton's Failure" and penned by John Claughton, a Master of Eton from 1984 to 2001, the letter offered a public apology for the school's role in producing a national elite fundamentally unfit for purpose. Recognising that Eton has and likely will continue "to educate the global elite," Claughton argued that "its most important mission will be to ensure that its pupils are saved from the sense of privilege, entitlement and omniscience that can produce alumni such as Boris Johnson, Jacob Rees-Mogg, Kwasi Kwarteng, and Ben Elliot and thereby damage a country's very fabric." "Sadly," he concluded, "I failed in that purpose."

In many ways Claughton's intuition is correct. As we have shown, schools like Eton and their old boys continue to have a grossly outsized advantage in reaching the top of British society. And while it is not for us to say whether this "damages" the "fabric" of Britain, we have certainly shown that these schools, by recruiting the children of the very rich, are predisposed to produce alumni who mingle socially conservative politics with a sense of entitlement.

Dismantling these dominant channels of elite recruitment will, however, take far more than altering their character. This has been attempted before and while the power of Britain's elite institutions has not gone unchallenged, they have traversed the last two centuries with remarkable ease. Their continued success is partly due to an error in how we have tried to tackle entrenched privilege in the United Kingdom. For too long, we have hoped that we could weaken channels of elite recruitment by lifting up the bottom. We hoped that if we made everyone richer or that if we gave everyone the chance to go to school or university, we could uncouple privilege and opportunity. But this hasn't worked and we would argue that it cannot work. Lifting up the bottom will do little to undermine elite reproduction in a setting where the wealthy can turn out meritorious children. Paradoxically, the most striking impact of focussing on the disadvantaged appears to be that elites today feel the need to articulate their connection and proximity to ordinary people, and tell the story of their success as though they were the beneficiaries of reforms aimed at opening up British society.

But the continuation of the status quo is not inevitable.[64] We have seen elite institutions become more open to women and subsequently seen them push for greater equality. We are also starting to see, albeit slowly, more people of colour in the elite and with that, notable changes in how elites think about race and empire. This is laudable but not enough. Changing the elite will require changing the set of institutions that produce the elite. Such reforms may be unpopular, not least because many of these elite institutions inspire reverence and awe, but this does not mean they are sacrosanct.

We need to undermine the power of private schooling because educational institutions that largely cater to the wealthy will always inculcate a "sense of privilege, entitlement and omniscience." We need to reform admissions at Oxbridge because the people in power thirty years from now should not be determined by A level results and interviews with Oxbridge dons. And we need to reduce wealth inequality not because it is wrong for parents to want the best for their kids, but because, to borrow from the legendary philosopher G. A. Cohen, we need to make it harder for wealthy families to indulge in inequality-generating inclinations that are harmful to society at large.[65] If we don't do these things, we will instead be consigned to the pernicious cosplay of an elite masquerading as common people.

Methodological Appendix

In this appendix we set out to provide an honest and transparent account of how our seven-year multi-method longitudinal research design unfolded. We also address a number of more technical and conceptual issues, including how our own backgrounds affected the research process, the various statistical techniques we used in our analysis, how we conducted interviews, our approach to confidentiality, and the key methodological limitations of the study.

Elites Critiquing Elites: Why Who We Are Matters

Some readers may consider our analysis in this book a little rich considering our own fairly elite positions within UK academia. We are mindful of the need to reflect on how our own social backgrounds impacted the research in this book. In some ways we share many important characteristics. We are both white male professors at two of Britain's most elite universities. This privileged position variously affected this research.[1] No doubt it helped smooth access to survey and interview participants, and it may have been central to the decision of the *Who's Who* team to share their data with us in the first place. Certainly, many respondents were keen to mention in emails and during interviews that they were alumni of Oxford or LSE. Our own positions, then, acted as exactly the kind of elite signal we have analysed in this book, and we are aware that many of our participants may not have agreed to take part if we were more junior, employed at different institutions, or not white men. We have directly benefited, in short, from the mechanisms we seek to critique.

It is also likely that our positions and profiles, and those of the other interviewers who worked on the project with us—Katie Higgins, Eve Worth, and Vlad Bortun—affected the interview findings we generated. For example, the fact that we are all white British or white other may have restricted the stories that interviewees of colour felt able to tell.[2] Similarly, our profiles as academics with a reputation for doing critical work on elite reproduction may have elicited a particular desire among interviewees to distance themselves from eliteness, or emphasise the meritocratic nature of one's success. We do not see this kind of dynamic necessarily as a limitation, however, as it still reveals something important about how elites seek to be seen by other elites.

Yet despite these important similarities, we are also different in significant ways, with unique class backgrounds and personal orientations to the British elite.

Sam is from a privileged upper-middle-class family. He was brought up in a wealthy area of Bristol and while he was growing up his dad worked as an economist and his mum as a social work lecturer. Many of the themes in this book speak directly to his own lived experience. Growing up in a family at the top end of the wealth distribution, Sam's life and career has undoubtedly been shaped by the insulation of parental wealth. His parents supported him during several unpaid internships at newspapers in his early twenties, and provided £50k to help him and his wife put down a deposit on their first flat. Sam also attended an elite HMC private school, Bristol Grammar School, from the ages of 11 to 16. While Sam has discussed elsewhere the role his schooling played as a catalyst for a career writing critically about class inequality, the most relevant point here is that like others interviewed in this book, he has always felt some embarrassment and discomfort mentioning his schooling in public, occasionally even omitting it from certain narrations of his biography.[3]

Aaron's background is more complicated. For a portion of his childhood he was brought up by a single mother in Essex and lived in poverty. They were homeless for a time, ran out of electricity periodically, and often relied on the generosity of friends and family. By the time he finished secondary school, his mum had retrained to become a teacher, and around this time she married a financial advisor who influenced Aaron's career trajectory. Aaron attended a comprehensive school (FitzWimarc) in Essex until 16 and then a grammar school for sixth form, but only passed one of his A levels. He worked various routine jobs until his early twenties before deciding to do an Access Course, which got him into the University of Essex. His changing class background no doubt helped him successfully apply for jobs at elite universities and yet, at the same time, working in these universities has sometimes left him feeling insecure and unsettled.

Analysing *Who's Who*

What we describe as *Who's Who* is actually two separate but connected data sources: (1) *Who's Who is* the current directory of every individual included in the published version of the book, consisting of around 39,434 short biographies.[4] This represents approximately 0.05 percent of the current UK population (or 1 in every 2,000 people).[5] When a person in *Who's Who* passes away, their record is transferred into (2) *Who Was Who.* We combined these datasets and treated them as one, referring to it collectively as *Who's Who.* Together, these two datasets contain 142,995 records.

A nontrivial number of individuals are known by two or more names and therefore have multiple entries (for example, name changes due to marriage). We excluded duplicate records (identified using a matching algorithm) and retained only those with full and current (or latest available) information for each individual. There is also some missing data. For example, a small number do not provide their year of birth; we removed these individuals from our cohort analysis. This gives us a final sample of 124,939 individuals (including 32,613 in the current version of *Who's Who*).

Once we had collected the data, we had to decide how to analyse it. We knew that time would be central to the story we wanted to tell, but there were some features of *Who's Who* that limited how we could include time in our analysis. We wanted to include current entrants, and so this stopped us from using age at death. We were interested in the year in which people were first included in *Who's Who,* but this was only available for recent cohorts. This pushed us towards *birth* cohorts, which is what we use for most of the analyses in this book, focussing on those born between 1830 and 1979. This allows us to cover over a century of British society, ranging from approximately 1897 (when the oldest people in our sample would have been about 67) to the present day. Cohorts reflect the formative effects of exposure to social events that persist over time.[6] We define cohorts as five-year periods, for example, 1930 to 1934 and 1895 to 1939, and sometimes as ten-year periods. We take this approach to maximize the sample size for each cohort and to smooth out any year-on-year fluctuations. The smallest cohort contains 1,397 individuals, and the largest contains 5,773. Most co-horts (twenty out of twenty-eight) have more than 4,000 individuals. We restricted our analysis to these years because the number of individuals born before 1830 and after 1979 is smaller (fewer than 1,000 individuals) and therefore less statistically reliable.

One of the reasons *Who's Who* is so interesting is that it contains lots of information that is almost completely missing from other data sources. This includes the schools and universities people attended, and their recreations. When people receive their *Who's Who* form, it is usually partially filled out based on publicly available information. The entrant is then able to update it, filling in any blank spaces. Entrants are specifically asked for these pieces of information but this does not mean that everyone completes it all. We therefore do have missing data and we touch on this where appropriate below.

Schools

We categorise schooling into six groups: (1) Clarendon Schools (cur-rently around 0.19 percent of school pupils age 13 to 18), (2) private schools in the Headmasters' and Headmistresses' Conference (HMC) (currently 2.3 percent of all pupils), (3) other private schools (currently 7 percent of all pupils), (4) any other school, (5) the twelve most elite girls schools, and (6) the private schools that are members of the Girls School Association. The Clarendon Schools are the nine male-only schools most synonymous with the term "old boys."[7] The HMC schools constitute a wider network of around 200 schools (although the number has changed somewhat over time), largely male-only (including the Clar-endon Schools).

We derive a list of other private schools from two sources: (1) the cur-rent list of registered private schools in the United Kingdom and (2) avail-able histories of previously private schools. This group is less clearly defined because school status has changed over time for many schools.

We choose the elite girls schools in our dataset based on their success at sending their graduates to Oxford and Cambridge.[8] We focussed on the top twelve schools because we wanted to create a group of girls schools that educate a similar number of students to the nine male Clarendon Schools—approximately 6,000 pupils.

We then plotted the proportion of people in *Who's Who* born in specific cohorts that attended one of these types of school. These time-series plots allow us to narratively explore changes in elite recruitment.

To formally assess changes in the composition of *Who's Who* between cohorts, we estimated structural break models for each school type.[9] A structural break represents a durable change in the social processes producing a trend in, for example, GDP or anything that can be measured over time. We used endogenous techniques to detect structural breaks, where the algorithm uses only the data to detect the breakpoints. As Bai and Perron explained in their development of these models, methods testing for multiple structural breaks therefore assume the timing and number of structural breaks are unknown a priori and are ideal for testing "the effectiveness of policy changes" by comparing "the estimated break date with the effective date of a policy change."[10] This does not mean we are testing the impact of specific reforms; instead, we are searching the data *inductively* for shifts.

We used annual data (140 observations) with a three-year moving average to estimate these models. Following the applied econometric literature, we stipulated in all models that the minimal number of observations between structural breaks would be twenty-one years, which represents a trimming percentage of 15 percent. This ensures that estimated break points are not random noise but significant shifts in the series. There are more than 12,000 possible combinations for each time series; we selected the best-fitting model according to the Bayesian information criterion and the residual sum of squares.

Universities

We followed a similar procedure for universities, focussing on three types of university: 1) Oxford or Cambridge, collectively known as Oxbridge, 2) London-based Russell Group universities, composed of the London School of Economics, King's College London, University College London, Queen Mary, and Imperial, and 3) Russell Group universities outside of London, which are the universities of Birmingham, Bristol, Cardiff, Durham, Edinburgh, Exeter, Glasgow, Leeds, Liverpool, Manchester, Newcastle, Nottingham, Queen's in Belfast, Sheffield, Southampton, Warwick, and York. To conduct this analysis we collected statistics on the size of these universities over time using archival sources.[11]

Calculating Risk Ratios

In the text we often say that one group is five times more likely than another group to get into the elite. When we use this phrase we are really talking about risk ratios. These are easy to understand. If 10 percent of group A get into the elite and 5 percent of group B get into the elite, then group A is twice as likely to get into the elite. Calculating risk ratios requires four pieces of information. The number of people in group A and group B and the number of people in group A and group B who get into the elite. *Who's Who* can tell us the proportion of the elite who attended a certain school or university, but it does not have information on how many people went to a particular school or university. In other words, to answer the questions most readers really care about (how much more likely are some people to get into the elite) we needed to compare the people in *Who's Who* to an underlying population drawn from census data and other archival sources. This allowed us to calculate these risk ratios. The underlying population we refer to varies depending on the analysis in question—as we make clear in the text—but broadly speaking we used one of two approaches. The most common is the birth cohort, where we compare the people in a particular socio-demographic group to the rest of the population born in that period. When we are looking at the chances of being in the latest edition of *Who's Who*, we compare recent entrants to the over-35 population. We do this because very few people in *Who's Who* are under age 35 (around 0.6 percent of current members) and this is commonly considered the age at which occupational trajectories solidify.[12] More details on these analyses can be found in our paper on schools, "The Decline and Persistence of the Old Boy," although note that in this earlier paper we use odds ratios, which is a similar but slightly different approach.[13]

Recreations

We analysed the recreations data using two different methods. First, we used dictionary methods to identify the proportion of people born in a given cohort who reported participating in a particular activity by directly counting the number of times certain terms were reported. To do this, we began by focussing on words used more than 100 times across all individuals. We then looked at the main trends among these commonly cited terms, identifying three large clusters of recreations, or cultural modes (what we call "aristocratic," "highbrow," and "ordinary") that share similar trajectories across time and accord with historical and sociological literature on elite cultural consumption (hunting, shooting, and polo, for instance, were clustered in "aristocratic," the arts, theatre, opera, and classical music in "highbrow," and family, friends, football, and pets in "ordinary"). The vast majority of entrants used at least one of the key words coded in this analysis (for more information on our hand-coding procedure, see the paper we published on this topic in *American Sociological Review*).[14]

There are several limitations to dictionary methods. First, although our analysis covers a high proportion of all words used, it does not categorise every one of them (words like Wittgenstein, skipping, and portacenare, which appeared fewer than 100 times, fell outside our categorization). We may thus overlook patterns in the data that exist beyond our hand-coded categories. Second, dictionary methods may struggle to reveal changes in entrants' *combination* of recreations because they ignore the relationship between words. That is, by focusing on "shooting" we may fail to capture how this term is used in relation to other activities, such as "sailing" and "golf," which together may represent a distinct mode of culture.

To address these issues, we turned to a second method—a semi-automated content analysis procedure (ReadMe)—to re-examine the trends in how *Who's Who* entrants report their recreations over time.[15] Here we initially hand-coded 600 entries, marking whether respondents reported interests in our aristocratic, highbrow, or ordinary categories. We then recorded all possible combinations of these categories; for example, a respondent may blend highbrow activities ("the arts") and ordinary ones ("spending time with my family"). Once completed, we plugged the hand-coded entries into a machine learning algorithm that then read the rest of the entries and calculated the proportion of entries (within a margin of error) in each single or combined category. We validated this method by testing how accurately it estimated our coding framework. To do this, we hand-coded an additional 600 entries and used the first set of hand-coded entries to predict the second set. ReadMe was very successful, predicting the proportions to within a few percentage points of the hand-coded results. We then again used the first set of hand-coded entries to calculate the proportion of all entries in each category for entrants who turned 20 in a given period (1850 to 1859, 1860 to 1869, . . . , 1980 to 1989).

Surveying the Elite

Who's Who contains lots of rich information but it does not tell us everything we would want to know. In particular, we were keen to understand a little more about entrants and their political preferences. Fortunately, the publishers of *Who's Who* kindly agreed to send a survey out on our behalf to all the current entrants for whom they had an email address. *Who's Who* usually communicates with entrants via email, but understandably it did not want to share those personal email addresses with us. We therefore created a survey, with the help of research assistant Asif Butt, which the organization then emailed out.

The survey helped us collect data missing from *Who's Who*: ethnicity, parental occupation, and subjective perception of class identity (both now and early in life). We then asked a series of attitudinal questions which were largely drawn from other surveys conducted on nationally representative populations or which are commonly used to describe the UK population. Most of these came from the British Social Attitudes survey or YouGov polls. The reason we took this approach is because we wanted to be able to compare the people in our sample to the rest of the British population. Some of the questions we asked were not in the national surveys and in these instances, we commissioned YouGov to collect new data for us so that we had comparable data.

We began data collection in mid-March 2022 and closed it in mid-October of the same year. We had responses from 4,075 people (a response rate of 17.4 percent) and, after removing those who finished less than 80 percent of the survey, we had a sample size of 3,160 (13.5 percent).

In Figure A.1 we compare the demographic characteristics of *Who's Who* with the demographic characteristics of the respondents in our survey. The sample is not a perfect mirror of the underlying population but it is not radically different and this gives us confidence that the people who responded to our survey are not unrepresentative of the wider group within *Who's Who*.

Survey Experiments

Around 54 percent ($n = 1,722$) of the people who responded to our survey told us that we could contact them again. In the spring of 2023, we sent another online survey, but this time included some short experiments. We sent the survey to 1,399 people and 716 responded, a response rate of

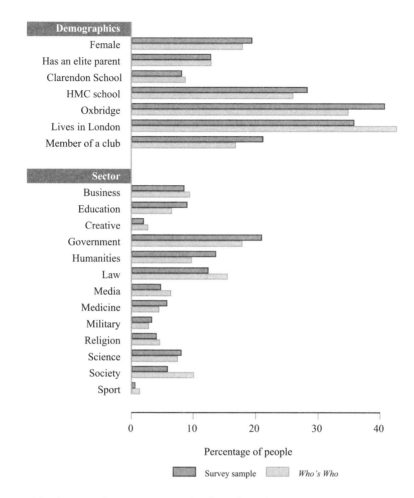

A.1 The demographic composition of *Who's Who* and survey respondents.

51 percent. These experiments were intended to explore whether elites, like the rest of us, are subject to certain kinds of bias. They were relatively simple and only involved two options. Sometimes this was a treatment and control, while others compared two treatments. We describe each of these below.

Status quo bias: Most people exhibit status quo bias, a propensity to prefer decisions that don't involve change. We tested status quo bias in two ways. First, we used a question developed by Sheffer and colleagues, which asks people to imagine they are a government minister who has to choose between two economic policies.[16] One plan is to keep growth high and to run a high deficit. The other is to reduce growth and lower the deficit. The only difference between the two scenarios is which one is presented as the status quo. That is, do you want to *keep* growth and the deficit high / low or do you want to do something different?

Status quo bias with self-interest: We also ran an experiment which explored whether self-interest would alter the degree to which people favoured the status quo. We asked our respondents to:

> Imagine there is a CEO who has to make a difficult decision. The share price of his company has plummeted because a negative press story led to a fall in consumer confidence. The CEO has to decide between two courses of action.
>
> Action 1: Typically, when the share price has fallen in the past, the senior management team has drawn up plans to buy supplies from lower quality providers and strategically reduce some salaries to save money. When these plans have been implemented before, this decision has temporarily reduced the firm's debt because of lower costs. One other implication of this potential plan is that, in the short run, there is a chance it increases the dividends for shareholders, including board members.
>
> Action 2: Another option, which has been proposed in light of this crisis, would involve buying supplies from higher quality providers and strategically increasing some salaries to boost productivity. The expectation is that this plan would temporarily increase the firm's debt because of higher costs. One possible consequence of this plan is that there is a chance it temporarily reduces the dividends for shareholders, including board members.

The other version of this vignette flipped the order, changing the action that was presented as the status quo option.

Sunk cost bias: Next we considered sunk cost bias. A sunk cost is a cost that has already been incurred and is thus non-recoupable. Sunk cost bias is the propensity to take account of sunk costs in current decision-making. For our purposes, we were interested in whether people would be willing to continue funding a government programme that is not working. In previous work, there is good evidence that people will invest more money into an existing failing policy if the sunk cost (the money already invested in the program) is larger.[17] We wanted to explore this sunk cost bias in a slightly different way to see whether the degree of sunk cost bias varied depending on the policy context. We presented one of the following two scenarios and asked respondents to make a decision (the parts in bold are the aspects of the vignette that varied):

Five years ago the government **[reduced capital gains tax in order to foster more investment and incentivise businesses to increase productivity through funding research and development]** // **[implemented a retraining program that provides income support to people who are out of work while they learn new skills]**. Although costing £500 million and increasing borrowing, **[this reduction in capital gains]** // **[this program]** was projected to eventually fully cover the lost revenue.

The **[policy]** // **[program]** is now about to end, and it turns out that after five years, the return has been only £300 million. That is, £200 million less than what was originally projected. The government department running the program has now asked to extend the tax change by a year, costing another £100 million of government funds, in order to provide **[additional encouragement to business to invest more in research and development]** // **[encouragement to people still trying to find work to get jobs in their chosen field]**.

The department's officials project that, by the end of the year, these measures will recover the remainder of the original investment of £200 million, plus return the additional £100 million asked for.

We then asked people whether they would accept the proposal for re-investment.

Desert Island Discs *and the salience of inequality:* We also asked survey respondents to imagine they were going on BBC *Desert Island Discs* and that they needed to pick a music track and a book. Broadcast almost every week since around 1942,[18] the show's format is straightforward. Each week a "castaway"—usually a noteworthy person—is asked to choose eight songs or pieces of music they would take with them if they were to be stranded on a desert island.

In the spirit of the show, we asked our survey respondents to tell us one music track and one book they would choose if they were asked to appear on the show. Before we asked these questions, we randomly assigned half of respondents another question. This was supposed to increase the salience of inequality and highlight their privileged economic position. We focussed on this because researchers have found that people will moderate their tastes to appear less highbrow when the reason they are better off is perceived to be the result of pecuniary motivations.[19] We tried to observe whether priming people to think about the salience of inequality and their position in the income and wealth distribution would elicit a similar kind of response.

Performing Ordinariness in an Online Profile

We included a further question on this second survey which asked the following:

> A close friend of yours was just appointed as the CEO of a FTSE 250 company in the UK. She has been asked to write an online profile that will be shared via email with all of the company's employees so that they can get to know her a bit better. Your friend asks you for advice about what she should talk about in the profile.

We then asked respondents to select from the options below what they thought the person should include in their profile:

- She grew up in a mining village where her grandfather worked in the pits.
- Her father was a headteacher.
- She won a partial scholarship at a private school.
- She is a Gold Patron of the Tate Modern in London.
- She performs the violin in an orchestra.
- She loves long walks with her cocker spaniel.
- She enjoys romantic comedies.

This aimed to see whether our elites recognise a symbolic market for ordinariness in the way they think about their own and their friends' public self-presentation.

A Note on Statistical Tests

In some places in the text, usually in the context of our survey experiments, we report a *p*-value. These are not the most intuitive statistics to understand, but the key thing to know is that most researchers would treat *p*-values less than 0.05 as evidence that the difference we are observing between two groups is unlikely to be explained by the idiosyncrasies of the particular people who participated in this experiment. When we run statistical tests, we are usually trying to understand differences between *all of the people* in two or more particular groups (for example, men and women in the elite). But we can rarely ask everyone in those groups to answer our questions and so we usually only ask a few of them (that is, we ask a sample of the men and women in the elite). The assumption we make is that the people we spoke to are pretty similar to the people we did not speak to. The problem is that the people who actually respond to a survey on any given day may be different in important ways from the people who do not respond, and this means that if we had sent the survey out on a different day, the results could be slightly different. This variation between possible samples of the underlying population means that we cannot be sure the differences we are seeing in our data reflect the "true" differences we would have seen if we could have asked everyone who is in those groups. The *p*-value tells us the probability that we would see the result that we do in our data if the true difference in the underlying population was really 0. If the *p*-value is really low (for example, less than 0.05), then we might conclude that it is very unlikely that we would see the same results if the true difference was 0 and thereby conclude that there is some meaningful difference between men and women in the elite.

How We Conducted Interviews

We complemented these surveys with a total of 214 interviews. To aid our longitudinal analysis, these were organised into four birth cohorts (1900–1920; 1921–1940; 1941–1960; 1961–present). We conducted at least thirty interviews in each cohort.

Seventy interviews, predominantly those in the two earliest birth cohorts, were taken from the *National Life Stories* archive at the British library.[20] Here we matched all individuals in the archive who were also included in *Who's Who* before selecting seventy interviewees that reflected the demographic coordinates of the underlying *Who's Who* data.

An additional 144 interviews were conducted by ourselves and our post-doctoral researchers Eve Worth, Katie Higgins, and Vladimir Bortun between November 2021 and June 2023. The vast majority of this sample was drawn from the 1,722 people who responded to the survey described above and who, in the survey, indicated that they would be willing to be interviewed.

The sampling strategy for both sets of interviews aimed to reflect the underlying demographic coordinates of *Who's Who*. However, we also sampled theoretically in a number of areas to capture the experience of particular social groups that emerged as salient in our quantitative analysis. In this way, we conducted at least twenty interviews with the following groups; elites from working-class backgrounds (featured in Chapter 2), men educated at Clarendon Schools (Chapter 5), those whose parents were in the top 1 percent of the wealth distribution (Chapter 4), Oxbridge graduates (Chapter 6), Black British and Asian British elites (Chapter 9), and those in the wealth elite (that is, those in the top 1 percent of the wealth distribution themselves).

Table A.1 provides details of the demographic coordinates of the interview sample. In the online appendix (https://github.com/asreeves/born-to-rule) readers can also find a table providing individual details for all interviewees, including their pseudonym, gender, ethnicity, university, and schooling.

Interviews were semi-structured, lasted from one hour to three hours, and were structured across four common sections. We began with a set of questions that probed class background and education. These included questions about subjective class origin, parental occupation, income, and wealth, as well as schooling, and (where applicable) university. We then asked interviewees to describe their own career trajectory, allowing them to narrate the key moments and critical junctures in their own words. Here we also asked them why they thought they had been able to reach their position and whether they consider themselves to be a member of the British elite. Third, we asked about lifestyle and recreations, and how this had changed over their life course. And, finally, we asked a set of more specific attitudinal questions about inequality in Britain, social mobility, feminism, and empire. A copy of our interview topic guide can be found in the online appendix. Readers should also note that we provide additional qualitative data in the appendix on each of the main themes presented in the book. For example, we provide additional data on deflecting privilege, cultural tastes, distance from necessity, varieties of feminism, and the legacy of empire.

A Note on Confidentiality

We take anonymity and confidentiality extremely seriously. Many of the questions we asked were intimate and provocative, and being identifiable could have a serious bearing on our participants' careers and wider

Table A.1 Demographics of Our Interviewees

	Birth cohorts											
	1900–1920			1921–1940			1941–1960			1961–1980		
Socio-demographics	% in Who's Who	N	% our interviewees	% in Who's Who	N	% our interviewees	% in Who's Who	N	% our interviewees	% in Who's Who	N	% our interviewees
Total number of interviews		32			48			90			44	
Women	5	9	28.13	6.4	8	16.67	16	39	43.33	24	27	61.36
Attended Clarendon School	16	6	18.75	13	8	16.67	10	16	17.78	11	1	2.27
Attended elite girls school	10	2	6.25	9	0	0.00	6	19	21.11	6	7	15.91
Attended Oxbridge	37	10	31.25	36	27	56.25	33	39	43.33	36	14	31.82
Ethnic minority	1	0	0	1.5	4	8.33	1.75	17	18.89	3.9	19	43.18
Member of a club	45	15	46.88	38	22	45.83	29	26	28.89	21	4	9.09

reputations. Our concern was thus not only that interviewees might be identifiable to the general reader, but also that they may be recognisable to colleagues in their field. For this reason, we took a number of steps to ensure anonymity. First, we refer to all participants with pseudonyms. Second, we modified the characteristics of some interviewees, or details about their lives, in order to ensure they would not be identifiable. In masking certain details, we avoided making changes that would be likely to affect the reader's capacity to evaluate our arguments (such as major changes to demographic characteristics).

Finally, readers will notice that we have not anonymised interview data taken from the *National Life Stories* archive at the British Library. We have made this decision on the basis that these interviews are publicly available and can be searched online. Other studies that have used this data have taken a similar approach.

Probate Data and Measuring Wealth in the Survey

The Principal Probate Registry, established on 12 January 1858, was tasked with keeping a copy of every will proved in England or Wales after 1858.[21] This data includes the name of the deceased, their date of death, and the valuation of the assets in their will. These are published online in probate calendars for every year between 1858 and 1995, when they stopped publishing the complete probate calendars online. With the help of a small number of people (including Dr. Naomi Muggleton and a band of research assistants), we downloaded these calendars and extracted their information, generating 18.6 million records. We have also downloaded by hand the probate records for a sample of parents who died after 1995 and compared them to the wealth distributions produced by Alverado and his colleagues covering the period since 1995.[22] The value of these records is that they give us a measure of wealth at death. Probate records generally underestimate true wealth.[23] People often gift their wealth to friends and family before they die or they put it in trusts, and probate only covers those assets which an executor must dispose of in accordance with the will, unlike inheritance tax which covers all assets.[24] However, the basic assumption we make is that while the value of probate may under-report actual wealth, the *rank order* of wealth holders in probate and inheritance data will be approximately the same. That is, someone in the top 1 percent of the inheritance tax distribution will also be in the top 1 percent of the probate distribution. We recognise this may not always be true and our adjustments for hidden wealth address this explicitly. In that process, we impute more hidden wealth to aristocrats and other very rich people because we think they are more likely to have their wealth in trusts. In the absence of better data, we have made some assumptions here which we believe are plausible.

To calculate these distributions, we situated the probate records of the members of *Who's Who* in the context of all people who died in the United Kingdom that year. This matters because many people die without any wealth and so the distribution of wealth at death is really the distribution of wealth at death of those with sufficient assets to warrant a probate in the first place. The proportion of people who require probate has increased over time. In the 1890s, only 15 percent of people who died required their will to be proved. This means that the threshold for the top 1 percent of the whole probate distribution (including those who left nothing) would start at around the 93.3 percentile among the observed probates. Later, in the 1950s, around 41 percent of people died requiring their will to be proved. This means that in this period the threshold for the top 1 percent of the probate distribution (including those who left nothing) would start at around the 97.6 percentile among the observed probates. We used this process to calculate the thresholds for different parts of the probate distribution (which we call the wealth distribution in the main text). These include the top 10 percent and the top 1 percent.

We used this probate data in two ways. First, we matched individuals in *Who's Who* to their probate records based on their names and dates of death. We were able to do this for 46,809 people. Second, we also wanted to match the probate records to the parents of the people in *Who's Who*. Here, with the help of Artem Volgin, we collected genealogical records for 70,303 people in *Who's Who* using a variety of genealogical sources. This was possible because most people in *Who's Who* tell us the name of their parents. We were able to find good matches for around 90 percent of these 70,303 people (and when we manually checked the mismatches, we found no correlation between a mismatch and the valuation of the probate record). This allowed us to place both the people in *Who's Who* and their parents in the probate distributions when they died. We matched probate records for parents of 34,782 individuals in *Who's Who*.

None of these procedures are perfectly accurate and this is because the matching process can introduce errors. We tried to validate our matched data in the following ways. First, by comparison with the *Oxford Dictionary of National Biography* (*ODNB*), a collection of articles written by historians on influential people in British history.[25] These biographies frequently contain the probate valuation and we found that 87 percent were closely matched to our probate figures. Among those that were mismatched, our data mostly underestimated wealth, and so if anything, our erroneous data is likely to be an underestimate.

Second, we went through half of all the parents and half of all of the individuals in *Who's Who* unmatched to a probate record to see if we could find any missing data. This involved manually going through the probate records to see if we could manually find the person without relying on a naming matching algorithm. This also increased the accuracy of our matching process.

Overall, we would stress that, if anything, elite reproduction is higher than we can discern with the probate data. This is particularly true since WWII where it is possible the accuracy of the data declines as tax evasion increases and the way the probate services reports certain values changes over time.

Our measure of wealth in the survey was different from how wealth is measured in the probate data and so these should be viewed as different indicators of the same underlying phenomenon. In the survey, we asked people to tell us how much wealth they had, and for most people, this is probably an underestimate of their gross wealth and therefore less accurate than the probate process. Moreover, wealth at death will be lower than wealth among those aged 50–70 (which is the age of most of the people in our survey). Wealth is typically at its height between 50 and 70 and may decline somewhat thereafter as people disburse their wealth or use it up through various forms of spending. Finally, the probate distribution is based only on those who died, while the wealth distribution is based on the whole population. For these reasons we have conducted some simulation analyses which adjusted for the age effects on wealth (that is, we estimated each individual's wealth at age 55 based on existing data on the age distribution of wealth and then recalculated the proportion of families who came from the top 1 percent). We find that this operation does not materially impact our results.

Genealogical Data

We also collected detailed genealogical records for 105 people who were in *Who's Who* at the end of the nineteenth century. We focus on the past because we wanted to see how wealth moves down family trees, but there are also challenges with tracing genealogies for people who are currently alive because the data is far less complete. Maddie Sheldon provided invaluable research assistance on this part of project. She used genealogical websites as well as other resources to trace the following family relationships: spouses, children and their spouses, grandchildren and their spouses, siblings and their spouses, nieces and nephews and their spouses. This data collection served three purposes. First, it enabled us to calculate the likelihood of having a descendent in *Who's Who*, both for those in *Who's Who* and not. Second, we could then dig into these family histories to uncover how processes of elite reproduction played out in their family tree. In particular, we were able to examine deviant cases, people of high wealth but low elite reproduction or low wealth but high elite reproduction. Third, it allowed us to see patterns of elite reproduction that do not just rely on data on fathers and son, which has traditionally been the focus. We stopped at 105 families because collecting data for new families stopped adding information to what we knew about the proportion of descendants in *Who's Who*. We used the same process for the twenty-five people of colour, and Adele Williams was absolutely essential to completing this task.

Judges

In Chapter 7 we look at whether family background may influence the decisions made by judges on the United Kingdom's Supreme Court. Here we use the amazing data collected and originally analysed by Professor Chris Hanretty in his book on the topic.[26] For those interested in how Professor Hanretty has coded "left-leaning" court decisions, we encourage people to look at his book, but they include decisions where public authorities win over companies or where an "economic underdog . . . wins in disputes between two individuals or two companies." What we add to the analysis is that we track the wealth at death of the parents of these judges and we then see whether the presence of a judge born into the top 1 percent is correlated with "left" outcomes.

Limitations and Future Research

Our research design is far from perfect and we encountered a number of methodological limitations. We have touched on several of these already, such as the conceptual limitations of *Who's Who* as a measure of the elite (Chapter 1) and the ethical issues raised by our use of an algorithm to identify minority ethnic elites in the past (Chapter 8). Briefly here, though, it is worth mentioning a few further issues.

The biggest of these is *Who's Who* itself. We did not construct the dataset ourselves and this creates two challenges. The first is transparency. Despite our best efforts, we have not been able to get very detailed information about how the selection process works (especially the more informal aspects of it) and how this might have changed over time.[27] The interviews we conducted with the coordinator of the selection process suggest that there has not been a great deal of change in the criteria governing the selection of reputational members over the last forty to fifty years, but we cannot be sure. On top of this, we know little about the people on the panel making these determinations. *Who's Who* defends this opacity by arguing that it avoids politicking for admission, a problem which has plagued similar publications.[28] The second challenge with using *Who's Who* is that social scientists usually want to control their research object and define who is included and who is excluded.[29] We are effectively outsourcing these decisions to people who made their decisions without reference to social scientific thinking and may therefore have missed people that social scientists might consider elite (for example, major donors to political parties that are not in *Who's Who*). It is difficult to sidestep these issues when studying elites. Even when scholars use seemingly clear definitions, such as focusing on members of the British Academy (a national scientific elite), there is still some opacity to the selection process underpinning inclusion which is just as subject to bias. The advantage of *Who's Who* is that its longevity and public profile means that it captures an elite widely recognisable in the actual social world, and therefore may be preferable to sociological formulations based on theory.

The second limitation is the disconnect between what elites say and what they actually do. Our interviews have helped us understand people's life histories, but such interviews may be less suited to documenting how power gets deployed or what priorities inform the work of our interviewees. Given that the operations of power are often hidden from view, this is perhaps an inevitable problem and not easily solvable via any research design. However, we would acknowledge that deploying ethnographic methods may have provided a valuable additional lens for understanding how elites operate.

The final limitation concerns causality. In many cases we cannot confidently claim that the relationships we document in this book are causal relationships. At the same time, it is important to be clear about what this means. For most social scientists, causality is rooted in being able to see what the world would have been like if you could change just one aspect of a given situation. For example, does wealth *cause* elite reproduction? To know the answer to this we would need to take a bunch of people and assign some to live in wealthy families and others to live in less wealthy families and then see what happens. If we wanted to know whether the causal relationship between wealth and elite reproduction had changed over time, we would need to run this kind of experiment at multiple different moments in time. This is clearly impossible. Even more plausible strategies for identifying causal effects via natural experiments are rare in this space. The truth is, to address the kinds of big historical questions we are tackling in this book, it is very hard to meet the threshold for a truly causal claim. While we acknowledge that our results are not necessarily causal, they are underpinned by the most comprehensive dataset of the British elite that has ever been produced.

Notes

Introduction

1. "Henry" and all other names derived from those interviewed in this book are pseudonyms. We have also modified certain details about some interviewees, like Henry, to ensure anonymity. For example, Henry *has* been feted in a national newspaper, but using different words to those we use below. We set out our approach to confidentiality in the Methodological Appendix.

2. The centre of the financial services industry and its associated industries, such as law, in the heart of London is commonly referred to as the City. See David Kynaston, *City of London: The History* (New York: Vintage, 2012).

3. A Magic Circle law firm is the term used to describe the five most prestigious law firms in the City. See Louise Ashley, "Making a Difference? The Use (and Abuse) of Diversity Management at the UK's Elite Law Firms," *Work, Employment and Society* 24, no. 4 (December 2010): 711–27, https://doi.org/10.1177/0950017010380639.

4. Jo Littler, "Just like Us?: Normcore Plutocrats and the Popularisation of Elitism," in *Against Meritocracy* (New York: Routledge, 2017); Rachel Sherman, *Uneasy Street: The Anxieties of Affluence* (Princeton, NJ: Princeton University Press, 2017); Anu Kantola and Hanna Kuusela, "Wealth Elite Moralities: Wealthy Entrepreneurs' Moral Boundaries," *Sociology* 53, no. 2 (2018): 368–84, https://doi.org/10.1177/0038038518768175.

5. Oliver Hahl, Ezra W. Zuckerman, and Minjae Kim, "Why Elites Love Authentic Lowbrow Culture: Overcoming High-Status Denigration with Outsider Art," *American Sociological Review* 82, no. 4 (August 2017): 828–56, https://doi.org/10.1177/0003122417710642; Sherman, *Uneasy Street;* Mike Savage, *The Return of Inequality: Social Change and the Weight of the Past* (Cambridge, MA: Harvard University Press, 2021).

6. Sam Friedman, Dave O'Brien, and Ian McDonald, "Deflecting Privilege: Class Identity and the Intergenerational Self," *Sociology* 55, no. 4 (August 2021):

716–33, https://doi.org/10.1177/0038038520982225; Bruno Cousin, Shamus Khan, and Ashley Mears, "Theoretical and Methodological Pathways for Research on Elites," *Socio-Economic Review* 16, no. 2 (April 2018): 225–49, https://doi.org/10.1093/ser/mwy019; Sherman, *Uneasy Street;* Vegard Jarness and Sam Friedman, "'I'm Not a Snob, But . . .': Class Boundaries and the Downplaying of Difference," *Poetics* 61 (April 2017): 14–25, https://doi.org/10.1016/j.poetic.2016.11.001; Kantola and Kuusela, "Wealth Elite Moralities."

7. Michèle Lamont and Sada Aksartova, "Ordinary Cosmopolitanisms: Strategies for Bridging Racial Boundaries among Working-Class Men," *Theory, Culture & Society* 19, no. 4 (August 2002): 1–25, https://doi.org/10.1177/0263276402019004001; Rachel Sherman, "'A Very Expensive Ordinary Life': Consumption, Symbolic Boundaries and Moral Legitimacy among New York Elites," *Socio-Economic Review* 16, no. 2 (April 2018): 411–33, https://doi.org/10.1093/ser/mwy011.

8. Littler, "Just like Us?"; Vegard Jarness and Magne Paalgard Flemmen, "A Struggle on Two Fronts: Boundary Drawing in the Lower Region of the Social Space and the Symbolic Market for 'Down-to-Earthness'," *British Journal of Sociology* 70, no. 1 (2019): 166–89, https://doi.org/10.1111/1468-4446.12345.

9. *Who's Who* was first published in 1849 but those early editions looked quite different. Most of the people included in the book were connected to aristocracy and it was largely based on information in the public domain, including "political bias." It was only in 1897 when *Who's Who* was taken over by A&C Black that it became the biographical reference work that we know today, based largely on a questionnaire sent to entrants. Those early records are not digitized by *Who's Who,* and so not included in our data.

10. Aaron worked with Charles Rahal to develop the script and has since become a collaborator on a number of projects. *Who's Who* granted us access to the entire data set but asked us to sign a non-disclosure agreement for that data.

11. Erzsébet Bukodi and John H. Goldthorpe, "Elite Studies: For a New Approach," *Political Quarterly* 92, no. 4 (2021): 673–81, https://doi.org/10.1111/1467-923X.13072.

12. A list of automatic appointments can be found in our online appendix.

13. Fabien Accominotti, "Consecration as a Population-Level Phenomenon," *American Behavioral Scientist* 65, no. 1 (January 2021): 9–24, https://doi.org/10.1177/0002764218800144.

14. Karl Marx and Friedrich Engels, *The German Ideology,* vol. 1 (International Publishers Co., 1845); Gaetano Mosca, *The Ruling Class* (New York: McGraw-Hill, 1939); C. Wright Mills, *The Power Elite* (Oxford: Oxford University Press, 1956).

15. The Clarendon Schools are named after a Royal Commission in 1861 which examined the state of British education, but only looked at nine schools. The nine schools comprised seven boarding schools (Charterhouse, Eton, Harrow, Rugby, Shrewsbury, Westminster, and Winchester) and two-day schools (Merchant Taylors' and St Paul's).

16. John Scott, *Who Rules Britain?* (Cambridge, MA: Polity, 1991); Gregory Clark, *The Son Also Rises: Surnames and the History of Social Mobility* (Princeton, NJ: Princeton

University Press, 2015); although Clark, contrary to the rest of this paragraph, would probably articulate the drivers of this continuity in genetic rather than institutional terms; Daniel Smith, *The Fall and Rise of the English Upper Class: Houses, Kinship and Capital Since 1945* (Manchester: Manchester University Press, 2023).

17. Perry Anderson, "Origins of the Present Crisis," *New Left Review* 1, no. 23 (February 1964): 26–53.

18. David Cannadine, *The Decline and Fall of the British Aristocracy* (New York: Vintage Books, 1999); William Doyle, *Aristocracy and Its Enemies in the Age of Revolution* (Oxford: Oxford University Press, 2009).

19. Gareth Williams and Ourania Filippakou, "Higher Education and UK Elite Formation in the Twentieth Century," *Higher Education* 59 (2010): 1–20; Simon Kuper, *Chums: How a Tiny Caste of Oxford Tories Took Over the UK* (London: Profile Books, 2022).

20. Ralph Miliband, *The State in Capitalist Society* (London: Basic Books, 1969).

21. Scott, *Who Rules Britain?*, 153.

22. Scott, *Who Rules Britain?*

23. Scott, *Who Rules Britain?*

24. Decades later, and writing shortly after the financial crisis of 2008, the journalist Owen Jones came to a similar conclusion about the continuation of "the establishment"—although notably he argues that "social composition" was "not central" to his analysis or understanding of this group. Owen Jones, *The Establishment: And How They Get Away with It* (London: Penguin, 2015).

25. Anthony Sampson, *Who Runs This Place?: The Anatomy of Britain in the 21st Century* (London: John Murray, 2005); W. L. Guttsman, *The British Political Elite* (MacGibbon & Kee, 1963); Aeron Davis, *Reckless Opportunists: Elites at the End of the Establishment* (Manchester: Manchester University Press, 2018).

26. Anthony Sampson, *Anatomy of Britain* (London: Hodder & Stoughton, 1962).

27. Sampson, *Who Runs This Place?*

28. Sampson, *Who Runs This Place?*

29. Matthew Goodwin, *Values, Voice and Virtue: The New British Politics* (London: Penguin, 2023).

30. Goodwin, *Values, Voice and Virtue.*

31. Goodwin, *Values, Voice and Virtue.*

32. Göran Therborn, *What Does the Ruling Class Do When It Rules?: State Apparatuses and State Power under Feudalism, Capitalism and Socialism: Set 3,* illus. ed. (London: Verso, 2008); Mills, *The Power Elite.*

33. Bukodi and Goldthorpe, "Elite Studies."

34. Peter Barberis, *The Elite of the Elite: Permanent Secretaries in the British Higher Civil Service,* 1996; R. K. Kelsall, *Higher Civil Servants in Britain* (London: Routledge & Kegan Paul, 1966); Erzsébet Bukodi, John H. Goldthorpe, and Inga Steinberg, "The Social Origins and Schooling of a Scientific Elite: Fellows of the Royal Society

Born from 1900," *British Journal of Sociology* 73, no. 3 (2022): 484–504, https://doi.org/10.1111/1468-4446.12958.

35. Jean-Pascal Daloz, "Elite Distinction: Grand Theory and Comparative Perspectives," *Comparative Sociology* 6, no. 1 (June 2007): 27–74, https://doi.org/10.1163/156913307X187397.

36. Cannadine, *The Decline and Fall of the British Aristocracy;* Leonore Davidoff, *The Best Circles* (London: Ebury Press, 1986).

37. Shamus Khan, *Privilege: The Making of an Adolescent Elite at St. Paul's School* (Princeton, NJ: Princeton University Press, 2011); Sherman, *Uneasy Street;* Ashley Mears, *Very Important People: Status and Beauty in the Global Party Circuit* (Princeton, NJ: Princeton University Press, 2020).

38. Jennifer Hall-Witt, *Fashionable Acts: Opera and Elite Culture in London, 1780–1880* (Lebanon, NH: University Press of New England, 2007); Maura A. Henry, "The Making of Elite Culture," in *A Companion to Eighteenth-Century Britain,* ed. H. T. Dickinson (Oxford: Blackwell, 2002), 311–28, https://doi.org/10.1002/9780470998885.ch24; Dave O'Brien and Lisa Ianni, "New Forms of Distinction: How Contemporary Cultural Elites Understand 'Good' Taste," *Sociological Review* 71, no. 1 (January 2023): 201–20, https://doi.org/10.1177/00380261221128144; Daniel R. Smith, *Elites, Race and Nationhood: The Branded Gentry* (New York: Palgrave MacMillan, 2016).

39. R. A. Peterson and R. M. Kern, "Changing Highbrow Taste: From Snob to Omnivore," *American Sociological Review* 61, no. 5 (1996): 900–907.

40. Jennifer C. Lena, *Entitled: Discriminating Tastes and the Expansion of the Arts* (Princeton, NJ: Princeton University Press, 2019).

41. Magne Flemmen, Vegard Jarness, and Lennart Rosenlund, "Social Space and Cultural Class Divisions: The Forms of Capital and Contemporary Lifestyle Differentiation," *British Journal of Sociology* 69, no. 1 (2018): 124–53; Will Atkinson, "The Context and Genesis of Musical Tastes: Omnivorousness Debunked, Bourdieu Buttressed," *Poetics* 39, no. 3 (July 2011): 169–86, https://doi.org/10.1016/j.poetic.2011.03.002; Tak Wing Chan, "Understanding Cultural Omnivores: Social and Political Attitudes," *British Journal of Sociology* 70, no. 3 (2019): 784–806, https://doi.org/10.1111/1468-4446.12613; S. Friedman, "Cultural Omnivores or Culturally Homeless? Exploring the Shifting Cultural Identities of the Upwardly Mobile," *Poetics* 40, no. 5 (October 2012): 467–89.

42. Friedman, O'Brien, and McDonald, "Deflecting Privilege"; Kantola and Kuusela, "Wealth Elite Moralities"; Khan, *Privilege: The Making of an Adolescent Elite at St. Paul's School;* Aaron Koh, "Doing Class Analysis in Singapore's Elite Education: Unravelling the Smokescreen of 'Meritocratic Talk,'" *Globalisation, Societies and Education* 12, no. 2 (April 2014): 196–210, https://doi.org/10.1080/14767724.2014.888308.

43. Although the performance of domesticity by the royal family in the Victorian era helped the monarchy distance itself from ideas of greed and debauchery. Laura

Clancy, *Running the Family Firm: How the Monarchy Manages Its Image and Our Money* (Manchester: Manchester University Press, 2021).

44. Michael Useem, *The Inner Circle: Large Corporations and the Rise of Business Political Activity in the U.S. and U.K.* (New York: Oxford University Press, 1986); G. William Domhoff, *Who Rules America?* (Englewood Cliffs, NJ: Prentice-Hall, 1967); Philip Stanworth and Anthony Giddens, *Elites and Power in British Society* (Cambridge: Cambridge University Press, 1974).

45. John H. Goldthorpe, Catriona Llewellyn, and Clive Payne, *Social Mobility and Class Structure in Modern Britain* (Oxford: Clarendon Press, 1980).

46. M. Savage and K. Williams, "Elites: Remembered in Capitalism and Forgotten by Social Sciences," *Sociological Review* 56 (2008): 1–24.

47. Thomas Piketty, *Capital in the Twenty-First Century*, trans. Arthur Goldhammer (Cambridge MA: The Belknap Press of Harvard University Press, 2014); Cousin, Khan, and Mears, "Theoretical and Methodological Pathways for Research on Elites"; Christoph Ellersgaard, Anton Grau Larsen, and Martin Munk, "A Very Economic Elite: The Case of the Danish Top CEOs," *Sociology 47* no. 6 (2013): 1051–71.

48. Alun Francis, "Rethinking Social Mobility for the Levelling Up Era," Policy Exchange, 14 October 2021.

49. Charlotte Dargie and Rachel Locke, "The British Senior Civil Service," in *Bureaucratic Elites in Western European States: A Comparative Analysis of Top Officials*, ed. Edward C. Page and Vincent Wright (New York: Oxford University Press, 1999), 178–204.

50. Claire Maxwell and Peter Aggleton, "Schools, Schooling and Elite Status in English Education—Changing Configurations?," *L'Année sociologique* 66, no. 1 (April 2016): 147–70; W. D. Rubinstein, "Education and the Social Origins of British Élites 1880–1970," *Past & Present* 112, no. 1 (August 1986): 163–207, https://doi.org/10.1093/past/112.1.163; Anthony Abraham Jack, *The Privileged Poor: How Elite Colleges Are Failing Disadvantaged Students* (Cambridge, MA: Harvard University Press, 2019).

51. Our twelve girls schools are: Cheltenham Ladies' College, North London Collegiate School, St Paul's Girls' School, Oxford High School for Girls, Queen's College on Harley Street, St. Leonard's in St Andrews, Clifton High School for Girls, King Edward VI High School for Girls in Birmingham, Roedean, Godolphin & Laytmer Girls' School, Wycombe Abbey, and the Benenden School. Eve Worth, Aaron Reeves, and Sam Friedman, "Is There an Old Girls' Network? Girls' Schools and Recruitment to the British Elite," *British Journal of Sociology of Education* 44, no. 1 (November 2022): 1–25, https://doi.org/10.1080/01425692.2022.2132472. There are 351 HMC schools in 2024, but this group was smaller in the past and we focus on those schools that have been in the HMC for a longer period of time.

52. Sol Gamsu, "The 'Other' London Effect: The Diversification of London's Suburban Grammar Schools and the Rise of Hyper-selective Elite State Schools," *British Journal of Sociology*, 69, no. 4 (December 2018): 1155–74, https://doi.org/10.1111/1468

.4446; Jane Gingrich and Ben Ansell, "Sorting for Schools: Housing, Education and Inequality," *Socio-Economic Review* 12, no. 2 (April 2014): 329–51, https://doi.org/10.1093/ser/mwu009.

53. Mills, *The Power Elite;* Jack, *The Privileged Poor.*

54. Mills, *The Power Elite,* 64–67, 278–83.

55. Jones, *The Establishment.*

56. Goodwin, *Values, Voice and Virtue.*

57. Early work on how social background and current economic circumstances inform the social attitudes and policy preferences of the British elite suggests there is only a weak relationship, while more recent studies, largely focussing on politicians, have discerned a left-wing disposition among those from working-class backgrounds. See Nicholas Carnes and Noam Lupu, "The Economic Backgrounds of Politicians," *Annual Review of Political Science* 26, no. 1 (2023): 253–70, https://doi.org/10.1146/annurev-polisci-051921-102946; Tom O'Grady, *The Transformation of British Welfare Policy: Politics, Discourse, and Public Opinion* (Oxford: Oxford University Press, 2022).

58. Olúfẹ́mi O. Táíwò, *Elite Capture: How the Powerful Took Over Identity Politics* (London: Pluto Press, 2022).

59. Benjamin I. Page, Jason Seawright, and Matthew J. Lacombe, *Billionaires and Stealth Politics* (Chicago: University of Chicago Press, 2018).

60. See also Kevin L. Young, Seth K. Goldman, Brendan O'Connor, and Tuugi Chuluun, "How White Is the Global Elite? An Analysis of Race, Gender and Network Structure," *Global Networks* 21, no. 2 (2021):365–92.

61. Nirmal Puwar, *Space Invaders: Race, Gender and Bodies Out of Place,* illus. ed. (Oxford: Berg Publishers, 2004).

62. Aline Courtois, *Elite Schooling and Social Inequality: Privilege and Power in Ireland's Top Private Schools* (London: Palgrave Macmillan, 2018); Pere Ayling, *Distinction, Exclusivity and Whiteness: Elite Nigerian Parents and the International Education Market* (Singapore: Springer, 2019).

63. Rubén A. Gaztambide-Fernández, *The Best of the Best: Becoming Elite at an American Boarding School* (Cambridge, MA: Harvard University Press, 2009); Brian Stoddart, "Sport, Cultural Imperialism, and Colonial Response in the British Empire," *Comparative Studies in Society and History* 30, no. 4 (1988): 649–73.

64. Piketty, *Capital in the Twenty-First Century.*

65. Facundo Alvaredo, Anthony B. Atkinson, and Salvatore Morelli, "Top Wealth Shares in the UK over More than a Century," *Journal of Public Economics* 162 (2018): 26–47.

66. Peter W. Cookson and Caroline H. Persell, "English and American Residential Secondary Schools: A Comparative Study of the Reproduction of Social Elites," *Comparative Education Review* 29, no. 3 (1985): 283–98.

67. Cas Mudde, "The Populist Zeitgeist," *Government and Opposition* 39, no. 4 (2004): 541–63, https://doi.org/10.1111/j.1477-7053.2004.00135.x.

1. Who Are the British Elite?

1. John Scott, "Transformations in the British Economic Elite," in *Elite Configurations at the Apex of Power* (Leiden: Brill, 2003), 155–73.

2. Documenting whether levels of interest have changed over time is difficult, but the words "elite," "elites," and "inequality" are at their highest level over the past 200 years according to Google's Ngrams database, which is a measure of the frequency that words or phrases are used in books. There are limitations to using these data in exactly this way but the magnitude of the change is still striking.

3. These are all quotations from statements made in the British House of Commons, which can be found on Hansard (https://hansard.parliament.uk).

4. Shamus Rahman Khan, "The Sociology of Elites," *Annual Review of Sociology* 38, no. 1 (2012): 361–77.

5. Khan, "The Sociology of Elites."

6. Matthew Goodwin, *Values, Voice and Virtue: The New British Politics* (New York: Random House, 2023).

7. Goodwin, *Values, Voice and Virtue.*

8. Olúfẹ́mi O. Táíwò, *Elite Capture: How the Powerful Took Over Identity Politics* (London: Pluto Press, 2022).

9. Murray Milner Jr., *Elites: A General Model* (Cambridge: Polity, 2014); Tom Bottomore, *Elites and Society,* rev. ed. (London: Routledge, 2006).

10. Ben W. Ansell and David J. Samuels, *Inequality and Democratization: An Elite-Competition Approach* (New York: Cambridge University Press, 2015); Thomas Piketty, *Capital and Ideology* (Cambridge, MA: The Belknap Press of Harvard University Press, 2020).

11. Erzsébet Bukodi and John H. Goldthorpe, "Elite Studies: For a New Approach," *The Political Quarterly* 92, no. 4 (2021): 673–81, https://doi.org/10.1111/1467-923X.13072.

12. Táíwò, *Elite Capture;* Philip Stanworth and Anthony Giddens, *Elites and Power in British Society* (Cambridge: Cambridge University Press, 1974).

13. "*Who's Who*—A Brief History, 1849–1998," in *Who's Who* (London: Bloomsbury Press, 1998), 1–16.

14. C. Wright Mills, *The Power Elite* (Oxford: Oxford University Press, 1956); Stanworth and Giddens, *Elites and Power in British Society.*

15. Gaetano Mosca, *The Ruling Class* (New York: McGraw-Hill, 1939).

16. A list of some of the automatic appointments is available on the *Who's Who* website.

17. This is an important feature of their influence—a distinction the theorist Pareto characterised as the difference between "governing" and "non-governing" elites. Vilfredo Pareto, *The Mind and Society* (New York: Harcourt, Brace, 1935).

18. Floyd Hunter, *Community Power Structure: A Study of Decision Makers* (Chapel Hill: University of North Carolina Press, 1953).

19. "*Who's Who*—A Brief History, 1849–1998"; Jeremy Paxman, "Who's New in *Who's Who*?," *Daily Telegraph,* 1 December 2007, https://www.telegraph.co.uk/news/features/3634850/Jeremy-Paxman-Whos-new-in-Whos-Who.html.

20. In certain countries, including the United States, there are long-standing concerns that some entrants pay for inclusion in *Who's Who*. Tucker Carlson, "The Hall of Lame," *Forbes,* 8 March 1999, https://www.forbes.com/forbes-life-magazine/1999/0308/063.html.

21. "*Who's Who*—A Brief History, 1849–1998."

22. Dave Griffiths, Andrew Miles, and Mike Savage, "The End of the English Cultural Elite?," *Sociological Review* 56, no. 1 (2008): 189–209; Stanworth and Giddens, *Elites and Power in British Society;* Colin D. Harbury and David M. Hitchens, *Inheritance and Wealth Inequality in Britain* (George Allen and Unwin: London, 1979).

23. Richard Fitzwilliam, "*Who's Who*: A Book That Speaks Volumes," *Daily Express,* 6 December 2010, https://www.express.co.uk/expressyourself/215657/Who-s-Who-A-book-that-speaks-volumes; Paxman, 'Who's New in *Who's Who*?'; '*Who's Who*," in *Wikipedia,* 6 June 2023, https://en.wikipedia.org/w/index.php?title=Who%27s_Who&oldid=1158900538.

24. "*Who's Who*—A Brief History, 1849–1998."

25. Ann Donald, "The Good, the Bad, and the High-Born," *Herald,* 22 March 1998, https://www.heraldscotland.com/news/12301999.the-good-the-bad-and-the-high-born/.

26. Katie Higgins, "Dynasties in the Making: Family Wealth and Inheritance for the First-Generation Ultra-Wealthy and Their Wealth Managers," *Sociological Review* 70, no. 6 (November 2022): 1267–83, https://doi.org/10.1177/00380261211061931; David McCrone, *Who Runs Edinburgh?* (Edinburgh: Edinburgh University Press, 2022).

27. Social Mobility Commission, "Cross-Industry Toolkit for Measuring Class: For Employers," Social Mobility Commission, accessed 3 November 2023, https://socialmobilityworks.org/toolkit/measurement/; Francis Green et al., "Who Chooses Private Schooling in Britain and Why?," 2017, https://discovery.ucl.ac.uk/id/eprint/10043039/. Around 6–7 percent of school children are attending a private school, but around 10 percent have attended a private school at some point.

28. Arun Advani, George Bangham, and Jack Leslie, "The UK's Wealth Distribution and Characteristics of High-Wealth Households," *Fiscal Studies* 42, no. 3–4 (September 2021): 397–430, https://doi.org/10.1111/1475-5890.12286.

29. It is worth noting that the aristocracy do make up a small percentage of *Who's Who* entrants, despite their positions being hereditary rather than achieved. However, regardless of origin, their titles still represent positions of influence and many also hold occupational positions that would qualify them for *Who's Who* entry anyway.

30. Fitzwilliam, "*Who's Who*"; Paxman, "Who's New in *Who's Who?*"

31. Fitzwilliam, "*Who's Who.*"

32. Anthony B. Atkinson, *Inequality* (Cambridge, MA: Harvard University Press, 2015); Thomas Piketty, *Capital in the Twenty-First Century,* trans. Arthur Goldhammer (Cambridge, MA: Harvard University Press, 2014); Thomas Piketty and Emmanuel Saez, "The Evolution of Top Incomes: A Historical and International Perspective," *American Economic Review* 96, no. 2 (May 2006): 200–205, https://doi.org/10.1257 /000282806777212116.

33. Roger Burrows, Richard Webber, and Rowland Atkinson, "Welcome to 'Piket-tyville'? Mapping London's Alpha Territories," *Sociological Review* 65, no. 2 (May 2017): 184–201, https://doi.org/10.1111/1467-954X.12375; Lisa A. Keister, "The One Percent," *Annual Review of Sociology* 40, no. 1 (2014): 347–67, https://doi.org/10.1146/annurev -soc-070513-075314.

34. Khan, "The Sociology of Elites."

35. "Lord Ashcroft Admits 'non-Dom' Tax Status," 1 March 2010, BBC News, http://news.bbc.co.uk/1/hi/uk_politics/8542744.stm.

36. Michael White, "Call Me Dave Is Nothing Short of a Jacobean Revenge Biog-raphy," *The Guardian,* 22 September 2015, https://www.theguardian.com/politics/blog /2015/sep/22/call-me-dave-is-nothing-short-of-a-jacobean-revenge-biography.

37. William K. Carroll and J. P. Sapinski, *Organizing the 1%: How Corporate Power Works* (Black Point, NS: Fernwood, 2018); Francois Denord, Mikael Palme, and Bertrand Réau, eds., *Researching Elites and Power: Theory, Methods, Analyses* (Cham, Switzerland: Springer Cham, 2020).

38. Karl Marx and Friedrich Engels, *The German Ideology,* vol. 1 (International Publishers Co, 1845).

39. Karl Marx and Friedrich Engels, *The Communist Manifesto* (1848; repr., London: Penguin, 2002).

40. John Scott, *Who Rules Britain?* (Oxford: Polity, 1991).

41. Ralph Miliband, *The State in Capitalist Society* (London: Basic Books, 1969); Scott, *Who Rules Britain?*

42. Mosca, *The Ruling Class;* Pareto, *The Mind and Society.*

43. Pareto, *The Mind and Society.*

44. Mosca explains that this minority holds onto power because it is organised and seems to assume that its capacity to organise itself to hold onto power is because it possesses superior qualities that make it elite. There is implicit a kind of class bias which seems to assume that the non-elite are unruly and unable to govern themselves and pursue collective goals. See Bottomore, *Elites and Society.*

45. Bottomore, *Elites and Society;* Jonathan Wolff, *Why Read Marx Today?* (Oxford: Oxford University Press, 2003).

46. Mosca, *The Ruling Class.*

47. Anthony Sampson, *Anatomy of Britain* (London: Hodder & Stoughton, 1962); Henry Fairlie, "Political Commentary," *Spectator,* 23 September 1955, http://archive .spectator.co.uk/article/23rd-september-1955/5/political-commentary.

48. Perry Anderson, "Origins of the Present Crisis," *New Left Review,* no. 1/23 (February 1964): 26–53; Tom Nairn, "The English Working Class," *New Left Review,* no. 1/24 (April 1964): 43–57.

49. Mills, *The Power Elite.*

50. Mills, *The Power Elite.* See also Heather Gautney's *The New Power Elite* (New York: Oxford University Press, 2022), which updates Mills's analysis.

51. Michael Useem, *The Inner Circle: Large Corporations and the Rise of Business Political Activity in the U. S. and U.K.* (New York: Oxford University Press, 1986).

52. Mills, *The Power Elite.*

53. Neil Cummins, "Where Is the Middle Class? Evidence from 60 Million English Death and Probate Records, 1892–1992," *Journal of Economic History* 81, no. 2 (2021): 359–404; W. D. Rubinstein, "New Men of Wealth and the Purchase of Land in Nineteenth-Century Britain," *Past & Present,* 92, no. 1 (1981): 125–47; David R. Green et al., *Men, Women, and Money: Perspectives on Gender, Wealth, and Investment 1850–1930* (Oxford: Oxford University Press, 2011).

54. Advani, Bangham, and Leslie, "The UK's Wealth Distribution." We did have people who reported their wealth being £2–4m and were married. In this instance, we randomly selected 20 percent of these individuals because we assumed that some of them would have underestimated their joint wealth.

55. Atkinson, *Inequality.*

2. A Life Less Ordinary

1. Anu Kantola and Hanna Kuusela, "Wealth Elite Moralities: Wealthy Entrepreneurs' Moral Boundaries," *Sociology* 53, no. 2 (April 2019): 368–84, https://doi.org/10 .1177/0038038518768175; Rachel Sherman, *Uneasy Street: The Anxieties of Affluence* (Princeton, NJ: Princeton University Press, 2017); Marte Mangset, "What Does It Mean to Be Part of the Elite?: Comparing Norwegian, French and British Top Bureaucrats' Understandings of the Elite Concept When Applied to Themselves," *Comparative Sociology* 14, no. 2 (2015): 274–99.

2. Owen Jones, *The Establishment: And How They Get Away with It* (London: Penguin, 2014).

3. Sherman, *Uneasy Street;* Kantola and Kuusela, "Wealth Elite Moralities."

4. René Levy, "Structure-Blindness: A Non-Ideological Component of False Consciousness," *International Journal of Sociology and Social Policy* 11, no. 6/7/8 (January 1991): 61–74, https://doi.org/10.1108/eb013146.

5. Sherman, *Uneasy Street*.

6. M. D. R. Evans and Jonathan Kelley, "Subjective Social Location: Data From 21 Nations," *International Journal of Public Opinion Research* 16, no. 1 (March 2004): 3–38, https://doi.org/10.1093/ijpor/16.1.3.

7. NatCen, "40 Years of British Social Attitudes: Class Identity and Awareness Still Matter" (London: NatCen, 2023), https://natcen.ac.uk/news/40-years-british -social-attitudes-class-identity-and-awareness-still-matter.

8. Sam Friedman, Dave O'Brien, and Ian McDonald, "Deflecting Privilege: Class Identity and the Intergenerational Self," *Sociology* 55, no. 4 (2021): 716–33.

9. This is also a theme highlighted in a series of recent media articles—see and https://www.vice.com/en/article/nexz9k/here-are-16-more-stories-of-rich-kids -pretending-not-to-be-rich?fbclid=IwAR2Nz1gsFkdMm7pUv4nhIy3XQLDVDtutO ILA_dmVZzpD6DLvZQ_aeW3Mkbw.

10. By "Objective" class we refer here to occupational class using the 3-class ver sion of the ONS National Statistics Socio-Economic Classification.

11. This is in line with a range of sociological studies showing the emotional dis-comfort people exhibit when discussing class and social position—see Beverley Skeggs, *Formations of Class and Gender: Becoming Respectable* (London: SAGE, 1997); Ali Meghji, *Black Middle-Class Britannia: Identities, Repertoires, Cultural Consumption* (Manchester: Manchester University Press, 2019).

12. Jonathan J. B. Mijs, "Inequality Is a Problem of Inference: How People Solve the Social Puzzle of Unequal Outcomes," *Societies* 8, no. 3 (2018): 64.

13. See, for example, Rohyn Fivush, Jennifer G. Bohanek, and Marshall Duke, "The Intergenerational Self: Subjective Perspective and Family History," in *Self Continuity: Individual and Collective Perspectives* (New York: Psychology Press, 2008), 131–43.

14. Umut Erel and Louise Ryan, "Migrant Capitals: Proposing a Multi-Level Spatio-Temporal Analytical Framework," *Sociology* 53, no. 2 (April 2019): 246–63, https://doi .org/10.1177/0038038518785298; Arnd-Michael Nohl et al., "Cultural Capital during Migration—A Multi-Level Approach for the Empirical Analysis of the Labor Market Integration of Highly Skilled Migrants," *Forum Qualitative Sozialforschung/ Forum: Qualitative Social Research* 7, no. 3 (May 2006), https://doi.org/10.17169/fqs -7.3.142.

15. As Rachel, a senior doctor, summed up of this intergenerational sense of self: "I am kind of standing on their [my upwardly mobile family's] shoulders."

16. See more generally Liz Moor and Sam Friedman, "Justifying Inherited Wealth: Between "the Bank of Mum and Dad" and the Meritocratic Ideal," *Economy and So-ciety* 50, no. 4 (October 2021): 618–42, https://doi.org/10.1080/03085147.2021 .1932353; Friedman, O'Brien, and McDonald, "Deflecting Privilege."

17. *Yes Minister* (British Broadcasting Corporation [BBC], 1980).

18. A minor but important point here is that these narratives frequently focused on somewhat extreme and likely uncommon examples of how elite closure operated in the past, that is, by explicitly recruiting someone on the basis of the school they

attended. Pointing towards these stories serves an important rhetorical function because it masks how, even in the nineteenth century, acquiring elite positions was generally more complicated than this. These stories, then, serve to draw somewhat exaggerated distinctions between the past and the present.

19. A range of recent studies, for example, has demonstrated elites' insistence that their advantaged position is attributable to talent and hard work. See Elisabeth Schimpfössl, *Rich Russians: From Oligarchs to Bourgeoisie* (New York: Oxford University Press, 2018); Katharina Hecht, "'It's the Value That We Bring": Performance Pay and Top Income Earners' Perceptions of Inequality," *Socio-Economic Review* 20, no. 4 (October 2022): 1741–66, https://doi.org/10.1093/ser/mwab044; Kantola and Kuusela, "Wealth Elite Moralities"; Lauren A. Rivera, *Pedigree: How Elite Students Get Elite Jobs* (Princeton, NJ: Princeton University Press, 2015).

20. Susan Ostrander, *Women of the Upper Class* (Philadelphia: Temple University Press, 1986).

21. Bethany Bryson, "'Anything but Heavy Metal': Symbolic Exclusion and Musical Dislikes," *American Sociological Review* 61, no. 5 (1996): 884–99; Bonnie H. Erickson, "Culture, Class, and Connections," *American Journal of Sociology* 102, no. 1 (1996): 217–51.

22. Vegard Jarness and Magne Paalgard Flemmen, "A Struggle on Two Fronts: Boundary Drawing in the Lower Region of the Social Space and the Symbolic Market for 'down-to-Earthness'," *British Journal of Sociology* 70, no. 1 (2019): 166–89, https://doi.org/10.1111/1468-4446.12345; Vegard Jarness and Sam Friedman, "'I'm Not a Snob, but . . .': Class Boundaries and the Downplaying of Difference," *Poetics* 61 (April 2017): 14–25, https://doi.org/10.1016/j.poetic.2016.11.001; Jørn Ljunggren, "Elitist Egalitarianism: Negotiating Identity in the Norwegian Cultural Elite," *Sociology* 51, no. 3 (June 2017): 559–74, https://doi.org/10.1177/0038038515590755; Shamus Khan, *Privilege: The Making of an Adolescent Elite at St. Paul's School* (Princeton, NJ: Princeton University Press, 2011), https://press.princeton.edu/titles/9294.html; Sherman, *Uneasy Street;* Kantola and Kuusela, "Wealth Elite Moralities"; Oliver Hahl, Ezra W. Zuckerman, and Minjae Kim, "Why Elites Love Authentic Lowbrow Culture: Overcoming High-Status Denigration with Outsider Art," *American Sociological Review* 82, no. 4 (August 2017): 828–56

23. Vegard Jarness and Magne Paalgard Flemmen, "A Struggle on Two Fronts: Boundary Drawing in the Lower Region of the Social Space and the Symbolic Market for 'down-to-Earthness'," *British Journal of Sociology* 70, no. 1 (2019): 166–89, https://doi.org/10.1111/1468-4446.12345. See also Lisa Mckenzie, *Getting By: Estates, Class and Culture in Austerity Britain* (Bristol, England: Policy Press, 2015); Sam Friedman, *Comedy and Distinction: The Cultural Currency of a "Good" Sense of Humour* (London: Routledge, 2014);

24. Pierre Bourdieu, *Distinction: A Social Critique of the Judgement of Taste* (London: Routledge, 2010), 472.

25. "Pulp—Common People Lyrics," accessed 19 July 2023, https://www.lyrics.com /lyric/9568316/Common+People.

3. Cultural Chameleons

1. Adrian Wooldridge, *The Aristocracy of Talent: How Meritocracy Made the Modern World* (London: Allen Lane, 2021), 36.

2. Some of these findings are also reported in Sam Friedman and Aaron Reeves, "From Aristocratic to Ordinary: Shifting Modes of Elite Distinction," *American Sociological Review* 85, no. 2 (April 2020): 323–50, https://doi.org/10.1177/0003122 420912941.

3. Thorstein Veblen, *The Theory of the Leisure Class* (1899; repr., Mineola, NY: Dover Publications, 1994); Pierre Bourdieu, *Distinction: A Social Critique of the Judgement of Taste* (London: Routledge, 2010); Jennifer C. Lena, *Entitled: Discriminating Tastes and the Expansion of the Arts* (Princeton, NJ: Princeton University Press, 2019); Mikael Holmqvist, *Leader Communities: The Consecration of Elites in Djursholm* (New York: Columbia University Press, 2017).

4. Veblen, *The Theory of the Leisure Class.*

5. Georg Simmel, "Fashion," *American Journal of Sociology* 62, no. 6 (1957): 541–58.

6. Charles Harvey and Mairi Maclean, "Capital Theory and the Dynamics of Elite Business Networks in Britain and France," *Sociological Review* 56, no. 1_suppl (1 May 2008): 103–20, https://doi.org/10.1111/j.1467-954X.2008.00764.x.

7. Bourdieu, *Distinction.*

8. Pierre Bourdieu, *The Rules of Art: Genesis and Structure of the Literary Field* (Cambridge: Polity Press, 1996); Pierre Bourdieu, *The Field of Cultural Production: Essays on Art and Literature* (Cambridge: Polity, 1993).

9. Semi Purhonen et al., *Enter Culture, Exit Arts?: The Transformation of Cultural Hierarchies in European Newspaper Culture Sections, 1960–2010* (London: Routledge, 2018).

10. Michele Lamont and Annette Lareau, "Cultural Capital: Allusions, Gaps and Glissandos in Recent Theoretical Developments," *Sociological Theory* 6, no. 2 (1988): 153–68, https://doi.org/10.2307/202113.

11. Tony Bennett et al., *Culture, Class, Distinction* (London: Routledge, 2009); Richard A. Peterson and Roger M. Kern, "Changing Highbrow Taste: From Snob to Omnivore," *American Sociological Review* 61, no. 5 (October 1996): 900–907, https://doi .org/10.2307/2096460.

12. Alan Warde, "Cultural Hostility Re-Considered," *Cultural Sociology* 5, no. 3 (9 January 2011): 341–66, https://doi.org/10.1177/1749975510387755; Bennett et al., *Culture, Class, Distinction.*

13. Lena, *Entitled.*

14. Vegard Jarness, "Modes of Consumption: From 'What' to 'How' in Cultural Stratification Research," *Poetics* 53 (December 2015): 65–79, https://doi.org/10.1016/j .poetic.2015.08.002; Sam Friedman, *Comedy and Distinction: The Cultural Currency of a "Good" Sense of Humour* (London: Routledge, 2014); Josee Johnston and Shyon Baumann, *Foodies: Democracy and Distinction in the Gourmet Foodscape* (New York: Routledge, 2009).

15. Tom F. M. ter Bogt et al., "Intergenerational Continuity of Taste: Parental and Adolescent Music Preferences," *Social Forces* 90, no. 1 (September 2011): 297–319, https://doi.org/10.1093/sf/90.1.297.

16. David Cannadine, *The Decline and Fall of the British Aristocracy* (New York: Penguin, 2005); Maura A. Henry, "The Making of Elite Culture," in *A Companion to Eighteenth-Century Britain* (Hoboken, NJ: John Wiley & Sons, 2002), 311–28, https://doi.org/10.1002/9780470998885.ch24.

17. John Scott, *Who Rules Britain?* (Oxford: Polity, 1991).

18. Kristen Richardson, *The Season: A Social History of the Debutante* (New York: W. W. Norton, 2019).

19. Cannadine, *The Decline and Fall of the British Aristocracy.*

20. Veblen, *The Theory of the Leisure Class.*

21. W. D. Rubinstein, "New Men of Wealth and the Purchase of Land in Nineteenth-Century Britain," *Past & Present,* no. 92 (1981): 125–47.

22. Pamela Horn, *High Society: The English Social Elite, 1880–1914* (Stroud, Gloucestershire: Sutton, 1992); Scott, *Who Rules Britain?*

23. Noel Gilroy Annan, *Our Age: Portrait of a Generation* (London: Weidenfeld & Nicolson, 1990); Robert Skidelsky, *John Maynard Keynes: 1883–1946: Economist, Philosopher, Statesman* (New York: Penguin, 2013).

24. Annan, *Our Age.* Annan characterised this as where one "plays cricket, is scratch at golf and has a fine seat on a horse" but is also likely to be suspicious of "anyone who knows about art, music or literature" (p. 37).

25. Jonathan Rose, *The Intellectual Life of the British Working Classes* (New Haven, CT: Yale University Press, 2021).

26. Immanuel Kant, *Critique of Judgment* (Cambridge, MA: Hackett, 1987).

27. Wooldridge, *The Aristocracy of Talent.*

28. Skidelsky, *John Maynard Keynes.*

29. Simon J. Potter, *Broadcasting Empire: The BBC and the British World, 1922–1970* (Oxford: Oxford University Press, 2012).

30. For example, the removal of the Latin requirement from the entrance exam to Oxford was partly pushed through by scientists—against the wishes of the Humanities faculty—who thought it stopped them from recruiting the best students.

31. Robert Hewison, *Culture and Consensus (Routledge Revivals): England, Art and Politics since 1940* (New York: Routledge, 2015).

32. For more details see Friedman and Reeves, "From Aristocratic to Ordinary."

33. Mike Featherstone, *Consumer Culture and Postmodernism,* 2nd ed. (Thousand Oaks, CA: SAGE, 2007); *Entitled,* 2019, https://press.princeton.edu/books/hardcover/9780691158914/entitled.

34. Mike Savage, *Social Class in the 21st Century* (London: Pelican, 2015); Hewison, *Culture and Consensus.*

35. Hewison, *Culture and Consensus.*

36. This is described in detail in the Methodical Appendix section

37. A limitation of our analysis is that its focus on *all WW* entrants runs the risk of masking recreational heterogeneity *within* the British elite. Yet, there is a surprising degree of homogeneity across potentially important subsamples. There are, however, potentially important differences by occupation. For example, members of the military are consistently more likely to participate in aristocratic practices, whereas people from the cultural industries are much more likely to participate in highbrow activities. See Friedman and Reeves, "From Aristocratic to Ordinary" for more details.

38. Omar Lizardo, "How Cultural Tastes Shape Personal Networks," *American Sociological Review* 71, no. 5 (1 October 2006): 778–807, https://doi.org/10.1177/000312240607100504.

39. Giselinde Kuipers, "Television and Taste Hierarchy: The Case of Dutch Television Comedy," *Media, Culture & Society* 28, no. 3 (1 May 2006): 359–78, https://doi.org/10.1177/0163443706062884; Friedman, *Comedy and Distinction;* Johnston and Baumann, *Foodies.*

40. Shamus Rahman Khan, *Privilege: The Making of an Adolescent Elite at St. Paul's School* (Princeton, NJ: Princeton University Press, 2012). Perhaps the most notable examples of the careful elite selection of popular culture come from the appearances of high-profile politicians, such as Tony Blair, on *Desert Island Discs.* Blair reputedly convened a focus group before deciding what music tracks to play.

41. Andrew Miles and Lisanne Gibson, "Everyday Participation and Cultural Value in Place," *Cultural Trends* 26, no. 1 (2 January 2017): 1–3, https://doi.org/10.1080/09548963.2017.1275129. Significantly, this trend does not appear to reflect wider shifts in the United Kingdom. For example, time-use research conducted in Britain over a similar period illustrates that UK residents are generally not spending more time with friends and family than in the past. Jonathan Gershuny and Oriel Sullivan, *What We Really Do All Day: Insights from the Centre for Time Use Research* (London: Pelican, 2019).

42. Charles Allan McCoy and Roscoe C. Scarborough, "Watching 'Bad' Television: Ironic Consumption, Camp, and Guilty Pleasures," *Poetics* 47 (December 2014): 41–59, https://doi.org/10.1016/j.poetic.2014.10.003.

43. Lizardo, "How Cultural Tastes Shape Personal Networks."

44. Thomas Piketty and Arthur Goldhammer, *Capital in the Twenty-First Century* (Cambridge, MA: Harvard University Press, 2014); Danny Dorling, *Inequality and the 1%* (London: Verso Books, 2019).

45. Rachel Sherman, *Uneasy Street: The Anxieties of Affluence* (Princeton, NJ: Princeton University Press, 2017); Oliver Hahl, Ezra W. Zuckerman, and Minjae Kim, "Why Elites Love Authentic Lowbrow Culture: Overcoming High-Status Denigration with Outsider Art," *American Sociological Review* 82, no. 4 (1 August 2017): 828–56, https://doi.org/10.1177/0003122417710642; Daniel R. Smith, *Elites, Race and Nationhood: The Branded Gentry* (New York: Palgrave MacMillan, 2016).

46. Florence Sutcliffe-Braithwaite, *Class, Politics, and the Decline of Deference in England, 1968–2000* (Oxford: Oxford University Press, 2018); Hewison, *Culture and Consensus Revivals);* Sherman, *Uneasy Street.*

4. Silver Spoons

1. "Five Times David Cameron Let His Mask Slip," *The Independent,* 11 May 2016, https://www.independent.co.uk/news/people/david-cameron-gaffes-controversial-comments-the-queen-nigeria-afghanistan-a7023981.html.

2. Sam Friedman and Daniel Laurison, *The Class Ceiling: Why It Pays to Be Privileged* (Bristol, UK: Policy Press, 2019).

3. Gregory Clark, *The Son Also Rises: Surnames and the History of Social Mobility* (Princeton, NJ: Princeton University Press, 2015).

4. Erzsébet Bukodi, John H. Goldthorpe, and Inga Steinberg, "The Social Origins and Schooling of a Scientific Elite: Fellows of the Royal Society Born from 1900," *British Journal of Sociology* 73, no. 3 (2022): 484–504, https://doi.org/10.1111/1468-4446.12958.

5. Clark, *The Son Also Rises.*

6. Shay O'Brien, "The Family Web: Multigenerational Class Persistence in Elite Populations," *Socio-Economic Review,* 23 June 2023, mwad033, https://doi.org/10.1093/ser/mwad033.

7. David Cannadine, *The Decline and Fall of the British Aristocracy* (New York: Penguin, 2005).

8. Cannadine, *The Decline and Fall of the British Aristocracy.*

9. W. D. Rubinstein, "Education and the Social Origins of British Élites 1880–1970*," *Past & Present* 112, no. 1 (August 1986): 163–207, https://doi.org/10.1093/past/112.1.163; *Democracy and Prosperity,* 2019, https://press.princeton.edu/books/hardcover/9780691182735/democracy-and-prosperity.

10. Aaron Reeves et al., "The Decline and Persistence of the Old Boy: Private Schools and Elite Recruitment 1897 to 2016," *American Sociological Review* 82, no. 6 (1 December 2017): 1139–66, https://doi.org/10.1177/0003122417735742; Aeron Davis and Karel Williams, "Elites and Power after Financialization," *Theory, Culture & Society* 34, no. 5–6 (September 2017): 3–26, https://doi.org/10.1177/0263276417715686.

11. Walter Scheidel, *The Great Leveler: Violence and the History of Inequality from the Stone Age to the Twenty-First Century* (Princeton, NJ: Princeton University Press, 2017).

12. Neil Cummins, "The Hidden Wealth of English Dynasties, 1892–2016," *Economic History Review* 75, no. 3 (2022): 667–702, https://doi.org/10.1111/ehr.13120; Facundo Alvaredo, Anthony B. Atkinson, and Salvatore Morelli, "Top Wealth Shares in the UK over More than a Century," *Journal of Public Economics* 162 (2018): 26–47.

13. Christoph Houman Ellersgaard, Anton Grau Larsen, and Martin D. Munk, "A Very Economic Elite: The Case of the Danish Top CEOs," *Sociology* 47, no. 6 (2013): 1051–71.

14. One potentially surprising finding is that the children of the aristocracy are not higher. Probate records do not include "settled personalty," which include trust funds, and we know that trust funds have been one way that aristocratic families have transferred wealth to their children for a long time. See Katharina Pistor, *The Code of Capital: How the Law Creates Wealth and Inequality* (Princeton, NJ: Princeton University Press, 2019). This fact bolsters our supposition that the estimates we produce here are almost certainly underestimates of the true level of elite reproduction.

15. Maren Toft, "Upper-Class Trajectories: Capital-Specific Pathways to Power," *Socio-Economic Review* 16, no. 2 (April 2018): 341–64, https://doi.org/10.1093/ser/mwx034; Marianne Nordli Hansen and Maren Toft, "Wealth Accumulation and Opportunity Hoarding: Class-Origin Wealth Gaps over a Quarter of a Century in a Scandinavian Country," *American Sociological Review* 86, no. 4 (2021): 603–38; Andreas Fagereng, Magne Mogstad, and Marte Rønning, "Why Do Wealthy Parents Have Wealthy Children?," *Journal of Political Economy* 129, no. 3 (March 2021): 703–56, https://doi.org/10.1086/712446.

16. Stephane Cote et al., "The Psychology of Entrenched Privilege: High Socioeconomic Status Individuals from Affluent Backgrounds Are Uniquely High in Entitlement," *Personality and Social Psychology Bulletin* 47 (May 2020): 014616722091663, https://doi.org/10.1177/0146167220916633.

17. Paul K. Piff et al., "Higher Social Class Predicts Increased Unethical Behavior," *Proceedings of the National Academy of Sciences* 109, no. 11 (2012): 4086–91; Sean R. Martin, Stéphane Côté, and Todd Woodruff, "Echoes of Our Upbringing: How Growing up Wealthy or Poor Relates to Narcissism, Leader Behavior, and Leader Effectiveness," *Academy of Management Journal* 59, no. 6 (2016): 2157–77.

18. Pierre Bourdieu, *Distinction: A Social Critique of the Judgement of Taste* (London: Routledge, 2010).

19. Douglas B. Holt, "Distinction in America? Recovering Bourdieu's Theory of Tastes from Its Critics," *Poetics,* 25, no. 2–3 (November 1997): 93–120, https://doi.org/10.1016/S0304-422X(97)00010-7; Vegard Jarness, "Modes of Consumption: From 'What' to 'How' in Cultural Stratification Research," *Poetics,* 53 (December 2015): 65–79, https://doi.org/10.1016/j.poetic.2015.08.002; Will Atkinson, *Class, Individualization and Late Modernity: In Search of the Reflexive Worker* (Houndsmill, Basingstoke: Palgrave Schol, 2010).

20. Annette Lareau, *Unequal Childhoods: Class, Race, and Family Life, 2nd Edition with an Update a Decade Later,* 2nd ed. (Berkeley: University of California Press, 2011); Diane Reay, *Miseducation: Inequality, Education and the Working Classes* (Bristol, UK: Policy Press, 2017).

21. Orian Brook, Dave O'Brien, and Mark Taylor, *Culture Is Bad for You: Inequality in the Cultural and Creative Industries* (Manchester: Manchester University Press, 2020); Friedman and Laurison, *The Class Ceiling.*

22. Louise Ashley, *Highly Discriminating: Why the City Isn't Fair and Diversity Doesn't Work* (Bristol, UK: Bristol University Press, 2022).

23. Robert D. Mare, "A Multigenerational View of Inequality," *Demography* 48, no. 1 (January 2011): 1–23, https://doi.org/10.1007/s13524-011-0014-7.

24. O'Brien, "The Family Web"; Lareau, *Unequal Childhoods.*

25. Rohyn Fivush, Jennifer G. Bohanek, and Marshall Duke, "The Intergenerational Self: Subjective Perspective and Family History," in *Self Continuity: Individual and Collective Perspectives* (New York: Psychology Press, 2008), 131–43; Clark, *The Son Also Rises;* Fagereng, Mogstad, and Rønning, "Why Do Wealthy Parents Have Wealthy Children?"

26. Lawrence Stone and Jeanne C. Fawtier Stone, *An Open Elite?: England 1540–1880* (Oxford: Oxford University Press, 1995); Parul Bhandari, *Money, Culture, Class: Elite Women as Modern Subjects* (New York: Routledge, 2019).

27. Luna Glucksberg, "Gendering the Elites: An Ethnographic Approach to Elite Women's Lives and the Reproduction of Inequality," in *New Directions in Elite Studies* (New York: Routledge, 2017); Sylvia Junko Yanagisako, *Producing Culture and Capital: Family Firms in Italy* (Princeton, NJ: Princeton University Press, 2002); Laura Clancy and Katie Higgins, "A Feminist Intervention in Elite Studies," British Sociological Association Conference, 2021; Jeremy Greenwood et al., "Marry Your Like: Assortative Mating and Income Inequality," *American Economic Review* 104, no. 5 (May 2014): 348–53, https://doi.org/10.1257/aer.104.5.348; Eve Worth, "Women, Education and Social Mobility in Britain during the Long 1970s," *Cultural and Social History* 16, no. 1 (2019): 67–83.

28. On networks and elites more broadly, see Anton Grau Larsen and Christoph Houman Ellersgaard, "Identifying Power Elites: K-Cores in Heterogeneous Affiliation Networks," *Social Networks* 50 (2017): 55–69.

29. Richard Allen, "Confidante Who Lived Next Door," *The Standard,* 12 April 2012, https://www.standard.co.uk/hp/front/confidante-who-lived-next-door-6299202 .html.

30. Yanagisako, *Producing Culture and Capital;* Clancy and Higgins, "A Feminist Intervention in Elite Studies"; Stone and Stone, *An Open Elite?;* Bhandari, *Money, Culture, Class.*

31. We also focussed on people who had spent a significant part of their lives in the United Kingdom.

32. Parliamentary Archives, "The House of Lords Goes to India: The Sinha Peerage Case | Parliamentary Archives: Inside the Act Room," 5 August 2021, https://archives .blog.parliament.uk/2021/08/05/the-house-of-lords-goes-to-india-the-sinha-peerage -case/.

33. Eleni Karagiannaki, "The Scale and Drivers of Ethnic Wealth Gaps across the Wealth Distribution in the UK: Evidence from Understanding Society," 2023, Centre for Analysis of Social Exclusion (CASE) and the International Inequalities Institute, LSE, https://eprints.lse.ac.uk/119885/.

34. Facundo Alvaredo et al., The World Inequality Database, 2023, https://wid .world/.

35. John H. Goldthorpe, "Social Class Mobility in Modern Britain: Changing Structure, Constant Process," *Journal of the British Academy* 4, no. 89–111 (2016); Richard Breen, *Social Mobility in Europe* (Oxford: Oxford University Press, 2004).

36. Christoph Houman Ellersgaard, Jacob Aagaard Lunding, Lasse Folke Henriksen, and Anton Grau Larsen, "Pathways to the Power Elite: The Organizational Landscape of Elite Careers," *Sociological Review* 67, no. 5 (2019):1170–92.

37. Richard Breen, "Educational Expansion and Social Mobility in the 20th Century," *Social Forces* 89, no. 2 (December 2010): 365–88, https://doi.org/10.1353/sof.2010 .0076.

5. Old Boys

1. Brian Simon, *The Two Nations and the Educational Structure, 1780–1870* (London: Lawrence & Wishart, 1981).

2. David Charles Douglas, George Malcolm Young, and W. D. Handcock, *English Historical Documents, 1833–1874* (East Sussex, England: Psychology Press, 1996).

3. We are indebted to research assistant Yasha Bajaj for calculating these figures.

4. Robert Verkaik, *Posh Boys: How English Public Schools Ruin Britain* (London: Oneworld Publications, 2018); Richard Beard, *Sad Little Men: Inside the Secretive World That Shaped Boris Johnson* (New York: Vintage, 2022).

5. David Kynaston and Francis Green, *Engines of Privilege: Britain's Private School Problem*, illus. ed. (London: Bloomsbury Publishing, 2019); Sol Gamsu, "Financing Elite Education: Economic Capital and the Maintenance of Class Power in English Private Schools," *Sociological Review* 70, no. 6 (November 2022): 1240–66, https://doi .org/10.1177/00380261221076202.

6. For more details on this part of our analysis see Aaron Reeves et al., "The Decline and Persistence of the Old Boy: Private Schools and Elite Recruitment 1897 to 2016," *American Sociological Review* 82, no. 6 (December 2017): 1139–66, https://doi .org/10.1177/0003122417735742.

7. See counterfactual analysis included in Reeves et al., "The Decline and Persistence of the Old Boy."

8. Peter W. Cookson Jr. and Caroline Hodges Persell, *Preparing for Power: America's Elite Boarding Schools* (New York: Basic Books, 1987).

9. Thomas James Henderson Bishop, *Winchester and the Public School Elite: A Statistical Analysis* (London: Faber, 1967).

10. See online appendix in Reeves et al., "The Decline and Persistence of the Old Boy."

11. For a detailed examination of the relationships between educational reform and meritocracy in Britain over the twentieth century, see Peter Mandler, *The Crisis of the Meritocracy* (Oxford: Oxford University Press, 2020).

12. Our use of structural break tests is explained in depth in the Methodological Appendix.

13. Simply identifying structural breaks in these time series does not definitively confirm that the decline in Clarendon alumni is driven by educational reform. We explored this further by estimating time-series regression models examining whether the long-run decline is associated with four measures of educational outcomes that can be viewed as proxies for these reforms: (1) the proportion of government spending on education (percent GDP) when any given cohort was age 10, (2) the proportion of the adult population without any formal schooling when any given cohort was age 35, (3) the number of children enrolled in school when any given cohort was age 10 (as a proportion of children age 0 to 14), and (4) the number of people attending university when any given cohort was age 20 (as a proportion of the population age 15 to 24). Even adjusting for these four potential confounders, our models indicate that greater government spending on education, more people with some formal schooling, more children in primary school, and more university students *predict fewer Clarendon alumni in Who's Who.* For more details see Reeves et al., "The Decline and Persistence of the Old Boy."

14. John Scott, *Who Rules Britain?* (Oxford: Polity, 1991).

15. Adrian Wooldridge, *The Aristocracy of Talent: How Meritocracy Made the Modern World* (Dublin: Penguin, 2023).

16. Shamus Khan, *Privilege: The Making of an Adolescent Elite at St. Paul's School* (Princeton, NJ: Princeton University Press, 2011), 9.

17. Many argue that elite schools have been particularly adept at adapting and responding to such reform—see G. William Domhoff, *Who Rules America? The Triumph of the Corporate Rich,* 7th ed. (New York: McGraw-Hill Education, 2013); Khan, *Privilege.*

18. It is important to be careful about assuming that means-tested here means low income. St Paul's school, for example, introduced a new scheme in 2016 that offered more generous support to families with a household income less than £126,000. So, while most of these families are not in the top 1 percent, many of them are very far from being on low incomes.

19. Verkaik, *Posh Boys;* see also Beard, *Sad Little Men.* Although texts like Beard's tend to rely on the autobiographical reflections of the author.

20. Verkaik, *Posh Boys.*

21. Mitchell L. Stevens, Elizabeth A. Armstrong, and Richard Arum, "Sieve, Incubator, Temple, Hub: Empirical and Theoretical Advances in the Sociology of Higher Education," *Annual Review of Sociology* 34, no. 1 (2008): 127–51, https://doi.org/10.1146/annurev.soc.34.040507.134737.

22. Khan, *Privilege.*

23. Claire Maxwell and Peter Aggleton, *Elite Education: International Perspectives* (New York: Routledge, 2015); Max Persson, "Contested Ease: Negotiating Contradictory Modes of Elite Distinction in Face-to-Face Interaction," *British Journal of Sociology* 72, no. 4 (2021): 930–45, https://doi.org/10.1111/1468-4446.12874; Emma Taylor, "'No Fear': Privilege and the Navigation of Hierarchy at an Elite Boys' School in England," *British Journal of Sociology of Education* 42, no. 7 (3 October 2021): 935–50, https://doi.org/10.1080/01425692.2021.1953374; Rubén A. Gaztambide-Fernández, *The Best of the Best: Becoming Elite at an American Boarding School* (Cambridge, MA: Harvard University Press, 2009); Khan, *Privilege.*

24. Pierre Bourdieu, *The State Nobility: Elite Schools in the Field of Power* (Cambridge: Polity Press, 1998). 180–184

25. Claire Maxwell and Peter Aggleton, "Creating Cosmopolitan Subjects: The Role of Families and Private Schools in England," *Sociology* 50, no. 4 (2016): 780–95; Joan Forbes and Claire Maxwell, "Bourdieu Plus: Understanding the Creation of Agentic, Aspirational Girl Subjects in Elite Schools," *International Perspectives on Theorizing Aspirations: Applying Bourdieu's Tools* (London: Bloomsbury, 2018), 161–74.

26. Janet Howarth, "Public Schools, Safety-Nets and Educational Ladders: The Classification of Girls' Secondary Schools, 1880–1914," *Oxford Review of Education* 11, no. 1 (1985): 59–71.

27. There is perhaps one notable absence from this list: Manchester High School for Girls. This is a school which is frequently discussed in the historical literature around top girls schools. It is true that Manchester was among the best schools in the early part of the twentieth century. However, this seems to have changed after 1940. There are very few alumni from Manchester that attend Oxford after 1940 in our data and it is noteworthy that, unlike many of the other schools on this list, they are no longer one of the most academically successful schools.

28. June Purvis, *History of Women's Education in England* (Maidenhead, UK: Open University Press, 1991).

29. Gillian Avery, *The Best Type of Girl: A History of Girls' Independent Schools* (London: Andre Deutsch, 1991).

30. Claire Maxwell and Peter Aggleton, "Schools, Schooling and Elite Status in English Education—Changing Configurations?," *L'Année sociologique* 66, no. 1

(April 2016): 147–70; Joan Forbes and Bob Lingard, "Elite School Capitals and Girls' Schooling: Understanding the (Re)Production of Privilege through a Habitus of 'Assuredness'," in *Privilege, Agency and Affect: Understanding the Production and Effects of Action,* ed. Claire Maxwell and Peter Aggleton (London: Palgrave Macmillan, 2013), 50–68, https://doi.org/10.1057/9781137292636_4.

31. Maxwell and Aggleton, "Schools, Schooling and Elite Status in English education."

32. Geoffrey Walford, *The Private Schooling of Girls: Past and Present* (London: Routledge, 1993).

33. Geoffrey Walford, *Private Education: Tradition and Diversity* (London: A&C Black, 2006).

34. Nancy Mitford, *The Pursuit of Love* (London: Hamish Hamilton, 1945).

35. Walford, *The Private Schooling of Girls.*

36. Avery, *The Best Type of Girl.*

37. Sara Delamont, "The Contradictions in Ladies' Education," in *The Nineteenth-Century Woman,* ed. Sara Delamont and Lorna Duffin (London: Routledge, 2012).

38. Sarah Aiston, "A Good Job for a Girl? The Career Biographies of Women Graduates of the University of Liverpool Post-1945," *Twentieth Century British History* 15, no. 4 (January 2004): 361–87, https://doi.org/10.1093/tcbh/15.4.361.

39. Ellen Jordan, "Making Good Wives and Mothers"? The Transformation of Middle-Class Girls' Education in Nineteenth-Century Britain," *History of Education Quarterly* 31, no. 4 (1991): 439–62.

40. Carol Dyhouse, "Good Wives and Little Mothers: Social Anxieties and the Schoolgirl's Curriculum, 1890–1920," *Oxford Review of Education* 3, no. 1 (1977): 21–35.

41. C. Wright Mills, *The Power Elite* (New York: Oxford University Press, 2000).

6. Bright Young Things

1. "Bright Young Things," National Portrait Gallery, accessed 31 January 2024, https://www.npg.org.uk/collections/search/group/1356.

2. Joseph A. Soares, *The Decline of Privilege: The Modernization of Oxford University,* illus. ed. (Stanford University Press, 2002); Claire Hann and Danny Dorling, "A Changed Institution," *Oxford Magazine* 2019, no. 411 (2019).

3. University of Oxford, "Admissions Statistics," accessed 15 July 2023, https://www.ox.ac.uk/about/facts-and-figures/admissions-statistics; University of Cambridge, "Undergraduate Admissions Statistics," Text, 19 May 2021, https://www.undergraduate.study.cam.ac.uk/publications/undergraduate-admissions-statistics; Daniel I. Greenstein, "The Junior Members, 1900–1990: A Profile," in *The History of the University of Oxford,* vol. 8, *The Twentieth Century,* ed. Brian Harrison (Oxford: Oxford University Press, 1994), chapter 3, https://doi.org/10.1093/acprof:oso/9780198229742.003.0003.

4. Walter Rüegg, ed., *A History of the University in Europe,* vol. 3, *Universities in the Nineteenth and Early Twentieth Centuries* (Cambridge: Cambridge University Press, 2004).

5. Robert David Anderson, *Universities and Elites in Britain since 1800,* vol. 16 (Cambridge University Press, 1995); A. H. Halsey, *Decline of Donnish Dominion: The British Academic Professions in the Twentieth Century* (Oxford: Oxford University Press, 1995); A. H. Halsey, "Oxford and the British Universities," in *The History of the University of Oxford,* vol. 8, *The Twentieth Century,* ed. Brian Harrison (Oxford: Oxford University Press, 1994), chapter 22, https://doi.org/10.1093/acprof:oso/9780198229742 .003.0022.

6. HESA, "Higher Education in Numbers," Universities UK, accessed 3 November 2023, https://www.universitiesuk.ac.uk/latest/insights-and-analysis/higher -education-numbers.

7. Anderson, *Universities and Elites in Britain since 1800.*

8. Of course, it is worth noting the composition of this comparison group of non-graduates clearly changes as more people go to university, becoming less affluent, less middle-class, and less based in the south-east. But equally across the period examined here university graduates remained in the minority. The number of people in any given cohort attending university did not reach above 10 percent before the 1990s.

9. Paul Wakeling and Mike Savage, "Entry to Elite Positions and the Stratification of Higher Education in Britain," *Sociological Review* 63, no. 2 (2015): 290–320.

10. Konrad H. Jarausch, "Higher Education and Social Change: Some Comparative Perspectives," in *The Transformation of Higher Learning 1860–1930: Expansion, Diversification, Social Opening and Professionalization in England, Germany, Russia and the United States,* ed. Konrad H. Jarausch (Stuttgart: Klett-Cotta, 1982), 9–36.

11. Roy Lowe, "The Expansion of Higher Education in England," in *The Transformation of Higher Learning 1860–1930: Expansion, Diversification, Social Opening and Professionalization in England, Germany, Russia and the United States,* ed. Konrad H. Jarausch (Stuttgart: Klett-Cotta, 1982), 37–56; John Roach, *Public Examinations in England 1850–1900* (Cambridge University Press, 1971).

12. Anderson, *Universities and Elites.*

13. L. W. B. Brockliss, *The University of Oxford: A History,* illus. ed. (Oxford: Oxford University Press, 2016); Christopher N. L. Brooke, *A History of the University of Cambridge,* vol. 4, *1870–1990* (Cambridge: Cambridge University Press, 1992).

14. M. C. Curthoys and Janet Howarth, "Origins and Destinations: The Social Mobility of Oxford Men and Women," in *The History of the University of Oxford,* vol. 7, *Nineteenth-Century Oxford, Part 2,* ed. M. G. Brock and M. C. Curthoys (Oxford University Press, 2000), chapter 24, https://doi.org/10.1093/acprof:oso/9780199510177.003 .0024.

15. JR de S. Honey and M. C. Curthoys, "Oxford and Schooling," *The History of the University of Oxford* 7 (2000): 545–69.

16. M. L. Stevens, E. A. Armstrong, and R. Arum, "Sieve, Incubator, Temple, Hub: Empirical and Theoretical Advances in the Sociology of Higher Education," *Annual Review of Sociology* 34 (2008): 127–51.

17. Curthoys and Howarth, "Origins and Destinations."

18. Noel Annan, *Our Age: English Intellectuals Between the World Wars: A Group Portrait* (New York: Random House Inc, 1991).

19. Annan, *Our Age.*

20. Anthony Sampson, *Anatomy of Britain* (London: Hodder & Stoughton, 1962).

21. Soares, *The Decline of Privilege.*

22. Sampson, *Anatomy of Britain;* David Kynaston, *Modernity Britain: 1957–1962* (New York: Bloomsbury Paperbacks, 2015).

23. Soares, *The Decline of Privilege.*

24. Soares, *The Decline of Privilege;* A. H. Halsey, "The Franks Commission," in *The History of the University of Oxford,* vol. 8, *The Twentieth Century,* ed. Brian Harrison (Oxford University Press, 1994), chapter 26, https://doi.org/10.1093/acprof:oso /9780198229742.003.0026.

25. Hann and Dorling, "A Changed Institution."

26. Hann and Dorling, "A Changed Institution."

27. Soares, *The Decline of Privilege.*

28. Soares, *The Decline of Privilege.*

29. Soares, *The Decline of Privilege.*

30. Soares, *The Decline of Privilege;* Greenstein, *The Junior Members, 1900–1990.* People from the professions in 1911 were over-represented at Oxford (an odds ratio of ~8) but this advantage declined as the size of the professions grew within the population in general. By 1971, the odds ratio had fallen to 2, suggesting the odds of attending Oxford were twice as high if your father was occupied in a profession.

31. Soares, *The Decline of Privilege.*

32. Alan Smithers, "A Levels 1951–2014" (Buckingham: Centre for Education and Employment Research, University of Buckingham, 2014); Paul Bolton, "Education: Historical Statistics," *House of Commons Library* SN / SG / 4252 (November 2012); Ken Mayhew, Cécile Deer, and Mehak Dua, "The Move to Mass Higher Education in the UK: Many Questions and Some Answers," *Oxford Review of Education* 30, no. 1 (2004): 65–82.

33. Peter Mandler, "Educating the Nation I: Schools," *Transactions of the Royal Historical Society* 24 (December 2014): 5–28, https://doi.org/10.1017/S0080440114000012.

34. Brockliss, *The University of Oxford.*

35. Smithers, "A Levels 1951–2014"; Bolton, "Education."

36. Phillip Brown, "Cultural Capital and Social Exclusion: Some Observations on Recent Trends in Education, Employment and the Labour Market," *Work, Employment and Society* 9, no. 1 (1995): 29–51; David Kynaston and Francis Green, *Engines of Privilege: Britain's Private School Problem* (London: Bloomsbury, 2019).

37. Brockliss, *The University of Oxford.*

38. Brockliss, *The University of Oxford.*

39. C. Wright Mills, *The Power Elite* (Oxford: Oxford University Press, 1956).

40. Diane Reay, Gill Crozier, and John Clayton, "'Strangers in Paradise'?: Working-Class Students in Elite Universities," *Sociology* 43, no. 6 (December 2009): 1103–21, https://doi.org/10.1177/0038038509345700.

41. Anthony Abraham Jack, *The Privileged Poor: How Elite Colleges Are Failing Disadvantaged Students* (Cambridge, MA: Harvard University Press, 2019).

42. Aaron Reeves et al., "The Decline and Persistence of the Old Boy: Private Schools and Elite Recruitment 1897 to 2016," *American Sociological Review* 82, no. 6 (1 December 2017): 1139–66, https://doi.org/10.1177/0003122417735742; Eve Worth, Aaron Reeves, and Sam Friedman, "Is There an Old Girls' Network? Girls' Schools and Recruitment to the British Elite," *British Journal of Sociology of Education* 44, no. 1 (November 2022): 1 25, https://doi.org/10.1080/01425692.2022.2132472.

43. W. D. Rubinstein, "Education and the Social Origins of British Élites 1880–1970," *Past & Present* 112, no. 1 (August 1986): 163–207, https://doi.org/10.1093/past/112.1.163; William D. Rubinstein, "The Social Origins and Career Patterns of Oxford and Cambridge Matriculants, 1840–1900," *Historical Research* 82, no. 218 (November 2009): 715–30, https://doi.org/10.1111/j.1468-2281.2008.00470.x.

44. The proportion of people in *Who's Who* who did not attend Oxbridge but who came from families in the top 1 percent of the wealth distribution has been relatively stable over time, at around 15 percent. Similarly, the proportion of people who did attend Oxbridge and came from families in the top 1 percent has pretty consistently floated around 25 percent.

45. This is actually below the annual income for the top 1 percent in the population as a whole, which in 2019 was £120,000. This suggests that the very richest people in the United Kingdom are slightly less likely to get their kids into Oxbridge. University of Oxford, "FOI 20200523," accessed 15 July 2023, https://www.whatdotheyknow.com/request/667009/response/1590075/attach/html/2/FOI%2020200523%203%20Letter.pdf.html.

46. Mills, *The Power Elite.*

47. Brockliss, *The University of Oxford.*

48. Toby Young, "Class," in *The Oxford Myth,* ed. Rachel Johnson (London: Weidenfeld and Nicolson, 1988).

49. Reay, Crozier, and Clayton, "'Strangers in Paradise'?"; Anthony Abraham Jack, "(No) Harm in Asking: Class, Acquired Cultural Capital, and Academic Engagement at an Elite University," *Sociology of Education* 89, no. 1 (2016): 1–19; Kalwant Bhopal and Martin Myers, *Elite Universities and the Making of Privilege: Exploring Race and Class in Global Educational Economies* (Abingdon, Oxon: Routledge, 2023).

50. Pamela Roberts, *Black Oxford: The Untold Stories of Oxford University's Black Scholars* (Oxford: Signal Books, 2013).

51. Clare Hopkins, *Trinity: 450 Years of an Oxford College Community* (Oxford: Oxford University Press, 2005).

52. Brockliss, *The University of Oxford.*

53. Young, "Class."

54. Pierre Bourdieu, *The State Nobility: Elite Schools in the Field of Power* (Oxford: Polity, 1996).

55. Edward Chaney, *The Evolution of the Grand Tour: Anglo-Italian Cultural Relations since the Renaissance* (London: Routledge, 2000).

56. *Daily Telegraph,* "Obituary of Sir Peter Daniell," 2002, https://www.telegraph .co.uk/news/obituaries/1398272/Sir-Peter-Daniell.html.

57. Bourdieu, *The State Nobility.*

58. Young, "Class."

7. How Elites Think

1. Karl Marx and Friedrich Engels, *The German Ideology,* vol. 1 (International Publishers Co, 1845); C. Wright Mills, *The Power Elite* (Oxford: Oxford University Press, 1956).

2. Mills, *The Power Elite.*

3. Owen Jones, *The Establishment: And How They Get Away with It* (London: Penguin, 2014).

4. Matthew Goodwin, *Values, Voice and Virtue: The New British Politics* (London: Random House, 2023).

5. This claim has been developed in Aeron Davis, *Reckless Opportunists: Elites at the End of the Establishment* (Manchester: Manchester University Press, 2018).

6. Benjamin I. Page, Jason Seawright, and Matthew J. Lacombe, *Billionaires and Stealth Politics* (Chicago: University of Chicago Press, 2018); Lior Sheffer et al., "Nonrepresentative Representatives: An Experimental Study of the Decision Making of Elected Politicians," *American Political Science Review* 112, no. 2 (2018): 302–21; Nicholas Carnes and Noam Lupu, "The Economic Backgrounds of Politicians," *Annual Review of Political Science* 26, no. 1 (2023): 253–70; Cristian Márquez Romo and Hugo Marcos-Marne, "If Unequal, Don't Change It? The Inequality-Redistribution Puzzle among Political Elites," *Current Sociology* (2023), https://doi.org/10.1177/001139212 31186447.

7. Adrian Wooldridge, "The New Elite: The Rise of the Progressive Aristocracy," *The Spectator,* 12 April 2023, https://www.spectator.co.uk/article/the-new-elite-the -rise-of-the-progressive-aristocracy/; Jones, *The Establishment.*

8. Peter Walker, "Suella Braverman Rails against 'Experts and Elites,' in Partisan Speech," *The Guardian,* 15 May 2023, https://www.theguardian.com/politics /2023/may/15/suella-braverman-rails-against-experts-and-elites-in-partisan-speech.

9. Jeremy Corbyn, "Engagements - Hansard - UK Parliament," accessed 17 July 2023, https://hansard.parliament.uk/Commons/2019-05-15/debates/603A3DE6 -2DF7-42C8-AFEE-D076A0EE790F/Engagementshighlight=pockets+super -rich+elite.

10. Page, Seawright, and Lacombe, *Billionaires and Stealth Politics;* Benjamin I. Page, L. M. Bartels, and J. Seawright, "Democracy and the Policy Preferences of Wealthy Americans," *Perspectives on Politics* 11, no. 1 (March 2013): 51–73; Benjamin I. Page and Martin Gilens, "Testing Theories of American Politics: Elites, Interest Groups, and Average Citizens," *Perspectives on Politics* 12, no. 3 (2014): 564–81.

11. Page, Seawright, and Lacombe, *Billionaires and Stealth Politics.*

12. Pablo Beramendi et al., "Introduction: The Politics of Advanced Capitalism," in *The Politics of Advanced Capitalism,* ed. Pablo Beramendi et al. (Cambridge: Cambridge University Press, 2015), 1–64, https://doi.org/10.1017/CBO9781316163245.002.

13. Ben W. Ansell and David J. Samuels, *Inequality and Democratization: An Elite-Competition Approach* (New York: Cambridge University Press, 2015); Ben W. Ansell, *Inward Conquest: The Political Origins of Modern Public Services* (Cambridge: Cambridge University Press, 2020).

14. David Kynaston and Francis Green, *Engines of Privilege: Britain's Private School Problem* (London: Bloomsbury, 2019); Simon Burgess, Claire Crawford, and Lindsey Macmillan, "Access to Grammar Schools by Socio-Economic Status," *Environment and Planning A: Economy and Space* 50, no. 7 (October 2018): 1381–85, https://doi .org/10.1177/0308518X18787820; Jon Andrews, Jo Hutchinson, and Rebecca Johnes, 'Grammar Schools and Social Mobility—The Education Policy Institute" (London: Education Policy Institute, 2016), https://epi.org.uk/publications-and-research /grammar-schools-social-mobility/; V. Boliver and A. Swift, "Do Comprehensive Schools Reduce Social Mobility?," *British Journal of Sociology* 62, no. 1 (March 2011): 89–110.

15. John H. Goldthorpe, "Understanding—and Misunderstanding—Social Mobility in Britain: The Entry of the Economists, the Confusion of Politicians and the Limits of Educational Policy," *Journal of Social Policy* 42, no. 3 (July 2013): 431–50, https://doi.org/10.1017/S004727941300024X.

16. Mills, *The Power Elite.*

17. Jacques A. Hagenaars and Allan L. McCutcheon, *Applied Latent Class Analysis* (Cambridge: Cambridge University Press, 2002).

18. There are a limited number of questions we can include in our analysis here, but the basic shape of our results does not vary if we, for example, take out the question on racism and replace it with the question about feminism.

19. Goodwin, *Values, Voice and Virtue.*

20. It is worth noting here that to define class position we use objective class origins as well as subjective class origins to identify the working class and middle class.

That is, "working class origin" people need to have had a parent who worked in a routine manual occupation and identify as working class. We use both to avoid the complex cases where people's subjective class origins might differ from the objective class origins because we suspect this might be correlated with political ideology.

21. Richard D Wiggins et al., "Are Right-Wing Attitudes and Voting Associated with Having Attended Private School? An Investigation Using the 1970 British Cohort Study," *Sociology*, 7 April 2023, 00380385221141386, https://doi.org/10.1177/00380385221141386.

22. Robert Ford and Will Jennings, "The Changing Cleavage Politics of Western Europe," *Annual Review of Political Science* 23, no. 1 (2020): 295–314, https://doi.org/10.1146/annurev-polisci-052217-104957.

23. Brendan Apfeld et al., "Higher Education and Cultural Liberalism: Regression Discontinuity Evidence from Romania," *Journal of Politics* 85, no. 1 (January 2023): 34–48, https://doi.org/10.1086/720644; Ralph Scott, "Does University Make You More Liberal? Estimating the within-Individual Effects of Higher Education on Political Values," *Electoral Studies* 77 (June 2022): 102471, https://doi.org/10.1016/j.electstud.2022.102471; although, see Elizabeth Simon, "Demystifying the Link between Higher Education and Liberal Values: A within-Sibship Analysis of British Individuals' Attitudes from 1994–2020," *British Journal of Sociology* 73, no. 5 (2022): 967–84,https://doi.org/10.1111/1468-4446.12972.

24. Colin Jerolmack and Shamus Khan, "Talk Is Cheap: Ethnography and the Attitudinal Fallacy," *Sociological Methods & Research* 43, no. 2 (2014): 178–209.

25. We tested some other kinds of decision-making which we discuss in the online appendix.

26. Hal R. Arkes and Catherine Blumer, "The Psychology of Sunk Cost," *Organizational Behavior and Human Decision Processes* 35, no. 1 (1 February 1985): 124–40, https://doi.org/10.1016/0749-5978(85)90049-4.

27. Sheffer et al., "Nonrepresentative Representatives."

28. Chris Hanretty, *A Court of Specialists: Judicial Behavior on the UK Supreme Court* (New York: Oxford University Press, 2020).

8. Radical Women

1. Lena Edlund and Rohini Pande, "Why Have Women Become Left-Wing? The Political Gender Gap and the Decline in Marriage," *Quarterly Journal of Economics* 117, no. 3 (August 2002): 917–61, https://doi.org/10.1162/003355302760193922; Rosalind Shorrocks, "Cohort Change in Political Gender Gaps in Europe and Canada: The Role of Modernization," *Politics & Society* 46, no. 2 (2018): 135–75.

2. Lola Olufemi, *Feminism, Interrupted: Disrupting Power* (London: Pluto Press, 2020); Patricia Hill Collins, *Black Feminist Thought: Knowledge, Consciousness, and the Politics of Empowerment* (New York: Routledge, 2022).

3. Lisa A. Keister, Sarah Thébaud, and Jill E. Yavorsky, "Gender in the Elite," *Annual Review of Sociology* 48, no. 1 (2022): 149–69, https://doi.org/10.1146/annurev-soc-020321-031544.

4. Luna Glucksberg, "Gendering the Elites: An Ethnographic Approach to Elite Women's Lives and the Reproduction of Inequality," in *New Directions in Elite Studies* (Abingdon, Oxon: Routledge, 2017), chapter 11; Sylvia Junko Yanagisako, *Producing Culture and Capital: Family Firms in Italy* (Princeton, NJ: Princeton University Press, 2002); Laura Clancy and Katie Higgins, "A Feminist Intervention in Elite Studies," British Sociological Association Annual Conference, online, April 2021; Silvia Federici, "Social Reproduction Theory: History, Issues and Present Challenges." *Radical Philosophy* 204 (2019): 55–57.

5. Elaine Chalus, "Women's Political Roles," in *Elite Women in English Political Life c.1754–1790,* ed. Elaine Chalus (Oxford University Press, 2005), chapter 2, https://doi.org/10.1093/acprof:oso/9780199280100.003.0003.

6. Luis Galan-Guerrero, "The Reform of the British Civil Service: Life Cycle, Family, and Class in the Treasury, c. 1847–1914" (PhD thesis, University of Oxford, 2022); Elaine Chalus, *Elite Women in English Political Life c. 1754–1790* (Oxford: Oxford University Press, 2005).

7. Gail Chester, *"Who's Who,"* in *Encyclopedia of Life Writing: Autobiographical and Biographical Forms,* ed. Margaretta Jolly (London: Routledge, 2001).

8. Chester, *"Who's Who."*

9. Pippa Norris and Joni Lovenduski, *Political Recruitment: Gender, Race and Class in the British Parliament* (Cambridge: Cambridge University Press, 1995); Ronald Inglehart and Pippa Norris, *Rising Tide: Gender Equality and Cultural Change around the World* (Cambridge: Cambridge University Press, 2003).

10. P. Paxton and S. Kunovich, "Women's Political Representation: The Importance of Ideology," *Social Forces* 82, no. 1 (September 2003): 87–113; Lori Beaman et al., "Powerful Women: Does Exposure Reduce Bias?," *Quarterly Journal of Economics* 124, no. 4 (November 2009): 1497–1540, https://doi.org/10.1162/qjec.2009.124.4.1497; Lori Beaman et al., "Female Leadership Raises Aspirations and Educational Attainment for Girls: A Policy Experiment in India," *Science* 335, no. 6068 (February 2012): 582–86, https://doi.org/10.1126/science.1212382.

11. Simone de Beauvoir, *The Second Sex,* trans. H. M. Parshley (Harmondsworth: Penguin, 1972); Betty Friedan, *The Feminine Mystique: Penguin Modern Classics* (London: Penguin Classics, 2010); Germaine Greer, *The Female Eunuch* (London: Harper Perennial, 2020).

12. Rosalind Shorrocks, "A Feminist Generation? Cohort Change in Gender-Role Attitudes and the Second-Wave Feminist Movement," *International Journal of Public Opinion Research* 30, no. 1 (2018): 125–45.

13. Paul Bolton, "Education: Historical Statistics," *House of Commons Library* SN/SG/4252 (November 2012).

14. Eve Worth, *The Welfare State Generation: Women, Agency and Class in Britain since 1945* (London: Bloomsbury Academic, 2022); ONS, "Births in England and Wales—Office for National Statistics," accessed 16 July 2023, https://www.ons.gov.uk /peoplepopulationandcommunity/birthsdeathsandmarriages/livebirths/bulletins/births ummarytablesenglandandwales/2021; Man Yee Kan, Oriel Sullivan, and Jonathan Gershuny, "Gender Convergence in Domestic Work: Discerning the Effects of Interactional and Institutional Barriers from Large-Scale Data," *Sociology* 45, no. 2 (2011): 234–51.

15. David Neumark and Wendy Stock, "The Effects of Race and Sex Discrimination Laws" (working paper 8215, National Bureau of Economic Research Cambridge, MA, 2001).

16. This is based on a linear extrapolation from a simple regression model.

17. Sarah Childs and Mona Lena Krook, "Should Feminists Give Up on Critical Mass? A Contingent Yes," *Politics & Gender* 2, no. 4 (December 2006): 522–30, https://doi.org/10.1017/S1743923X06251146; Mariateresa Torchia, Andrea Calabrò, and Morten Huse, "Women Directors on Corporate Boards: From Tokenism to Critical Mass," *Journal of Business Ethics* 102, no. 2 (August 2011): 299–317, https://doi.org/10 .1007/s10551-011-0815-z.

18. Helen Kowalewska, "Bringing Women on Board: The Social Policy Implications of Gender Diversity in Top Jobs," *Journal of Social Policy* 49, no. 4 (October 2020): 744–62, https://doi.org/10.1017/S0047279419000722; Torchia, Calabrò, and Huse, "Women Directors on Corporate Boards."

19. Fidan Ana Kurtulus and Donald Tomaskovic-Devey, "Do Female Top Managers Help Women to Advance? A Panel Study Using EEO-1 Records," *ANNALS of the American Academy of Political and Social Science* 639, no. 1 (January 2012): 173–97, https://doi.org/10.1177/0002716211418445.

20. Raghabendra Chattopadhyay and Esther Duflo, "Women as Policy Makers: Evidence from a Randomized Policy Experiment in India," *Econometrica* 72, no. 5 (2004): 1409–43; Grant Miller, "Women's Suffrage, Political Responsiveness, and Child Survival in American History," *Quarterly Journal of Economics* 123, no. 3 (August 2008): 1287–1327, https://doi.org/10.1162/qjec.2008.123.3.1287.

21. Lyn Kathlene, "Alternative Views of Crime: Legislative Policymaking in Gendered Terms," *Journal of Politics* 57, no. 3 (1995): 696–723, https://doi.org/10.2307 /2960189.

22. Pamela Paxton, Sheri Kunovich, and Melanie M. Hughes, "Gender in Politics," *Annual Review of Sociology* 33, no. 1 (2007): 263–84, https://doi.org/10.1146 /annurev.soc.33.040406.131651.

23. Olufemi, *Feminism, Interrupted;* Rogers Brubaker, *Trans: Gender and Race in an Age of Unsettled Identities* (Princeton, NJ: Princeton University Press, 2016).

24. There has been very little change in this over time too. If we consider all those born before 1940, around 18.6 percent of men and 16.3 percent of women in *Who's Who* were born into the top 1 percent of the wealth distribution. Similarly, if we choose

an alternative metric of elite birth (that is, whether the parents of the people in *Who's Who* had some postnominal title, for example, Bt), then we find that ~22 percent of both men and women were born to parents who had one of these titles. Women were slightly more likely than men (19 percent vs 15 percent) to have a parent in *Who's Who*. But, in general, women in the past were roughly as elite as men.

25. Orian Brook, Dave O'Brien, and Mark Taylor, *Culture Is Bad for You: Inequality in the Cultural and Creative Industries* (Manchester: Manchester University Press, 2020).

26. Shorrocks, "Cohort Change"; Edlund and Pande, "Why Have Women Become Left-Wing?"

27. Rosalind Shorrocks and Maria T. Grasso, "The Attitudinal Gender Gap across Generations: Support for Redistribution and Government Spending in Contexts of High and Low Welfare Provision," *European Political Science Review* 12, no. 3 (2020): 289–306.

28. Ben Baumberg-Geiger, Rob de Vries, and Aaron Reeves, "Tax Avoidance and Benefit Manipulation: Views on Its Morality and Prevalence," in *British Social Attitudes 34*, ed. Elizabeth Clery, John Curtice, and Roger Harding (London: NatCen Social Research, 2017), 12–37.

29. Additionally, in terms of their experience of gendered-specific advantages, around 50 percent of the elite men we surveyed agreed that their gender has made it easier to succeed, while only 10 percent of women thought this was true for them.

30. Marlene LeGates, *In Their Time: A History of Feminism in Western Society* (New York: Routledge, 2001). Although, for a critique of delineating feminism in terms of waves, see Olufemi, *Feminism, Interrupted.*

31. Lynn Abrams, "Heroes of Their Own Life Stories: Narrating the Female Self in the Feminist Age," *Cultural and Social History* 16, no. 2 (2019): 205–24.

32. Ysenda Maxtone Graham, *Terms & Conditions: Life in Girls' Boarding Schools, 1939–1979* (London: Abacus, 2017); Gillian Avery, *The Best Type of Girl: A History of Girls' Independent Schools* (London: Andre Deutsch, 1991).

33. Daniel Kahneman, Jack L. Knetsch, and Richard H. Thaler, "Anomalies: The Endowment Effect, Loss Aversion, and Status Quo Bias," *Journal of Economic Perspectives* 5, no. 1 (March 1991): 193–206, https://doi.org/10.1257/jep.5.1.193.

34. Chalus, *Elite Women in English Political Life;* Glucksberg, "Gendering the Elites."

35. Lena Wängnerud, "Women in Parliaments: Descriptive and Substantive Representation," *Annual Review of Political Science* 12, no. 1 (2009): 51–69, https://doi.org/10.1146/annurev.polisci.11.053106.123839; Aaron Reeves, Chris Brown, and Johanna Hanefeld, "Female Political Representation and the Gender Health Gap: A Cross-National Analysis of 49 European Countries," *European Journal of Public Health* 32, no. 5 (October 2022): 684–89, https://doi.org/10.1093/eurpub/ckac122; Childs and Krook, "Should Feminists Give Up on Critical Mass?"

36. Abrams, "Heroes of Their Own Life Stories."

37. Childs and Krook, "Should Feminists Give Up on Critical Mass?"; Kowalewska, "Bringing Women on Board."

9. Centring Race and Empire

1. Commission on Race and Ethnic Disparities, *Commission on Race and Ethnic Disparities: The Report* (London: Government Equalities Office, 2021).

2. Commission on Race and Ethnic Disparities.

3. Dr. Shola Mos-Shogbamimu, "Liz Truss 'Most Racially Diverse Cabinet Ever' Is Only Skin-Deep," *Metro* (blog), 8 September 2022, https://metro.co.uk/2022/09/08/liz-truss-most-racially-diverse-cabinet-ever-is-only-skin-deep-17327706/.

4. Nirmal Puwar, *Space Invaders: Race, Gender and Bodies Out of Place,* illus. ed. (Oxford: Berg, 2004).

5. Roger Ballard, "The Construction of a Conceptual Vision: 'Ethnic Groups' and the 1991 UK Census," *Ethnic and Racial Studies* 20, no. 1 (1997): 182–94; Jonathan Burton, Alita Nandi, and Lucinda Platt, "Measuring Ethnicity: Challenges and Opportunities for Survey Research," *Ethnic and Racial Studies* 33, no. 8 (2010): 1332–49; Kevin Howard, "Constructing the Irish of Britain: Ethnic Recognition and the 2001 UK Censuses," *Ethnic and Racial Studies* 29, no. 1 (1 January 2006): 104–23, https://doi.org/10.1080/01419870500352439.

6. Richard Laux, "50 Years of Collecting Ethnicity Data—History of Government," 7 March 2019, https://history.blog.gov.uk/2019/03/07/50-years-of-collecting-ethnicity-data/.

7. Howard, "Constructing the Irish of Britain"; GOV.UK, "Gypsy, Roma and Irish Traveller Ethnicity Summary," accessed 17 July 2023, https://www.ethnicity-facts-figures.service.gov.uk/summaries/gypsy-roma-irish-traveller.

8. Ludi Simpson, Stephen Jivraj, and James Warren, "The Stability of Ethnic Identity in England and Wales 2001–2011," *Journal of the Royal Statistical Society Series A: Statistics in Society* 179, no. 4 (2016): 1025–49; Jivraj Stephen and Simpson Ludi, *Ethnic Identity and Inequalities in Britain: The Dynamics of Diversity* (Bristol, UK: Policy Press, 2015).

9. Monica McDermott and Annie Ferguson, "Sociology of Whiteness," *Annual Review of Sociology* 48 (2022): 257–76.

10. Liam Kennedy, "How White Americans Became Irish: Race, Ethnicity and the Politics of Whiteness," *Journal of American Studies* 56, no. 3 (July 2022): 424–46, https://doi.org/10.1017/S0021875821001249; Eric L. Goldstein, *The Price of Whiteness Jews, Race and American Identity: Jews, Race, and American Identity* (Princeton, NJ: Princeton University Press, 2008); Noel Ignatiev, *How the Irish Became White* (New York: Routledge, 2008); Thomas A. Guglielmo, *White on Arrival: Italians, Race, Color, and Power in Chicago, 1890–1945* (Oxford: Oxford University Press, 2004).

11. Rogers Brubaker, *Ethnicity without Groups* (Cambridge, MA: Harvard University Press, 2006).

12. David R. Williams, Jourdyn A. Lawrence, and Brigette A. Davis, "Racism and Health: Evidence and Needed Research," *Annual Review of Public Health* 40, no. 1 (2019): 105–25, https://doi.org/10.1146/annurev-publhealth-040218-043750; D. Pager and H. Shepherd, "The Sociology of Discrimination: Racial Discrimination in Employment, Housing, Credit, and Consumer Markets," *Annual Review of Sociology* 34 (2008): 181–209; David Olusoga, *Black and British: A Forgotten History* (London: Pan, 2017).

13. Tony Kushner, "'Without Intending Any of the Most Undesirable Features of a Colour Bar': Race Science, Europeanness and the British Armed Forces during the Twentieth Century," *Patterns of Prejudice* 46, no. 3–4 (1 July 2012): 339–74, https://doi.org/10.1080/0031322X.2012.701807; Shirin Hirsch and Geoff Brown, "Breaking the 'Colour Bar': Len Johnson, Manchester and Anti-Racism," *Race & Class* 64, no. 3 (January 2023): 36–58, https://doi.org/10.1177/03063968221139993; Olusoga, *Black and British.*

14. And even if they did, we still have the problem that being white is not entirely determined by skin colour nor is it only about how people self-identify. Ellis P. Monk Jr, "Inequality without Groups: Contemporary Theories of Categories, Intersectional Typicality, and the Disaggregation of Difference," *Sociological Theory* 40, no. 1 (2022): 3–27.

15. Sara Ahmed, *On Being Included: Racism and Diversity in Institutional Life,* illus. ed. (Durham, NC: Duke University Press Books, 2012).

16. Jeffrey W. Lockhart, Molly M. King, and Christin Munsch, "Name-Based Demographic Inference and the Unequal Distribution of Misrecognition," *Nature Human Behaviour,* 17 April 2023, 1–12, https://doi.org/10.1038/s41562-023-01587-9.

17. Pablo Mateos, Paul A. Longley, and David O'Sullivan, "Ethnicity and Population Structure in Personal Naming Networks," *PLOS ONE* 6, no. 9 (September 2011): e22943, https://doi.org/10.1371/journal.pone.0022943; Jens Kandt and Paul A. Longley, "Ethnicity Estimation Using Family Naming Practices," *PLOS ONE* 13, no. 8 (August 2018): e0201774, https://doi.org/10.1371/journal.pone.0201774.

18. Mateos, Longley, and O'Sullivan, "Ethnicity and Population Structure"; Lockhart, King, and Munsch, "Name-Based Demographic Inference."

19. We want to be clear, however, that using such tools is not an adequate substitute for collecting ethnicity data through self-identification (as we have done with our survey).

20. Lockhart, King, and Munsch, "Name-Based Demographic Inference."

21. McDermott and Ferguson, "Sociology of Whiteness."

22. Kojo Koram, *Uncommon Wealth: Britain and the Aftermath of Empire* (London: John Murray, 2022).

23. Gurminder K. Bhambra, *Connected Sociologies* (London: Bloomsbury Academic, 2014); Kathleen Paul, *Whitewashing Britain: Race and Citizenship in the Postwar Era* (Ithaca, NY: Cornell University Press, 1997).

24. Asian and Black British respondents were actually over-represented in our survey compared to the rest of *Who's Who.*

25. Although see Tomiwa Owolade, "Racism in Britain Is Not a Black and White Issue. It's Far More Complicated," *The Observer,* 15 April 2023, https://www.theguardian.com/commentisfree/2023/apr/15/racism-in-britain-is-not-a-black-and-white-issue-it-is-far-more-complicated.

26. This has not always been the case. In the past, Asian and Black British elites were far less likely to become part of the wealth elite once they were in positions of influence. Access to the wealth elite was severely limited for those who were more distant from what it meant to be white. For example, over 20 percent of the White British people in *Who's Who* were in the top 1 percent of the wealth distribution when they died, among those who died between 1950 and 1995. This is approximately the same as it is today. For "other" elites, the proportion in that group was also quite high, around 15 percent. However, for non-white elites we see much lower rates (~ 6 percent).

27. McDermott and Ferguson, "Sociology of Whiteness"; Although the relationships here are complex, see Stuart Hall and Doreen Massey, "Interpreting the Crisis," *Soundings,* no. 44 (Spring 2010): 57–71, https://doi.org/10.3898/136266210791036791.

28. Ignatiev, *How the Irish Became White;* W. E. B. Du Bois, *The Souls of Black Folk,* rev. ed. (New York: Dover Publications, 2016).

29. Ignatiev, *How the Irish Became White.*

30. Nicola Rollock, *The Racial Code,* 2023, https://www.penguin.co.uk/books/444010/the-racial-code-by-rollock-nicola/9780141997544.

31. Koram, *Uncommon Wealth.*

32. Joanna Burch-Brown, "Should Slavery's Statues Be Preserved? On Transitional Justice and Contested Heritage," *Journal of Applied Philosophy* 39, no. 5 (2022): 807–24, https://doi.org/10.1111/japp.12485; Olusoga, *Black and British.*

33. "Suella Braverman—2023 Speech to Conservative Party Conference," UKPOL.CO.UK, 3 October 2023, https://www.ukpol.co.uk/suella-braverman-2023-speech-to-conservative-party-conference/.

34. Koram, *Uncommon Wealth;* Olusoga, *Black and British.*

35. Anna Leach, Antonio Voce, and Ashley Kirk, "Black British History: The Row over the School Curriculum in England," *The Guardian,* 13 July 2020, https://www.theguardian.com/education/2020/jul/13/black-british-history-school-curriculum-england.

36. Olusoga, *Black and British;* Peter Fryer, *Staying Power: The History of Black People in Britain,* 3rd ed. (London: Pluto Press, 2018); Hakim Adi, *Black British History: New Perspectives* (Bloomsbury, 2019).

37. George Floyd was a Black man who was murdered by a police officer in Minnesota on 25 May 2020.

38. Brian Kwoba, Roseanne Chantiluke, and Athinangamso Nkopo, *Rhodes Must Fall: The Struggle to Decolonise the Racist Heart of Empire* (London: Bloomsbury, 2018).

39. McDermott and Ferguson, "Sociology of Whiteness."

Conclusion: Who Rules Britain?

1. Lawrence Stone and Jeanne C. Fawtier Stone, *An Open Elite?: England 1540–1880* (New York: Oxford University Press, 1995); Adrian Wooldridge, *The Aristocracy of Talent: How Meritocracy Made the Modern World.* (Dublin: Penguin, 2023); W. D. Rubinstein, "Men of Property. Some Aspects of Occupation, Inheritance and Power among Top British Wealthholders," in *Elites and Power in British Society,* ed. Philip Stanworth and Anthony Giddens (Cambridge: Cambridge University Press, 1974), 144–69.

2. BBC, "Theresa May: PM's Conference Speech," BBC News, accessed 30 March 2019, https://www.bbc.com/news/live/uk-politics-45732706.

3. Alun Francis, "Rethinking Social Mobility for the Levelling up Era" (London: Policy Exchange, 2021).

4. Oliver Hahl, Ezra W. Zuckerman, and Minjac Kim, "Why Elites Love Authentic Lowbrow Culture: Overcoming High-Status Denigration with Outsider Art" *American Sociological Review* 82, no. 4 (August 2017): 828–56, https://doi.org/10.1177/0003122417710642; Jo Littler, "Just like Us?: Normcore Plutocrats and the Popularisation of Elitism," in *Against Meritocracy: Culture, Power and Myths of Mobility* (New York: Routledge, 2017), chapter 4; Rachel Sherman, "'A Very Expensive Ordinary Life': Consumption, Symbolic Boundaries and Moral Legitimacy among New York Elites," *Socio-Economic Review* 16, no. 2 (April 2018): 411–33, https://doi.org/10.1093/ser/mwy011; Niall Cunningham, "Making and Mapping Britain's 'New Ordinary Elite,'" in *Disclosing Elite Ecologies* (New York: Routledge, 2021); Shamus Khan, *Privilege: The Making of an Adolescent Elite at St. Paul's School* (Princeton, NJ: Princeton University Press, 2011), https://press.princeton.edu/titles/9294.html.

5. Here we draw specifically on the hypothesis proposed by Hahl and colleagues in Hahl, Zuckerman, and Kim, "Why Elites Love Authentic Lowbrow Culture."

6. Michael J. Sandel, *The Tyranny of Merit: What's Become of the Common Good?* (London: Penguin, 2020); Jo Littler, *Against Meritocracy: Culture, Power and Myths of Mobility* (New York: Routledge, 2017).

7. C. Wright Mills, *The Power Elite* (Oxford: Oxford University Press, 1956); Ralph Miliband, *The State in Capitalist Society* (London: Basic Books, 1969).

8. Joni Lovenduski and Pippa Norris, "Westminster Women: The Politics of Presence," *Political Studies* 51, no. 1 (1 March 2003): 84–102, https://doi.org/10.1111/1467-9248.00414; S. Childs and M. L. Krook, "Critical Mass Theory and Women's Political Representation," *Political Studies* 56, no. 3 (October 2008): 725–36.

9. Nirmal Puwar, *Space Invaders: Race, Gender and Bodies Out of Place,* illus. ed. (New York: Berg, 2004).

10. "Britain's Council Tax Is Arbitrary, Regressive and Needs Fixing," *The Economist,* 25 January 2024.

11. Anthony B. Atkinson, *Inequality* (Cambridge, MA: Harvard University Press, 2015).

12. One obvious concern would be people who live in very expensive houses but whose incomes are low, such as retirees. The government could create a provision that, if the owner prefers, the state can become equity owners in the property with the individual. This level of taxation is actually far lower than property taxes at the start of the 1970s, when, on average, they were more than 1 per cent of property values.

13. This is one of the scenarios proposed by the Wealth Tax Commission. See Arun Advani, Emma Chamberlain, and Andy Summers, *A Wealth Tax for the UK* (London: LSE, 2020).

14. Thomas Piketty, *Capital and Ideology* (Cambridge, MA: Harvard University Press, 2020), 560.

15. Florian Scheuer and Joel Slemrod, "Taxing Our Wealth," *Journal of Economic Perspectives* 35, no. 1 (February 2021): 207–30, https://doi.org/10.1257/jep.35.1.207.

16. Thomas Piketty, *A Brief History of Equality* (Cambridge, MA: Harvard University Press, 2022), 163.

17. Scheuer and Slemrod, "Taxing Our Wealth."

18. Arun Advani and Hannah Tarrant, "Behavioural Responses to a Wealth Tax," *Fiscal Studies* 42, no. 3–4 (2021): 509–37, https://doi.org/10.1111/1475-5890.12283.

19. Katrine Jakobsen et al., "Do the Rich Flee Wealth Taxes? Evidence from Scandinavia," in *Paris-London Public Economics Conference 2021*, 2021, https://econ.lse.ac.uk/staff/clandais/cgi-bin/Articles/WealthMigration_slides2021.pdf; Edward Troup, John Barnett, and Katherine Bullock, "The Administration of a Wealth Tax," *Wealth Tax Commission Evidence Paper* 11 (2020), https://www.wealthandpolicy.com/wp/EP11_Administration.pdf.

20. Advani and Tarrant, "Behavioural Responses to a Wealth Tax."

21. Kenneth Scheve and David Stasavage, *Taxing the Rich: A History of Fiscal Fairness in the United States and Europe* (Princeton, NJ: Princeton University Press, 2016); Isaac William Martin, *Rich People's Movements: Grassroots Campaigns to Untax the One Percent* (Oxford: Oxford University Press, 2013); Claudio Riveros and Alejandro Pelfini, "Chilean Business Elites over Tax Reform Attempts (2014–2020)," *Estudios Sociológicos* 41, no. 121 (2023):159–88.

22. Luke Sibieta, *Tax, Private School Fees and State School Spending* (London: Institute for Fiscal Studies, 2023).

23. This is particularly important because the most expensive schools are also the most convincing when it comes to their charitable work. Removing charitable status would not affect schools like Eton, which now see themselves as a "charity for the advancement of education" rather than a school that does charitable work. Nicola Woolcock, "If We'd Stayed the Same since 1440, Eton Would Have Closed Years Ago," *The Times,* 19 July 2023, https://www.thetimes.co.uk/article/simon-henderson-if-wed-stayed-the-same-since-1440-eton-would-have-closed-years-ago-p0mwdhcth.

24. In our view, a student should be viewed as "privately educated" if they took either their GCSEs or their A levels at a private school.

25. Daniel Chandler, *Free and Equal: What Would a Fair Society Look Like?* (London: Allen Lane, 2023).

26. "Do Private Schools Harm or Benefit Britain?," YouGov, accessed 31 January 31 2024, https://yougov.co.uk/topics/politics/trackers/do-private-schools-harm-or-benefit-britain.

27. Bruce Sacerdote, "Experimental and Quasi-Experimental Analysis of Peer Effects: Two Steps Forward?," *Annual Review of Economics* 6, no. 1 (2014): 253–72, https://doi.org/10.1146/annurev-economics-071813-104217; Reyn van Ewijk and Peter Sleegers, "The Effect of Peer Socioeconomic Status on Student Achievement: A Meta-Analysis," *Educational Research Review* 5, no. 2 (1 January 2010): 134–50, https://doi.org/10.1016/j.edurev.2010.02.001.

28. Daniel McArthur and Aaron Reeves, "The Unintended Consequences of Quantifying Quality: Does Ranking School Performance Shape the Geographical Concentration of Advantage?," *American Journal of Sociology* 128, no. 2 (2022): 515–51; Jane Gingrich and Ben Ansell, "Sorting for Schools: Housing, Education and Inequality," *Socio-Economic Review* 12, no. 2 (1 April 2014): 329–51, https://doi.org/10.1093/ser/mwu009; Sol Gamsu, "The 'Other' London Effect: The Diversification of London's Suburban Grammar Schools and the Rise of Hyper-Selective Elite State Schools," *British Journal of Sociology* 69, no. 4 (2018): 1155–74.

29. See, for example, BBC, "Brighton and Hove: Free School Meals Increase Eligibility for Places," BBC News, 24 January 2024.

30. Danny Dorling, *Injustice: Why Social Inequality Still Persists* (Policy Press: Bristol, 2015).

31. University of Oxford, "Contextual Data," accessed 19 July 2023, https://www.ox.ac.uk/admissions/undergraduate/applying-to-oxford/decisions/contextual-data; Timea Walker, "Contextual Data," Text, 18 November 2022, https://www.undergraduate.study.cam.ac.uk/applying/contextual-data.

32. Angus Holford, "Take-up of Free School Meals: Price Effects and Peer Effects," *Economica* 82, no. 328 (October 2015): 976–93, https://doi.org/10.1111/ecca.12147.

33. Mark Fransham, "Increasing Evenness in the Neighbourhood Distribution of Income Poverty in England 2005–2014: Age Differences and the Influence of Private Rented Housing," *Environment and Planning A: Economy and Space,* 51, no. 2 (August 2018), 0308518X18792569, https://doi.org/10.1177/0308518X18792569.

34. Anna Mountford Zimdars, *Meritocracy and the University: Selective Admission in England and the United States* (London: Bloomsbury Academic, 2017).

35. There is, of course, a more fundamental challenge here which is the class-based inequalities in attainment. We are focussed on admissions processes here because our attention is on elite universities, but this does not mean we think those class-based inequalities are unimportant.

36. For example, in 2022, 29,247 young people took their A levels and 17.8 percent achieved three As or more (approximately 5,206 students). In that same year,

approximately 629 people from the North East applied to Oxford or Cambridge. See "A Level and Other 16 to 18 Results, Academic Year 2022 / 23," Gov.UK, accessed 31 January 2024, https://explore-education-statistics.service.gov.uk/find-statistics/a-level -and-other-16-to-18-results. Data on admissions for Oxford and Cambridge can be found on their admissions websites. See https://www.ox.ac.uk/about/facts-and-figures /admissions-statistics and https://www.undergraduate.study.cam.ac.uk/apply/statistics.

37. A similar policy in Texas boosted enrolment at top universities from historically marginalised students in rural areas, small towns, and midsize cities, including students from schools with large numbers of poor and minority students, although there is still work to be done to ensure marginalised students take up these offers. The policy also led to affluent people moving to poorer areas. The policy also increased college-related ambitions among minority students. Thurston Domina, "Higher Education Policy as Secondary School Reform: Texas Public High Schools After Hopwood," *Educational Evaluation and Policy Analysis* 29, no. 3 (September 2007): 200–217, https://doi.org/10.3102/0162373707304995; Stella M. Flores and Catherine L. Horn, "Texas Top Ten Percent Plan: How It Works, What Are Its Limits, and Recommendations to Consider," Civil Rights Project, 1 December 2016, https://escholarship .org/uc/item/4hm2n74b; Kalena E. Cortes and Andrew I. Friedson, "Ranking up by Moving out: The Effect of the Texas Top 10% Plan on Property Values," *National Tax Journal* 67, no. 1 (March 2014): 51–76, https://doi.org/10.17310/ntj.2014.1.02; Mark C. Long, Victor Saenz, and Marta Tienda, "Policy Transparency and College Enrollment: Did the Texas Top Ten Percent Law Broaden Access to the Public Flagships?," *The ANNALS of the American Academy of Political and Social Science* 627, no. 1 (1 January 2010): 82–105, https://doi.org/10.1177/0002716209348741; Kim M. Lloyd, Kevin T. Leicht, and Teresa A. Sullivan, "Minority College Aspirations, Expectations and Applications under the Texas Top 10% Law," *Social Forces* 86, no. 3 (1 March 2008): 1105–37, https://doi.org/10.1353/sof.0.0012.

38. L.W.B. Brockliss, *The University of Oxford: A History,* illus. ed. (Oxford: Oxford University Press, 2016).

39. Piketty, *Capital and Ideology;* Simon Jäger, Shakked Noy, and Benjamin Schoefer, "Codetermination and Power in the Workplace," *Journal of Law and Political Economy* 3, no. 1 (2022).

40. Jäger, Noy, and Schoefer, "Codetermination and Power in the Workplace"; Simon Jäger, Shakked Noy, and Benjamin Schoefer, "What Does Codetermination Do?," *ILR Review* 75, no. 4 (August 2022): 857–90, https://doi.org/10.1177/0019793 9211065727.

41. Alexander A. Guerrero, "Against Elections: The Lottocratic Alternative," *Philosophy & Public Affairs* 42, no. 2 (2014): 135–78.

42. Hélène Landemore, "Deliberation, Cognitive Diversity, and Democratic Inclusiveness: An Epistemic Argument for the Random Selection of Representatives," *Synthese* 190, no. 7 (2013): 1209–31.

43. John S. Dryzek et al., "The Crisis of Democracy and the Science of Deliberation," *Science* 363, no. 6432 (March 2019): 1144–46, https://doi.org/10.1126/science .aaw2694.

44. Dryzek et al., "The Crisis of Democracy."

45. Landemore, "Deliberation."

46. Peter Allen, *The Political Class: Why It Matters Who Our Politicians Are,* illus. ed. (Oxford: Oxford University Press, 2018).

47. Khan, *Privilege;* M. Savage, G. Bagnall, and B. Longhurst, "Ordinary, Ambivalent and Defensive: Class Identities in the Northwest of England," *Sociology-the Journal of the British Sociological Association* 35, no. 4 (2001): 875–92; Tony Bennett et al., *Culture, Class, Distinction* (London: Routledge, 2009); Katharina Hecht, "A Relational Analysis of Top Incomes and Wealth: Economic Evaluation, Relative (Dis) Advantage and the Service to Capital," 2017; Sherman, "'A Very Expensive Ordinary Life'."

48. Vegard Jarness and Sam Friedman, "'I'm Not a Snob, But . . .': Class Boundaries and the Downplaying of Difference," *Poetics* 61, no. Supplement C (April 2017): 14–25, https://doi.org/10.1016/j.poetic.2016.11.001; Hahl, Zuckerman, and Kim, "Why Elites Love Authentic Lowbrow Culture"; Vegard Jarness and Magne Paalgard Flemmen, "A Struggle on Two Fronts: Boundary Drawing in the Lower Region of the Social Space and the Symbolic Market for 'down-to-Earthness'," *The British Journal of Sociology* 70, no. 1 (2019): 166–89, https://doi.org/10.1111/1468-4446.12345.

49. John Scott, *Who Rules Britain?* (Oxford: Polity, 1991); Philip Stanworth and Anthony Giddens, *Elites and Power in British Society* (Cambridge: Cambridge University Press, 1974); Aaron Reeves et al., "The Decline and Persistence of the Old Boy: Private Schools and Elite Recruitment 1897 to 2016," *American Sociological Review* 82, no. 6 (December 2017): 1139–66, https://doi.org/10.1177/000312241 7735742.

50. Daniel Laurison and Sam Friedman, "The Class Pay Gap in Higher Professional and Managerial Occupations," *American Sociological Review* 81, no. 4 (August 2016): 668–95, https://doi.org/10.1177/0003122416653602.

51. Magne Paalgard Flemmen et al., "Forms of Capital and Modes of Closure in Upper Class Reproduction," *Sociology* 51, no. 6 (December 2017): 1277–98, https://doi .org/10.1177/0038038517706325; Maren Toft, "Upper-Class Trajectories: Capital-Specific Pathways to Power," *Socio-Economic Review* 16, no. 2 (April 2018): 341–64, https://doi.org/10.1093/ser/mwx034.

52. M. L. Stevens, E. A. Armstrong, and R. Arum, "Sieve, Incubator, Temple, Hub: Empirical and Theoretical Advances in the Sociology of Higher Education," *Annual Review of Sociology* 34 (2008): 127–51; Pierre Bourdieu, *The State Nobility: Elite Schools in the Field of Power* (Oxford: Polity, 1996); David Kynaston and Francis Green, *Engines of Privilege: Britain's Private School Problem* (London: Bloomsbury, 2019); Gillian Avery, *The Best Type of Girl: A History of Girls' Independent Schools* (London: Andre

Deutsch, 1991); Diane Reay, Gill Crozier, and John Clayton, "'Strangers in Paradise'?: Working-Class Students in Elite Universities," *Sociology* 43, no. 6 (December 2009): 1103–21, https://doi.org/10.1177/0038038509345700; Robert David Anderson, *Universities and Elites in Britain since 1800,* vol. 16 (Cambridge: Cambridge University Press, 1995).

53. For a recent exception see Anthony Abraham Jack, *The Privileged Poor: How Elite Colleges Are Failing Disadvantaged Students* (Cambridge, MA: Harvard University Press, 2019); Reay, Crozier, and Clayton, "'Strangers in Paradise'?"

54. Benjamin I. Page, Jason Seawright, and Matthew J. Lacombe, *Billionaires and Stealth Politics* (Chicago: University of Chicago Press, 2018); David E. Broockman, Gregory Ferenstein, and Neil Malhotra, "Predispositions and the Political Behavior of American Economic Elites: Evidence from Technology Entrepreneurs," *American Journal of Political Science* 63, no. 1 (2019): 212–33.

55. Nicholas Carnes and Noam Lupu, "The Economic Backgrounds of Politicians," *Annual Review of Political Science* 26, no. 1 (2023): 253–70, https://doi.org/10.1146/annurev-polisci-051921-102946; Allen, *The Political Class.*

56. Laura Nader, "Up the Anthropologist: Perspectives Gained from Studying Up," ERIC, 1972, https://eric.ed.gov/?id=ED065375.

57. Aeron Davis, *Reckless Opportunists: Elites at the End of the Establishment* (Manchester: Manchester University Press, 2018).

58. Karl Marx, *Capital,* vol. 1 (London: Penguin, 2004); Jonathan Wolff, *Why Read Marx Today?* (Oxford: Oxford University Press, 2003).

59. Beverley Skeggs, "Introduction: Stratification or Exploitation, Domination, Dispossession and Devaluation?," *The Sociological Review* 63, no. 2 (May 2015): 205–22, https://doi.org/10.1111/1467-954X.12297; Fiona Devine et al., *Rethinking Class: Cultures, Identities and Lifestyles* (Basingstoke: Palgrave Macmillan, 2005); Imogen Tyler, *Revolting Subjects: Social Abjection and Resistance in Neoliberal Britain* (London: Zed Books, 2013); Imogen Tyler, "Classificatory Struggles: Class, Culture and Inequality in Neoliberal Times," *Sociological Review* 63, no. 2 (1 May 2015): 493–511, https://doi.org/10.1111/1467-954X.12296.

60. Ufuk Altunbuken et al., *Power Plays: The Shifting Balance of Employer and Worker Power in the UK Labour Market,* The Economy 2030 Inquiry (London: Nuffield Foundation, 2022); Nicola Ingram and Sol Gamsu, "Talking the Talk of Social Mobility: The Political Performance of a Misguided Agenda," *Sociological Research Online* 27, no. 1 (March 2022): 189–206, https://doi.org/10.1177/13607804211055493; John Hills, *Good Times, Bad Times: The Welfare Myth of Them and Us* (Bristol, UK: Policy Press, 2014).

61. Guido Alfani, *As Gods Among Men: A History of the Rich in the West* (Princeton, NJ: Princeton University Press, 2024).

62. Florence Sutcliffe-Braithwaite, *Class, Politics, and the Decline of Deference in England, 1968–2000* (Oxford: Oxford University Press, 2018).

63. Partygate is a political scandal in the United Kingdom about gatherings of government and Conservative Party staff during the COVID-19 pandemic in 2020 and 2021, when public health restrictions prohibited most gatherings.

64. Peter Turchin, *End Times: Elites, Counter-Elites and the Path of Political Disintegration* (New York: Allen Lane, 2023).

65. G. A. Cohen, *If You're an Egalitarian, How Come You're So Rich?*, rev. ed. (Cambridge, MA: Harvard University Press, 2001).

Methodological Appendix

1. Laura Nader, "Up the Anthropologist: Perspectives Gained from Studying Up," ERIC, 1972, https://eric.ed.gov/?id=ED065375; Sherry B Ortner, "Access: Reflections on Studying up in Hollywood," *Ethnography* 11, no. 2 (1 June 2010): 211–33, https://doi.org/10.1177/1466138110362006.

2. Joy Adamson and Jenny L. Donovan, "Research in Black and White," *Qualitative Health Research* 12, no. 6 (July 2002): 816–25, https://doi.org/10.1177/104323 02012006008.

3. Sam Friedman, "The Limits of Capital Gains: Using Bourdieu to Understand Social Mobility into Elite Occupations," in *Bourdieu: The Next Generation,* ed. Jenny Thatcher et al. (London: Routledge, 2015), chapter 8.

4. "*Who's Who*—A Brief History, 1849–1998," in *Who's Who* (London: Bloomsbury Press, 1998), 1–16; Colin Bell, "Some Comments on the Use of Directories in Research on Elites, with Particular Reference to the Twentieth-Century Supplements of the Dictionary of National Biography," in *British Political Sociology Yearbook,* vol. 1, *Elites in Western Democracy,* ed. Ivor Crewe (London: Croom Helm, 1974), 161–71.

5. Aaron Reeves et al., "The Decline and Persistence of the Old Boy: Private Schools and Elite Recruitment 1897 to 2016," *American Sociological Review* 82, no. 6 (December 2017): 1139–66, https://doi.org/10.1177/0003122417735742.

6. N. B. Ryder, "The Cohort as a Concept in the Study of Social-Change," *American Sociological Review* 30, no. 6 (1965): 843–61.

7. Today, not all Clarendon schools are male-only. Westminster (since 1973), Shrewsbury (since 2008), and Charterhouse (since the mid-1970s) now take women in the sixth form (ages 16 to 18). Rugby has been fully co-educational since 1992. However, across most of the period we are interested in (1830 to 1979), these schools were male-only. Even HMC schools—the weaker version of the old boys network—only provided about 3 percent of places to women during the 1970s, see Geoffrey Walford, *Life in Public Schools,* vol. 204 (London: Routledge, 2011).

8. For more information on these schools, see Eve Worth, Aaron Reeves, and Sam Friedman, "Is There an Old Girls' Network? Girls' Schools and Recruitment to the British Elite," *British Journal of Sociology of Education* 44, no. 1 (November 2022): 1–25, https://doi.org/10.1080/01425692.2022.2132472.

9. Jushan Bai and Pierre Perron, "Computation and Analysis of Multiple Structural Change Models" (working paper no. 0998, Center for Interuniversity Research in Quantitative Economics, Montreal, CN, 1998); Jushan Bai and Pierre Perron, "Estimating and Testing Linear Models with Multiple Structural Changes," *Econometrica* 66, no. 1 (1998): 47–78, https://doi.org/10.2307/2998540; More information on how we conduct these tests can be found in Reeves et al., "The Decline and Persistence of the Old Boy."

10. Bai and Perron, "Computation and Analysis of Multiple Structural Change Models," 3.

11. L. W. B. Brockliss, *The University of Oxford: A History,* illus. ed. (Oxford: Oxford University Press, 2016); HM Treasury, *University Colleges (Great Britain) (Grant in Aid): Return to an Order of the Honourable the House of Commons* [Parl. H. of c. 1902. Reports and Papers], 252 (London: H.M.S. Office, multiple years), https://catalog .hathitrust.org/Record/009894183; Robert David Anderson, *Universities and Elites in Britain since 1800,* vol. 16 (Cambridge: Cambridge University Press, 1995); University of London, *The Historical Record (1836–1926)* (London: University of London Press, 1926); Francis Michael Longstreth Thompson, *University of London and the World of Learning, 1836–1986* (London: Hambledon Press, 1990).

12. John H. Goldthorpe, Catriona Llewellyn, and Clive Payne, *Social Mobility and Class Structure in Modern Britain* (Oxford: Clarendon Press, 1980).

13. Reeves et al., "The Decline and Persistence of the Old Boy."

14. Sam Friedman and Aaron Reeves, "From Aristocratic to Ordinary: Shifting Modes of Elite Distinction," *American Sociological Review* 85, no. 2 (April 2020): 323–50, https://doi.org/10.1177/0003122420912941.

15. Daniel Hopkins and Gary King, "A Method of Automated Nonparametric Content Analysis for Social Science," *American Journal of Political Science* 54, no. 1 (2010): 229–47.

16. Lior Sheffer et al., "Nonrepresentative Representatives: An Experimental Study of the Decision Making of Elected Politicians," *American Political Science Review* 112, no. 2 (2018): 302–21.

17. Sheffer et al., "Nonrepresentative Representatives."

18. Julie Brown, Nicholas Cook, and Stephen Cottrell, eds., *Defining the Discographic Self: Desert Island Discs in Context* (Oxford: Oxford University Press, 2017).

19. Oliver Hahl, Ezra W. Zuckerman, and Minjae Kim, "Why Elites Love Authentic Lowbrow Culture: Overcoming High-Status Denigration with Outsider Art," *American Sociological Review* 82, no. 4 (August 2017): 828–56, https://doi.org/10.1177 /0003122417710642.

20. British Library, *National Life Stories* (London: British Library, 1987).

21. C. D. Harbury and D. M. Hitchens, *Inheritance and Wealth Inequality in Britain* (London: George Allen and Unwin, 1979); Facundo Alvaredo, Anthony B. Atkinson, and Salvatore Morelli, "Top Wealth Shares in the UK over More than a Century,"

Journal of Public Economics 162 (2018): 26–47; Neil Cummins, "Where Is the Middle Class? Evidence from 60 Million English Death and Probate Records, 1892–1992," *Journal of Economic History* 81, no. 2 (2021): 359–404.

22. Alvaredo, Atkinson, and Morelli, "Top Wealth Shares in the UK."

23. Harbury and Hitchens, *Inheritance and Wealth Inequality in Britain.*

24. Harbury and Hitchens, *Inheritance and Wealth Inequality in Britain.*

25. Henry Colin Gray Matthew and Brian Harrison, eds., *The Oxford Dictionary of National Biography* (Oxford: Oxford University Press, 2004).

26. Chris Hanretty, *A Court of Specialists: Judicial Behavior on the UK Supreme Court* (New York: Oxford University Press, 2020).

27. "*Who's Who*—A Brief History, 1849–1998."

28. "*Who's Who*—A Brief History, 1849–1998."

29. Erzsébet Bukodi and John H. Goldthorpe, "Elite Studies: For a New Approach," *Political Quarterly* 92, no. 4 (2021): 673–81, https://doi.org/10.1111/1467-923X.13072.

Acknowledgments

This project has taken seven years to complete and at its heart is a research partnership that has been driven by friendship and equality. We have incurred many debts along the way. We are especially grateful to *Who's Who,* who showed tremendous faith in us and this research project and without whom this book would simply not exist. We would also like to register our thanks to Harvard University Press for publishing the book, for our editor Joy de Menil, who has provided vital improvements on every page of the manuscript, Emeralde Jensen-Roberts, who helped us keep all of the moving parts aligned, and Grigory Tovbis, who helped us over the final hurdles. We would also like to thank Ian Malcolm, who helped shepherd the book through the proposal stage, two anonymous reviewers, and the members of the Harvard University Press Board of Syndics, who all provided crucial feedback.

This book would not have been possible without the support of the European Research Council. We had been working on this project for a number of years when Aaron was awarded a Starting Grant of just over £1m. This funding allowed us to massively expand the scope of the research and hire a group of brilliant postdoctoral researchers who have made crucial contributions to different aspects of the project. Naomi Muggleton helped us extract the probate records from digital files, while Eve Worth, Katie Higgins, and Vlad Bortun all conducted some of the interviews we use in the book. Each also helped us in various other important ways, providing advice and insight on areas where we lacked expertise. Alongside them, we are especially grateful for the input of Charlie Rahal. He was instrumental in helping us get access to the *Who's Who* data in the first instance and has been an important source of advice on various aspects of this book. Aaron would also like to thank the University of Melbourne (and Rebecca Bentley in particular) for hosting him for one month during a crucial phase of this book.

This book draws on a lot of data, and a large number of research assistants have helped us collect, clean, and check the accuracy of these datasets. These include Maria Izabel Bahia, Yasha Bajai, Ava Bergsman, Asif Butt, John Davies, Luke Elford, Ioanna Gkoutna, Ben Goodair, Molly Graham, Nicole Jedding, Paul Moore, Jeremy Pye, Rachel Pye, Cherise Regier, Alexandra Rottenkolber, Maddie Sheldon, Brian Treacy, Artem Volgin, and Adele Williams. The work they did was sometimes not very glamorous, but it was essential and we are grateful to them all.

We would also like to recognise our research participants: the several thousand entrants of *Who's Who* who kindly filled out our survey, and particularly those who gave up their time to be interviewed. This research would have been impossible without their insight, generosity, and candid honesty.

One reason writing a book is so challenging is because it gradually becomes more difficult to see parts of the text where the tempo drops or where the arguments go astray. The way to solve this problem is to rely on friends and colleagues to read drafts and help pinpoint weaknesses in the text. We had a number of readers who offered valuable comments, including Louise Black, Vlad Bortun, Rob de Vries, Katie Higgins, Marte Mangset, Richard Pye, Aarash Saleh, Mike Savage, Laura Sochas, Andy Summers, Anders Vessen, Hannah Wilson, and Eve Worth.

Finally, we would like to thank our families: our parents (Sarah and Richard, Pat and Andy), our partners (Beth and Louise), and our kids (Amelie, Jude, and Ellis, and Cora and Skye). We know that supporting us during this intense period has been challenging, and we truly appreciate your patience, kindness, and love.

Index

Addis, Richard, 77
Addison, Lynda, 74
Ahmed, Sara, 204
Alford family (Charles, Edward Fleet, Josiah), 111–112
Anatomy of Britain (Sampson), 10, 51, 141–142
Annan, Noel, 141
aristocracy: British elite and, 22; British wealth elite and, 36; collapse of, 96; continuing influence of, 271n29
aristocratic character of elite culture (1890–1920), 67–69, 89–90
Arts Council, 17, 71, 74, 84
Ashcroft, Michael, 31–32
Ashley-Smith, Jonathan, 77
Ashmore, Edward, 77
Asian and Black elite, 202–203, 204–206; class origins of, 207; political orientation of, 206–209. *See also* elite people of colour
Asian and Black wealth elite, 207–211, 296n26
Atallah, Naim, 70
Atkinson, Anthony, 31, 229
author backgrounds and professional interests, 4–5, 241–243
Ayling, Pere, 17

Badenoch, Kemi, 200
Bagehot, Walter, 64
Bakewell, John, 79, 80
Bank of England's Court of Directors, elite and, 64–65
Baring, George, 120, 140–141
Barnes, Josephine, 141, 192

Bathurst family (Charles, Charles, Jr., Benjamin, Rupert, William), 108
BBC, 71, 74
Benenden School, 130–131
Benn, Tony, 95
Berlin, Isaiah, 79
Bhopal, Kalwant, 149
bias: social desirability, 172–173; status quo, 195–196, 249–250; sunk cost, 173–174, 250–251; survivorship, 198–199
birth cohort: everyday recreation among elite and, 82–84; ideological configurations among the elite and, 166–167
Blair, Tony, 164
Blakiston, Herbert, 150
Bloomsbury Group, 69–70, 71, 90
Bourdieu, Pierre, 59, 66, 100, 128, 152–153
Braverman, Suella, 158, 200
"bright young things" era, 135–136, 140–141
British elite: ambivalence about status, 40–41; benefits of privilege, 224–225; change and continuity of, 8–11; class and, 95–96; colonial past and, 17, 109–111; comparing contemporary to historical, 50–52; conception of in *Who's Who*, 22–26; control over resources in multiple domains, 31–32; defining, 21–31; deflecting privilege, 42–47; demography of contemporary, 26–31; denying their influence in interviews, 39–40; description of, 34–38; early-twentieth-century accounts of elite identity, 53–58; elite theory and, 31–34; ethnic diversity in, 205–206; impression management and, 4, 61, 225–227; members'

Index

British elite (*continued*)
  claim of ordinariness (*see* ordinariness);
  meritocratic legitimacy of upward story, 41,
  47–50; narratives of opening up of opportunity, 50–52; number of, 6; number of people
  of colour in, 200–202; power and, 21, 22;
  presentation of self within, 221–222; recommendations for change in, 227–234; sense of
  being better than other people, 58. *See also*
  Asian and Black elite; education; elite women
British elite ideology, 17, 157–178; elite reproduction and, 157–158, 168–172, 177–178;
  elites *vs.* the people, 158–160; elite women
  and, 182–186; political behaviour and, 172–174;
  race-ethnicity and, 206–209; spending on
  education, 160–162; tax policies, 159–160,
  162–164; wealth and wielding influence,
  175–177; wealth elite and political ideology,
  164–168; of women elites, 179–180, 183–186
British Library interviews, 53–58
British Social Attitudes survey, 159, 189–190, 248
British Supreme Court, class and behaviour of
  judges on, 174
Bukodi, Erzsébet, 95–96
business occupations, British elite and, 28, 30,
  36, 38

Calder, John, 70
Cambridge, entrants in *Who's Who* who live in,
  26, 29
Cambridge University, 9; private girls schools
  sending alumni to, 130–131; reforming
  admission to, 231, 232–233. *See also*
  Oxbridge
Cameron, David, 31–32, 95, 135
capital gains tax: British elite attitudes towards,
  162–163; sunk cost bias and, 173–174
capitalist class: continuity in British, 9–10; as
  ruling class, 32, 33
career success: claim of merit as reason for,
  51–52; claim of natural intelligence as reason
  for, 125–126; claim of personality traits as
  reason for, 124–125; claim of possession of
  "good judgment" as reason for, 125
Carew family (Charles Robert Sydenham,
  Nichola, Peter Gawen), 107
Carr, Alan, 54–55, 56
Casely-Hayford family (Augustus, Joseph,
  Joseph Ephraim, Margaret, Victor), 111
Casson, Hugh, 140
causality, 261
Chalus, Elaine, 181
Chamberlain, Ruth, 107

Charterhouse, 7, 121, 303n7
Chattopadhyay, Raghabendra, 182–183
Cheltenham Ladies College, 130, 131
child-rearing, wealth effect on, 100–102
Churchill, Winston, 25
Clarendon Report, 115, 116
Clarendon Schools, 7, 264n15; declining
  influence in elite reproduction, 116, 117–118,
  119–121, 282n13; elite recruitment and, 14–15,
  224; entrants in *Who's Who* and, 27, 122–123,
  131, 170; merit and, 123–126; military elite
  and, 118; as model for American private
  schools, 18; Oxbridge attendance, elite,
  and, 146; relation to British elite and,
  115–116; student selection at, 126–127;
  wealth distribution of students at, 123.
  See also individual schools
Clark, Gregory, 96
Class Ceiling, The (Friedman), 5
class identity, elite and deflecting privilege,
  42–47
class origin: behaviour of judges and, 174; of
  British wealth elite, 35; downplaying elite,
  223; of elite people of colour, 207; of entrants
  in *Who's Who,* 27; ideological orientation
  and, 169–170, 173–174; social justice and, 177;
  sociology of elites as sociology of, 237–238;
  of women elites, 179–180
Claughton, John, 238
Cleese, John, 77
Cleverly, James, 200
Clifton High School for Girls, 130
Cocker, Jarvis, 61–63
Cohen, G. A., 239
colonial past, elites and, 17, 109–111. *See also*
  empire
Commission on Racial and Ethnic Disparities,
  200
"Common People" (Pulp), 61–63
Communist Manifesto (Marx & Engels), 32
concerted cultivation, family wealth and, 100–101,
  102
confidence, family wealth and, 100–101
confidentiality, research, 254, 256, 263n1
Conservative cabinet, diversity in, 200
Corbyn, Jeremy, 158
corporate boards, adding workers to, 234
Council Taxes, 162, 228–229
Court of Specialists, A (Hanretty), 174
Courtois, Aline, 17
Crawford, John, 68
creative occupations, elite in, 28, 30, 36,
  186–187

Index

creative thought, claim private schools fostering, 128

critical mass theory, gender equality and, 182, 199

cultural capital, 67, 153

cultural egalitarianism, elite and, 226

cultural emulation, elite distinction and, 65–66, 89–90

cultural intermediaries, role in legitimising elite, 66–67

cultural omnivorousness: among British elite, 73–82, 90; elite distinction and, 67, 90; publicly ordinary, privately distinct, 82–87

culture wars, gender and, 184, 185

Cummins, Neil, 99–100

Daloz, Jean-Pascal, 11

Daniell, Peter, 135–136, 140, 148, 152

Davidoff, Leonore, 11

De gustibus non Est disputandum, 75–78

Delamont, Sara, 133

demographics: of British wealth elite, 35–37; of contemporary British elite, 26–31

Desert Island Discs (radio program), 12, 65; elite choices exhibiting cultural omnivorousness, 78–82; interview question about, 87–88, 91; research methodology and, 8, 251–252

Digby, John, 68

distance from necessity concept, elites and, 100

distinction, family wealth and sense of, 100–102

Du Bois, W. E. B., 210

Duflo, Esther, 182–183

Durham University, 137, 231

economic position: of British wealth elite, 35; of entrants in *Who's Who,* 27

economic power, centrality in elite theory, 33–34

economic roots of women's progressive politics, 186–189

education: British elite on spending on, 160–162; of British wealth elite, 35; changing composition of British elite and, 117–121; elite recruitment and, 114; elite school decline and reform in, 118–121; of entrants in *Who's Who,* 27; as occupation of British wealth elite, 28, 30, 36; old girls network and, 130–134; persistence of the old boy and, 122–123. *See also* Clarendon Schools; girls private schools; Headmasters' and Headmistresses' Conference (HMC) schools; private schools; *individual schools*

Education Act of 1944, 119, 120–121

educational curricula, 71–72, 126, 127–128, 139

educational inequality, proposals to address, 230–233

educational reform, 118–121, 282n13, 282n18

education model, colonialism and, 17

Elementary Education Act (1890), 119

elite, defining, 6–8, 21–22

elite capture, 16

elite culture: aristocratic character (1890–1920), 67–69, 89–90; decline of deference in (1950–), 73–82, 90; elite distinction and, 11–13, 65–67; highbrow (*see* highbrow culture); ordinary elite distinction, 87, 89–91; publicly ordinary, privately distinct, 82–87, 90

elite distinction, 11–13, 65–67; ordinary, 87, 89–91; private, 82–87

elite identity: elite distinction and, 11; elite schools and, 128–129

elite networks: over last 200 years, 106–109; Oxbridge reinforcing, 148–152

elite people of colour: colonial ties of, 109–111; elite reproduction among, 109–111, 112–113; as entrants in *Who's Who,* 26, 28; on legacy of empire, 214–217; political orientation of, 206–209; underrepresentation of, 200–202. *See also* Asian and Black elite

elite recruitment: analysis of persistence of, 3–4; continuity in, 224; education and, 114; family wealth and, 95–97; need for reform of, 238–239; private schools and, 130–134; public schools and, 122–123; resurgence of, 13–15; sociology of, 13–14, 235–236

elite reproduction, 113–114; among people of colour, 109–111, 112–113; British elite ideology and, 157–158, 168–172, 177–178; confidence and risk-taking inculcated by family wealth and, 100–104; extended families and, 104–109; link between wealth and, 96, 111–114, 228–230; occupation and, 98–99; perpetuation of, 224–225; persistence of Oxbridge in, 136–139; power of, 97–100; role of wealth in extended-family, 111–113; role of women in, 181; significance of, 15–17, 171–172, 177–178, 226–227; transition from family- to school-mediated, 152–153

elite studies, proposed areas to study, 235–238

elite taste, 12

elite theory, 31–34

elite universities: hub function of, 148; private school link with, 146–147; sieve function, 140; women elite and access to, 182. *See also* Oxbridge; Russell Group universities; *individual universities* elite women: being political with small *p*, 195–197; economic roots of progressive politics, 186–189; elite women *vs.* women in the elite, 181–182; experience of sexism, 191, 192, 193–195, 198–199; feminism and, 180, 181–182, 191–193; ideological orientation, 182–186; political attitudes of, 179–180; political behaviour of, 180; rise in, 179–180; rule-bending and, 189–191; survivorship bias and, 198–199

Elliot, Ben, 238

Ellis, Frederick George and Thomas Evelyn, 107

empire: class origin and attitude towards, 169; elite women and attitudes towards legacy of, 184, 185–186; military elite and decline in, 118; politics of race and, 209–211; wealth elite's attitudes towards, 164–166; white elites and elites of colour on legacy of, 214–217

entitlement, British elite and, 53–58

equalisation of wealth, elite reproduction and, 113–114

"establishment," 16, 158

Establishment Right: elites of colour aligned with, 206; elite women identifying as, 186; within the elite, 165–168

ethnic categories, 202–206

ethnic diversity, in British elite, 200–202, 205–206

ethnicity of British elite, 7; algorithmic approach to identifying, 204–205; political orientation and, 206–209

Eton College, 7, 9, 15, 115; "Eton's Failure," 238; influence of, 120, 121; Oxford and, 134; political elite and, 116, 238; student performance on standardised tests, 121; student selection at, 126–127

"Eton's Failure" (Claughton), 238

everyday recreations, elite and, 82–87

experiments on cultural tastes of British elite, 7–8, 248–253

extended family network: colonial ties and people of colour, 109–111; elite reproduction and, 104–109, 111–113

family-mediated elite reproduction, 152–153

family wealth: confidence and risk-taking inculcated by, 100–104; extended family and, 104–109; hidden, 99–100; overrepresentation in elite and, 97–100; Oxbridge attendance and, 147; recruitment to influential positions and, 95–97; role in elite reproduction, 111–113

Fedirici, Silvia, 181

feminism, women elites and, 180; elites of colour on need for continued, 209; elite women on need for continued, 184, 185; varieties of, 191–193

Fisher Act (1918), 119, 120

Fivish, Robyn, 46

Flemmen, Magne, 58–59

Forbes, Joan, 132

Fry, Roger, 70

Galetti, Monica, 83

Gaztambide-Fernandez, Ruben, 128

gender: inclusion in British elite and, 26, 27; Oxbridge attendance and reaching elite status, 151–152

gender equality, elite women on, 191–193

genealogical data, 259

geographic associations, entrants in *Who's Who* and, 26, 29

Georgina, Lady Kennard, 106, 108

Giddens, Anthony, 74

girls private schools, 130–134, 267n51; alumni in *Who's Who*, 131–132; ambivalent aims of, 117, 133–134; as engines of inequality, 117; as incubators of elite identities, 132; instilling confidence in students, 195; as sieves, 132–133; as temples, 132

Girls' Schools Association (GSA), 116, 131

Godolphin and Latymer School, 130

Goldthorpe, John, 13, 95–96

Goodwin, Matthew, 10, 16, 21, 158, 167

governing elites, 32–34, 270n17

government health spending, British elite and, 162, 163

government policy preferences / priorities: of Asian and Black wealth elite, 208–209; of elite, 163–164; of elite women, 183–186; of wealth elite, 163–164

grade standardization, decline in elite school influence and, 121

"great equalisation," 95–96

Greer, Germaine, 25–26

Grenfell family (Edward, Henry), 64, 65

Hahl, Oliver, 58

Hamilton, Richard, 74

Hanretty, Chris, 174, 259

Harisinghji, Shri Sir, 214–215

Harrow, 7, 9, 15, 116, 121

Headmasters' and Headmistresses' Conference (HMC) schools: alumni in *Who's Who*, 14–15, 122–123, 131; decline in power of, 116, 117;

ideological orientation of alumni, 171; people of colour at, 205

Heathcoat-Amory, John and Muriel Mary, 107

Hecht, Katharina, 51

Henderson, John, 56–58

highbrow culture: belief in civilizing influence of, 70–72; decline of dominance among elite, 73–82, 90; rise of (1920–1950), 69–73, 90; rising inequality and expression of, 87–89

highbrow identity, British elite and, 53–58

Holden, Blanch, 107

Hollingworth, Clare, 72

Horgan, Sharon, 80–81, 91

House of Lords, proposal to replace, 234

Howarth, Janet, 130

How the Irish Became White (Ignatiev), 209–210

Huston, Victoria, 83

ideological configurations among the elite. *See* British elite ideology

Ignatiev, Noel, 209–210

Imperial, 138, 231

imperial institutions, elites of colour and work for, 215–216

imposter syndrome, British elite and, 48

impression management, British elite and, 4, 61; elite claims of ordinariness and, 225–227

income tax, British elite attitudes towards, 162

incubators: girls private schools as, 132; private schools as, 126, 128–129

inequality: elite and, 18, 159; elite claims for ordinariness and rise in, 4, 225–226; expression of highbrow taste and rising, 87–89, 90–91; women elites and concern about, 183

influence: of aristocracy, 271n29; elite and political, 16, 157–158, 175–177; elite denying in interviews, 39–40; elite distinction and, 22–23; inclusion criteria for *Who's Who* and, 22, 23

inheritance tax, 229

intergenerational self, 46

interviews of British elite, 8, 39–40; conducting, 253–254, 255; disconnect between what elites say and what they do and, 260–261

invidious distinction, 66

Jack, Anthony Abraham, 145

Jarness, Vegard, 58–59

Jerolmack, Colin, 172

Johnson, Boris, 95, 135, 238

Johnson, Len, 203

Jones, Owen, 16, 41, 158, 265n24

judges, class origin of, 174, 259

Kantola, Anu, 58

Kennard, George Arnold Ford, 107

Kennedy, John Maxwell, 55

Keynes, John Maynard, 71

Khan, Sadiq, 83, 200

Khan, Shamus, 21, 22, 31, 58, 121, 127, 172

King Edward VI High School for Girls, 130

King's College London, 137, 138

Kuusela, Hanna, 58

Kwarteng, Kwasi, 238

Lamont, Michelle, 67

Landemore, Hélène, 234

Langdon, Philip, 148

Lareau, Annette, 67, 100–101

Lasdun, Denys, 53

latent class analysis (LCA), on ideological coherence of wealth elite, 164–168

Laurison, Daniel, 5

law, as occupation of British wealth elite, 28, 30, 36

Lawrence, D. H., 70

Lena, Jennifer, 11–12

Littler, Jo, 225

Lizardo, Omar, 86

local politics, women elite and focus on, 197

London, British elite living in, 26, 29, 35

London-based universities, reaching elite and attendance at, 138–139

London School of Economics (LSE), 137, 138, 231

Lopes, Henry, 107–108

MacWilliam, Alexander, 71

Mallinson, Anthony, 55, 140

Manchester, entrants in *Who's Who* who live in, 26

Manchester High School for Girls, 283n27

Mankiewicz, Alice, 108

marriage practices, among British elite, 107–108

Marx, Karl, 6, 32, 33–34, 157–158

Maxwell, Claire, 127–128, 132

May, Theresa, 158, 225

media, as occupation of British elite, 28, 30, 36

Melody Maker (magazine), 81

men: Oxbridge attendance and reaching elite status, 151–152; as preponderance of entrants in *Who's Who*, 26, 27, 28

Merchant Taylors', 7

merit / meritocracy: career success and claims due to, 51–52; claims elite position due to, 41, 47–50, 203, 226; private schools and rhetoric of, 121, 123–126; racism and, 213

Metacritic (website), 80
methodology, 241–261; analysing *Who's Who*, 243–247; author backgrounds, 241–243; confidentiality, 254–256; genealogical data, 259; interviews, 253–254, 255; judges, 259; limitations and future research, 260–261; probate data and measuring wealth in survey, 256–258; survey experiments, 248–253; survey of elite, 248
migration stories, British elite with, 46
Miliband, Ralph, 9, 32
military, as occupation of *Who's Who* entrants, 28, 30
military elite, decline of, 118
Mills, C. Wright, 6; on factions within elites, 164; on power elite, 33–34, 157; on two Harvards, 134, 145, 148
Mirrlees Review, 229
misrecognition: elite distinction and, 66–67, 90; rise of highbrow culture and, 69–73, 90
Mitford, Nancy, 133, 136
Montgomery, Bernard Law, 56–57
moral legitimacy: elite claims of ordinariness and, 225–226; elite disidentification and claim of, 41; elite insecurity about own, 58–59, 87–89
Morse, Jeremy, 53–54, 120
Mosca, Gaetano, 6, 32–33
Moss, Kate, 80, 81–82, 91
Mudde, Cas, 18

name discrimination, 217
narratives of opportunities to join elite opening up, 50–52
National Life Stories archives, 8, 253, 256
nepotism, elite reproduction and, 56–58, 152–153
"new elite," 10, 16, 21, 158
New Labour Left, elite and, 164, 165–168; elites of colour aligned with, 206; elite women aligned with, 185
NME (magazine), 81
non-governing elites, 32–33, 270n17
North London Collegiate School, 130, 131
nouveau riche, 66, 89–90

O'Brien, Shay, 96
occupational domains, elite reproduction and, 98–99
occupational recruitment: nepotism and, 56–58, 152–153; Oxbridge and changes in, 143
occupations: of elite women, 186–187; of entrants in *Who's Who*, 28–30; ideological orientation of elite and, 166; of wealth elite, 35–36, 37

"old boy," persistence of, 122–123
old boys network, 48, 52, 130, 303n7
old girls network, 130–134
100 Great Black Britons, 110
Onomap, 7, 204
ordinariness: cultural currency of, 235; elite signalling and, 13; elite's quest for, 1–4, 13, 39–40, 221–224; historical elite and claims of, 53; performing in online profile, 252; satiric song about elite longing for, 61–63; symbolic market for, 58–61, 225–227
ordinary elite distinction, 87, 89–91
origin stories, of British elite, 12, 41, 42–43, 45–46, 47–50
Osborne, George, 135
Ostrander, Susan, 58
"Other" ethnic category: empire and, 214; political orientation, 206–207, 218; politics of race and empire and, 209–210; underrepresentation in elite, 201
Oxbridge: change in recruitment / admission processes, 142, 143, 144–145, 152, 232–233, 239; changes in culture at, 141, 142–143; composition of student population at, 136; curriculum changes at, 71–72, 139; elite recruitment and, 13, 14, 15; end of certainty of elite destination by attending, 143–145; entrants in *Who's Who* and, 27; ethnic diversity at, 205–206; fluctuations in role in elite reproduction, 138–143, 224; hub function of, 148–152; improved academic performance of students, 145; persistent role in elite reproduction, 136–139; political preferences of graduates, 172; racism at, 150; relationship with British elite, 139–140; sexism and, 151; social divisions at, 145–147. *See also* Cambridge University; Oxford University
Oxford, entrants in *Who's Who* who live in, 26, 29
Oxford Dictionary of National Biography, 110, 258
Oxford High School for Girls, 130
Oxford University, 9; "bright young things" at, 135–136; entrance exam for, 140, 144; private girls schools sending alumni to, 130–131; reforming admission to, 231, 232–233; relation to British elite, 1; ties with Eton, 134. *See also* Oxbridge
Oxford University Press, 5

Page, Benjamin, 159
Pareto, Vilfredo, 32–34, 270n17
people of colour. *See* Asian and Black elite; elite people of colour
Peppiatt, Hugh, 142, 143, 149, 221–222

Index

Persson, Max, 127–128

Piketty, Thomas, 31, 234

political activism: of Asian and Black elite, 211–213; of elite women, 180, 195–197; of wealth elite, 175–177

political attitudes / orientation of British elite. *See* British elite ideology

political behaviour: of British elite, 172–174; of elite women, 180

political elite: Clarendon Schools and, 115–116, 238; from wealthy families, 95

political influence, elite and, 16, 157–158, 175–177

political significance of British elite, 16–17

political sociology, elite studies and, 236–237

politics: elite reproduction and, 226–227; influence of British elite on, 157–158; as occupation of *Who's Who* entrants, 28, 30. *See also* British elite ideology

popular culture: elite distinction and, 12–13; rise of, 73–82

populism, attitude towards elites and, 18

Posh Boys (Verkaik), 124

positional elites, 6, 23

positional power, 4, 33–34

Pound, Ezra, 70

poverty reduction, elite opinions on, 171, 173–174, 184, 208–209

Powell, Anthony, 136

power: of British elite, 21, 22; of elite reproduction, 97–100; positional, 4, 33–34; proposal to redistribute, 233–234; reducing private schools' propulsive, 230–232, 238–239; signalling, 13, 25–26, 133

power elite, 33–34, 157

Power Elite, The (Mills), 145

private lives, public presentation *vs.*, 12–13

private schools: categorising schools for research, 244–245; elite recruitment and, 13, 14–15; habits of thought and, 127; hierarchy in, 116; ideological orientation of elite and, 170–171; as incubators of elite identity, 126, 128–129; link with elite universities, 146–147; meritocracy claims and, 123–126; reducing propulsive power of, 230–232, 238–239; sense of specialness inculcated by, 126–130; as sieves selecting certain students, 126–127; as temples of distinct curriculum / knowledge, 126, 127–128; trend in alumni included in *Who's Who,* 122–123. *See also* Clarendon Schools; girls private schools; Headmasters' and Headmistresses' Conference (HMC) schools; *individual schools*

Privilege (Khan), 127

privilege, deflecting, 2, 42–47, 48–50

Privileged Poor, The (Jack), 145

probate records, analysis of, 7, 34, 96, 256–258

professional public sphere, increase of women in, 181

professions, nepotism and favouritism and entry into, 56–58, 152–153

Progressive Left: elites and, 165–168; elites of colour aligned with, 206; elite women aligned with, 185, 186–189; rise of, 167–168

progressive politics, economic roots of elite women's, 186–189

prosopography, 236

public attitudes: elite as out of step with, 158–160; towards elite, 41; towards elite if considered upwardly mobile, 59–61, 62

Pulp (band), 61–63

Pursuit of Love, The (Mitford), 133

Puwar, Nirmal, 17, 201, 227

p-value, 252–253

Queen Mary, 138

Queen's College on Harley Street, 130

race: being white and on the Right, 206–209; entrants in *Who's Who* and, 26, 27, 28; legacy of empire and, 214–217; politics of race and empire, 209–211; progress towards equality and, 200–202; wealth elite's attitudes towards, 164–166; who counts as "white," 202–206

racism: as driver of change among elite people of colour, 211–214; elite women on continued, 184, 185; experience of racism as driver of change, 211–214, 217–219; Oxbridge and, 150

Rajan, P. T., 150

Ramasamy, Selvaraju, 77

Reay, Diane, 149

recreations, elite, 7, 65; analysis of, 246–247; aristocratic, 67–69; changing lifestyle of British elite and, 223; decline of elite claiming only highbrow, 73–82, 90; highbrow, 54–55, 69–73; rise of popular and everyday among elite, 73–87, 90

Rees-Mogg, Jacob, 95, 238

Reith, John, 71

religion, as occupation of *Who's Who* entrants, 28, 30, 118

reputation, inclusion in elite and, 23–24

Rhodes, Mary, 108

risk ratios, 246

risk-taking, family wealth and, 102–104

Rivera, Lauren, 51

Roedean School, 130

Rugby School, 7, 140, 303n7
rule-bending, elites and, 189–191
ruling class, 9, 32, 33–34
Russell Group universities: elite reformation and restricting admission to 10 percent of privately educated students, 230–232; reaching elite and attendance at, 137, 138, 139

Saez, Emmanuel, 31
Sampson, Anthony, 10, 50–51, 141–142
scarcity: aristocratic culture and, 69; invidious distinction and, 66
Schimpfössl, Elisabeth, 51
Scholey, David, 64–65
School Certificate, 119, 120–121
school-mediated elite reproduction, 152–153
scientific elite, class origins of, 95–96
Scott, John, 9–10, 21, 32, 170
"Season," the, 68
second-wave feminism, women elite and, 181–182, 194
self-presentation, shift in elite, 12
sexism: elite women's experience of, 191, 192, 193–195, 198–199; at Oxbridge, 151
S. G. Warburg and Co., 64–65
Shah, Monisha, 74
Shaw, Roy, 72
Sherman, Rachel, 41, 58
Shrewsbury School, 7
sieves: elite universities as, 140; girls private schools as, 132–133; private schools as, 126–127
signalling power, 13; girls private schools and, 133; of *Who's Who*, 25–26
Sinha, Satyendra Prasanna, 110
Slade, Douglas, 181
"smart set," at Oxbridge, 149
snobbishness, 75–78; cultural omnivorousness and, 81–82
Soares, Joseph, 143
social clubs, Oxbridge, 148–149
social desirability bias, 172–173
social origins of elite attending Oxbridge, 147
society elites, 98
sociology of elite recruitment, 235–236
sociology of elites, as sociology of class, 237–238
Solomon, David, 72
specialness, private schools and sense of, 126–130
"stains," at Oxbridge, 149, 153
state, role in legitimising elite, 66
State Nobility, The (Bourdieu), 152
statistical tests, 252–253
status quo bias, 195–196, 249–250

Steel, David, 140
Stevens, Mitchell, 126
St Leonard's in St Andrews, 130
St Paul's School, 7, 116
St Paul's School for Girls, 130
Strachan, Michael, 140
strategies of condescension, 59
Stratton, Allegra, 77
structural test breaks, changes in power of elite schools and, 119–121
students of colour, experience at Oxbridge, 149–151
Sunak, Rishi, 4, 116, 200
sunk cost bias, 173–174, 250–251
survey experiments, 7–8, 248–253
survey of British elite, 7–8, 248, 249; measuring wealth in, 256–258; uncovering political behaviour via, 172–174
survivorship bias, elite women and, 198–199

Táíwò, Olúfẹ́mi O., 16
taxation: weakening link between wealth and elite reproduction and reform of, 228–230; women elite and, 184
tax avoidance, elite women and men and, 190
tax increases: Asian and Black wealth elite and, 208; British elite attitude towards, 159–160, 162–164; proportion of men and women supporting, 187–188
Taylor, Emma, 127–128
temples: girls private schools as, 132; private schools as, 126, 127–128
Thatcher, Margaret, 228
transparency, research and, 260
trans people: elites of colour and, 209; elite women and, 184
Trinity College, Oxford, racism and, 150

UK Social Mobility Commission, 14
United States, private schooling in, 18
universities: categorising for research, 245; increase in attendance, 137. *See also* Oxbridge; Russell Group universities; *individual schools*
University College London, 138, 231
university graduates reaching elite, 138–139
University of Edinburgh, 26, 137, 231
University of Exeter, 231
upper-class identity, embrace of self-consciously, 53–58
upward mobility: British elite's origin stories of, 45–46, 47–50; education and, 161; political preferences and types of, 172; public attitude

towards elites considered upwardly mobile, 59–61, 62; study of, 13–14
Ure, Alexander and John, 112
Useem, Michael, 33

Vaithianathan, Kanthiah, 215
Values, Voice and Virtue (Goodwin), 10
Varah, Chad, 140
VAT: British elite attitudes towards increase in, 162; exemption for private schools, 230
Veblen, Thorstein, 66, 69
Verkaik, Robert, 124

Wakefield, Victoria, 83
Warburg, Siegmund, 64–65
Warhol, Andy, 74
Waugh, Evelyn, 136
wealth of entrants in *Who's Who*, 27–28; influence wielded via, 175–177; link with elite reproduction, 228–230; measuring in survey, 256–258; positional power and, 4
Wealth and Assets Survey, 34
wealth distribution, restructuring of, 96
wealth elite, 6, 31; Asian and Black, 207–211, 296n26; Clarendon Schools and, 117; defined, 34; description of, 34–38; on education spending, 161–162; ethnicity and membership in, 207–208; on government health spending, 162; on government policy priorities, 163–164; identifying, 34; ideological coherence of, 164–168; ideological orientation of, 167, 168–169; number of British, 34; political influence and activism of, 175–177; on tax increases, 159, 163; women and, 187–188
wealth tax: British elite attitudes towards, 162; weakening link between wealth and elite reproduction and, 229–230
Wernher, Harold Augustus and Julius Charles, 108
Westminster School, 7, 121, 303n7
white, who counts as, 202–206

white elite, 204–205; class origins of, 207; legacy of empire and, 214–217; political orientation of, 206
whiteness, 210, 219; preponderance of entrants in *Who's Who* and, 26, 27, 28
Who's Who: analysing, 243–247; changing educational composition of entrants, 117–121; conception of British elite in, 22–26; consistent inclusion of elites of colour in, 214–215; as data source on elite, 5, 6–7; education of women in, 131–132; extended family elite networks constructed from, 105–109; inclusion criteria, 6, 22, 23, 24–25; increase of women in, 179, 180, 181, 182; limitations of, 30–31; people of colour in, 200–202, 214–215; signalling power of, 25–26; as source on British wealth elite, 36–37
WikiTree, 105
Winchester College, 7, 9, 15, 116, 120
women: education of those in *Who's Who*, 131–132; number of entrants in *Who's Who*, 26, 27, 28; over-representation among elites of colour, 205–206; Oxbridge attendance and reaching elite status, 151–152; role in elite reproduction, 181; on work ethic, 129. *See also* elite women
Women of the Upper Class (Ostrander), 58
Woolf, Virginia, 70
work ethic: as driver of academic success, 129–130; Oxbridge attendance and lack of, 140, 141
working-class identification: elite embrace of, 223; progressive left orientation and, 169, 170, 171–172
Wycombe Abbey, 130

Yes Minister (TV comedy), 50
Young, Toby, 149, 153
Yousaf, Humza, 200

Zephaniah, Benjamin, 77